THE MARK OF Oppression

A PSYCHOSOCIAL STUDY OF THE AMERICAN NEGRO

BY *Abram Kardiner,* M.D.
AND *Lionel Ovesey,* M.D.

(The research on which this book is based was done with the technical assistance of William Goldfarb, Robert Gutman, Ethel D. Kardiner, and Zeborah Suesholtz)

Martino Publishing
Mansfield Centre, CT
2014

Martino Publishing
P.O. Box 373,
Mansfield Centre, CT 06250 USA

ISBN 978-1-61427-754-5

Cover design by T. Matarazzo

Printed in the United States of America On 100% Acid-Free Paper

THE MARK OF Oppression

A PSYCHOSOCIAL STUDY OF THE AMERICAN NEGRO

BY *Abram Kardiner,* M.D.
AND *Lionel Ovesey,* M.D.

(The research on which this book is based was done with the technical assistance of William Goldfarb, Robert Gutman, Ethel D. Kardiner, and Zeborah Suesholtz)

W · W · NORTON & COMPANY · INC · *New York*

First Edition

ERRATUM

The legend following the authors' names on the title page of *The Mark of Oppression* should read:

With the Assistance of
William Goldfarb, Robert Gutman,
Ethel D. Kardiner, and Zeborah Suesholtz

Advice to the Reader

In times as troubled as ours the impact of some types of sociological investigation is extremely uncertain and, by the same token, the role of the investigator is correspondingly uneasy. Some such investigative endeavors are susceptible to partisan interpretations in accordance with interests and issues that are not of the essence, but are rather adventitious to the actual matter in hand. Under these conditions the investigator has a hard choice to make. He can either continue his dispassionate inquiries and keep the record straight about what are the facts and what are the emotional reactions to these facts, or he can declare for himself a moratorium on investigation and submit to the fear that his efforts will be misused for ends he does not approve. In the study that follows we have chosen the former course and elected to accept such risks of misuse as may attend it. It is with this anticipation that we wish to make clear our purpose and intent.

This book is conceived and written as an inquiry, not as a polemic. It is conceived and written on the premise that group characteristics are adaptive in nature and therefore not inborn, but acquired. A great mass of published material drawn from a wide variety of cultures amply substantiates this premise. The material in the book is arranged in a sequence that supports this thesis. The conclusions flow from the weight of evidence. Hence, the book does not describe Negro racial characteristics; it describes the personality he acquired while being obliged to adapt to extremely difficult social conditions. Anyone who wishes to quote from the conclusions of this book to uphold any other thesis risks doing injustice to the material in the book, to the intentions of the authors, and to the Negro people. The authors will give no comfort or support to those who wish to use some part of this work out of its conceptual and sequential context in order to hurt the interests of the Negro people.

The scientific position of the authors has been well stated by other social scientists with whom they concur. This position is clearly defined in the following quotations:

> "The prospect of a continuing inferior status is essentially unacceptable to any group of people. For this and other reasons, neither colonial exploitation nor oppression of minorities within a nation is in the long run compatible with peace. As social scientists we know of no evidence that any ethnic group is inherently inferior."—From *Tensions That Cause Wars*, Edited by Hadley Cantril, University of Illinois Press, 1950.
>
> Signed:
>
> Gordon W. Allport
> Gilberto Freyre
> Georges Gurvitch
> Max Horkheimer
> Arue Naess
> John Rickman
> Harry S. Sullivan
> Alexander Szalai

> "16. Lastly, biological studies lend support to the ethic of universal brotherhood; for man is born with drives toward cooperation, and unless these drives are satisfied man and nations alike fall ill. Man is born a social being who can reach his fullest development only through interaction with his fellows. The denial at any point of this social bond between man and man brings with it disintegration. In this sense, every man is his brother's keeper. For every man is a piece of the continent, a part of the main, because he is involved in mankind."
>
> —The concluding point of the UNESCO "Statement on Race," July 18, 1950.

This book is a part of the methodical investigation upon which the thesis contained in these two quotations rests.

Abram Kardiner
Lionel Ovesey

Contents

Preface

This book has a twofold purpose. First, it demonstrates the application of psychodynamics to a specific problem in the social sciences. In this sense, it is a pilot study in a sociological technique. Second, the demonstration involves a specific type of subject matter which has unique properties of its own. Both facets of this work, the technique and the subject matter, are equally important, and each requires special orientation.

The technique is not new. It was developed over the past fifteen years and was first put in definitive form in 1939 with the publication of *The Individual and His Society*.[1] The general thesis of this book held that human personality varied with the conditions to which it must adapt. There was nothing original about this thesis. That human nature varied according to tribal custom was known to Herodotus. The new technique, however, furnished this common-sense conclusion with a specific bill of particulars. It provided a method for correlating personality traits with the institutional sources that gave them origin. The subject matter in this first book consisted of two "primitive" societies [2] described by Ralph Linton. There were no accompanying personality studies. The technique was an extrapolation of principles established by psychodynamics in the study of neurosis and personality structure. The book demonstrated that the human unit had a definite place in the development of social processes, that he had to be studied genetically in his specific cultural milieu, and that cultural institutions left a definite imprint upon him. This imprint was called *basic personality*, and it varied as the institutions varied.

[1] Kardiner, A., *The Individual and His Society*, Columbia University Press, 1939.

[2] The Marquesas and the Tanala.

The technical innovation of making the human unit the focal object of study was bound to affect the conclusions that were drawn from the study of institutions alone. It was also likely to affect the conclusions of those who followed the thesis of Freud in *Totem and Taboo*. Both anthropologists and protagonists of the latter aspects of Freud found the procedure distasteful, and hoped it was a passing fad. Nevertheless, several anthropologists undertook this new plan of research, but without convincing results because the material and psychodynamics were faulty. Others took up the concept of basic personality and attempted to use it as an operational tool. Many felt obliged to invent new catchwords to convey the idea of basic personality, and before long there were a dozen variations on the market, no two writers using the same term. This constituted a serious error. It put the emphasis on the wrong factors. The concept of basic personality had no operational value at all. The effective tool was the psychodynamic technique. Moreover, none of the works published prior to 1944 had any verification in the personal histories or personality surveys of the actual people living in the various cultures that were studied. The necessity for such material had been clearly indicated in the pioneer studies of the Marquesas and the Tanala.

The proof of the thesis contained in *The Individual and His Society* required verification on the personalities, and it was with this anticipation that the study of the people of Alor had been launched. This research was planned to meet the required specifications. There were, in addition to the ethnographic account, eight personality studies and thirty-seven Rorschach tests. All of this material was gathered in the field by Cora Du Bois. The Rorschachs were given to Emil Oberholzer to be interpreted "blind." He knew nothing about the nature of the project or the origin of the subjects. Neither did he participate in the study of the culture in a research seminar. The institutional set-up was studied first. This furnished the basis for the prediction of the type of personality the Alorese were likely to have. Next, the biographies were studied. The correspondence between the predicted and actual results was very close. Dr. Oberholzer then delivered his report on the Rorschach tests. Here, the coincidence with the data from the institutions and the biographies was strikingly high. The findings were published in two separate works, *The People of Alor* [3] and *The Psychological Frontiers of Society*.[4]

The latter volume also contained an account of American personality as reflected in Plainville, a middle-western community described by James West. For this study there were only five biographies and no Rorschachs. The same kind of analysis was done on Plainville as on Alor, but with far less success. The study was sharply criticized on several counts. Many critics held that the evidence was too scanty. Others felt that the basic personality described for Plainville was not really derived from the source material, but was predetermined by the study of neuroses in our culture. Still others pointed out that the basic personality did not take into account class differences. There was some truth to all of these allegations. Actually, the procedure used was not incorrect; it was incomplete and lacked demonstrative value. The data were too diffuse and general and insufficiently checked by projective tests. The methodology, however, was basically sound. It attempted to describe the motivational sources of the personality, rather than the mimetic tendencies derived either from tradition or from changes in the style of living. An accurate correlation between personality function and social institutions must be based on the former, not on the latter. It is precisely here that we quarrel with much of the recent work of social scientists in this field.

This question of the sources from which one draws conclusions about basic personality, or its many synonyms, is not just an academic one. It is a serious matter—as are all questions pertaining to contemporary cultures. Social engineering in today's crisis will not allow for much margin of error, if any. Unfortunately, the point of view of most of the social scientists who deal with this problem is strictly behavioristic, and the end product is capable of no generalizations that can be applied to any culture other than the one they describe. The recent rash of books on so-called "national character," both American and foreign, is a case in point. Most of these studies owe no responsibility to any set of verified or verifiable postulates, clinical procedures, or projective tests. Nor are they supported by so much as even a bit of direct source material. The

[3] Du Bois, Cora, *The People of Alor*, University of Minnesota Press, 1944.

[4] Kardiner, A., and Associates, *The Psychological Frontiers of Society*, Columbia University Press, 1945.

authors do make many good observations, but the problem is to find a place for these observations in some consistent and verifiable scheme of personality and social functioning. They describe sources from which imitative (mimetic) and learned systems of behavior proceed, but not the motivational (integrative) systems which give origin to basic personality.[5]

It is difficult to account for so great a discrepancy in the scientific formulation of a construct, such as personality or character, that enjoys the widest possible usage. Such discrepancies can only be attributed to the fact that the various workers approach this question with different preconceptions and different technical methods of investigation. According to one's tools, one looks for evidence to suit them. However, to write about personality without a consideration of integrative systems is to read *Hamlet* with Hamlet removed. Such accounts of "national character," based on the observable fashions of the day, can be done only by those whose knowledge of motivation is on the newspaper level. The traits that are described by this procedure reflect the impact on the socially oriented aspects of the ego of those public and exposed influences which arrive through mass media. Why is it that none of these traits will ever show up in a Rorschach or Thematic Apperception Test, except perhaps to give the framework in which a motivation is cast? It is because such tests register *integrative* systems. Traits that owe their origin to fashions and vogues are not integrated, but suggested and changeable.

[5] We regret that we must introduce such technical matters in a preface, that are better treated later in the text. But the question of procedure is so vital that it forms the backbone of the aforelying work. All psychologies are efforts to interpret the totality of experience, which is initially perceived as an indivisible whole. The two dominant psychologies of today are behaviorism and psychodynamics. The former relies primarily on its adjunct learning theory, the latter on unconscious motivation. They approach two different aspects of total experience, and their methods of inference and deduction vary accordingly. It is not a question of whether one is right and the other is wrong. Each has its place. The technique of psychological analysis can be compared with the procedure in algebra called factoring, where the total quantity in question can be factored for different recurrent quantities. Thus, "mimetic," "learned," and "integrative" systems of behavior are factors in a total experience which never consists of one to the exclusion of the other two. Drawing on mimetic and learned as against integrative factors exclusively gives a distorted and selective description of the total experience which is misleading. One cannot describe the influence of mimetic or learned systems without reference to integrative, because the latter is the selective agent and is for the greater part unconscious; the learned depend on memory processes, the mimetic on suggestion, and both are conscious to a high degree.

The public transmission of attitudes is a legitimate and vital area of sociological research. Mimetic factors cannot and should not be omitted from any discussion of group mores. Their choice, popularity, and impact should be studied as part of the definition of immediate social goals and mass morality. They are subject to gradual change, and vogues of twenty years ago are as dated as if they belonged to the remote past. Whatever these attitudes reveal, they do not reveal national character. The place of these phenomena cannot be decided until an adaptational frame of reference for following the course of social processes is constructed. At present, there is no such frame of reference. Where then do learned and mimetic systems come in? These points are discussed in the text. Suffice it here to indicate that the integrative systems exercise a constant polarizing influence on both learned and mimetic systems. In short, if one wishes to look for the dynamo of motivation, one must look to integrative systems. This is where Freud's contribution lay and this is what explains personality and neurotic configurations.

This discussion is germane to the chief technical objective of this book, namely that the psychodynamic analysis is a technique for demonstrating the effects of cultural pressures on human beings. It is therefore a tool of high sociological value. This demonstration was already made in *The Psychological Frontiers of Society*. However, the best documented study, the Alorese, was of little interest to sociologists. The impact was lost in part because the Alorese are "savages," and the striking lessons in that culture seemed of dubious relevance to our own. It is this fact, perhaps more than any other, which made it necessary that the psychodynamic technique be applied to contemporary societies, if the lesson were to be binding. The present study is one of a series now in the making.

We were obliged to recognize, after the initial attempt with Plainville, that so complex a society as American would have to be studied in segments. Among the segments of American society, the one that lends itself easily to direct study is the Negro. The basic reason for his accessibility is that the Negro occupies a unique position in American culture, being separated from the majority white group by a caste barrier. The Negro still bears the psychological scars created by caste and its effects. It is these scars that we have chosen to call "the mark of oppression." They are not only the hang-over of slavery, but are implemented today in the attenuated form of oppression called "discrimination." Hence, in electing to study the Negro, we are studying a social group demarcated by a color line and subjected to discriminatory treatment. Otherwise, the Negro is a participant in American culture insofar as he is permitted to participate.

American Negro sociology is one of the best documented in the world. It requires strong justification to write still another book on the subject. After the works of Frazier,[6] Myrdal,[7] Drake and Cayton,[8] Dollard,[9] and others, any book that covers the same territory is likely to be anticlimactic. The justification is based on the fact that this work does not cover the same ground, for our data derive from the examination of new source material, namely the Negro individual himself. The project then becomes the study of the impact on Negro personality of the specific and identifiable social pressures. These pressures are subsumed under the heading of "discrimination" and have been described with encyclopedic thoroughness by Myrdal and others. Many of their effects will not be directly measurable on the individual Negro, but may show themselves in the creation of other socially recognizable phenomena, like lack of social cohesiveness. However, in order to understand these secondary phenomena, a prior knowledge of the Negro personality becomes imperative. This is the gap in Negro sociology that this work purports to fill. It will also test out the hypothesis that many social phenomena of Negro life can at least in part be explained through this knowledge.

This formulation of the methodological procedure immediately raised new questions: Whom shall we study, how many, and what sampling shall we take?

Whom shall we study resolved itself to the question: Who has sufficient incentive to expose his inner life to the scrutiny of another person? The answer was: Those who had something to gain from so doing. Thus, the lure of therapeutic gain was held out to some of the subjects. This, however, raised the perennial issue about

[6] Frazier, E. Franklin, *The Negro Family in the United States*, University of Chicago Press, 1939, and *The Negro in the United States*, Macmillan, 1949.

[7] Myrdal, Gunnar, *An American Dilemma*, Harper, 1944.

[8] Drake, St. Clair, and Cayton, H. R., *Black Metropolis*, Harcourt, Brace & Co., 1945.

[9] Dollard, John, *Caste and Class in a Southern Town*, Harper, 1937.

whether neurotic individuals are people. This issue is discussed in the text. The incentive of a scientific cooperation was held out to others, and finally we paid some of our subjects. All subjects but one were active and functioning members of the community; the single exception was a criminal and a drug addict.

The question of how many was resolved by the amount of time we thought we could spend on the entire project. The total time span from the inception of the study to the publication of this book was five years. It took four years to work up twenty-five cases adequately and one year to write the case summaries and the remainder of the text. The original case records were too voluminous to publish. They were abstracted, condensed, and presented in psychodynamic order. Twenty-five cases is a very small number from the standpoint of gathering vital or employment statistics, but it is a very large number from the standpoint of psychodynamic analysis. Let the reader recall that Freudian psychodynamics were set forth on the basis of five published case histories. Nevertheless, we choose to call this study a pilot study. We would have preferred one hundred cases; but this would have meant deferment of publication indefinitely, and the increment of scientific gain would not have been commensurate with the sacrifices involved. This is a qualitative, not a quantitative study. In this sense, our conclusions are tentative and await statistical validation.

The next question was that of status sampling. The most accessible subjects were the white-collar workers, but we did manage to induce a sufficient number of "lower" and "upper" class subjects to cooperate. Thus, we used the concept of status in the sense that it is determined by vocation and income. This has its defects, but we were not prepared to make an issue of the common use of the concept of class as used in American sociology. Since all the subjects in this volume were urban Negroes, at least during the time they were studied, we are in no position to judge how far the conclusions hold for rural Southern Negroes. This would require separate investigation. However, many of the subjects were raised in the South, and the caste system strikes at all Negroes, North and South, urban and rural. We feel it safe to predict that the differences are not in quality, but only in quantity.

The last and most troublesome issue of all was the appraisal of the impact of this study on the white man and on the Negro. We are fully aware that any discussion of the Negro in America is a touchy subject, one in which very few escape the opportunity for prejudgments that are emotional rather than rational in origin. To those who already have prejudgments this book will have but little value. The data of this book are arranged in an order of causality, and as has been demonstrated in earlier research, man in his personality make-up is the product of the adaptive maneuvers he is obliged to institute in order to function in his environment. Adaptive patterns are not inherited; each individual creates them anew according to need, within the framework of culturally determined possibilities.

We have also had some concern about the impact of this work on the Negro, who may consider it an intrusion on his privacy on the grounds that much had better been left unsaid. To follow this excessive precaution would mean to abandon a useful implement for social research because its conclusions hurt the sensibilities of those investigated. This same consideration would apply equally to any living culture. We hope that what is learned from this study can be of great help to the white man and Negro alike. We rest our claim that this work will do more good than harm on the belief that the truth about what happens to the individual who is subject to discrimination can help free those who perpetrate it and those who suffer from it alike.

The labors of this book have been unevenly divided. All but one of the twenty-five cases were studied by Lionel Ovesey, M.D. The remaining case was studied by a colleague who prefers to remain anonymous. This was the major part of the work involved and the most time-consuming. The case summaries were written by Dr. Ovesey. The remainder of the book was written by Abram Kardiner, M.D., who also participated in drawing up the psychodynamic conclusions from the original protocols. Dr. Kardiner was also responsible for the over-all planning of the book. Dr. Ovesey moreover helped in editing all of the book. Robert Gutman, A.B., assisted in preparing the chapter on the Social Environment of the Negro. William Goldfarb, Ph.D., M.D., did the Rorschach analyses and wrote the chapter on the Rorschach Experiment. The Rorschach tests were administered by Zeborah Suesholtz, M.A., The Thematic Apperception Tests (for ten cases) were done by Ethel D. Kardiner, A.B., the results of which are only partly recorded. We also owe a great debt to the students in the Sociology Seminar for their criticisms of the undertaking and for their supplementary research that highlighted many points we could not study ourselves. Our greatest indebtedness is to the twenty-five subjects who gave us the rare privilege of looking into their inner lives.

We are greatly indebted to Dr. E. Franklin Frazier for advice concerning the book as a whole. We owe to the Department of Sociology gratitude for the opportunity to test the material in the Graduate Seminar at Columbia University. We have also been aided and advised by Dr. Sandor Rado, Dr. Viola Bernard, and Dr. Aaron Karush of the Department of Psychiatry, The Psychoanalytic Clinic for Training and Research, Columbia University. We wish also to thank Regina Ovesey and Ethel D. Kardiner, who read the manuscript and made many valuable suggestions during its preparation.

We wish to acknowledge our debt to the following individuals and clinics who cooperated in the procurement of subjects: Drs. Mamie and Kenneth Clark of the Northside Center for Child Development; Nettie Terestman of the Psychosomatic Clinic, Columbia-Presbyterian Hospital; Dr. M. Ralph Kaufman and Frances Siegel of the Psychiatric Clinic, Mt. Sinai Hospital; the Psychoanalytic Clinic for Training and Research, Columbia University; the New York City Bureau of Child Guidance; the Community Service Society of New York; the several individuals whose names must be kept hidden in order not to identify the subjects they referred.

Abram Kardiner
Lionel Ovesey

Departments of Psychiatry and Sociology,
Columbia University

PART ONE

The White Man and the Negro: A Comparative Sociology

CHAPTER ONE
Introduction

I. THE FRAGMENTATION OF THE SOCIAL LIFE OF MAN BY THE SOCIAL SCIENCES

THERE IS no work in any of the social sciences which does not by implication claim certain immunities on grounds that the author is a specialist. The historian has a scope which takes in all other social sciences; but, in practice, he feels, like the evolutionary biologist, that only certain broad social movements are his sphere of interest, not the minutiae of adaptation of the human individual. The anthropologist has as his domain the great variety of adaptational and institutional forms which man has developed during his long attempts at adaptation. The economist has his own specialty of observing and correlating certain facts pertaining to man's efforts at producing and distributing goods for human use. The same is true of the political scientist who studies the principles and conduct of government. So it is with all the others.

These specialties do not add up to a total of human adaptation. A synthesis of these social sciences cannot be effected by listening to each separately. The result can only be confusion. Each specialty selects a limited segment of experience and develops a frame of reference suited to deal with the limited selection. The rest of the totality is left to other specialists, each of whom has his own little segment and his own frame of reference. Moreover, no two specialists in the same field will agree on a common frame of reference. In fact, each new investigator or compiler considers it his sacred obligation to invent a new frame of reference, just to be original, which no one takes the trouble to learn, except the students on whom he foists it. Because of the semantic difficulties involved in frames of reference in all the social sciences that have no fixed language like mathematics, the confusion in the social sciences is considerable. A synthesis in the social sciences can only take place in one mind, and under a uniform frame of reference. The need for such synthesis is implicitly conceded by every writer when he admits that there are historical, social, or psychological phenomena, of which he is ignorant.

Psychology is the science of adaptation. It focuses on the minutiae of adaptation of the individual to the environment, natural and human. It is, therefore, the discipline best suited to be the instrument for a synthesis of the social sciences, all of which, in the final analysis, concern themselves with the impact the particular phenomena they study have upon man. At present, however, such an undertaking is impossible. For this failure, psychology itself must bear a good deal of the onus, because the confusion in the various psychologies is as marked as it is in all the other social sciences. All psychologies are still occupied with fundamentals and, in consequence, are in no position to undertake a major job of synthesis. Nevertheless, there is a limited area in which the little that is decisively known about human adaptation can be safely used in an exploratory manner toward such a synthesis.

There are many psychological techniques today. Psychology is not a homogeneous science, and different techniques are suited to different problems. Those who invoke the aid of psychology do not always specify what problems they want solved. Nor are they in any position to recommend which psychology is best suited for their particular problem.

There are three techniques which compete for the attention of the social scientist: behaviorism, Kurt Lewin topology, and psychodynamics. The authors do not claim to be experts in the first two. We can only make out a case for the usefulness of psychodynamics on the basis of previous experience. Psychodynamics is not the only discipline that can be of use to us; but it does give us information that no other discipline can.

All social sciences today are directed by certain implied assumptions. One of these is that by knowledge and reason man can in a measure govern his fate. This assumption is not new; it is at least as old as Plato and has had many revivals in twenty-five hundred years. There is something new, however, in the application of this old assumption. It is today capable of implementation through a more complete and usable knowledge of the adaptive functions of the human mind. This assumption is at least as valid as its opposite, that man can govern his fate by blind obedience to a superior power. His obligations then are limited to soliciting the favor or avoiding the wrath of the established deity. The assumption of the social sciences is more in conformity with the *Zeitgeist*, for better or for worse. The religious assumption always ends up in handing the affairs of man to a group who claim to be the earthly plenipotentiaries of the great superior power. They profess to have a magical insight into the affairs of man. On this basis, they claim to have a monopoly on the control of his anxieties.

Psychology has been one of the discoveries of man which he has used with the intent of *self-help* on various levels. Of these, social self-help is one of the most recent. Psychology, in order to be the instrument of social synthesis, must be based upon a knowledge of the growth of human personality from its inborn equipment at birth to the adult functioning individual. Just as no psychology can investigate man in a vacuum, so the social sciences must interpret their findings in relation to those laws which govern the functioning of the mind, the emotions, and the physiological organism.

Why do we need psychology? Why doesn't common sense suffice? Firstly, because there is no such thing as a single type of common sense that all humanity draws on except for a few universal methods of dealing with the real world, e.g., manipulation, overcoming physical obstacles, etc. Human social life is on a much more highly integrated level; therefore, a knowledge of the functioning of the entire personality is indispensable. Not all social phenomena originate in pure or specialized forms of common sense. Religion, for example, is a universal social phenomenon which is the product of emotional rather than rational thinking.

Our knowledge of the relation of emotion to mental processes enables us to attempt to answer some pertinent questions that lie in the no man's land between psychology and the other social sciences. Chief among these are the following: What is the influence of a given social environment on the human personality? What is the influence of this personality on the society? What are the motivational sources of social institutions? Can we evaluate the effectiveness of a given institutional structure by an examination of the human unit that lives under its influence?

In a limited way this book attempts to answer some of these questions for a segment of our own society. In order to follow the technique, certain assumptions upon which the procedure is based must be set down.

II. THE HUMAN MIND: CONSCIOUS AND UNCONSCIOUS PROCESSES[1]

The human mind cannot be understood from the conscious psychologic data it produces. It is a complex apparatus for adaptation; that is, it facilitates adjustment to external realities and to other human beings, and it mediates between the inner needs of man and the outer world. In this connection, its ultimate function is to insure man's survival in his environment, natural and human. The organism is constantly engaged in directing its behavior in such a way to the outer world as to yield it the required satisfactions. We call the psychologic event that intervenes between a need, or a wish, and its satisfaction a *motivation*. It follows, then, that motivation has a goal mechanism. The goal itself may be achieved immediately, or it may be deferred for a long time. A more important aspect of motivation is that the goal mechanism may take place on either of two levels. It can be verbalized and avail itself of any of the devices for communication. This is the level of full awareness, i.e., consciousness. It may also exist on a non-verbal level and not be accessible to any of the devices for communication, neither between one individual and another nor even between one portion of the organism and another. This is only a different way of saying it is unconscious.

Thus, when we examine the purely conscious portion of the events in the mind, we see only the end products of a complex series of events. In certain types of motivation, these end products tell a complete story of need tension and goal-directed behavior. In other types of motivation, the examination of these conscious end products makes no such sequential concatenation, whatsoever.

[1] An exceptionally clear statement of the psychological activity of the human mind is contained in an article by Sandor Rado: "Mind, Unconscious Mind, and Brain," *Psychosomatic Medicine*, August, 1949, Vol. XI, No. 3. In the discussion that follows, we have drawn freely on Dr. Rado's concepts and terminology.

On the contrary, some of these strange types of motivation seem not to be goal directed, and if they are, their goals are not apparent, neither to the subject in whom they occur, nor to anyone else. Freud devised a technique for investigating and discovering the meaning of these obscure motivational patterns. These meanings must be inferred from indirect evidence, and to the latter he gave the name of unconscious tension, emotion, or thought. Thus, where we introduce these inferred unconscious factors into the context, then the hitherto meaningless series acquires a plausible and meaningful consistency.

These unconscious processes occur in representational forms that are disguised either through symbolization, condensation, or several other processes which render them incapable of overt recognition. The grand purpose of this complex maneuver is to prevent these motivations from becoming known, because their acknowledged presence would expose the subject to some danger.

Not all unconscious or non-aware processes take their origin in the necessity of preventing danger or what is so considered by the subject. Some processes undergo a form of automatization in the interests of economy of effort. The acquisition of learning in all forms reduces many processes to automatization, because it saves effort and increases speed, dependability and predictability of performance. Into this category, for example, fall such processes as walking and talking.

A large variety of memories must be stored on unconscious levels purely in the interests of keeping the awareness levels free to deal with new oncoming stimuli. These remain on immediate recall. In this category belong all memories of the past that are neutral, i.e., not of a painful character, whose influence on the personality is already recorded in the habitual modes of response. Here also are factual memories, i.e., the earth is round, items like the multiplication table, convictions, clichés, stereotypes, etc. The chief function of keeping these on a non-awareness level is to make it unnecessary for the individual to solve every new problem afresh. Old solutions of problems are rushed in and time need not be taken to work out new ones. This is in the interests of economy of effort. However, such automatization is not without its dangers. It is a two-edged sword. It is exactly this category of memories and attitudes that militates against effective adaptation on the personal and social plane. It may very well be that the old solution is unsuitable to the new perception.

Then there are a group of memories, emotions and tensions that are kept on a non-awareness level by an active repressing force whose function is *protective*, i.e., to prevent pain or anxiety from flooding the awareness levels, the effects of which may be paralyzing. However, in many instances, the repression is not completely effective; it is not completely banished from activity in the personality. Instead, the repressed tensions may either establish contact with repressed memories, or add their influence to the understanding and meaning of current events. In such circumstances, the repressed material undergoes an elaboration which terminates in some attempt at satisfying the repressed tension on non-aware levels, or in a disguised, but conscious form. Such a tension can force itself into awareness in some distorted manner, or failing that, may seek a physiological discharge like hypertension, gastric spasm, diarrhea, etc. Another form for such discharge into a harmless channel can take place in a dream; however, only in a very disguised or condensed form, so as to escape detection. The purpose of this maneuver is to effect discharge without exciting fear.

The psychological processes described above do not take place in society, but only in the individual. How then can we bridge the gap between the individual and society, since the latter is decidedly not an organism? We cannot take the mystical position that society is "something more than a group of individuals" without qualifying in any way the relation of the individual to this "something more." We cannot posit a "superorganic factor" and attribute to its mystical action all that we do not know and cannot examine. There is a way out of this theoretical impasse, through the help of psychology, and this way has been demonstrated in five cultures studied by Kardiner and his associates.[2] These studies established that the mental and emotional processes of a group of people who live under the same institutional and environmental conditions have a certain similarity which was called *basic personality*. This is acquired through progressive integration during the entire life cycle but with special emphasis on childhood. This integrative series is important because it is the moti-

[2] Kardiner, A., *The Individual and His Society*, Columbia University Press, 1939, and Kardiner, A., and Associates, *The Psychological Frontiers of Society*, Columbia University Press, 1945.

vational source of group action. This is readily confirmed, for example, by the relation that a religion has to an entire culture.

However, the establishment of this fact, that people who live under the same institutions have a certain common personality, is not a complete answer to the question of the relation of the individual to social processes. The concept of basic personality rests primarily on integrated (unconsciously determined and automatized) behavior. There are in addition other factors which are of the highest importance in the interaction between an individual and his social institutions. Two of these, learned and mimetic behavior, are psychological processes that are conscious in origin and, like integrative behavior, operate from within the individual. Psychological processes are not, however, the only determinants. There are also social influences that stem from the institutions themselves. These preserve the stability of the institutional structure or promote continuous change. All of these enter upon the definition of the relation of the individual to social processes. Some of these factors are readily accessible to direct observation, i.e., learned and mimetic systems. Others are made visible only through the indirect study of unconscious motivation in the individual, i.e., integrative systems. The operation of learned systems is quite well known. The study of mimesis in social processes has not yet been reduced to a technique, though in the ensuing work it will be seen what a powerful role it plays in human social adaptation. The integrative series is central in this work because it has the capacity for polarizing both learned and mimetic systems toward itself. Thus, if we study the integrative series in a given group, we can form a concrete idea of the manner in which basic personality influences all the other mental and emotional processes. This will give us the picture of *total adaptation* that we are looking for.

III. THE VALUE OF THE KNOWLEDGE OF UNCONSCIOUS LEVELS FOR THE SOCIAL SCIENCES

The position that the social sciences must take, in view of the evidence accumulated thus far, is that the completed human personality in any given society has at its disposal certain ready-at-hand reaction types, integrated through the agency of institutionalized directives as well as through chance influences. It is the former in which we are chiefly interested, because these are common to all constitutents who live in the society. The chance influences are variables; the institutionalized ones are constants. A hasty comparison of the reactions of a minority group like the Negro makes the conclusion imperative that they are in some ways different from the reactions of the surrounding whites. There are two ways in which these differences can be explained. One is based on scientific logic. We have already touched on this way. It maintains that the divergent reactions of the Negro are expressions of specific social pressures to which the white man is not subject. This is the essential thesis of this book. The other way is based on the emotional and concretistic thinking typical of infantile thought. It is magical and coincidental. It makes use of a difference which is readily at hand and easily noticeable, namely skin color. Some are quick to conclude that the skin color and the other differences are related. That is to say, they are the way they are because they are Negroes. This is the thesis of the racists. It is a particularly simple, direct, and convenient rationalization for those who have something to gain from such a conclusion.

The lesson that psychodynamics teaches is that these ready-at-hand reaction types are not idiosyncratic and hence traceable to *racial* differences, but to differences in the integrative or upbuilding process which characterizes the human personality. They are determined by variations in the specific characters of the parents, mores, customs, and conditions to which the individual must adapt from birth to adulthood. This is merely another way of saying that human personality varies with the environmental influences.

Human personality is generally considered a gratuitous and more or less private concern. It is supposed to have something to do with how one impresses others, how one can "put himself over." This is an American stereotype that has little to do with personality as a vehicle for human interaction. It fails to recognize that the personality and its inner organization are the supreme implements for adaptation in its widest sense. It is not a matter to be dismissed lightly. It is of the highest social importance. Institutional changes proceed from dynamic sources within the personality. For this reason, a knowledge of the composition and structure of the personality in specific groups is a basic preliminary to social engineering.

How do we study personality? The peripheral manifestations of the personality—overt behavior and conscious, reporting levels of awareness—furnish an inventory of personality traits. Many of these peripheral traits are grotesque. They seem to have no bearing on any of the other personality traits, according to the canons of common sense. To explain these oddities of personality functioning, we need to know the organization of the unconscious, nonreporting levels. These can be discovered in two ways, best used in combination: (1) studying the whole past trajectory of the experience of the individual; (2) studying the total functioning of the individual over a limited span of time. A structural inventory can then be made of the techniques of adaptation used by the subject under study. This gives us an opportunity to coordinate the experience of the individual with his patterns of adaptation.

The study of a group like the Negro confronts us with a unique situation. The culture in which the Negro lives is American. Hence, we expect to find in the Negro an American personality—the same basic patterns of adaptation we find in the white man, insofar as these are determined by social conditions common to both. In addition, we expect to find the results of the impact of those conditions that are different for the Negro. These come under the heading of social discrimination. They force the Negro to live within the confines of a caste system which not only interferes seriously with all varieties of social mobility through class lines, but, simultaneously, tends to stifle effective protest by the threat of hostile retaliation from the majority whites. Such oppression cannot but leave a permanent impact on the Negro's personality.

In order to demonstrate these effects, we shall have to order our presentation in a certain way. The problem of controls becomes central. How do we know that our sampling is correct or representative? We do not know if we study the sample alone, but we have at hand a ready basis for comparison. Our constant control is the American white man. We require no other control. Both he and the Negro live under similar cultural conditions with the exception of a few easily identifiable variables existing for the Negro only. This means that we can plot the personality differences of the Negro in terms of these variables against the known personality of the white.[3]

[3] There is another roundabout way of controlling our conclusions. We could study the Negro in a community where he enjoys the same status mobility as the white, as is the case, for example, in Brazil. However, in order to use this control, we would first have to establish a norm for the white Brazilian, and then compare it with the Negro Brazilian—an undertaking that would destroy the unity of this book.

Our presentation, then, must begin with a description of the white man's culture, personality and social goals. We then need a survey of the history of the Negro in the United States, together with the conclusions that can legitimately be drawn from this history. These conclusions pertain particularly to the psychology of being a slave and the psychological changes brought about by the "Emancipation." After that, we need a description of the present social environment of the Negro, with a special emphasis on those features which differ from the white. We then proceed to examine Negro personalities in vivo and structure them psychodynamically. We shall, in addition, use the Rorschach Test on each of these and note the correspondences and the discrepancies. These Rorschachs have all been interpreted "blind," i.e., from the protocols without any previous knowledge on the part of the Rorschach reader of either the subject or his personality. Finally, from these various sources, we shall attempt to draw some conclusions about those features of personality that are common to all Negroes. We naturally expect that the main similarities will lie in the reactions to caste and class.

The question can be raised at this point whether there is such a thing, in the Negro, as a basic personality in the sense that this term has been used in two previous works.[4] That depends on what one means by basic personality; if we were studying the Negro in his native African habitat, that is what we would be looking for. However, in this book our objective is not to establish a Negro basic personality because the institutional background of the Negroes we are studying is American. We confine ourselves to the task of establishing the effects of caste and class on this personality.

The crucial issue is the use that can be made of this information once we have established it. First, it can define precisely the areas of personality functioning that are affected by the caste system and the intra-group class struggle. This technique becomes, therefore, a method of diagnosing the effect of social pressures on the individual. This information can then be used to explain other aspects of Negro social life, such as social cohesion, religion, marriage, crime, etc. Finally, efforts at alleviation of the problems created by caste and class can be based on the knowledge that we have so gained. This, then, is the scope of our book.

[4] Kardiner, *op. cit.*

CHAPTER TWO
The Social Environment of the White Man

I. THE INTERACTION BETWEEN SOCIAL INSTITUTIONS AND PERSONALITY

THE STUDY of personality organization is a contribution of psychodynamics. Its relation to the social sciences is defined by two objectives: (1) to determine the effects of a given institutional structure upon the individual, and (2) to establish the relation between personality organization and the effectiveness of the functioning of the society as a whole. In other words, the study of personality is a method of checking on the efficacy of the institutional structure upon the human unit. If this technique has any practical uses, this is the information it can give—and no other. It is of no value to study personality as an adjunctive technique in the social sciences merely to make an inventory of group idiosyncrasies. This technique is a pragmatic one. Patterns of social organization are not intrinsically either good or bad; they are effective if they lead to higher patterns of cooperation, diminish the anxiety that pervades a society, and reduce the amount of mutual aggression. A pattern of social organization is ineffectual if it leads to heightened anxiety and mobilizes greater quantities of mutual distrust and mutual aggression. Ultimately, such a pattern must lead to mutual extermination.

During the past few years several books have appeared that purport to describe the American personality in American culture. The most important of these are Mead's *And Keep Your Powder*

Dry,[1] and Gorer's *The American People*.[2] These appraisals of American culture and personality have one common characteristic: they are drawn without any established frame of reference, and there is no conceivable way for checking the correctness or incorrectness of their observations and conclusions. More important, these observations, right or wrong, owe no responsibility to any scheme of human personality. One of them makes the attempt to derive these traits from institutionalized practices, but in doing so, extravagant claims are made for isolated events in childhood without adequate proof that they start an integrative series.

This does not mean that the above writers have not made some very shrewd observations about American group traits. It does mean, however, that in evaluating these traits we are completely disoriented as regards their origin and their relative importance in the total functioning of the personality. Here it is necessary to establish a hierarchy of priorities. In the two works previously mentioned,[3] we used the simple classification of primary and secondary institutions. We saw the basic personality as a product of the primary institutions. The secondary institutions, in turn, were derived from the basic personality. This formulation was an oversimplification, and in practice it could account for only a small, though important, group of social phenomena. It was correctly pointed out by critics that some institutions were difficult to place in either category of primary or secondary; and, further, no room was left for the role of tradition. The entire scheme remained airtight and failed to account for many group traits whose existence could not be denied. Perhaps this classification of primary and secondary institutions stemmed from the attempt to establish relations between institutions, and not from the adaptation of the individual. From the point of view of personality functioning this scheme derives from the exclusive use of *integrative* systems as our guides. This procedure is *not* incorrect, it is incomplete. For, in addition to integrative systems operating in man on lower levels of consciousness, there is a group of *learned* systems, and still another group that is purely *mimetic*.

[1] Mead, Margaret, *And Keep Your Powder Dry*, Morrow, 1942.
[2] Gorer, Geoffrey, *The American People*, Norton, 1948.
[3] Kardiner, A., *op. cit.*

Integrative systems

These derive from practices that may be either institutionalized or not institutionalized. For example, the monogamous family is an institutionalized practice; but neglect of children in Alor [4] is not an institutionalized practice. There are no overt instructions to parents that children should be neglected. This neglect of children derives incidentally from another institutionalized practice that obliges the woman to raise the vegetable foods. Notwithstanding the incidental origin of maternal neglect in Alor, the consequences of maternal neglect are registered in a long integrative series of traits. Moreover, no learning toward any specific social end is involved in this particular integrative series. Children here are not *taught* to mistrust their parents. This consequence is an unwanted, unforeseen by-product of an integrative series. On the other hand, sex mores and bowel training do have a social end in view; they are inducted for purposes which suit the community. Here we have a combination of both a learned and an integrative series.

An integrative system is an habitual pattern of response inducted by some form of direct experience that has intimate connections with intellectual, emotional, and hedonic levels of personality functioning. It takes its origin during infancy and childhood, early in the developmental years. It is unconsciously determined, an automatic, involuntary response that is not subject to higher cortical control. It involves the kind of learning that is shown by the automatization of a conditioned reflex; but it is not self-contained or isolated. If some appetite or drive is involved, the reactions set off can be compounded and diffused, so that the influences of the resulting integrative system can spread over areas that have no connection with the original social purpose for which it was designed. For instance, these systems can be symbolically extended.

Let us take bowel training as a typical example of an integrative system. The ethics of bowel training are founded primarily on the basic attitude of the community toward excreta. This is determined partly by tradition and partly by the social significance of excreta. If excreta are poisonous (Pomo Indians) and can be used as magical

[4] Kardiner, A., and Associates, *The Psychological Frontiers of Society*, Columbia University Press, 1945; also Du Bois, Cora, *The People of Alor*, University of Minnesota Press, 1944.

bait, then evacuation must take place secretly and excreta buried, so they cannot be found. If excreta are used as fertilizer, as in China, then they are not buried, but treasured as a valuable life-giving substance. If they are regarded as filthy, disgusting, and unaesthetic (Western urban culture), then the training incorporates these specific meanings. This is the *learned* part of the system.

However, since the learning to live in accordance with this social directive involves certain somatic reflexes that must be placed under voluntary control, another system is built up around the evacuating function that is entirely adventitious. This system depends on the amount of rage and anxiety that are involved in the learning process. Some of the end products of this *integrative* system are:

(1) To oneself	"I am good and powerful," or "I am no good and weak"
(2) To the activity	retention = control = self-mastery; ideas about all things that can be retained, such as money (stinginess)
(3) To the parent	defiance, hostility, obstinacy, rebelliousness, untidiness, negativism, *or* excessive obedience, conscientiousness, meticulousness

Learned systems

A learned system is also inducted by direct experience, but it involves only mnemic functions of the mind. It is entirely conscious and is completely subject to voluntary control. It operates, therefore, primarily on the thought level, but it may have variable connections with emotional and hedonic levels of functioning. There is one type of learning that has few of the latter, e.g., the multiplication table. Once learned, it is within recall when needed, and has no influence on other personality functions. It can also be compounded or represented symbolically. Man's extraordinary facility in compounding his knowledge and mastery of the outer world depends on this kind of learning and its elaboration by the intellect.

Mimetic systems

Mimetic systems are essentially imitative, but have no integrative function, except when they are remotely connected with some integrative system. For example, the wearing of short hair by women is essentially mimetic. This can be imitated because it is a fashion or a vogue and the woman need have no knowledge of the underlying social trend symbolic of the wish for equality with men, or the disparagement of femininity. Pure fashion, like length of skirts or fabrics in style, is mostly mimetic. But, even so, it has status implications, and so cannot be purely mimetic. The same can be said of vogues, clichés, slogans, styles, manners; they are in a large measure idiosyncratic, but not entirely free of emotional implications.

We can see from this classification that none of these systems exists in pure form and each can only be characterized from its predominant function. Therefore, in discussing personality with respect to origins, it is well to bear in mind whether a trait is predominantly of integrative, learned, or mimetic origin.

It is a common feature with writers, who undertake to speak of group or national character, to concentrate all their attention on the peripheral, non-integrative traits, as if the integrative systems could be taken for granted, or are of no importance. Why make such an issue about this detail? For the study of society, it is, in fact, crucial. We must divide traits from the point of view of origin and function; otherwise, we shall have nothing but an inventory which merely tells us that one group has this set of traits and another group that set of traits. Such an inventory has descriptive value only. It leaves us with no tools when our job becomes one of social engineering.

It is an essential task of social psychology to divide institutions in accordance with the character of the influence they exert, their purpose, and their source of origin. It is also the task of social psychology to track down personality traits to institutional origins, or, if this cannot be done, then to assign them to other categories. To deny the importance of this differentiation is to create great confusion in defining the relations of personality to experience.

Some group characteristics, despite our attempts to be systematic, cannot be easily classified, either as to purpose or as to source of origin—apart from tradition. When a given trait is traditional, that is supposed to settle its position permanently. Thus, one investigator, much occupied with contemporary cultures, told us that in the legislature of a country he had studied, every representative has the right to vote against the majority. His opposition is recorded, and, for the moment, nothing is done about it. But when he leaves the legislative chambers, he is very likely to be shot. This is recorded as a feature of "national character"—to kill those who oppose the majority. The attitude to opposition in defining political strategy is one that is likely to vary from time to time. This is an emergency characteristic that can be invoked by any group irrespective of basic personality or of tradition.

Our approach, therefore, places the supreme emphasis on the derivation of personality differences from integrative systems originating in fixed institutional practices. A list of these key integrative systems follows: [5]

- Maternal care
  - Constancy of attention—or abandonment
  - Feeding regularity
  - Surrogate parents, activities of
  - Help in learning processes—walking, talking
  - Pre-walking and post-walking care
  - Weaning—age, methods
  - Sphincter control—when inducted, associated ideas (cleanliness, obedience, etc.)
- Induction of affectivity
  - Solicitation of response; handling, play, fondling
  - Maternal attitudes to child—care or neglect, honesty to children or practice of deception
  - Insistence on obedience and presence or absence of reward systems—superego formation
- Early disciplines
  - Consistency
  - Punishment-reward systems—when punishment is inflicted, place of choice for inflicting bodily pain, etc.
- Sexual disciplines
  - Masturbation, interdicted or permitted, attitudes of elders—neglect, ridicule, castration threats, tolerance, or used as placebo

[5] Kardiner, A., and Associates, *op. cit.*

- Playing with opposite sex—permitted openly or tacitly, attitude of elders

Institutionalized sibling attitudes
- Rivalries encouraged or suppressed
- Aggression—controls

Induction into work
- Age—duties, rewards, degree of participation
- Differences between sexes
- Attitude to work—division of economic responsibilities

Puberty
- Alteration of participation in society
- Premature or deferred
- Parental aid in preparation for marital status

Marriage
- Mating mores
  - Difficulties in mating created by parents
- Position of woman, freedom of choice
- Economic status requirements
- Fidelity requirements, freedom of divorce

Character of participation in society
- Status differentiation
- Function differentiation
- Life goals

Factors that keep the society together
- Superego formation
- Cooperative and antagonistic phases
- Permitted and controlled activities—sanctions

Projective systems
- Religion
- Folklore

Reality systems, derived from empirical or projective sources

Arts, crafts, and techniques

Techniques of production
- Differentiation of function
- Participation in distributed products—status differentiation, degrees and controls of prestige

Surveying this list in terms of its relevancy to our present problem—the influence of the institutional environment of the Negro upon his personality—we can legitimately conclude that there will be differences from the white man with respect to caste, and also to class. All Negroes live within the institutional confines of the same caste. All Negroes, therefore, are likely to have certain features in common when contrasted with whites. On the other hand, inside the caste, not all Negroes are of the same class. We can expect this difference to define still another set of traits, because certain characteristics are likely to owe their origin to dissimilarities in the experiences of a specific class.

We have stated several times that the white man and his culture define the ambit within which the Negro personality must develop. This is our control system. There is, however, one serious drawback to its use: there have been no studies as yet to establish the differences in personality organization in the white man according to class. Hence, we are working with a limited control system because the inventory we shall use in this study represents a white personality organization as seen largely through middle-class individuals. Too much should not be made of this limitation. There are likely to be deviations from middle-class practices in both lower and upper classes. However, the mores tend to gravitate to middle-class standards because American culture is predominantly middle-class in ethos, if not in practice. This is insured by social mobility. There has been up to now more progression from lower to middle class, than vice versa.[6]

II. THE WHITE MAN'S SOCIAL ORGANIZATION AND SOCIAL GOALS

The effective social unit into which the individual is born and stays until *social maturity* is the monogamous family. The father is the titular head and bears the responsibility for the economic basis for family life. The family is a social and economic unit. Its orientation is patriarchal, but with qualifications; it is not so much authority, as responsibility that devolves upon the father. Authority is more nominal than real. The function division between father and mother is still, as always, based on the biological fact that child-bearing and

[6] We are fully cognizant of the loose and unsettled connotation of such terms as upper, middle, and lower classes. However, since these terms are used both in common parlance and in sociological treatises, we do not feel it is incumbent upon us to invent a new classification. By using these terms as we do throughout this work, we imply no value or moral judgment. The specific sociological connotations applied to class in this study are defined elsewhere.

the necessity for proximity of mother and child in the formative years gives the female less time and mobility to assume other responsibilities. This particular fact, that the mother is the chief caretaker of the child, leaves a special imprint on the development of affectivity and the capacity for idealization and also supplies a powerful motive to the child for the acceptance of discipline.

The family unit occupies a closed place in the entire social organization. Whatever may change outside the family, this unit has long since demonstrated its expediency, notwithstanding the many tensions that exist within it. It is the one place in our social organization where positive feeling, and not utility, is the basis of interaction. In every other relationship (excluding friendship and kindred forms of voluntary interaction), the family unit is obliged to act on the basis of mutual utility, largely through the medium of money.

The place of subsistence varies greatly in the entire social organization. In the lower classes, subsistence is the chief objective; in the middle classes, it is subsistence plus varying degrees of prestige and opportunities for excess enjoyment of particularized kinds, all of which are subsumed under the general term "standard of living." The social goal of enjoying more and suffering less privation takes up most of the emotional drive of the middle classes. This group is much concerned with power for the sake of standard of living—power to command services of various kinds. "Self-betterment" in the middle classes has these particular goals—though the particular forms of implementation vary widely. Since the objectives are similar for everyone, the competitiveness runs very high. The middle class of all the groups, has the highest degree of mobility and can move easily across the various gradations of the status–class–prestige–power complex. Strong indications exist, however, that the opportunities for enterprise and mobility are rapidly shrinking.

In the lower classes, with their limited objectives for subsistence, competitive struggle is equally keen, because the opportunities for selling labor power are subject to the whims and vicissitudes of the economy of the nation as a whole. Depression—or the vanishing opportunity for selling labor power—is the great nemesis of the lower, i.e., labor power, classes.

In the upper classes, power is the chief objective of pursuit. This is a topic of highest importance, but outside our focal interests.

This is a convenient place to put a crucial question. What is the use of studying personality structure relative to social functioning, if, by the examples used up to this point, all strains in the social fabric of human interaction are expressed by anxiety and rage? The noteworthy feature of these emotions lies in their emergency function (Rado). They warn the subject of impending danger (anxiety) and set the organism into a preparatory state (rage) for combat against it. It is quite true that any individual in any culture can feel anxiety and rage. It does not, however, follow that these emotions should, therefore, be the chief objects of study. They are merely the common currency into which all maladjustments are ultimately translated; they can be taken for granted. We must seek instead the failures of the defensive activities of the mental apparatus. It is these failures that expose the emergency emotions. This is where the accepted norm of personality integration in a given society either succeeds or fails in its social adaptive function. In other words, we are implying that the personality structure in a given society must have a certain margin of compatibility with the objectives of the society as a whole. How, for example, could a society like the Comanche or Roman survive, if the accepted patterns for personality formation led to a human unit that was passive and unenterprising? Neither society could have long survived.

How do these considerations bear upon our present problem? How do they affect the Negro living within a caste system of the white man's culture? The Negro is allowed only limited participation. This means that the expressions of his personality are strangled off by preventing the achievement of goals for which he is equipped. Under these circumstances something must give way. There are three possibilities: (1) either the basic mores of the caste-confined group must change; or (2) the mores remain the same, but with an increase in fear and rage, against which new defenses must be erected; or (3) a little of each can take place. We expect to find all three in the Negro. Meanwhile, we select as our standard of comparison the personality integration of the white middle class.

Parental care

Here we find male and female functions sharply divided. Activities in relation to sex differentiation are sharply defined, with some permissible overlapping. The father works, the mother takes care of house and children. The care by the mother is the persistent influence in infancy and early childhood. However, the question of what constitutes good maternal care personality-wise is less well-established than what constitutes poor maternal care. Neglect is the chief item in poor care, because it means that the infant must deal with tensions and discomforts with which it has no independent means of coping. This results in the failure to satisfy feelings of dependency that are realistic and normal for the growing child. Failure of dependency, in turn, can easily lead to failure to take an interest in the outer world of things and phenomena. Intellectual development can lag on this account. The positively toned affects are strangled off, and the child must fall back on its own limited resources. Feeding is only one of the many tensions which call for relief. The image of a helping nurse-mother is one of the normal consequences of good parental care. Excessive maternal care can, on the other hand, create a proclivity to passivity. Good maternal care lays the basis for idealization of the parent. This insures continued expectations from her, and lays a strong foundation for the acceptance of discipline, the purpose of which the child does not know, and which momentarily interferes with the child's comfort. This is true especially for disciplines that are concerned with cleanliness—sphincter control—and later for sexual disciplines, that are devised chiefly to prevent pleasurable uses of the genitals. This is a very ancient taboo, the source of which no one knows, no one questions, and everyone obeys on the tacit assumption that it harms the child.

The battle over the induction of sphincter control can be a long and bitter fight, referred to in the vernacular as "the Battle of the Pot." This is a battle which the child is bound to lose; however, before he loses, he can wage a persistent fight which ultimately creates certain fixed constellations in his character. These all pertain to obedience and compliance and a great many defenses against them. Such a fight engenders a good deal of aggression which is incapable of adequate discharge. The disposition of this aggression may end in far-flung techniques for dealing with it. For example, an excessive sense of responsibility, overconscientiousness, and diligence can, as a result of this "Battle of the Pot," restrict the individual's sense of spontaneity, so that all activity becomes surrounded by an aura of obedience. The result in character formation is the obsessional character.

The constellations structured around sphincter control give rise to fixed *values* concerning cleanliness and dirt, values that are all adventitious to the evacuating function. The functions of retention and expulsion may become distorted in meaning; thus, retention can become an act of fear or aggression. These affects may remain concealed from conscious awareness, but find expression through psychosomatic channels. The parting with feces may become associated with the idea of loss and take on the meaning of impoverishment. Thus, the evacuative function can acquire adventitious meanings connected with money, poverty, stinginess and the like. Expelling something may become associated with the idea of freeing oneself of something noxious, like a painful situation or stimulus.

It is held by some that all attitudes pertaining to systematization, order and constructiveness derive from this source. Whether a specific erotism is at the basis of this or not is an open question; that definite attitudes are derived from it is beyond question.

The problem of sexual disciplines in childhood is a very complex and difficult one. It is a long-standing custom—as old as Western civilization—that sexual activity is denied both existence and expression. It has been amply shown, from the study of other and "primitive" societies, that this assumption is not universally true for all societies. Some societies recognize and permit sexual activity in childhood. In our culture, this activity is considered an aberration when it is observed, and strictly forbidden, either by direct prohibition or by implication. Actually, our sexual disciplines have the effect of terrorizing children against its manifestations or exercise. It is erroneously assumed that the "sexual instinct," being inborn, develops, or rather, shows itself in completed form when it is socially permissible to do so. This is not the case. It is an inborn propensity, to be sure; but its development follows an integrative pattern. This means, in effect, that the instinct, though present, may, under certain conditions of development, become either distorted or paralyzed. Sexual deviations and disturbances of potency must, therefore, of necessity run high in our Western culture, because sexual functioning is associated with fear.

Our sex morality is a very old cultural lag. Certain biological facts lie at its basis. The human child becomes sexually mature, i.e. capable of procreation, at puberty. However, man is the only mammal who has the concept of social maturity, which does not in our society—in fact, in no other, either—correspond to the time of sexual maturity. There is a discrepancy of several years. During this time sexual development is supposed to stand still. It does not; hence, *sex morality*, i.e. postponement of sexual maturity until social maturity. Sex morality, therefore, must have the basic function of preventing irresponsible parenthood. It is one of the cornerstones of any social structure. Its absence would destroy our entire social organization—even if it were possible to take care of our excess population. However, regardless of the purpose of our sex morality, our methods of terrorizing children out of sexual activity take their toll in neurosis and deviant behavior. One may argue that this is the inevitable price for social order; but it would seem that sex morality could be implemented by means more skillful than terrorization.

The consequences of this brutal or polite terrorization are many. The attachment to the parent of the opposite sex is exaggerated, greater tax is placed on the imagination, and introversion is stimulated. Ultimately, at social maturity the sexual drive may become crippled on the executive end. Not the least harmful consequence is the spoiling of the attitude to the normal sexual object. Sexual activity becomes synonymous with crime, and the sexual object is either feared or hated. In other words, our sex morality imposes on the growing child adventitious attitudes to the sexual impulse, alterations in the capacity to execute the sexual act, alterations in attitude to those who stimulate sexual interest, and alterations in the feelings to those who impose the discipline, i.e. their power for good or harm becomes exaggerated.

This is a convenient place to discuss the significance of that almost universal constellation called by Freud the oedipus complex. No one with any clinical experience can deny the existence of this complex. However, the interpretation of its significance varies somewhat. Because of its universality, Freud was of the opinion that it was a phylogenetically predetermined constellation, and not a precipitate of experience. This is not the case. It is phylogenetically determined only in the sense that man is helpless at birth and forms a marked attachment to the stronger figures about him. The oedipus complex in any culture is the result of the impeding of sexual development. Obstacles to sexual objects and goals force the child to turn, in fantasy, to the parent of the opposite sex for sexual gratification. This fantasy is generally repressed through the threat of parental punishment. The oedipus complex, if unresolved, becomes a focal point of inhibitions toward sexual objects. These inhibitions are only the remote descendants of the original parental taboos. The oedipus complex does not, however, have the same configuration in every culture—though all show some variant of it, depending on the prevailing social organization. If the social organization is such that the maternal uncle is the disciplinarian, it is he who appears as the father figure. If the organization is polyandrous (Marquesan) the secondary husbands, who take care of the child, may appear in place of the actual father. There is no need here to labor this point; there is little doubt that the persistence of the oedipus complex is a definite indication of retardation of development.

Our disciplines further give rise to special values associated with sex, such as chastity, marital fidelity, etc. They are also the starting point for certain myths, like those pertaining to Adam and Eve, who were driven out of the Garden of Eden because they discovered sex. They give rise to doctrines that have done man and society inestimable harm, like the Doctrine of Original Sin, in the light of which man is an animal fallen from grace—a grace that he can never regain. Man as a fallen angel, with practically no chance of redemption, can only exalt the past and make of our ancient progenitors the true repository of all our wisdom. He gives them the ultimate credit for the know-how of living. These are some of the values that became hitched to our sex morality. Asceticism and prudery are still other consequences. In Puritan ethics the highest personal achievement lies in self-mastery over the demands of the sexual urge. That the Puritan, on the basis of his self-righteous abstinence, takes the license to persecute others, remains either entirely hidden or partakes of the original virtue of self-control.

Punishment-reward systems — Conscience and ego-ideal

One of the functions of the socializing process is to render the individual susceptible, via his own immediate parents, to the acceptance of the ideas and social objectives furnished by the group. This is essentially where the effects of good parental care pay off. The child learns very early in life that parental care and affection are not gratuitous, but are contingent on conformity with parental demands. This type of "learning" is very different from learning that putting a finger on a hot stove hurts. It is the former that gives the human unit the capacity for interaction with others in his group. And the first steps in this learning process take place in the home.

In the white middle-class family, the father is the focal point of conformity disciplines—no matter who actually administers them. These take the form of admonitions, scoldings, reproaches, and more rarely, beatings. The Western custom of beating on the buttocks probably originates in sphincter control. The compelling force that makes the child tractable with regard to these disciplines is the knowledge that parental affection or support can be withdrawn. Thus, if the gratifications of child from parent are high, there is strong likelihood that disciplines are readily absorbed and the parental ideal internalized. This, in turn, lays the basis for the automatic action of the fear of withdrawal of approval and love. This mechanism we call conscience.

The operation of conscience and its formation is still a very obscure subject. Consistency of parental disciplines, with certainty both on the reward and punishment side, is a great aid to learning and internalizing the disciplines concerned. However, a general criticism can be made of middle-class mores in this regard. The emergence of the obsessional character, which is an extreme, to be sure, emphasizes that we, as a culture, are strong on the punishment-reward systems pertaining to nursery morality, but weak in the application of the same principle in the larger areas of social interaction. Conscience is strongest in the infantile disciplines, weakest in its application to business morality. In consequence, we get perverse combinations in our culture of individuals whose "morality" is impeccable when it pertains to nursery mores, but who are capable, without disturbances of conscience, of great dishonesty and cruelty in other types of interaction.

However, on the whole, there is generally a strong tendency in middle-class mores to internalize discipline and to have disturbances of conscience when these mores are breached. Children, who cannot be disobedient at home, may take it out on their teachers in school or in the mores of the streets. In order for a child to internalize disciplines, there must be a considerable margin of satisfactions over frustrations from the parent. Otherwise, the child has little to gain from obedience or conformity, and little to lose by delinquency.

Once the child is convinced of the affectionate and protective role of the parent, and that through this influence many securities and gratifications can be enjoyed, he has a strong motivation for the retention of such boons and for the establishment of a lien on still others that are supposed to be at the disposal of the parent. This is called the magical projection of powers onto the parent. Directional disciplines like learning the multiplication table do not need conscience mechanisms. Suppression of aggression or sexual impulses do invoke conscience, and if the suppression becomes automatized, we have an inhibition, in which the conscious control is lost.

It is easy to see from this scheme that neglected children cannot have strong internalization of discipline. It does not pay off.

The importance of the entire internalization process lies in its relation to the society as a whole. Where discipline is internalized, i.e. automatized, there is less need for police and punishment systems.

We can pause here for a moment to appraise the effects and social relevancy of our patterns of rearing children. The personality gets off to a good start. It develops a strong capacity for affective response and strong tendencies to idealize the parents. Disciplines are easily internalized and this lays the foundation for effective conscience reactions. The tension points are the tendency to overprotect, with the attending encouragement of passive attitudes, and the distorted patterns established by reactions to disciplines. These may end in sexual and characterological distortions, psychosomatic patterns of release, lowering of self-esteem, and in ambivalent feelings to parents, which are then easily displaced onto other authoritarian figures.

The success or failure of the adaptive process will depend on how the characterological configurations are suited to the social role the individual chooses or is forced to play. And this, in turn, is at least partially determined by the common ideal which in our society is success and accomplishment. The individual has some freedom in the choice of his social role, and he can, in a measure, escape the extreme hardship of being placed in a role he is ill-equipped by character to play. He can choose a passive social role. Thus, many people who possess inherited wealth escape the entire conflict of competitive living by merely clipping coupons, and have no other social role.

Adolescence

The dominant characteristic of adolescence is the transition from childhood dependency to a preparation for the adult role. This role is determined by ability and by the status of parents. In the middle classes, this is the age of apprenticeship. In the lower classes, it is the beginning of adult life, work, and responsibility, accompanied by a subordinate position in the family.

Psychologically, it is the time of preparation for heterosexual relationships. During this period both sexes encounter innumerable obstacles in the form of social taboos. This is where the basic patterns laid down in childhood either lead to a break-through to successful heterosexual adjustment, or the basis is laid for neurotic decompensation later.

It is also the age of revolt and disillusionment. Father-hatred, deflation of religious ideals, and home-leaving are symptomatic of this revolt, though home-leaving is very uncommon in urban centers in the middle classes. It is more common in rural centers among farm families. The underlying factors are, however, the same: too little compensation for obedience and too many sexual restrictions.

Adulthood

The real test of successful personality integration comes with the assumption of adult responsibilities. The first test situation lies in the capacity to compete effectively without serious inhibitions or self-inflicted, painful (masochistic) elaborations. When inhibitions predominate, the individual must be satisfied with lesser ends, but there is always a big reservoir of unconscious hatred against employers, rivals, or those who achieve the accepted goals.

The accepted goals in the middle classes are expressed chiefly in "standard of living" comforts, conveniences, slight increments of pleasure at high cost. Keeping up with these standards is the common ideal, because it is impossible to escape from them. Needs are created by every vehicle of communication: radio, newspapers, magazines. The comforts and conveniences of owning this or that gadget are stressed, so that nobody can have much self-respect without owning one. All this is placed within the reach of everyone by the simple device of mortgaging future earnings at high interest rates for the immediate possession of these comfort gadgets. The self-esteem of the individual is tied to the extent to which he can own and display these tokens of well-being. Even if the individual has no characterological blocks, and is successful at work and enterprise, the social ideal gives him no peace of mind. The gadgets he buys are built for limited viability and with an eye for replacement. So, to keep up with the social ideal, the individual must not only mortgage his future earnings, but also sacrifice his peace of mind in order to augment his margin of security against want—real, fancied, or artificially stimulated. "Getting along" does not mean fixity of status, but taking a position on an escalator of endlessly increasing needs. What is the effect of this on the personality—granted that there are no inner blocks to achievement? It means an endless though attenuated tension and anxiety for achievement and satisfaction. The acceptance of a lower standard of living can only come in advancing age when physical and emotional resources are at an ebb. Even then it will be accepted with protest; at best, with resignation.

The second test of adulthood is successful mating. This is where the integrational systems begun in childhood come home to roost. Difficulties may arise in the affective or in the sensual areas. In the former, various degrees of anxiety and mistrust prevail; in the latter, there appear defects in the executive aspects of sexual activity. Sexual deviation, neurosis, and ultimately distorted attitudes toward children can take place.

We must add, parenthetically, that the vicissitudes here described are those which occur when no external obstacles, like a caste system, prevail. A caste restriction augments all those anxieties that have to do with social acceptance. To these there is no end, whether it is in courts of law, in getting credit, in being unable to get a job. All the anxieties of the whites are multiplied many times for the Negro in the same relative status.

Old age

This is the time of greatest anxiety for a major proportion of our population. Years ago, when vested interests could be accumulated as protection against this anxiety, old-age security could be a fixed objective of living. Today, those who live by labor power are no longer able to accumulate excess earnings for future use. These earnings are either insufficient or are all taxed away. The devaluation of money has the same effect. Adequate social security measures would offer a stop-gap, but, at the present time, these function chiefly at the cost of lowering the standard of living.

Personality, values, and social role

In our culture, we do not cultivate a specialized personality, as, for example, did the Comanche.[7] They cultivated a personality that had high development of the manipulative skills, fearlessness of the environment, high courage and daring enterprise. So essential were these traits for the survival of the group that all aberrations of personality which terminated in passivity—like homosexuality, transvestitism, and the like, were strictly interdicted. A certain number of inverts will occur in any society, no matter what the method of upbringing happens to be. These occurred in Comanche. However, these "queer ones" were tolerated only if the social role of soldier was not jeopardized by their aberrations.

In our society a large variety of social roles are available and character variations fit themselves into suitable role-categories.[8] Character must always be measured by the yardstick of commonly accepted values. We do not live in a time when the one who suffers the most gets the highest social regard. Our time is one in which the most daring enterprise and accomplishment—even at the expense of dishonesty—gets the highest prestige. For the consummation of the socially approved goal of success, daring and ruthlessness are requisite. A high degree of competitive aggression is essential. Behind the success are two other goals: power and security.

[7] Kardiner, A., and Associates, *The Psychological Frontiers of Society*, Columbia University Press, 1945.

[8] There is a good deal of confusion in the literature concerning the difference between "personality" and "character." Many use the two terms interchangeably. It can be supposed that when the term "national character" is used, it connotes the same thing that is connoted by "basic personality." However, this loose usage creates a good deal of confusion. When we speak of "personality" in a comparative sense, we mean the total adaptational equipment of the individual, insofar as it is culturally determined. This includes all integrative, learned, value, and mimetic systems. "Personality" becomes, therefore, a term that can be used to describe the differences in equipment between an Eskimo and an Okinawan. For the sake of clarity, this differentiation should be preserved. However, when we want to describe the difference between two Eskimos, the term "character" is more appropriate; for it describes the predominant and habitual patterns of interpersonal relationships within the ambit of the same culturally determined personalities.

The former is available only to a relatively few in executive positions; but *security*, except for the base line of subsistence, must be defined for each individual for himself.

All these values—success, power, security—are all egocentric. It is the individual (and his family) against the field. Notwithstanding these egocentric goals, the individual in our society has a high capacity for relatedness to others.

The impetus to accomplishment is the convention we call social mobility—that is, the ability to move from one status to another. Though this is rapidly vanishing, it is still a powerful incentive. We have not yet reached the point where vested interests are handed down and status is inherited. This situation of free mobility makes for a good deal of restlessness and instability which is considered quite normal. The individual, however, remains isolated, confronted by a world of ceaseless competition which engenders a good deal of anxiety.

The socially relevant features of the personality that our culture fosters can be evaluated in accordance with two criteria: (1) how far they permit the achievement of approved social goals; and (2) how far they permit social cohesion and various patterns of interrelatedness.

The personality has too many spurious blocks placed in its path of development, which later act as interferences with the capacity to achieve goals. Our sex mores—particularly when they are related to children—encourage too many forms of passivity, which destroy pugnacity and competitiveness. The importance of sexual intimidation is that it is one of the first encounters the individual has with the control of an inborn drive. The chief instrumentality for establishing sexual inhibition is the fear of withdrawal of parental love and support. Inhibitions are contagious. Once they are laid down in the sexual area, they tend to affect other action systems which have no direct relationship to sexual objects. In spite of the barrage of stimuli, from radio and the educational system, which emphasize relative degrees of excellence, the individual cannot follow the goal of combativeness in a direct and unimpeded route. There is always the possibility of neurotic elaboration, such as compensatory mechanisms for feelings of inferiority and suppression of jealousy and envy.

The capacity for strong feelings of interrelatedness—love, fellow-identification, friendship, ability to form groups for concerted action—are all generally high in their potential. Actually, they are vitiated in one's public existence (in contrast to one's "private" life) by the high competitiveness that exists. Among the features that indicate such relatedness are the ability to feel inferiority, superiority, hatred, envy, love and friendship, depression, and the pressure of conscience. These are not inborn capacities, nor are they emergency reactions, like fear and rage. They are end products of integrated systems which are not present in all cultures. The Alorese,[9] for example, have little capacity for relatedness to others, and hence their capacity for social cohesion is destroyed.

Projective systems—Religion—Folklore—Social ideologies

Religion in our society today does not have the force of a true projective system as was demonstrated in such cultures as Tanala,[10] Marquesas,[10] and Alor.[9] We have retained only the form of religion. Institutionalized religion today has more advice to give on the concrete problems of living, and social and political issues, than it is concerned with the fate of the soul after death. Owing to a complex development we cannot discuss here, the state has largely taken over functions formerly exercised by the church. Salvation as a goal of life has long since disappeared. Its place has been taken by actual satisfactions, here and now, all through the medium of "standard of living." People now demand that government take a more responsible role in helping them to achieve security. The growth of constructive social legislation has taken the place of prayer. A good deal of the type of thinking formerly cast in religious terms is now expressed in the form of social ideologies. The heresy of former years is today the social and political sin of nonconformity. However, the form of religion does survive and in some quarters exercises considerable influence in strengthening traditional morality. There is the paradoxical situation of being interested in both social security and salvation *after* death, but, more particularly *before*. The social well-being of the individual is now hardly ever considered either as a reward for good behavior or the wages of sin. To those who are interested in freezing our social thinking to the traditional molds, the unwillingness of man today to accept his

[9] Kardiner, A., and Associates, *The Psychological Frontiers of Society*, Columbia University Press, 1945.
[10] Kardiner, A., *The Individual and His Society*, Columbia University Press, 1939.

social fate as a part of the will of God is a dangerous premise and one that makes for social unrest. But it is probably here to stay, and few people today will accept starvation as punishment for sins for which they either have no sense of responsibility or which belong to the category of nursery transgressions. There is too much common knowledge about what social well-being depends on, for any religion to exercise its influence toward social stability by threats of a fall from grace or dire punishments after death.

For true expressions of personality structure we must look elsewhere—in traditional and living folklore and social ideologies or movements.

Living folklore was once a spontaneous manifestation, at least until the early twenties. Since then, it has been subject to a kind of benevolent censure, so that more recently the imagination of creative writers has had the short tether of censorship attached to it. All this occurs before the public gets its chance to approve or disapprove by patronage.

We are a song-singing nation, with constant hunger for changes in musical rhythm and melodic style, and also for changes in the content of lyrics. However, some of them remain perennial: the motif of nostalgia for "home," the South, the idealization of the usually deserted mother. All these were hangovers of the frontier days when men left their early habitats to make their fortunes elsewhere. These motifs are fast vanishing. The broken romance, the comfort of expatiating on one's sorrows, the "blues," loneliness, and the praises of love, June-moon style—all these motifs are still with us. To this literature and music the Negro has made a significant contribution, in that his innovations of style, especially rhythm, are widely imitated.

The screen—more recently characterized by its sterility—was once a popular vehicle of expression for fantasy needs. Some of the stars, like Charlie Chaplin, were universal in their appeal, especially to urban citizens. Chaplin represented most effectively the common wish to retreat from a bewildering world, and to escape from the dilemma of either being crushed by the struggle to achieve socially approved goals of success and power, or succumbing to a hopeless resignation and flight from them. Evil is represented by power and wealth, and Charlie never locks horns with them except by accident.

Other screen and radio entertainment exploit the success saga, the rags to riches, the "crime doesn't pay" motif—all of which have recently lost their conviction. They all had the function of comforting the individual for his failings, holding out hope that justice and equity would triumph. Through all of these, the implicit idealization of brutality and criminality is manifest. However, these vehicles of expression are no longer spontaneous, but must correspond to a code of subjects and treatment that will not disturb the status quo. The current sterility is due to this censure.

The subject of ideologies deserves treatment in a separate treatise. It is the most complex of social manifestations resulting from the interaction between personality organization and changes in social functioning. There is no homogeneity in ideologies; they split along the lines of interest of specialized groups. Social ideologies are really not ideologies at all; they are projected plans about social action or social organization. What social ideology one holds is the expression of both personality organization and the status held in the present scheme of things. For the greater part, social ideologies are not thought out privately by each individual. They tend to be stereotyped and fought about with the aid of catchwords and clichés. What is more important as an indicator of powerful existing tensions is the amount of emotion that is wrapped up in these ideologies—chiefly, hatred and aggression, in explosive proportions. This is something most people do not want to think about; they would rather emote about it vehemently. The effort to capture popular support for this or that ideology will in the long run be of no avail. The final acceptance of any ideology depends entirely on its ability to satisfy the basic needs of the people involved. A society either works or it does not work, and what may have been effective a century ago may not be so today. The lag is concealed in the emotions built about vested interests—public or private.

Value systems

Today, value systems are among our most controversial issues, as regards both origin and function. A *value* can be defined in terms of some of its attributes: it is, first of all, a social directive, implicit or explicit. It can exist in the form of "do's" and "don't's." It is *social* in character, in that clashes concerning values form the base for the most violent personal and group attractions and repulsions.

In origin, they are related to super-ego functions, i.e., conscience and ego-ideal, and, if there is such a thing, values belong to the social super-ego. To this system can belong:

(1) accepted appraisals of interpersonal relations: ego, honesty, loyalty, shrewdness.
(2) achievements: e.g., salvation, success.
(3) approved types of gratification: e.g., aesthetic, those pertaining to order, systematization, efficiency.
(4) approved goals: e.g., respectability, status, strength, skill.

The simplest of all value systems are those that are easily subsumed under the captions of "good" or "bad." There are some values that are permanent, others transient. War, for example, introduces a group of spurious values, which tend to disappear. Heroism in war has much prestige attached to it; but this prestige does not last very long in peacetime. It is even difficult to find values that are universal and valid during all kinds of social vicissitudes. For example, respect for the life of the individual is an almost universal value; but in certain social situations, this value yields to some prior interest for the moment.

In Western society, heroism is of high value. Beginning with Homer, there is a long series of sagas about heroic exploits. One would gather from these that heroism is a universal value. It is not. In a culture like Alor, there are no heroes: the chief protagonist (who in Western society is called the "hero") is anything but heroic. He is generally an insignificant nobody, whose fate is not decided by courageous and enterprising exploits, but by women and the father-in-law to be. It is no wonder that strength and skill do not have high standing in this culture. Even personal beauty—a decisive factor in sexual selection—has an equivocal standing. The reason for this can only be found in the influence of the remaining mores. A woman's fate is decided not by her personal beauty but by the wealth of her relatives.

What are the predominant American values? The most peripheral ones are naturally the ones that derive their polarized influence from the prevailing style of common endeavor. Success is, therefore, our dominant value; as a corollary to this, we can add *financial* success as measured in the ability to command prestige and service. The force of the value of success is measured also by the ability, through enterprise or "good luck," to avail oneself of the social mobility which is one of the credos of our culture.

"Liberty" is another value of highest importance to Americans. The high regard for "liberty" is traditional, and it means essentially that no one can become the vested interest of anyone but oneself. The attempts to justify slavery and social discrimination against the Negro in the face of this basic value are what Myrdal calls "The American Dilemma," [11] and which is a remarkable illustration of organized rationalization.

"Fair play" is another American value, based on the analogy between life and a football game. Fouling is disgraceful and heavily penalized. All this emphasizes the high value of competitiveness, but honest competitiveness.

This all too brief inventory of the white man's social environment and goals is merely intended as a backdrop for the discussion of Negro adaptation that follows. The social goals must be the same for the Negro as for the white. Their pursuit follows the principle of mimesis, modified only by the polarizing influence of character and temperament. It is the institutional and effective environment which molds the integrative systems. Here we must watch for differences between white and Negro: in the strength of parental attachment, of capacity to idealize, of realizable and unrealizable dependency cravings, of the development of affectivity potential with its unlimited effects on social cohesion. Most of all we must watch for differences in the respective self-esteem systems and in the disposal of the aggression generated by the frustrations of caste and class. Another area that bears watching is the effect of the total social situation on the relations between male and female in the Negro.[12]

[11] Myrdal, Gunnar, *An American Dilemma*, Harper, 1944.

[12] See discussion of American Basic Personality in *Psychological Frontiers of Society*, pp. 345–377.

CHAPTER THREE

The Social Environment of the Negro [1]

I. THE HISTORICAL BACKGROUND OF SLAVERY

For our purposes, the African background of the Negro is of importance only with regard to the extent that his aboriginal culture survived in his new habitat. There is a good deal of difference of opinion on this subject. Two authorities, Herskovits,[2] and Frazier,[3] differ widely in their interpretation. There is little doubt that vestigial remains of aboriginal African culture have survived into the present. Herskovits believes that African survivals can be discovered in almost every phase of current Negro life. This is undoubtedly a great exaggeration. The Negroes came from widely scattered areas of the West Coast of Africa. There may even have been, and probably was, some similarity in the institutions of the various aboriginal tribes. However, there is every reason to believe that the conditions of slavery were such that no aboriginal culture could survive the impact. This is the position of Frazier, and also our own. If there were survivals, they would have to be in areas that lie outside the main problems of human adaptation. We can assume that art forms, musical idioms, and the like can long survive in the

[1] The authors do not intend this chapter to be a summary of the vast literature dealing with the subject, and certainly not a substitute for it. The works of Frazier and Myrdal are still standard in this field. We have included the statement that follows rather as a text for discussion than as an exhaustive account of the Negro's social environment.

[2] Herskovits, Melville, *The Myth of the Negro Past*, Harper, 1942.

[3] Frazier, E. Franklin, *The Negro in the United States*, The Macmillan Company, 1949.

new environment. Even religion can do so—but only for a while.

This issue of origins and survivals is of some consequence because there are anthropologists who insist that many features of Negro life in America are what they are because they represent survivals of African culture. This is claimed to be especially true of the uterine family (a mother-child unit in the absence of the father), which is supposed to be common in West Africa. We propose to show that the present state of the Negro family structure is a function of the social adaptation of the Negro in America and not an aboriginal survival.

The basic issue in this question is whether ways of living have an adaptive function or whether they exist irrespective of such function. We can point to many features of our own institutional structure that are functionally useless, yet, nevertheless, persist. This would seem to upset the assumption that all institutions have an adaptive function. Some of these institutions in our culture, which have outlived their usefulness, are either given new explanations, or no explanations at all are given, for no one knows what the original function was. In other words, it is the way it is because it has always been that way. Such an answer merely begs the question because of ignorance. In the case of the uterine family, such as it is, we are on much safer ground. We find it limited in the Negro to the lower classes. This means, in effect, that the pull, when possible, is toward the middle classes with their orthodox American family structure. The so-called uterine family is not institutionalized, but the accidental end product of transient socioeconomic conditions. The father deserts because his masculine prerogatives are undermined by the inability to find consistent and gainful employment.

The most conspicuous feature of the Negro in America is *that his aboriginal culture was smashed*, be it by design or accident. The importance of this basic fact for the Negro in America cannot be overestimated. It means, in effect, that the old types of social organization and all their derivatives could not continue, but a new type of emergent adjustment derived from the new conditions would have to be established. This kind of situation has arisen many times in human history. The incentives for such emergent changes in adaptation are usually the inadequacy of the environment in which the group finds itself. The movement of the Comanche

Indians from the plateau to the plains was caused by such exhaustion of the adaptive possibilities in the old environment. This led to the attempt to make a fresh start in a new one. This is an example of a voluntary change of environment to improve the living conditions of the group.

The Negro did not come to America under such circumstances. It was not necessity that brought him here, but a forced transportation against his will. Also, for the greater part, his communication with other slaves was limited by the conditions of slavery. In other words, when we say that Negro culture was destroyed, we are implying three things: (1) that the old types of organization were rendered useless; (2) that the minimal conditions for maintaining a culture, or for developing a new one, were lacking; and (3) that his adoption of American culture was, by the same token, limited. Hence, the term *acculturation* cannot be applied to the Negro, at least not during slavery.

This raises an important question, What are the minimal conditions for the continuation of a culture? They are as follows:

(1) Its constituents must be able to survive in sufficient numbers to be able to propagate.

(2) The institutions must have a functional relevance to the problems that confront the group. For example, the old Tanala[4] culture was smashed by the exhaustion of dry rice and the necessity for seeking valleys for wet rice cultivation. Here the family organization could not continue because it was unsuited to the new environment. The resultant family breakdown had far-reaching consequences.

(3) The relations between the various statuses in the society—age, sex, and social role—must be able to continue in such a way that mutual aggression and antagonism do not disrupt essential co-operation.

(4) Minimal instinctual satisfaction must be permitted each constituent to preserve a workable balance between frustration and gratification. Otherwise, the comfort and the effectiveness of the constituents are destroyed.

(5) Each constituent must be permitted minimal access to participation in the whole culture. A caste system destroys this to a large measure.

[4] Ralph Linton in Kardiner, A., *The Individual and His Society*, Columbia University Press, 1939.

(6) Emotional reciprocal interaction between each other must be permitted the various constituents. This is also destroyed by a caste system.

In the light of these criteria, we can compare the Negro under slavery with the Ghetto Jew. The latter did not have his culture destroyed, but rather the whole culture was transplanted to a new environment—the Ghetto. Full participation in his own culture inside the Ghetto was permitted the Jew, but only limited participation in the master culture outside of it. Family organization, religion, tradition could continue unchanged. The ideals of the group were drawn from traditional sources, and the ideals of accomplishment were drawn from the intrinsic culture. The master culture in which the Ghetto was located was treated with disdain, and its ideals were rejected. The subservient position the group had to the master culture was, to a good measure, canceled out by the exaggerated value of the intrinsic culture. The extrinsic culture was "foreign." It was this contrast that kept the culture of the Jews alive for two thousand years.

The case of the Negro was completely different from that of the Jew. There was not only limited participation in the extrinsic culture, but this could only take place by identification with the master's status. In other words, participation was vicarious—through the agency of another person. Moreover, slavery destroyed the intrinsic culture by depriving the old institutions of functional relevance and by destroying the functional interaction of various statuses. All of the latter were leveled to one status, that of a vested interest belonging to someone else. Minimal instinctual gratification had to be permitted to preserve the utility of the slave, but much of his comfort and effectiveness were destroyed. Reciprocal action between members of the intrinsic group (slave) was extremely limited, and with the extrinsic group (master) was completely absent. There was also another disrupting feature: one of the statuses—the female—had more participation with the extrinsic group through her value as a sexual object and as a mother surrogate. This was immediately better for the female, but it sowed seeds for a serious disruptive influence in the intrinsic group.

II. THE PSYCHOLOGY OF SLAVERY

We can best begin our discussion on the psychology of slavery by describing several types of human relationships: (1) to a machine; (2) to a domesticated animal; (3) to a slave; and (4) to an equal.

The relationship to a machine is governed entirely by *utility*. The machine is created by man to serve a specific utilitarian end, and if it is effective, a high degree of dependency can be attached to it. It then becomes an extension of some organ of man—of a foot, hand, eye, ear. An automobile is an extension of the foot, used for transportation; a lathe is an extension of the hand; a telescope an extension of the eye, a radio an extension of the ear, etc. A simple tool like a hammer needs no attention other than to use it when necessary; when not needed, the tool has no existence and has only a potential utility. In the case of more complex tools, like an automobile, the properties of the apparatus must be maintained in good condition to keep the potential utility in constant readiness. This means that the conditions for functioning must be preserved: it must be oiled, parts must be replaced, etc. The greater the care bestowed to preserve this potential utility, the greater the effective utility will be. However, regardless of the amount of care devoted to the machine, it cannot be said to have *needs* to which the owner must respond. A machine has no needs; it has only conditions under which it will function.

The relationship of man to a domesticated animal, such as a horse, is quite like that to a machine, but with one exception: an animal has *needs* and not merely conditions—like oiling—for effectiveness. Food, for example, is a condition for effectiveness, as well as a need. But sexual appetite in a horse is a *need* without qualification. This need can interfere with the utility value of the animal. Hence, what man does to the animal is to castrate it, thus obviating any interference from that source to its utility. There is thus no opportunity for the animal to influence his master except where the utility of the animal is concerned.

The relation of a man to a slave is quite the same as to a horse, and yet there are important differences. It is the same, insofar as the prime objective is to exploit the utility value of the slave, and to perpetuate the conditions which favor his maximum utility. All other conditions for cultural existence are ignored or prevented by force. It would have been uneconomical to castrate the male Negroes, because in permitting propagation, his utility was greatly enhanced, notwithstanding the time lost by the females to bear the infants and pay a minimal amount of attention to them. In order to carry out the program of maximum utility of the slave, it was necessary to suppress all cultural practices which were injurious to utility and permit only those over which no control could be exercised.

Thus, physiological needs, including sexual activity, would have to be satisfied. Entertainment of the kind the slaves could create among themselves, while at work or after, could be permitted. But a family organization, either of the kind to which they were accustomed in their native habitat, or like that of the whites, could not be permitted. Thus, the only permissible kind of family organization would be one that would not interfere with utility. This set of conditions prescribes in a large measure what kind of family organization was possible. Neither paternity nor permanent marriage could be recognized, for this would interfere with the free mobility of the slave for sale purposes.

The chief conclusion that emerges from these considerations is that *reciprocity of feeling* between master and slave was destroyed. There was no possibility for emotional interchange. If a slave was sick, he would be treated like a sick horse, to restore his utility. The rage or protest of the slave could be *ignored* or treated with violence. The only really effective form of protest was *flight.*

Communication between slaves could not be completely destroyed, but its effectiveness could be impaired by the limited opportunities for concerted action. However, organized revolts and flight could and did take place, but never on a scale that permanently benefited the status of the slave. The forces arrayed against him were too great.

The relation between equals is characterized by complete emotional reciprocity. There is no barrier between identification of equals capable of mutual influence. For example, the anger of one party will influence the overt behavior and emotional tone of the other party. The latter is free to register his protest. Reconciliation is possible between equals, but not necessarily submission. If there is submission, it is of a voluntary and not of a coercive kind. In large groups of equals, the reciprocal influence is maintained by certain *conventions.* For example, property rights are largely a convention among equals; their force is maintained by mutual support of the conventions, and the invocation of commonly ordained agencies of enforcement, should one of the parties violate the convention. This is effected through police and courts of law. Reciprocity is also extended among equals to all forms of positive affects, such as love, sexual union among the sexes, marriage, friendship, and the like. Reciprocity of feeling also involves the convention of access to conviction. One can argue with a friend or a fellow citizen in the attempt to get his consent to common action. He is not forced or commanded.

If *culture* is the name for the collective methods or patterns of social adaptation, then it follows that whatever culture or cultures the Negroes had to start with could not survive under these new conditions, except in the form of fragmentary remnants. As regards the *new* culture in which the slave found himself, this was forced upon him. But, even here, he could only adopt those features of the culture in which he was permitted limited participation. He was thus obliged to learn the new language and adopt a new religion, which was not evolved out of his old cultural conditions, but was foisted on him as a new credo, with no bearing—except in one detail to be discussed below—on his current problem of adaptation.

One cannot, therefore, speak of a new Negro culture that would spring up emergently from the new stipulations for living. The conditions of slavery were such that they not only destroyed the possibility of reciprocal interaction between master and slave, but, in a large measure, free emotional interaction between slaves was seriously impaired. No *culture* can arise under these limitations.

The fate of the Negro family under slavery is a case in point. Marriage was not recognized; paternity was not recognized. Offspring became the property of whoever owned the *mother*. The child-mother relationship had to be respected, at least until the utility potential of the child was realized, i.e. until the child was able to work, and, therefore, had a sale value. The biological father had no social significance, whether he was white or colored. There were, however, exceptions to this. White fathers occasionally did recognize and care for offspring from Negro mistresses. On the whole, marriage between Negroes was a loose arrangement without mutual obligations. However, slaveowners did recognize the fact that the cohesion of the slave group was greater where the family was allowed to remain intact, and that flight was commonest where the families were broken up.

This takes us to a feature of slavery, which altered the relations between white and Negro, and that is the relation of the white male to the Negro female. This could not be confined to the domain of pure utility, as it was with the male. The Negro female did have the opportunity for more emotional interaction with white masters by virtue of her sexual attractiveness. This can never be confined within the limits of *utility*. A white master (or his son) could become attached emotionally to his Negro mistress. He could care for his Negro offspring and could discriminate in their favor, or free them.

A second function of the Negro female, commonly underestimated, is the role of the Negro nursemaid. Here the attachment of the growing child to the Negro mammy could become very strong indeed, and even predispose the white male to a predilection for the Negro woman as a sexual object. There is little question that the Negro female was attractive to the white male for mating purposes. The universality of laws prohibiting marriage of whites and Negroes is an eloquent testimonial to this fact. These two features, the sexual usefulness of the female and her role as a mammy, could only have the effect of increasing the white man's fear of the Negro male, her rightful mate and legitimate possessor. This could not help but lead to the fantastic exaggeration in the white man's mind of the Negro male's sexual prowess. And this, in turn, would necessitate more repressive measures against the Negro male—all caused by the white man's guilt and anxiety. The necessity to "protect" the white female against this fancied prowess of the male Negro thus became a fixed constellation in the ethos of the South.

It is easy to see from this discussion what the destruction of a *culture* means. The most rudimentary type of family organization was not permitted to survive, to say nothing of the extensions of the family. The mother-child family with the father either unknown, absent, or, if present, incapable of wielding influence, was the only type of family that could survive in the new environment. This is known as the *uterine family*, and it is this type of family that is supposed to be common in the native African habitat of the Negro. Hence, it is regarded by some as a cultural *survival*. This is not the case. No matter what the type of family organization was in Africa

—it was an institutionalized type. Under the conditions of slavery, the uterine family was not institutionalized, but incidental to a host of conditions that held priority of claim.

The effects of the uterine family could, however, be enduring. There would be created a definite type of emotional relationship of mother-child, father-child, and of the siblings toward each other. These constellations, of course, would be of quite a different order than those created by the patriarchal family organization of Western culture. Let us track down the effects of the emotional patterns that prevailed in the Negro family.

The mother-child relationship must have been affected because the care the mother could give the child was limited. White children had priority, if the mother was a nursemaid or a mammy; if, in addition, she worked in the fields, she then could devote little or no time to her own children. The effects of this on the development of affectivity, or emotional potential, are well known. They are inevitably diminished.[5]

However, in comparison with the mother, the father image suffered a great deal more. It must not be forgotten that the white man's culture was *male-oriented.* In contrast, the anonymity or continuous absence of the father made the mother the central and focal point of the Negro family. The father could not be idealized as protector and provider, for he was neither. The mother could be idealized to a certain extent, and this is what actually happened. Thus, greater and more protracted proximity to the mother, together with her protective role, rendered her the central point of orientation in the family. In the lower classes this orientation still persists, and has been reinforced by conditions which perpetuated the higher status and prestige of the Negro female after emancipation.

Nor can it be overlooked that under conditions of slavery, it was the *white master*, who, despite his role as exploiter and persecutor, was also protector. And it was in this role that the white owner became an idealized, though hated figure. This idealization enhanced the adaptation of the Negro to the slave status. It strongly reinforced his unconscious perception of the white man's power. The identification of the Negro with his master was facilitated by the difference in status between house slaves and field slaves, the former being

[5] *See* Kardiner, *op. cit.*

more desirable. The competition and mutual hatred of field and house slaves did not help the Negroes as a group.

The psychological effects of the slave status on the individual were probably very complex; but a few features of this adaptation can be inferred with certainty:

(1) Degradation of self-esteem.
(2) Destruction of cultural forms and forced adoption of foreign culture traits.
(3) Destruction of the family unit, with particular disparagement of the male.
(4) Relative enhancement of the female status, thus making her the central figure in the culture, by virtue of her value to the white male for sexual ends and as mammy to the white children.
(5) The destruction of social cohesion among Negroes by the inability to have their own culture.
(6) The idealization of the white master; but with this ideal was incorporated an object which was at once revered and hated. These became incompatible constituents of the Negro personality.

Can anything be said about the slave status that was favorable from the adaptational point of view? Only one thing. There was an absence of strong pressure on the individual to achieve status, a feature that was very conspicuous in the white man's culture. When status is frozen, one cannot successfully direct one's aspirations toward goals that are beyond the possibility of attainment. Some inner peace can be achieved by ceasing to struggle for it. The adaptation of the slave was essentially by a process of passivity. Such adaptation can be at least partially effective, provided that all instinctual needs are satisfied—particularly hunger and sex.

Another compensatory feature of slavery was the vicarious participation in the culture through identification with the master. The slave could get some prestige by belonging to a wealthy or influential household. This, together with the gradations of status between field and domestic slaves, laid the base for status differentiation between Negroes. Gradations of color became a fixed method of determining status which persists to this day. In conclusion, it need hardly be said that the disadvantages of the slave state so far outweighed the advantages, that any comparison is ludicrous.

III. ADAPTATIONAL CHARACTERISTICS OF THE "EMANCIPATION"

The so-called "Emancipation" must have brought with it a great shock—apart from the moral triumph of the altered status, and the nominal equality that was conferred on the Negro. The first change was a complete alteration of the sense of responsibility. The absence of this feature was the only positive factor in the adaptation of the Negro as a slave. He had no responsibility for himself. With "Emancipation," he had to shift for himself, but without the possibility of equal participation in the culture of which he was now proclaimed a part. Mobility of status was nominally his, but actually, not at all. He had no more opportunity for participation than he had before, and, in addition, he had now to compete for opportunities to work, at a great disadvantage. His status was actually unchanged, though he had to surrender the dubious advantages of the slave state and enter into competition for which he was psychologically unprepared.

It must be noted that there were always *free* Negroes whose numbers were increased by a constant addition of slaves who were manumitted, especially on the death of a grateful master. The illegitimate children of Negro mistresses were favorite objects for manumission. These free Negroes had long since taken position in the society as minor landowners or craftsmen. The chief competition these Negroes had was white foreign labor. Thus, when the fact of "Emancipation" came, there was the example of the manumitted slaves to follow. Notwithstanding the history of the free Negro, "Emancipation" must have been a psychological shock to the freed slaves. Nothing more is meant by this statement than that it implied an abrupt change in the style of adaptation.

Most of the Freedmen became refugees hanging around the Union Army camps. This constituted the first alteration in adaptation. Funds had to be raised in the North for their care. Later, they were put to work as laborers, servants, or soldiers.[6] "The success or failure of individual Negroes in becoming established as free men capable of self-direction depended to a large extent upon their character, intelligence, and efficiency." [7]

[6] Frazier, *op. cit.*
[7] *Ibid.*, p 115.

The major problem of the adaptation of the Negro in connection with his "new" status was the inner acceptance of the demands that went with it, i.e. the shedding of the old methods of adaptation. Here arise two crucial questions in connection with Negro adaptation. These questions can best be stated in those terms by which we defined the relation of a man to his peers. First, could the Negro accept mutually reciprocal relations with the white? Second, was he ever given the opportunity to find out whether he could? The answer to the last question is no. The Negro was never given this opportunity of finding out, because "Emancipation" did not restore reciprocal emotional interaction between Negro and white on the basis of equality. The answer to the first question, therefore, remains unanswered. Our assumption is that he both could and would. In other words, the obstacles toward reciprocal interaction come from the white man. Why?

Most books about the "Negro question" deal with precisely this issue. And since this is not a book about this question, we need not repeat what has been said many times before by Dollard,[8] Myrdal,[9] and a host of others. The issue can be stated in simple terms: it is difficult to transform an object heretofore used as a vested interest into an object with whom you enjoy reciprocal emotional interaction. The white man has never made this shift in his own adaptation to the Negro. It is of no moment to consider the rationalizations used by the white man to justify his inability or refusal to do so. The blatant fact is that he has not done so. The social phenomena we shall consider in this book are evidence to the fact that the white man has not made this transition; he has only made grudging compromises. The result is the discrimination against the Negro, whether it takes the form of the withholding of the franchise or Jim Crowism. Needless to say, the inability to change a vested interest into an equal was strongest in those places where the vested interest was greatest; namely, in the South.

A sample of the distorted logic which characterizes the unwillingness of the white to alter his mode of thinking about the Negro is the following: "The black man is what God and Nature and circumstances have made him. That he is not fit to be invested with these important rights may be no fault of his. But the fact is patent

[8] Dollard, John, *Caste and Class in a Southern Town*, Harper, 1937.
[9] Myrdal, *op. cit.*

to all that the Negro is utterly unfitted to exercise the highest functions of the citizen. The government of the country should not be permitted to pass from the hands of the white man into the hands of the Negro." [10] This statement contains hatred, anxiety, and guilt, but most of all, a strong retaliatory fear. The way chosen to quiet these disturbing emotions on the part of the white was *more aggression* against the Negro, in the frantic effort to reinstate those conditions which prevailed during slavery. But since this was now impossible, and the Negro could not be made again into an object of pure utility, at least emotional reciprocity was withheld by the white.

Perhaps the most interesting feature of this quotation from the resolutions of a convention in South Carolina in 1867 is the presumed justification for the attitude of the white man: it was the alleged *racial character of the Negro.* This puts the cart before the horse. The so-called racial character of the Negro is the consequence of the many generations of being a slave. Now his character is being used as the pretext on which to keep him from equal participation in the society.

This type of thinking is what may be called *emotional,* in contrast to *rational* thinking. The really pernicious feature of emotional thinking is the concealment of the emotional objective even from the person who entertains it. If one, therefore, tries to dissuade a person with rational thought out of a position maintained by emotional thinking, one generally does not convince him of the error of his ways. Rather, one only accentuates the underlying emotion. The attempt to convince such a person is usually interpreted by him as a frustration, which tends to accentuate, not diminish the emotion. The fact is that the issue of what to do about the Negro was subject to violent oscillations, and was the pawn in conflicts that had deep economic roots. The promises made under the flush of Northern victory were never kept and the attempts by the Negro to induce the white man to live up to his promises failed. After a few short years of effort, the Negro finally had to accept the unhappy fact that "Emancipation" brought him only a formal change in status. And so it has remained ever since.

This is all one can say about the emotional attitude in the white

[10] Fleming, Walter L., *Documentary History of Reconstruction* (Cleveland, 1906), I, pp. 425–26.

man which lies at the basis of his discrimination against the Negro. The campaign of the whites for "white supremacy" has, on the whole, been successful. That is, the Negro has been put and kept in a subordinate status. The actual story of the Negro since slavery is the story of this attitude in practice. The logical conflicts caused by this attitude in the face of our acknowledged credo about the equality of man have been aptly described by Myrdal.[11] Nor does it matter much at what time since 1865 we make our survey of the social environment of the Negro; the essential facts are still basically the same. The Negro is still forced to accommodate himself to the conditions the white man imposes on him; the white man continues to "protect" his position by discrimination against the Negro. The conditions we elect to study concern the urban Negro.

IV. THE URBAN NEGRO AND HIS COMMUNITY[12]

The purpose of this brief summary of the socioeconomic conditions under which the Negro lives is to provide the institutional background for our conclusions about the Negro personality. The particular community we have selected as the chief source of our case material is Harlem in New York City. The conditions that prevail here are perhaps not identical with those in Chicago, Philadelphia, Washington, etc. They must, however, be quite similar. In fact, the material aspects of the Negro community are probably not very different from poor and ill-cared-for white centers in any American city, large or small; they are only more deteriorated. The social aspects, however, differ in certain configurations peculiar to the Negro. These differences reflect the pressures of caste.

The Negro population of New York City lives in a virtual, but not nominal segregation. Harlem is a section in which the Negro population is the great bulk of the total. This collection of Negroes into "sections" is the end product of progressive infiltration. Once a few Negroes begin to settle into a white neighborhood, the whites, after initial protests, move out. Other Negroes then come in and push outward, gradually taking over more and more of the vicinity, until they reach a point where white counterpressure, in the form of violence or extralegal restrictive covenants, becomes effective. Any

[11] Myrdal, *op. cit.*

[12] Robert Gutman provided technical assistance in the preparation of this section.

further increase in the Negro population is then at the expense of overcrowding.

Housing

Harlem was once a fashionable residential district for whites. Many of the buildings had fine appointments, but have been allowed to deteriorate through landlord negligence. Now, almost all of the dwellings in Harlem are in need of reconditioning. Most of the Negroes live as tenants; very few are landlords. A conspicuous feature of the Negro dwelling is the number of its inhabitants. More people occupy a given amount of space than is the case with whites. The overcrowding is far higher than in most congested white areas. In 1945, in one area of 530 square blocks lived approximately 280,000 Negroes. In one block there were 3,871 people. At such a population density, every person in the United States could live in one-half of New York City.[13] Frequently, more than one family occupies the same apartment. In this respect, statistics for Harlem are not available, but they undoubtedly reflect the national trend for non-white families, in whom the practice of sharing the living quarters of others is far more widespread than among whites. Thus, in 1947, non-whites in the United States maintained only 9 per cent of the households, but non-whites were the heads of 15 per cent of the subfamilies, 29 per cent of the secondary families, and 21 per cent of the families not in households.[14] There is also the custom of taking in lodgers. A large number of the Negro homes have from one to several lodgers, even in the fashionable section of Sugar Hill. In 1932, a study of 2,326 homes in Harlem revealed that 45 per cent had 4 persons or less per household, 52.1 per cent had from 5 to 10, and 2 per cent had more than 10. There were 3,314 lodgers, an average of more than one per household.[15] Today, of course, this rate must be much higher. Rentals are higher for comparable space than for whites because demand is greater.[16] The conveniences of living, such as refrigeration, hot and cold water, etc., are less abundant. All of this means that the Negro spends a good deal more of his

[13] *Demonstration in Harlem*, Urban Housing Management Association Publication, June, 1945, New York City.

[14] U.S. Department of Commerce, Bureau of Census, *Current Population Reports, Population Estimates*, Series P-20, No. 17, p. 2.

[15] *Report of the Subcommittee on Housing of the City-wide Citizen's Committee on Harlem*, New York City, 1942, p. 3.

[16] *Ibid.*, p. 2.

income on rent than does the white. He has less opportunity for privacy and family unity is disturbed.

Health

Sanitation is difficult under slum conditions and the incidence of disease is higher than in white neighborhoods. For example, the tuberculosis mortality for Negroes in New York City in 1945 was 15.2 deaths per 100 deaths from all causes as contrasted with the white rate of only 3.5.[17] Medical and hospital facilities are poorer for Negroes. They have less money to spend for medical care, and even if they can afford it, segregation limits the number of hospital beds available for them. These facts are best reflected in two sets of statistics—mortality rates and life expectancy. Infant mortality is far higher among Negroes than among whites. The following table lists the number of deaths under 1 year per 1,000 births in the entire United States: [18]

	White	*Non-White*
1945	35.6	57.0
1940	43.2	73.8
1935	51.9	83.2
1930	60.1	99.9
1925	68.3	110.8
1920	82.1	131.7
1915	98.6	181.2

The same trend holds for the total (infant and adult) mortality rate. The next table gives the national death rate by race per 1,000 population in the death-registration states: [19]

	1920	*1935*	*1943*	*1946*
White	12.6	10.6	10.7	9.8
Non-White	17.7	14.3	12.8	11.1

The next table contrasts life expectancy of whites with non-whites, again in the entire United States: [20]

[17] *United States Public Health Reports*, Vol. 63, Jan., 1948, No. 1, p. 18.

[18] U.S. Department of Commerce, *Historical Statistics of the United States, 1789–1945*, p. 46.

[19] U.S. Department of Commerce, Bureau of Census, *Statistical Abstracts of the United States*, 1948, p. 74.

[20] U.S. Department of Commerce, Bureau of Census, *Current Population Reports, Population Estimates*, Series P-25, No. 43, p. 4.

	MALE		FEMALE	
	White	*Non-White*	*White*	*Non-White*
1919–21	56.3	47.1	58.5	46.9
1929–31	59.1	47.6	62.7	49.5
1939–41	62.8	52.3	67.3	55.5
1950	65.5	58.8	71.1	62.8

These statistics speak for themselves. They go a long way toward explaining the frequency with which early parental death occurs in the case histories of the lower-class Negroes presented in this book. In all fairness to New York City, where vast public hospital facilities are provided, the health of the Negro population is undoubtedly better than the national figures in the above tables, particularly as regards infant mortality. However, no one can gainsay that the Harlem Negro's ability to secure adequate medical care is generally well below the white average.

The economic status of the Negro

The Negro, for obvious economic reasons, begins to work earlier than the white. Jobs are harder to get and he is more often unemployed. More Negroes are on work relief at any given time. He is hypersensitive to economic depression and is not as responsive to prosperity. Thus, it is a startling fact that in 1934, at the height of the depression, 43.2 per cent of all families in Harlem applied for relief.[21] More Negro females are in the labor force than white females. The Negro female starts work earlier and works until later in life. Sterner [22] points out that the white female gainful worker withdraws from the labor market at a much more rapid rate after the age of 25 than does the Negro female. The latter usually continues to work until about the age of 65. This difference between white and Negro women expresses the greater economic security of the white male. The Negro male does not have the same economic opportunities and hence cannot be as good a provider. The Negro female's chances for employment are better and more constant than those of the Negro male. "Negro working-class women always hold the purse-strings. Ill-paid and irregularly employed, the masses of Negro men have not succeeded in becoming steady providers for their families. In the country, also, Negro women are actually or po-

[21] "Negro Harlem: An Ecological Study," *American Journal of Sociology*, Vol. XLIII, No. 1, July, 1937.

[22] Sterner, Richard, *The Negro's Share*, Harper, 1943.

tentially economically independent." [23] These facts have, as we shall see, far reaching consequences for Negro social organization.

Labor conditions for the Negro can be summed up in the formula: "Last hired, first fired." This principle was most recently illustrated in the period of reconversion following World War II. Of seven industries studied by F.E.P.C., all but Chicago showed a heavier loss of jobs by Negro than by white workers, and a necessity on the part of Negro workers to accept the lowest paid jobs. By 1946, openings for professionals among Negroes had declined to a "scant few." [24] When he does work, the Negro is concentrated in those jobs where old-age compensation and systems of graduated promotion least exist. His labor, except for a very small proportion of the total Negro population, is in the lowest paid and most menial occupations. He is concentrated in unskilled and semi-skilled work. These are the jobs that require long and strenuous muscular effort. They carry the greatest physical danger and are most subject to disability. Most unskilled night work is reserved for Negroes. He has no significant control over the means of production in the form of capital goods, power, transportation, communications, or utilities. Negroes are least found in jobs that have an annual wage—the managerial and professional echelons. He is largely a day or week worker. In many jobs, where he can compete with whites, he will find a wage discrimination against him.

These facts are all borne out in a number of statistical tables. The following table classifies employed persons in the United States into socioeconomic groups by color for 1940: [25]

SOCIOECONOMIC GROUPING	PER CENT DISTRIBUTION	
	Negro	*White*
Professionals	2.6	7.5
Proprietors, managers, and officials	16.1	20.2
Clerks, etc.	2.2	19.5
Skilled workers and foremen	2.9	12.4
Semi-skilled	12.3	21.4
Unskilled	63.9	19.0
Total	100.0	100.0

The lack of employment opportunities in the most desirable cate-

[23] Davie, Maurice R., *Negroes in American Society*, McGraw-Hill, 1949, p. 208.
[24] Frazier, *op. cit.*
[25] Davie, *op. cit.*

gories is illustrated in the next table. It is a record of the non-agricultural placements made by the United States Public Employment Offices by race in the major occupational groups.[26] Each figure represents the percentage of applicants assigned, based on a total of 100 per cent for each grouping:

	White	*Non-White*
Professional and managerial	97.3	2.7
Clerical and Sales	97.8	2.2
Service	44.6	55.4
Skilled	95.7	4.3
Semi-skilled	87.8	12.2
Unskilled and other	75.5	24.5

This lack of opportunity markedly influences the choice of vocational training in Negroes. In 1942, a comparison was made of Negro and white opportunities for job assignment in the N.Y.A. program in New York City for both males and females.[27] The results are very revealing:

NUMBER AWAITING ASSIGNMENT

Shop	*Total*	*White*	*Negro*
	a. Male		
Machine	947	916	31
Sheet metal	168	156	12
	b. Female		
Sewing unit	217	29	188

The conclusion drawn was the following: "We may reasonably assume that where trainees know that jobs are easily found, as in the case of the garment trades, they will seek without any hesitancy the training that will equip them for these jobs."

The Negro in business

Negroes can rarely get credit from whites to start new businesses. They, therefore, cannot own or control large manufacturing establishments, large stores, or large wholesale trade businesses. Most capital for Negro business comes from savings. There were, how-

[26] U.S. Department of Commerce, Bureau of Census, *Statistical Abstracts of the United States*, 1948, p. 262.

[27] *Preliminary Report of the Sub-Committee on Employment of the City-wide Citizen's Committee on Harlem*, New York City, 1942, p. 9.

ever, a few Negro financial institutions which were started because credit was too difficult to get from whites. The impetus for these organizations came from Negro ministers.

These conditions force the Negro businessman largely into fields which do not compete with whites. These are predominantly the personal service fields, i.e., barber and beauty shops, cleaning and pressing establishments, funeral parlors, and the like. Businesses that cater to the *basic* needs of the Negro community—e.g., grocery stores, meat markets, coal and ice companies, bakeries, etc.—are usually run by whites. The majority of the Negro businesses in this class are restaurants.

Negro businesses are almost all small and rarely employ more than a few people. Most are owner operated. The vast majority—85 per cent—are one-man establishments.[28] More than one-third are conducted by women, especially beauty shops and eating places.[29] These businesses pay so poorly that most operators are obliged to have supplementary jobs. The shops and places of business are often quite squalid, with dirty and unattractive furnishings. Most operators must pay cash for the commodities they sell. This increases the markup, and prices are therefore frequently higher than among whites. Almost all customer transactions must be for cash. This causes these businesses to lose the clientele who are willing to buy on deferred payment. The majority of Negro businesses are outside the main Negro shopping areas. The choicest locations invariably belong to the whites.

The number of Negroes in business is extremely small. In Harlem, for example, in 1936, Negroes conducted only 18.6 per cent (1,928) of the 10,319 businesses.[30] The conditions are too unfavorable for successful operation. The Negro businessman must share, in addition, all the hardships and discomforts of the small businessman in America. In this type of business, there is no opportunity for the growth of a managerial or entrepreneur class.

The professions

These are difficult for the Negro to enter. The facts are too well known to require elaboration beyond the statistics furnished above.

[28] Frazier, *op. cit.*

[29] *Ibid.*

[30] The Mayor's Commission on Conditions in Harlem, "The Negro in Harlem," New York, 1936, pp. 23–24. (Unpublished report)

The "shady" occupations

The policy game, the numbers racket, houses of prostitution, gambling, and the like are among the most successful ventures in the Negro community. The reasons for this we shall subsequently discuss.

Negro participation in unions

There are many unions where Negroes have full participation. On the other hand, many unions exclude Negroes by provisions in their constitution or in practice. Other unions exclude them by indirect implications. Still others admit them, permit them to pay dues, but limit their participation and give them no voice. In general, however, Negro participation and activity in unions is steadily, even though slowly, on the increase.

Economic problems of the migrant

To the Southern Negro, the North is the land of opportunity. Migratory epidemics spread, especially during wartime, when the demand for urban labor is high. Migrant Negroes generally go alone; they do not usually go as families. Hence, the family as an economic unit tends to be broken in these moves from South to North. Upon arrival, they face the hardships that go with the transition from farm workers to city laborers. They do not have the requisite skills, nor do they have protection against competition with white workers. Notwithstanding these drawbacks, industrial and white-collar opportunities are developing for migrant Negroes.

The Negro family [31]

The organization of the Negro family in America is not a survival of the so-called uterine organization common in Africa, but rather, as we have already pointed out, an emergent necessity determined by the exigencies of the new environment. Any resemblance between the two is purely coincidental. During slavery the Negro family was an approximation of the white pattern. It was aided by white masters. This was for purposes of intraplantation stability. In some plantations three-generation families were kept intact. These

[31] The most authoritative analysis of the American Negro family is E. Franklin Frazier's, *The Negro Family in the United States,* University of Chicago Press, 1939. We have drawn freely from this source.

were temporary arrangements which were not institutionalized, but, at the time, happened to be best suited to the interests of the landowner.

Under these conditions, the mother-child tie had to be respected and the female became the emotional center of the family. When a male slave was sold, he went alone; when a female slave was sold, the children generally went with her, unless they were sufficiently grown to become independent pieces of property. The mother became the central figure and the prime authority. This can hardly be called a survival. This condition was fixed still more by the common practice of the whites, who used the female slaves as concubines. Whether free or slave, the Negro female had many advantages in permitting intimacies with white men. In other words, the Negro female broke the caste system and entered upon a limited emotional reciprocity with her white master. But no matter what variants were introduced into this situation, the Negro mother remained the center of her household, and the father, white or black, was distinctly in the background.

The situation with the "free" Negroes was about the same. Marriages were definitely less stable than in whites, and promiscuity was the rule. The female under these conditions retained her dominant position in the household. The stability of the Negro family and its resemblance to the white pattern increased according to the economic stability of the Negro male. Hence, the female-centered family is most characteristic of the South. This has one prominent variant in the form of the grandmother-centered family. Migration of males to the North was one of the strong contributors to the uterine family. In the North, the largest number of families with female heads is to be found in the lowest classes, i.e., those that are the worse off economically. This is the ultimate consequence of the higher economic value of the female and the greater relative economic insecurity of the male. During slavery, the female took the dominant role by virtue of her higher sexual value. After emancipation she retained this dominance, but this time through her greater economic value.

The Negro family, particularly in the lower classes, suffers a great deal of disorganization. Basic here is the lesser economic opportunity of the Negro male. His inability to meet familial obligations finds its ultimate expression in the large number of broken homes among

Negroes, as well as in the large number of families with female heads. In the United States in 1940, broken families were 28 per cent of all Negro families, but only 12 per cent of white families.[32] Likewise, the percentage of Negro families with female heads in cities with a total population of 100,000 or over ranged from 21 to 34.[33] These figures reflect not only a higher separation and divorce rate for Negroes, but also a higher desertion rate for Negro males, since the large number of homes with female heads is not accounted for solely by widowhood, divorce, and legal separation.

The economic necessity for sharing households—"doubling-up"—is another factor that contributes to Negro family disorganization. Many more Negro families have grandchildren living with them than do white families. More Negro households have relatives other than parents, grandparents, and children. The high proportion of lodgers has already been noted. Lodgers and "one person" families constituted 10 per cent of the total Negro population in 1940, whereas the corresponding figure for the white population was 5 per cent.[34]

These facts must be contrasted with the basic patriarchal orientation of the white family. A new source of difficulty in the Negro household is introduced by the tradition of expectancy of male dominance. In other words, a Negro female loses respect for her spouse whose economic condition prevents him from acting according to white ideals or prototypes. The unhappy economic plight of the Negro male not only contributes to the economic dominance of the Negro female, but also makes her psychologically dominant. Such a situation does not enhance family cohesion. It also renders the female less likely to make the effort to hold her husband or to try to get him back, once he is gone.

Perhaps the best index of family stability that is available is that of illegitimacy. For the United States as a whole in 1944 Negroes (non-whites) had about eight and a half times as much illegitimacy as whites.[35]

[32] U.S. Bureau of the Census, *Sixteenth Census of the United States, 1940, Population, Families, Types of Families.* Calculated from Table 7.

[33] Frazier, E. Franklin, *The Negro in the United States*, Macmillan, 1949.

[34] U.S. Bureau of the Census, *Sixteenth Census of the United States, 1940, Population, Families, Size of Family and Age of Head*, p. 122; and *Population, Characteristics by Age, United States Summary*, Vol. IV, Table 10.

[35] U.S. Department of Commerce, *Vital Statistics of the United States, 1944, Part II, Natality and Mortality Data for the United States, Tabulated by Place of Residence*, Table T, p. xvii.

The caste system

Caste carries with it the limitation of participation and a relegation to a position that is subordinate to whites. Negroes are excluded from intermarriage with whites, with some exceptions; from common housing with whites; from cliques, churches, and clubs with whites; from recreational situations that involve active joint participation; and from all situations where exclusiveness is an object.

This is the main issue of contention of Negro protest: the exclusion from participation and integration on the basis of color in all the varieties of social, educational, and political opportunities. This is the essence of *discrimination.* There is hardly a phase of living which is not encompassed by this type of discrimination against the Negro.

Practically no Negroes are included in white congregations. In fraternal orders and professional associations, in the fields of education, social welfare, religion, medicine, art, business, there is either discrimination against admitting Negroes, or segregation when they are admitted. The result of this has been the creation of active autonomous fraternal life among Negroes wherever it is possible. The same discrimination is practiced in connection with recreation like ball-playing, admission to swimming pools, etc. The Negro is not usually admitted to high-priced ladies specialty shops, but is not excluded from department store buying. He is kept out of high-priced restaurants, hair dressing parlors, beauty shops. He has his own.

In employer-employee relationships, Negroes are not denied participation, but remain in a subordinate position. Negroes are rarely, if ever, made foremen over whites.

In the North, Negroes are allowed to vote and the so-called Negro vote is sought after; but the Negro is rarely a political boss. Negroes occasionally do receive appointments which give them authority over whites. Thus, in federal and municipal civil service jobs there is less discrimination against Negroes; hence these jobs are eagerly sought by them.

Class structure of Negro society

"Class" is a very vague sociological concept. It generally conveys the connotation of varying degrees of prestige attached to relative position in a hierarchy of status. It implies a certain amount of hostile tension in the form of contempt or envy, and a desire on the part of those in the lower levels of the hierarchy to move into and acquire the values and assets of the upper levels.

Among Negroes, the traits to which values of class distinction are attached are: (1) occupation and steadiness of job; (2) education; (3) family organization; (4) housing, furnishing, and appurtenances of comfort or convenience; (5) relationship to the white world; (6) characteristic recreations and amusements; but most of all (7) skin color. The closer skin color approximates "white," the higher the status and the greater the mobility through class barriers.

This class structure differs in no way whatsoever from its prototype in white society. The only really distinctive feature is the augmentation of status by association with whites and that pertaining to skin color.

Professions and business have the highest status. In the middle class, steadiness of work in craftsman and service jobs rate highest. The lowest are unskilled labor and domestic work.

Tradition or distinguished ancestors play a part in establishing family respectability. This is a replica of white mores. The higher the position in the class structure, the more closely the white patterns of family tradition and strict sex morality are observed. In these strata, the women do not work.

The home owner has high prestige. Next is the swank apartment. In the middle group, comparative privacy of family, i.e., no boarders or distant relatives in the household, has "class" meaning. In the lower classes, boarders are the rule.

Political limitations

The one great limitation placed upon the Negro politically is the denial of the full rights of citizenship in the South. Myrdal [36] maintains that this denial was given special emphasis in the North as a moral issue. Also, it was consistent with the war aims of the North to stress emancipation and the franchise to enhance Northern morale. In the 70's, a compromise was reached, which ended the issue as a national one and it was handed over for local treatment in the South.

In the North, there is no serious attempt to deprive the Negro of the franchise, notwithstanding a deeply intrenched belief in the mental and moral inferiority of the Negro. There is also the con-

[36] Myrdal, *op. cit.*

viction that groups like Negroes add to the corruption of the practice of free and intelligent voting. In the South, the denial of the franchise is merely one of the ways of perpetuating the fiction that the Negro is still a slave. The rationalizations used in the South to "justify" this attitude need not concern us. It is only important to note that the maintenance of this attitude has cost the entire population of the South a very high price in the general backwardness of political culture. It has kept at a minimum organized and self-disciplined mass movements. Thus, the very people who carry out this mandate of inequality are never aware that they themselves are also its victims. In short, maintaining the political degradation of the Negro has cost the price of social and political retardation of the entire South.

In the North, the Negro vote is handicapped from exerting its proper influence through such practices as gerrymandering, and by non-voting. The blatant fact is that in proportion to the Negro voting population, the Negro gets practically no direct representation and neither does he collect his proportionate share of political favors. In the North, however, he has acquired a certain amount of bargaining power.

Inequality of justice

In the South, all forms of administering justice according to law are stacked against the Negro. In the North, there is a similar disposition, but it is considerably attenuated. Offenses of Negroes against Negroes are treated lightly. Only offenses of Negroes against whites are seriously treated. Negroes get higher sentences under these conditions than for the same offense against Negroes. The police are more likely to arrest under any suspicious circumstances. Negroes are treated with discourtesy, if not violence. Violence against the Negro and other forms of overt intimidation are confined largely to the South. Lynching is most commonly a rural small town affair.

Negroes are kept out of choosing residences freely and are confined to "Negro neighborhoods." There is no law which permits this practice. It is maintained by "gentleman's agreement." Negroes are not permitted in certain restaurants and hotels by the same convention. These are constant irritants to the self-esteem of the Negro.

Segregation and Jim Crow are forms of social discrimination that go with any caste system. Though essentially Southern, these practices continue in a lesser form in the North. The etiquette of address between Negro and white in the South is not observed in the North. In the South, he may be addressed by his first name, offered no handshake, forced to enter through the rear door, etc.

In the North, Negroes are not officially denied opportunities for education. Discrimination is no fixed policy, but subject to whims of individual administrators. The number of Negroes who apply for higher education is distinctly small. But here, other factors, especially economic, in conjunction with discrimination, play a decisive role.

Religion (See discussion in Chapter 12.)

Clubs, cliques and fraternal organizations

The Negro in America has been an inveterate joiner of clubs, cliques, and fraternal mutual help organizations. Many of these are of nation-wide scope, others purely local.[37] Those on a national scale with good organization (like the Elks) have had long viability and increased membership. Those that have a special interest to us are the small clubs and cliques which are in constant state of organization and dissolution. Their membership is small (10–50), takes on high-sounding names, and dedicates itself to purely social ends like dancing or other forms of entertainment. It is a feature of these clubs that they are torn asunder by the mutual antagonisms, rivalries, and the quest for leadership and prestige.

V. LIFE CYCLE OF THE NEGRO

The following impressions about the life cycle of the Negro represent a synthesis of material culled from the case histories and the vast source literature on the Negro. These impressions are definitely of no statistical value. However, they do show a qualitative trend in several directions and these we hold to be important.

The family constellation

In the group we designated as lower classes, the dominant characteristic of the family constellation is its unsettled quality. The dis-

[37] *See* Frazier, E. Franklin, *The Negro in the United States*, Macmillan, 1949, Chapter XV, for a complete account of the history and development of Negro clubs and fraternal organizations.

integration of the family unit before the subject is 16 to 20 years of age is frequent, and in many of those instances where the family remains otherwise intact, the father deserts either before the child is born or two or three years later. The death of one parent before the child reaches the age of eight is extremely common. The death of both parents before the child is five is also common. These early deaths reflect the higher incidence of disease and the greater mortality among Negroes.

The fate of the children when the father deserts or dies is always very uncertain. The remarriage of the mother once or twice brings the child in contact with step-siblings, who almost invariably treat the newcomer with hostility. Often, the children of these broken homes are taken care of by aunts, uncles, or various other relatives, and their lot under these conditions is a most unhappy one. These surrogates understandably resent the added economic burden. The children are constantly aware that they are not wanted, at best tolerated, and in return for the care they get, are expected to be obedient and servile to their benefactors. The consequences of the broken home for the children are disastrous in every possible sense. Nor is the lot of the abandoned wife very much better. These consequences we shall discuss later.

In the middle and upper classes, on the other hand, the family unit usually remains intact, whatever other characteristics it may have.

Maternal care

The frequency of husband abandonment in the lower classes generally forces the deserted mother to take care of the children; but in order to do so, her role as a parent suffers severely. She is obliged to work during the day and the child is neglected in the meanwhile. And when she returns from work, her disposition to the child is not prone to be very considerate. Fatigue and irritability are likely to be prominent reasons why the records indicate so frequently that the mother is ill-tempered, imposes severe and rigid discipline, demands immediate obedience, and offers only sporadic affection. In fact, this is the most common complaint, even by well-fed children, that the mothers in this group are often loveless tyrants. Coldness, scoldings, and frequent beatings are the rule. Exploitation of children by foster parents is extremely common. However, these features are not universal. In many instances, maternal care is good, notwithstanding hardships. Such instances are found mainly in lower-class families where the family unit has remained intact. The grandmother often takes over the maternal role while the mother is at work. This accounts for the frequency with which the grandmother is idealized in this group.

In the middle class, there is no consistent trend. Maternal care tends to vary directly with socioeconomic circumstances that are favorable to family stability. For this reason, maternal care is generally better than in the lower class, but as hardships develop, maternal rejection and lack of interest begin to appear. In cases where the grandmother takes some part in child-rearing, we do not see much of the idealized granny. As a general rule, she carries out maternal attitudes since she is more often an adjunct rather than a substitute for the mother. One of the features of middle-class maternal care is the favoritism of mothers for the lighter skinned children. This is an offshoot of improved socioeconomic conditions. It represents a shift from a preoccupation with basic subsistence to a preoccupation with status.

In the upper class, with its opportunities for family solidarity, maternal care approximates that found in whites of a similar socioeconomic level.

Paternal care

The common feature of paternal care in the lower class is its frequent absence. For many reasons that will become apparent, the father is the lesser figure in the household. The fathers frequently oscillate between two poles: they are either seclusive, taciturn, violent, punitive, and without interest in the children, or they are submissive to the mother. Often they are irresponsible or alcoholic. Uncles who assume care of children are generally resentful of their nephews, and when they have their own children, openly discriminate in favor of the latter. Grandfathers as paternal surrogates are usually no better than uncles. Nevertheless, kind, benevolent, and provident fathers do appear in this group. Here again, this occurs mostly when the father can achieve economic security and, with the assumption of full masculine prerogatives, is enabled to express more positive behavior toward his children.

In the middle class, the father, like the mother, shows no consistent trend. The caliber of paternal care tends to go hand in hand with economic opportunity. Middle-class fathers are generally good providers and hence, more responsible than those in the lower class. As in whites, their attitudes toward offspring vary widely. Some are rigid disciplinarians and delinquent in paternal functions, such as attention, interest, and affection. Others are excellent in all aspects of parenthood.

In the upper class, paternal care resembles that of white fathers of a similar status.

General discipline

The disciplinary treatment of children in the lower classes is characterized by its inconsistency. Obedience is often enforced toward ends the child does not understand. High standards of behavior are expected without the affectionate background that can act as an incentive to the child. Beatings without provocation are common; severe punishment for minor infractions, likewise. Such treatment mirrors the hardships and frustrations of the parents, which militate against parental patience and tolerance. Children cared for by uncles, and aunts, and other relatives or friends are generally subject to cruel treatment, and for the same reasons. On the other hand, moderate discipline, appeal to reason, and occasional appreciation for good behavior is found in those families where parental hardship is diminished.

In the middle class, discipline is generally moderate, and not usually enforced by cruelty. Tongue lashings and encouragement of high ideals are much more common. Occasionally, just as in whites, one finds parents in this group who impose a reign of terror. The disciplinary role is divided between both parents, with some predominance on the maternal side.

In the upper class, discipline tends to be somewhat stricter but enforced by appeal to reason and high emphasis on the status value of certain approved kinds of behavior.

Attitude toward siblings

This can be evaluated in two ways: by what the subject says about it and by the character of the current tie to the siblings. According to these standards, sibling attitudes in the lower class show that animosity and hatred are the rule, with complete severance of relations. But there are many variations of this motif. In some instances, attitudes to siblings are friendly, but ties are not currently maintained. In other cases, ties are maintained by a sense of duty, but attitudes are very hostile. In still other instances, the animosity is so violent that relations are on a homicidal basis. The deteriorated quality of sibling relationships is easily explained. The opportunities for affection and material necessities in the lower-class child are severely limited. In the struggle to obtain a share of these scarcities, the ensuing rivalry is bitter and enormously exaggerated, in contrast to that between more privileged children.

In the middle class, the picture changes considerably. Here, animosity is controlled and ties are maintained, notwithstanding an undercurrent of rivalry. In the upper classes, the attitude is about the same.

Sexual history

The sexual mores of the urban Negro is a subject that cannot be treated impressionistically. Nothing but an exhaustive statistical study like that of Kinsey [38] can show us anything like a predominant trend. However, we offer our available clinical data largely because of their remarkable consistency with middle-class white standards. This establishes the norm for our culture, and Negroes of all classes are heavily influenced by it.

In the lower class, the overt teachings about sex are Victorian for both males and females. However, although sex taboos are universally taught, explicitly or implicitly, it is rare that they are enforced with beatings. There is little intimidation. The boys learn about sex in the streets; masturbation generally begins early, six to eight. On the whole, masturbation does not play much of a role in the growing lower-class boy. This is due to the early opportunities for relations with women. First intercourse at seven or nine is not uncommon, and very frequent in early adolescence, usually with girls much older.

The sexual education of the lower-class female is a bit more thorough. She is generally taught Victorian morality. Masturbation is less common than among boys, and possibly about the same frequency as among whites in the same group. Shame is generally invoked as the chief sanction. Later, the emphasis is more that sex

[38] Kinsey, Alfred, *et al., Sexual Behavior in the Human Male*, W. B. Saunders Company, 1948.

should be associated with love. Generally, the girls are inducted into first intercourse earlier than whites, but even here, in the lower class, the impact of the Victorian indoctrination is surprisingly effective. Fidelity to husbands runs higher than would be expected from the frequency of family disruption, and sexual disturbance, i.e. frigidity, is quite frequent. The Victorian sexual ethic in the lower class hits chiefly the female. The male begins his sexual career with women earlier; potency disturbances among males, too, are not uncommon.

In the middle class, we have some difference between the sex education of males and females. There is more freedom in this group in discussing sex with parents, and we found few instances of intimidation. Masturbation is somewhat more frequent among the boys in this group than in the lower class; it is learned later and continued longer. First intercourse for males occurs earlier than in middle-class whites, but later than in lower-class Negroes. It is common for boys in this group to begin active sexual relations at fifteen to sixteen and continue regularly from then on. We find that sexual activity as a power symbol is much more common and, as in the upper classes, it is used in an ego-enhancing capacity. Here, also, sex relations with white women have a high demonstrative value in terms of pride and prestige.

The middle-class female is much like her white sister. Sex education is rigidly puritanical, masturbation not frequent, and sex as an expression of love is highly stressed. The same is true of continence as a virtue. There is, however, little terrorization. Where early intercourse takes place, the female tends to hold the man responsible in the event of pregnancy. Fidelity to one man is very common. Sexual disorders are likewise common, as are virgins at marriage. It is in this middle-class group that we find most of the "kept women." These women are generally much preoccupied with *status;* i.e. they prefer the trappings of middle-class status at the cost of middle-class "respectability."

The upper-class sex mores are about the same as in the middle class.

The most surprising fact about the sex life of the Negro—of all classes—lies in its marked deviation from the white stereotypes that exist on the subject. The Negro is hardly the abandoned sexual hedonist he is supposed to be. Quite the contrary, sex often seems relatively unimportant to him. The factors that weigh heavily to make this the case are the uniformly bad relations with females on an emotional level. This has many determinants. If the male comes from a female-dominated household, the relation to the mother is generally one of frustrated dependency and hostility. This does not conduce to good relations with the female. The sexual function does not occupy an airtight compartment in the mental life of man; it is tied to many other aspects of adaptation. It is, therefore, consistent with the general hardships of the adaptation of the male that his sex life suffers as a consequence. He fears the female much more than is apparent for intrinsic genetic reasons, and also, because his economic opportunities are worse than the female's. Hence, he is not infrequently at the mercy of the woman. Masculinity is closely tied to power in every form in our society. The male is much the more vulnerable to socioeconomic failure. He unconsciously interprets it as a loss in masculinity, i.e. as femininity. The inability to function successfully in the male sexual role can be one of the outcomes of this interpretation. This concept will be fully elaborated in the personality studies.

The frequent disregard of the female for sex is equally remarkable. She is just as handicapped as her white contemporaries. This reluctance exists notwithstanding earlier opportunities for induction into sex, and less real oppression by the sense of shame for breach of conformity—as is the case, for example, with illegitimate offspring. We shall discuss this problem at greater length later.

Marriage

In the lower class, multiple and discordant marriages are the rule. Two marriages are quite frequent and even three and four are not uncommon. The ethics of marriage in the lower class are entirely different from white middle-class standards. The status of "married" is entered upon more casually than among whites, the relationship is more tentative and provisional, and it is much more easily dissolved. Formal divorces are instituted only when one or the other of the divorced pair wants legalized remarriage. Otherwise, they simply break up, the husband usually doing the absconding. Hence, it is the female who more commonly seeks the formal divorce.

The basic reason for the instability of the lower-class marriage lies in the fact that it is generally entered on for economic purposes by the female. The wish to get away from an oppressive environment is a common inducement for the female to seek marriage precipitously, only to be disillusioned shortly after. "Love" is not a predominant motive for marriage in this group, and companionship between mates is rare. Forced marriages because of pregnancy are quite frequent.

The most prevalent complaints of the females in this group about their marriages are: the marriages are loveless; there is no companionship; the women are only bed mates; the husbands do not support them. The entire relationship is more often than not taken up with a power struggle between husband and wife, with the former usually in a submissive role, and the female holding dominance by virtue of her actual or potential capacity as a provider. The absence of affectionate relatedness is the predominant feature of these marriages.

In the middle class, which is predominantly a white-collar group, marital relations are better. There is more emphasis on romantic "love"; marriage is less just an economic convenience. The dominance-submission conflict in the lower class is somewhat toned down in this group because of the better economic chances of the male, but not to the extent that the male becomes a completely idealized figure.

In the upper class, we find a still greater ability to idealize each other's roles. Romantic relationships with high mutual regard are, therefore, more common. Here, however, status conflicts of one or the other mate are conducive to a great deal of distress to both.

Education and occupational opportunities

Education in the United States is compulsory, but this does not mean that the lower-class Negro child is necessarily exposed to similar learning opportunities as the white child. In the rural areas, hardly more than a token educational structure exists for most Negro children. The buildings are decrepit, the teachers inexperienced, the classes overcrowded, and planned supervision is lacking. Furthermore, attendance is markedly irregular, either because the child must work, or because of truancy which is ignored through lack of interest by the authorities. For these reasons, a great many rural Negro children fail even to complete grammar school. Most urban children, however, manage to go at least through public school and a considerable number get one year of high school. From this point on, the resistance to education of the lower-class children becomes enormous. There are three dominant reasons for this: first, Negro children in this group understandably fail to see the relevance of education to their opportunities in life; second, many are obliged to work half or full time; and third, the competition of street life with the school is too great, and the street, with its imitation of the struggle for existence, with its sexual opportunities, and those for adventure, generally wins. From this time on, school becomes a meaningless and unrewarding bore. This is equally true of both sexes. It is difficult to conceive of a more hopeless and dispirited group than a high school class of Negro adolescent girls; nor a more bored and resentful group than a high school class of Negro boys. Both seem equally aimless and befogged. They do not assume these attitudes through choice. The fault is society's, not theirs.

The opportunities of those who do undertake to learn a skill is very problematical. It is very common to read in a work record that a subject was trained as an automobile mechanic, but could never find employment in that capacity. He, therefore, had to become a dishwasher, handyman, porter, short-order cook, hospital orderly, and so on. Another record reads: began work at eight, bootblack and odd jobs; twelve to fifteen, apprentice presser; fifteen to twenty-five, presser, musician in dance band, chauffeur; twenty-five to thirty-five, Pullman porter, chauffeur, assistant superintendent. This is, by and large, the occupational fate of the lower-class male. The lower-class female has less of an occupational range, but better chances of using training and skill. Her chief employment is in domestic personal service as housemaid, cook, nursemaid, and the like, with longer periods of constant employment and on a market wage scale.

In the middle classes, school is continued longer and the group has at least a more hopeful attitude about the value of education and of learning a skill. The choice of occupation for both males and females is most frequently in the clerical group. Lately, there has been a big drift of the Negro into all varieties of federal and municipal civil service, where there are anti-discrimination regulations.

The upper classes tend to give their children the same educational opportunities as whites in the same class, with infinitely less chance of seeing it through. The males seek technological training. The females in this group do the same, but without the compelling necessity to work.

We have not taken into consideration any of the occupations which depend on exploitation of the Negro's interest in sports, gambling, numbers rackets, and the like. These interests furnish only a very few Negroes with an adequate livelihood.

Old age

The Negro shares all the hazards of old age that the white man does and a good deal more besides. It is easy to see from both the statistical data and those pertaining to the life cycle, that a very small proportion of Negroes have any opportunity at all to save enough money to be able to provide themselves with an old age free of discomfort and anxiety, let alone live to an old age. Their hardship is, therefore, all the more increased because they cannot share equally in the social security program. Since agricultural and domestic workers are excluded from social security benefits, the Negro is hit hard, even without discrimination. As it is, in the case of old-age benefits, they receive more than their ratio of the total population would warrant. That is, Negroes were 12 per cent of all those receiving old-age assistance, whereas they are only 7 per cent of the population sixty-five years and older.[39] Negroes receive less than whites in the same relief category, especially in some Southern states.[40]

In this connection, the female comes off better than the male. The grandmother is a common fixture in lower- and middle-class families. She can always earn her keep as a caretaker and nurse for the grandchildren. The aged father is much less welcome. He can do little and is generally resented by his children. However, in some cases, the father continues to be exploitive of his children's working capacity and is a parasitic figure. This is the exception. The aging father usually takes what crumbs he can get.

This completes our comparative survey of white and Negro social organization. We have focused on the points of difference that stem from caste and class. We are now in a position to examine the impact of these differences on the personality of the Negro. Let us proceed to the personality studies.

[39] Myrdal, *op. cit.*, pp. 358–59.
[40] *Ibid.*

PART TWO
Personality Studies

CHAPTER FOUR

The Personal Document as Sociological Source Material

AN AUTOBIOGRAPHY is the organized experience of an individual edited by his character and expectations. The subject records for us experience in a distinctive human environment, governed by conventions and rules. His vicissitudes are the record of a series of interactions between himself, as he was organized at a given time, and this environment, which has a certain fixed character.

There is no rigid standard according to which a biography can be documented. There are any number of frames of reference. All biographies taken from a psychodynamic point of view focus on the mental and emotional equipment with which the individual operates. They seek to describe how this equipment came into being, how it was molded by experience, and how it functions in a given set of circumstances. In order to write such a biography, we must know the values and reality systems within which the individual lives. This the subject does not tell us; he assumes we know it. He does not know his social environment as an arrangement of institutions. He only knows what experience affected him pleasantly or unpleasantly, what was gratifying, and what was frustrating.

Biography, as commonly understood, is a conventionalized account of the impact of character on events and relationships. Psychodynamics, however, relies not only on this highly conventionalized form of self-representation, but also on forms of experience the significance of which the subject does not comprehend. This includes the following: the relationship of the parts of a subject's narrative to each other, i.e., free associations; dreams, or experience while asleep; the consistency of trends over a whole life trajectory; and the consistency of his current experience with his established character.

In this book, we are depending in a large measure for the biography to give us information we cannot gather by the use of statistical data, opinion polls, or the like. We are looking for information about the effects of a certain type of social oppression on the human unit. Is there any consistency in the results? We cannot expect uniformity, but we can expect a certain *range* of consistency.

We have arbitrarily elected to present the material in the form of division into lower, middle and upper classes, with full recognition of the limitations of this classification. We are aware that it has many sources of error. For example, a subject may now be classified as "lower" but his parents were "middle." Many varying combines of this sort will be encountered. Nevertheless, we have no choice but to place each subject into one or the other group according to his current style of living. If we did not do this, we could not arrange the subjects in any order that would give us the necessary basis for comparison.

The procedure consisted of studying twenty-five Negroes of different sex, age, and status, sufficiently varied to cover as many aspects of Negro adaptation as possible. These cases were all studied by the psychoanalytic interview technique. The first few hours were spent in taking a life history, the remainder in relating daily vicissitudes through the agency of free associations, dreams, and reactions to the interviewer. Each case was continued long enough to yield a picture of the dominant problems of adaptation and a sampling of reaction types. The records were then condensed into the personality summaries as presented later in the book. All subjects but one were seen once, twice, or three times a week for a minimum of twenty to a maximum of more than a hundred visits. The average subject was observed over a period of four to six months. No subject but one was studied for less than three months. The single exception (H.N.) was seen only ten times in six weeks, but the data was sufficient for an adequate reconstruction of his personality. In a few cases, interviews continued for more than a year. Various incentives were used to induce subjects to participate in the study. Twelve were patients in psychotherapy; they related their life stories in return for aid in the solution of a personal problem. Eleven were paid subjects; two volunteered their services. The paid subjects were rewarded with $1.50 per interview, payable immediately on its conclusion, and a $20.00 bonus, paid at the end of the twentieth session. The bonus acted to insure the completion of twenty interviews, the required minimum for adequate study. Subjects thus earned $2.50 per interview.

Some of the records are those of subjects who sought treatment for some neurotic difficulty. The façade of the story may therefore be occupied with the neurosis. This added feature merely complicates the *form* in which the problems are handled; it does not destroy or distort their *content*. The latter answers the question: What is the Negro personality concerned with? The former answers the question: How are these problems dealt with? The reader should learn to place the neurotic superstructure in its proper perspective. The particular difficulty the subject stresses is merely a thread which leads to the deeper layers of the personality.

How valid is our sample if we include subjects with neuroses? This raises the old question: Are neurotics people? One could in the same vein ask the question: Are the insane people? Here, some distinctions are in order. To the census taker, those in asylums, neurotics and non-neurotics, are all people. To the psychiatrist, "people" can change their psychiatric status by the mere fact that they consult a psychiatrist. The same person who is your dinner partner may be a "worrisome or anxious person," who is not placed in a category of abnormals. This same person becomes a "neurotic" if he talks to a psychiatrist. There are vast areas in this country, particularly rural centers, where the word psychiatrist is completely unknown. There are, nevertheless, people with severe mental and emotional disorders in these areas. They are generally called "queer," which has no fixed connotation.

The term "neurotic" is, therefore, purely relative to the person making the judgment and for what reason this judgment is made. For purposes of this book, "neurotics" are people indeed—because it is difficult to find anywhere in our society any considerable number of people who are entirely free of neurotic traits. The majority of them do not consult psychiatrists. Does that render them any less neurotic? It does not. It merely means that the neurosis is not making enough trouble for the individual for his symptoms to be recognizable.

There is a technical reason why neurotics are people. It lies in the simple fact that the general personality functioning of the neurotic is the same as the so-called normal. There is only one difference. Some of the systems with which the personality functions are disordered and give rise to certain types of discomfort (like anxiety) or dysfunction (like impotence). Save for these usually localized disorders, the rest of the personality functions normally. Every subject in this study (with the single exception of H.N.), regardless of his conflict—neurotic or real—was capable of being a self-sustaining member of our society.

This is not true of the insane. Here the whole perceptive apparatus and the responses of the individual are seriously impaired. Judgment is faulty, and the actions based on these faulty judgments are completely out of keeping with the norms of behavior for both normals and neurotics. They often lead to destructive or otherwise antisocial behavior. This is generally why the insane are kept confined where they can do no harm. No psychotic individuals have, therefore, been included in this report.

Finally, a word of caution must be given the reader concerning all these personal documents that follow. They read much worse than they are. The psychodynamic exploration of personality functioning inevitably concentrates on sources of conflict. The result may look as if we find everything "bad." This is very far from the truth. In these records will be found some of the most extraordinary examples of effective adaptation that we have seen anywhere, in any group. In fact, as a group we must make the judgment that their adaptability is extraordinarily good considering the difficult conditions under which most of them live. Some of these subjects whose records are unrelieved from the persistent failure and frustration, nevertheless are able to salvage some happiness, now and then. We have not in every case paused to make as complete an inventory of the happier aspects of their lives. This is unintentional. This is the result of the focus of this work, rather than a complete picture of the reality.

The reader of these case histories must perform another task, not an easy one, of translating the findings about the Negro personality into terms of social relevancy. A psychodynamic study of any personality in any culture gives a distorted picture of the individual in his living environment. The psychodynamic picture is the "inside" of the personality; in the living environment we get the social façade. The aspect that counts in the social evaluation is the latter, but in order to understand this, we must know the former.

We can summarize the total picture of the personalities that follow in a few sentences. The Negro, in contrast to the white, is a more unhappy person; he has a harder environment to live in, and the internal stress is greater. By "unhappy" we mean he enjoys less, he suffers more. There is not one personality trait of the Negro the source of which cannot be traced to his difficult living conditions. There are no exceptions to this rule. The final result is a wretched internal life. This does not mean he is a worse citizen. It merely means that he must be more careful and vigilant, and must exercise controls of which the white man is free. This fact in itself, the necessity to exercise control, is distractive and destructive of spontaneity and ease. Moreover, it diminishes the total social effectiveness of the personality, and it is especially in this regard that the society as a whole suffers from the internal stresses under which the Negro lives.

CHAPTER FIVE
The Lower Class

I. MALE

S.C.

S.C. is a 27-year-old, unmarried, dark brown Negro. There is a perpetual sullen expression on his face. He speaks with a very thick Southern accent in a low, at times almost inaudible, mumble. He lives alone in a single, furnished room in a boardinghouse. During the day he is employed as a porter, and at night he is a student at a trade school, where he is learning to be a radio technician.

S.C. is a patient in psychotherapy. He dates the onset of his difficulties to World War II. At that time, following a long stretch of hazardous combat duty in Italy, he developed a typical traumatic neurosis of war: severe headaches, chronic fatigue, nervousness, terrifying nightmares, explosive irritability, insomnia, and loss of appetite. He was returned to the States for recuperation and the intensity of the symptoms abated, but they never completely disappeared. His chief complaints localized around the headaches and the fatigue, and in his attempts to get relief, he has drifted from clinic to clinic. No organic disorder was found and the many drugs with which he was treated had no effect. Finally, he was referred for psychiatric treatment.

S.C. was born and raised on a farm in the South. His mother was very sickly and died when he was five. He remembers her with kindness: "She was very nice to us—a very good mother." There is probably a good bit of idealization in his memory, which derives from the contrast with his step-mother, whom he hated. His father was an uneducated, but literate sharecropper, who demanded respect, but in return gave some warmth and affection. There are two siblings, an older brother and a younger brother. S.C. has little use for both and has not kept in touch with either of them. The father remarried when S.C. was eight. The step-mother was an illiterate domestic worker, who brought two small nieces with her when she joined the family. She rejected S.C. and his brothers in favor of these two nieces. They received what little affection she was capable of giving; the boys got only coldness, scoldings, and beatings. S.C. resented his father's remarriage: "That hurt me. We didn't want him to remarry. And my step-mother treated my two step-sisters nice and always played them against us and treated us rough."

The family's economic condition was always very poor. They lived in a decrepit four-room house in which the three brothers occupied a single room, all sleeping in the same bed. Food and clothing were scarce. As S.C. puts it: "We had a lot of hardship. It was pretty tough. We lacked for everything." Discipline was rather strict and was applied by both parents, but the final arbiter was the father. S.C.'s attitude toward his father's whippings is something on the order of it-hurt-him-more-than-it-did-me: "Looking back, I can see that when he whipped us it wasn't because he wanted to. Of course, he was no angel either. He used a razor strap and beat you around the legs and the rump." The step-mother attended the Protestant Sanctified Church and tried to force her religious beliefs on the three boys, but out of their hatred for her, they refused to attend. In the end, the two nieces were sanctified, but the three brothers were not. S.C. identified the preacher with his step-mother, and from his description, perhaps rightfully so. They both frustrated his dependency needs: "The preacher took everything. He had clothes and a car and we had nothing. We used to get one good meal a week and that was on Sunday, and the preacher, he would come over and eat that up. That's what turned me against religion." Neither the father nor the step-mother gave any sexual information and sex was never discussed in the home. S.C. and his brothers "picked up" their sexual knowledge "from the guys."

He did not begin school until the age of nine. He explains the late start on the basis of poverty; he did not have clothing suitable for attendance at school. His father finally managed to get on relief, and dressed by the government, S.C. was able to begin school. Here, he soon displaced to his teacher the resentment he felt toward his step-mother, and for the same basic reason: he felt the teacher discriminated against him in favor of other students. He protested and for his rebellion both the teacher and his father whipped him. After that, S.C. stopped fighting back; he "just didn't bother any more." This is good evidence that he learned his lesson well: self-assertion is dangerous and can only lead to aggressive retaliation. Scholastically, he had no trouble. As a matter of fact, he was the best student in his class—as far as he went. Unfortunately, he had to drop out at 15 while only in the sixth grade. This was due to an unhappy trick of fate which played right into his complex about discrimination. His older brother was working and broke his hand. This forced S.C. to drop out of school and go to work in his place, since the family could ill-afford to lose the income. After his brother got well, S.C. was not permitted to resume his education; instead he had to go on working. He now blames his brother for much of the frustrated ambition that lack of education has caused him.

For the next five years S.C. worked as a delivery boy. Finally, he decided there was no future for him in the South, and so he came to New York in search of opportunity. He worked first as a porter, later as a dishwasher. Then the war broke out and he entered the Army. In four years of service he rose no higher than the rank of Pfc., but not because he lacked ability. Here, again, he was motivated by his fear of self-assertion. He was offered advancement several times but always refused: "I didn't want no rank. Man get to be a sergeant, then his officer is on him, pretty soon everybody is on everybody else. I didn't want any of that. Even the Pfc. was forced on me. The Captain said I had to take it. He said I could get a better rating if I wanted to, but I couldn't see it that way."

Since his discharge from the Army he has had a number of unskilled jobs, but each invariably ends in the same way. He begins to feel he is being discriminated against and either quits in a rage or provokes his employer to fire him: "One trouble is holding a job. I never get along with the employer. Any person who has more authority than I, I like for them to talk to me right, like you was a human being or a person. Usually the man complains about my work or he says something I don't like and I get mad and either blow my top or say my little piece or quit. One thing it really started from was staying in the South—the discrimination, but now, even where there is no discrimination, if anybody says something, I jump right back. It ain't discrimination any more but it started with that."

The Great American Success Dream is his major aspiration: "Sometimes I daydreams so much I thinks I'm going to blow my top. I thinks crazy things, like a hill dug out and I have a house there with dynamos at the bottom to give electric powers, and then I thinks of a car I would like to have. In the Army I used to think of what I'd do when I came home, but I get here and everything is different. I thought I'd make a lot of money and have a home. This home would be two stories with a terrace and garden including grass and everything on top of the house. It was a house on a house, not an apartment. I want something nobody else has. That's a tendency with me. Men all dress alike. I think I should make my own style—do it my way. I don't want to get married now. I want a foundation first. I want to finish school. Then I can get a good job and bring up a family the way I want. I would like a good wife and two children—a boy and a girl—and I always thinks how good she is going to be. I just thinks of her as not having any faults. And I want my children to get an education. That's something I never had and it hurt me real bad."

His goals, unfortunately, far outdistance his capacity for their implementation. The problem is not in the lack of resources. These S.C. has in ample quantity. Rather, the difficulty stems from two obstacles, each of which reinforces the other. These are his lack of the necessary skills and the caste system, which blocks off avenues of solution. It is next to impossible for him to get technical training, but even if he gets it, his chances of putting it to use are practically nil. The result is a constant state of frustration, symptomatically expressed in a mixture of resentment, depression, and apathy. This is what lies behind his sullen expression. Throughout the interviews, S.C. repeatedly voices his hopelessness: "I never had a chance to go to school so I could never accomplish what I wanted. But suppose I do finish school. How'll I get a job being colored? I keep thinking all the time: Is that true that I won't even get a chance? I keep trying to tell myself it ain't true, but all the time there's a doubt." And again: "I just feel bad. I'm not sick. I just feel bad. It's not a sickness like I have a fever. It's nothing like that. I try to study, I try to read, but I just don't seem to be able to do it. Maybe it's just lazy. I just don't feel like doing anything at all. Regardless of what you do, you can't get anywhere. You work and you go to school and you work and you work and you go to school and you're still in the same place. Take this country right now. You work eight hours a day and all you get is $25 a week. You can't live—you can only exist. So what's the use? You can't see any reason for doing anything. There's no use trying—you just can't. There just ain't no use. That's the way I feel, so I act that way. I act the way I feel."

There is no escape from this frustration. S.C. is caught in a trap. In childhood, he was subject to discrimination against him. Now, under similar circumstances, he has little choice but to project upon the current social scene his childhood conflicts. This involves a perpetuation of the infantile patterns of adaptation. In order to understand how this operates, we must first define the childhood constellations and trace out their dynamic interconnections.

The early death of his mother produced several effects: it frustrated dependency needs; it doubled the significance of the father as a dependency object; it laid the foundation for mistrust of the woman—S.C. could not help but feel he was abandoned; it increased the intensity of sibling rivalry with his brothers since now there was only one parent for whose favor they could compete. The father's remarriage only made matters worse. It reinforced S.C.'s sense of abandonment, this time by a male, and it consolidated his distrust of women. The step-mother was not only a rival for the father's affection and interest, but, in addition, she actively rejected his sons in favor of her two nieces. Further, she then mistreated the boys and subjected them to a loveless discipline. Here we have a familial background almost entirely devoid of security. S.C., for one reason or another, felt himself threatened by every single member of the group. Let us track down the adult derivatives of these childhood relationships.

One thing we know for certain: S.C. isn't going to trust anyone—and this, indeed, is true. His original perception that people are dangerous makes it impossible for him to get close to anybody. Effective relations with people are further hampered by his low affectivity, an end product of the affect-hunger of his childhood. S.C. is a lone wolf. He has no friends, and for all practical purposes lives in a state of social isolation. He, himself, is well aware of this, and throughout the interviews he comments upon it repeatedly, invariably concluding with the same rationalization: "People only take advantage of you."

Sexual need forces him to attempt relationships with women, but these are doomed to failure from the outset. His occasional unions are entirely devoid of affection; instead they are predominantly colored by distrust and fear, derived from the image of his step-mother: "Women cause all my trouble. I don't have no confidence in them. Me and women just don't get along. Maybe my step-mother put me against them. My mother died when I was a baby. My step-mother was the only woman I ever knew. You can't trust any of them and every woman I meet proves what I think."

It is not long with every woman before S.C. becomes "disagreeable"; then follows incessant quarreling, and finally the union dissolves. Even sex, alone, is unsatisfactory. S.C. suffers from premature ejaculation. This difficulty is directly related to his perception of woman as a dangerous object. He sees her as a threat to his masculinity. His fear of castration is illustrated by the following comment, a spontaneous answer to a question by the interviewer concerning women: "One of my girl friend's nieces likes to cut guys. She has knives and when she blows her top she cuts them. I don't like knives —I'm allergic to them. I figure maybe sometime my girl friend and I will get into an argument and her niece will come to help her and will come after me with a knife. I hate to see a fellow run from a woman. I would have to stand there and do something. I figure some day she will do that to me and I won't run and I will have to pick up a brick or something and hit her. I figure it's best this shouldn't happen. I hate knives. I always have. So I figure the best thing to do is not to be around."

One would think from listening to S.C. that his main problem is with women. Actually, this is an artifact created by his defenses. His greatest difficulty lies in social and sexual competition with men, but he fears discussion of this conflict and diverts it always to women. The reason for this diversion is that S.C. has anxieties which he identifies as "homosexual," a concept most humiliating to him. This becomes apparent several times during the interviews, when, after a long pause, he unfailingly asks about "mens going with mens." Every attempt by the interviewer to elaborate this topic was met by blocking or running away; thus, on two occasions, he failed to appear for the subsequent session. As a matter of fact, these anxieties are not really homosexual at all, in the erotic sense of the term, but rather they represent an unacceptable wish to assume a passive-feminine, submissive position to some stronger man as an alternative to his own failure in the masculine role. He fantasies that in this relationship power and strength will be made available to him. However, unconsciously, he thinks of such a union as an erotic one, and hence, homosexual. Actually, it is a magical kind of dependency based on the prototype of the relationship between a father and a son. The explanation for this wish is very complex and is based on an interaction between individual and social dynamic forces.

The revival of infantile dependency needs in an adult unerringly represents a failure in adaptation. This is certainly true of S.C. We have already touched on the societal reasons for his failure. These consist of the caste system which effectively blocks his attempts to achieve ambitious goals. The individual basis of his failure has to do primarily with the inhibition of aggression. This takes root from the rivalry with the siblings, a struggle unconsciously symbolized in violent terms. A typical dream, one of several, illustrates this point:

I was staying with my brother and his wife. They invited some friends in and me and one of the fellows went for a walk. We were getting along very nice. Then all of a sudden we come to a disagreement and we both had knives. I had a big knife and he had a small knife. All of a sudden he pulled out two big old butcher knives. I started backing up. Then I ducked behind a house. I woke up sweating.

Thus, his brother, through a third party, attacks him. S.C. identifies the aggressor as a pool shark who once tricked him out of some money. The immediate stimulus for the dream was his brother's promise to back him financially in a business after he finished radio school. S.C. interpreted his brother's good wishes as a camouflaged attempt to exploit him: he would do all the work and his brother, as the backer, would insist on all the profits. S.C. simply cannot accept that his brother will help his efforts to be successful. His childhood experiences have taught him to be wary and he can foresee only violent opposition to his competitive strivings. Throughout therapy S.C. has several similar nightmares all having to do with bodily attack by his siblings and his cousins. These are invariably prompted by attempts to elevate his status. This means that he now conceives of any assertive activity designed to further his ambitions as a piece of violent aggression against his fellows which can only lead to retaliation in kind. A successful performance under such circumstances is hardly possible. The restrictions of the caste system make matters infinitely worse. What little assertion he can muster is foredoomed to failure. The effect this has on his already deflated self-esteem is disastrous. It would be low enough if he were a white man with similar inhibitions, but being a Negro really pushes it to rock bottom. The social realities, which relegate the Negro to a position of inferiority, serve to confirm S.C.'s feelings of worthlessness. His reaction is to reject his own race. This is really a projection of his own self-hatred: "They're always cursing in the street, and they go on, and they holler. I don't like it myself, so I don't expect others to like it. The majority of them are loud. O.K., so there are reasons, but I don't like it anyway. Then they don't want education. They won't go to school. They're always hollering 'discrimination.' Well, I discriminate against them myself, too."

His capacity for solidarity with other Negroes is thoroughly undermined. This results not only from the status conflict but also from his lack of affectivity and from his expectation of attack: "One thing I feel bad about—one thing I have a lot of resentment about—they don't try to help one another, the Negroes. Instead, they go against one another. Take Harlem. There's a lot of people there who don't want to work. They just want to wait 'til the other person gets some money. Then they'll knock him on the head, and get it away. I don't like that. That's what's holding all of us back. One guy is trying to advance and the majority pulls him back."

He is equally consistent in his attitudes toward "race leaders": "I don't think much of them. I think they're just advancing themselves, getting more power. They ain't trying to lead nobody. All they're doing is trying to advance themselves. Regardless of how big a man gets as long as he is social with me and talks to me, then O.K., but when he starts thinking he's God, then it's time to pull him down to size. I never really thought about who is the leader. I read a lot about what they is doing and saying, but it's mostly to advance themselves."

S.C. is no fool. He demonstrates an acute insight into the Negro's problem: "I read the other day about a white man who was a great fighter for the colored race. Then one day his daughter said she was going to marry a colored man and he blew his top. Now it's the same with these "race leaders." They won't let their daughters marry except for money. They want the man their daughters marry to have fifteen college diplomas and know all the right people. That's why they ain't no leaders. Any time you consider yourself better than others you can't fight for them. All they doing is fighting for their own clique. I don't see myself better than anybody and I don't see anybody better than me. I'm a man and he's a man, that's all. Some people have more money, but what's that? It's just money. I heard a woman say about a little girl, 'Why she looks so nice. She's dressed up like a little white girl.' That just burns me up! In other words she ain't no good unless she can be like a little white girl. That's the way all the colored are. They want to think and act like the white race. That's no good. They've got to start being and acting themselves before they can amount to anything. The people that are supposed to be educated are just as stupid in this as the uneducated."

S.C.'s failures—social and sexual—are represented in his unconscious as an emasculation. He sees himself as utterly unable to assume the masculine role. The following dream vividly demonstrates the extent of his castration:

There was people around and they all had dogs on a leash. They were all womens. I was in the center and I had a snake on a leash. When the women found out I had this snake they all started scattering and running. I didn't even know I had this snake until they started running, and then I looked down and saw this snake. I don't know if it was a black snake or a mixture of colors. The womens, they were all rich peoples like the kind you see on Park Avenue. They were all white. They had furs and they're the kind that takes dogs for a walk.

His associations, as well as their sequence, are extremely revealing. First, he discusses the taboos against intercourse with white women: "It's all right for the white man to have a colored woman, but if a colored man is seen with a white woman, they want to hang him." Next, he complains he can't make a living: "I been worrying myself to death trying to find a job. I found a couple at sixty-five cents an hour, but that's no good." This is followed by a pause of several minutes. He breaks the silence by remarking, "No thoughts. Maybe it's something I don't want to say." Finally, after another pause, he asks the interviewer why "some mens likes to be with other mens." The interviewer parried the question and S.C. paused again. He then said, "I'll ask another question. Could this nervous worrying cause you to smoke a lot? I used to smoke a cigarette a month. Now I smoke all day." He skipped the next session.

In these associations, S.C. tells us: sexual failure combined with social failure destroys masculinity and produces homosexuality. Repair can be achieved through oral incorporation (fellatio) of the penis. The dream is a simple wish-fulfillment, a magical attempt to refute his own awareness of total failure in the masculine role. He conjures up an illusory penis, so strong and so powerful, it must even be kept on a leash. This is an indication that the real situation is exactly the reverse. But in the dream he achieves the topmost level of masculine performance, couched in status terms: he successfully intimidates a wealthy, socially prominent white woman.

S.C. illustrates the neurotic elaboration into a social context of a psychosexual conflict terminating in so-called "passive homosexuality." Completely frustrated and blocked at every turn, he struggles with the wish to fall back upon the magical dependency of his childhood. He strikingly demonstrates the high cost, in energy and emotion, of going through adaptational maneuvers that serve no function except to maintain a precarious psychological balance.

O.D.

O.D. is a 29-year-old, dark-skinned Negro male, who works as an orderly in a hospital. He is tall, athletically built, and makes a very personable appearance. He is currently married for the second time and shares a single room with his wife in a private home. They have no children. His demeanor with the therapist is that of an Army enlisted man with an officer. He is formal, submissive, and deferential, frequently addressing the therapist as "Sir."

O.D. is a patient in psychotherapy. He comes to treatment because he has been having potency trouble for the past three years. He either fails to get an erection, or if he does, he has a premature ejaculation. These disturbances began following his discharge from the Army when he returned home to find his first wife living with another man. He attempted a reconciliation, but she rejected him, and thereafter he has been unable to perform sexually. He denies prior sexual difficulty. A year ago he remarried, but his impotence continued with his second wife. Finally, in disgust, she informed him that she had been forced to take a lover. She gave him an ultimatum: either he regain his "nature" or she would seek a divorce. At this point, thoroughly frightened that he might lose her, he applied for aid.

He was born and raised in a Northern metropolis. His mother and father separated when he was a few months old. He remained with his mother and only on rare occasions saw his father. The mother, a blues singer, remarried when he was two. The step-father was a chef and made a fair living. A son and a daughter were born of this marriage. The step-father worked out of town and was home only one day a week. O.D. remembers little about him. The mother stayed home and brought up the children. She was a warm and affectionate woman, but quite strict, demanding instantaneous obedience. Whippings were frequent and he recollects that his "fan was warmed a million times." The mother particularly insisted on neat and proper dress. As a result, he has always been self-conscious of his appearance. The children attended Sunday school regularly, but otherwise religion was not stressed. Sex was taboo and he does not remember a single mention of it by his mother during his childhood. Relations between the siblings were never cordial. He describes his half-brother as "mean and hateful." He speaks with more favor of his half-sister, but here, too, he is at best only lukewarm.

The step-father died when O.D. was eight and the family temporarily broke up. The mother went on the road as a singer, O.D. and his half-brother moved in with the maternal grandmother, while the half-sister stayed with relatives in the South. The grandmother could not support the two sons, and after a year they were placed in a foundling home. During the next four years they were farmed out to various private families, staying with each for several months. Throughout this period O.D. was very ashamed of being a "court kid." He felt unloved and unwanted. He expresses his drop in status in terms of clothing: "I didn't like the clothes they made me wear. I didn't feel dressed. If I'd been home with my mother, I wouldn't have been ashamed with the clothes she got me." One family he stayed with looked down on him not only for being a ward, but also for being so dark. The lady of the house could pass for white and her three children were very fair. O.D. and his step-brother were not allowed to associate with the lighter children, nor could they eat at the same table with them. They were fed separately and even given inferior food. The family ate heartily of a balanced diet, while the two foster children subsisted mostly on beans. Yet, in relating this mistreatment, O.D. finds it difficult to express open resentment:

"I really ought to hate her for it, but I don't. I just pity her. She didn't know what she was doing. I can't hate anybody. I can dislike them, but as far as hate, I never did that, at least not yet."

The mother married again when O.D. was twelve and once more the family was united. She gave up singing and resumed her duties as a housewife. The second step-father was a night-club comedian, who slept during the day and had little contact with the children. His role was mainly that of a breadwinner. He had a "bad disposition" and O.D. disliked him thoroughly.

At the age of fifteen O.D. entered a trade school and learned how to become an auto mechanic. He had few friends. He could not adjust himself to the social and sexual patterns of his contemporaries. He complains that the other boys thought only of carousing and sleeping with girls, activities forbidden to him by his mother, who warned him, "If a woman is good enough to go to bed with, she is good enough to marry." He could find no such girl. As a consequence his sexual experiences were delayed. His first date was at twenty-one, and his first intercourse shortly thereafter. Women were attracted by his handsome appearance and he began to have intercourse regularly.

He graduated from trade school at nineteen, but he could not find a job as an auto mechanic. For the next four years he held successive jobs as a dishwasher, a car washer, a beer joint porter, and a short-order cook. In 1942 he entered the Army. A girl he had been sleeping with accused him of being responsible for her pregnancy and insisted he marry her. He was most reluctant, but nevertheless, he agreed. He then failed to show up for three successive appointments with the minister. The baby was born out of wedlock, and the rejected bride, in a fury, swore out a warrant for his arrest. A trial followed and the judge confronted him with only two alternatives: "Marry her or go to jail. What do you want to do?" O.D. married her.

Three weeks after the marriage he was shipped overseas. During the whole two years he was away he did not have a single cheerful letter from his wife. She only castigated him for his initial refusals to marry her. Then he began to hear stories about his wife from Army buddies left behind in the States. It was rumored that he, after all, had not been the father. Further, she was now living with another man, one of his former friends. He returned home with a gun in his pocket. If the rumors were true, he intended to kill her. She met him at the door and would not let him in. As we would suspect, he did not carry out his threat. Instead of shooting, he fell on his knees and pleaded for forgiveness. He begged and cried, but it was no use; she remained adamant. It was following this incident that his potency difficulties began. A year later, he met and married his present wife, a college-trained librarian.

O.D. opened therapy with a statement of his failures to achieve economic success and play the desired masculine role with his present wife. He wants a family but she insists they will be in no position to have children until they secure an apartment and he makes enough money so that she can stop working. His search for more gainful employment has not been fruitful. He has failed a number of civil service examinations and has lacked the necessary skills for other jobs. His masculinity is further deflated in the relationship with his wife. She is an aggressive, quick-thinking, dynamic young woman and her word in the household is law. He is utterly incapable of being assertive with her. He uses her higher education and greater knowledge as a rationalization for his inhibition. She and her friends make him feel inferior.

Unfortunately for O.D., most discussions on family policy demonstrate in the end that his wife was right and he was wrong. This makes him even more fearful to express his opinions. His wife has begun to complain she never knows his views on anything. So, lately he has been perusing newspapers from cover to cover so that he will have ready answers for his wife's remarks on current affairs. The wide cultural gap between O.D. and his wife creates additional conflicts. He likes to listen to mystery stories on the radio, but he defers to her interest in programs of greater educational value that come at the same time. He enjoys Western movies, but his wife usually refuses to go. On the rare occasions that she does, she pointedly indicates her disapproval by going to sleep. It is invariably O.D. who gives in.

At first, as he describes these incidents, he denies any anger whatsoever. Challenged by the therapist, he finally admits to being "a little peeved" but he quickly "forgets all about it." He elaborates his inability to express anger: "Very seldom do I ever get angry. It takes two to make an argument and I don't argue. I just don't say any more. I just lay down and read a book. I don't do anything. I guess

I never been angry more than two or three times in my life that I can remember. Lots of times I think if I get pushed to a certain point I'll get mad, but it never gets to that point. I often wonder if I get angry what would I do."

He remembers only one time that he let himself go. His rage exploded with nearly fatal results: "A fellow named Rhubarb. This particular day was so ungodly hot! We were loading heavy equipment for the Normandy invasion. I took my truck down but Rhubarb wouldn't move so I could get in my place. I asked, 'Rhubarb, would you mind moving your truck? It's hot out here.' He said, 'You make me move!' I thought he was joking, but he wasn't. I asked three times, then I grabbed an English soldier's gun and pulled the trigger I don't know how many times, but it didn't fire. It wasn't loaded. Rhubarb moved the truck then. I felt cold. I was just as nervous! I had the shivers."

He is especially fearful of hurting a woman. He uses another rationalization to explain this fear. He argues that women are fragile and men should be chivalrous: "I don't think I'm afraid of them. It's just that to me a woman is something to be handled carefully like a delicate piece of china. The way I see most men treat them, beat them, kick them around, I think women should not be treated that way. I am too good to a woman. Some men kick their women around, and they get along all right, but I always treat them good and I always get hurt."

His submissiveness leads people to take constant advantage of him. They borrow money, and when they do not repay, he is too timid to ask for it. His fellow employees pile extra work on him, and he does it, too fearful to protest. He is unable to voice a contrary opinion in an argument, and if he is insulted, he cannot answer back. Instead of expressing his resentment at such treatment, he falls silent and broods. If the anger mounts, and there is danger that it may not be contained, he gets anxious: "I know one thing—I get scared when I get angry. I don't know what it is, fright or what, but I know I get nervous as the devil."

O.D.'s patterns of aggression are incorporated into his sexual behavior. During intercourse he worries that he might hurt his partner: "Every woman I ever went to bed with I've been very careful about that. I heard women talk they had men, who didn't care how they were punching. They didn't care how much they hurt a woman. I always ask my wife if I hurt her, and she says no. Some men have bigger penises than others and they try to put too much in. That is the worst of all. Then they can really mess her up. As a rule, if a man has a penis that is too big, a woman won't have anything to do with him, not if she values her life."

All the observations on O.D.'s behavior, derived from the therapeutic sessions with him, are confirmed in an interview with his wife: "Not once, never, since we got married, has he ever shown any anger toward me. Some men beat their wives. I wish just once he would flare up at me, rather than say 'yes' all the time. I slept with another man just once and I told him and even then he didn't get mad. I never know what he wants. He always says we'll do whatever I want. Like going to the movies—maybe it doesn't matter to him what he sees, but he never makes an issue of it. Then, the radio—if he turns on what he wants he gets uneasy and finally he turns back to my program. It makes me mad he doesn't have guts enough to listen to what he wants. And he wants me to buy his clothes because he's afraid he might buy something I don't like. I don't want him to worship me. I want him to express himself."

She is equally penetrating in her analysis of this marked dependency upon her: "He is dissatisfied with every job, stays only a while and leaves. I don't want to go on working all my life. I want a child but we can't get an apartment. He says, 'Go out and get pregnant and the Lord will provide,' but I see plenty of people every day at welfare places by whom the Lord is not doing so good. Then right after we got married he insisted on staying with my uncle and aunt. It was cramped. Intercourse was embarrassing. They could hear the springs. But he didn't want to leave. It didn't seem to bother him one bit. Then he has no sense about money. He spends it carelessly and he never questions where it comes from. He is very dependent on me. He gets very despondent when I tell him I'm fed up. I would have left him by now, but I'm afraid he will kill himself."

O.D. wants to play an aggressive male role. He wants to be master of the household, a father and a provider. He has rather childish fantasies of greatness and success: "I have some funny thoughts sometimes. I'll be thinking I am a big financier and everything I touch turns to money. Sometimes I am a famous boxer or an explorer. Sometimes I be a king way back in the old days. I daydreamed I was a doctor once and I was healing a lot of sick people. And once I daydreamed I was a prospector and found so much gold it was a pity." Actually, his main stock in trade is his appearance. He makes good use of his physical attributes to bolster his self-esteem. His wife attests to the success of his efforts: "I like him. He looks so good in a dress suit on Saturday night, and he's tall and handsome, and everybody likes him."

O.D.'s masculine aspirations are represented in his unconscious by the penis, the symbol par excellence of masculine power. This symbolic equation is illustrated by a dream expressing concern over his performance at a dance:

I dreamt my damn dick was cut in 4 equal parts, lengthwise, right up against my stomach. I told my wife, 'I'm sick.' She said, 'Well, you can't go to the dance like that.' I said, 'Don't worry. I'm well enough to go to the dance.' Then I woke up.

The injured penis symbolizes failure in the masculine role. He had the dream in anticipation of a dance he was to attend. This impending event apparently stimulated the fantasy that he would be a great success and make many a conquest over adoring women. The dream puts these fantasies to rest by representing him as castrated; i.e., he hasn't got what it takes. He puts an end to these ambitious fantasies because he fears his wife. But this solution of the problem does not satisfy him either. He now has anxieties that go with being impotent.

The explanation for his impotence lies in his fear that intercourse can terminate in castration. This fear is based on his conception of assertion as an exercise of masculine power that can be mediated sexually through the penis. We have already seen that he thinks of intercourse as an act of potential violence in which the penis is the organ of aggression. That is why his impotence invariably accompanies repressed hostility toward the woman. He dare not risk expression of this anger through intercourse for fear retaliation will take the form of injury to his genital. Seen in this light, the impotence is a protective device that inhibits masculine assertion and thus wards off retaliatory castration.

How does O.D. get this way? The trouble lies in the original relationship with his mother from which he has never extricated himself. Early in life he learned two maxims: (1) submission to maternal authority guarantees love and protection, and (2) rebellion is futile and leads only to rejection and punishment. O.D. took the easy way out. He became a good boy. To make the adaptation foolproof, he internalized his mother's dictates, and then responded to his conscience with automatic obedience and tight control of aggression. This control, and the manner in which he exercises it, are the dominant features of his adaptation. He does everything possible to prevent anger from reaching conscious levels. And when it does, he performs a masterly feat in controlling it by compliance, by anticipation, by deflection. How effective this control is can be seen from the fact that only once in his entire life did he lose it. Should his defenses break down he is confronted with an unpleasant fear of retaliation. It is this expectation of retaliation that produces such anxiety in O.D. upon any awareness of anger.

Unhappily, he has never considered himself strong enough to make his own way. In this connection, the obstacles society places in front of him for being a Negro have not made it any easier. As a result, he has remained tied to his infantile system of security. He simply shifts from his mother to his wife as the object of dependency and he continues to be a good boy. Such a security system demands the sacrifice of masculine prerogatives. This generates some hostility, but for the most part, the sacrifice is palatable as long as he is rewarded by dependency gratification. It is only when these dependency needs are frustrated that his aggression threatens to break its bounds.

G.R.

G.R. is a paid subject. He is a tall, well-proportioned, dark brown, 28-year-old Negro, who is employed as a porter. He has been married twice, but is now separated from his second wife and lives alone in a furnished room. He wears expensive, practically unused "hand-me-downs" that he has "begged" from his wealthy employers. The final result is a fashion plate, but one that expresses his own sense of style. Typical clothing consists of a checkered black-and-white sports jacket, white shirt with cuffs, colorful tie, black slacks, white socks, and black suede shoes. He not only is completely at ease in such clothes, but wears them with boldness and assurance. Toward the interviewer his demeanor is always one of respectful ingratiation. He addresses him as "Sir," smiles constantly, and creates an impression of bowing and scraping. Behind this cheerful façade, however, lies a chronic depression of mild intensity.

G.R. was born in the South in a country town of a few hundred people. His father was a poorly educated cook who deserted the family when G.R. was only a few months old. Little is known about the mother. She died when G.R. was three. He has only one memory of her, but it is a significant one: "When my mother died I just can remember I got in bed with her and they took me out. That's all I remember." The persistence of this image is a sure sign that his dependency longings remained unfulfilled. He had one sibling, a sister four years older. She is one of the few people from his childhood that he remembers with any fondness: "She's a very good person. We were very close together and she used to worry about me sometimes." After the mother's death, the two children lived for one year with the maternal grandfather, a sharecropper on a near-by farm. But the grandfather could not support them and when G.R. was four, he and his sister moved to a town of 12,000 to live with a maternal aunt and her husband. Here G.R. remained throughout his childhood.

The uncle was an uneducated, but literate laborer. He resented G.R.'s intrusion into his household, gave him no warmth, and treated him with considerable violence: "He was mostly a 'sometimes' person—sometimes he was all right, then again sometimes he was mean. He gave us plenty to eat but he was pretty cruel to us at times and didn't behave toward us as I would say a father would. When I was eight, his son and I was fighting, and my uncle come and slapped me off the porch and I fell and my jaw was swollen for days. I told him then that when I was twelve I would leave and make my own living." As we shall see, G.R. was true to his word.

The aunt was an illiterate housewife, who tried to shield him from the uncle's wrath and gave him some measure of affection. They had one son, two years older than G.R. He tried to emulate the father in his behavior toward the adopted children: "He picked on me all the time. Then we'd have to fight. Sometimes he'd win, sometimes he'd lose. Most the time I'd get a hatchet or an ax—anything I could get my hands on and run him off. He wouldn't bother me after that."

The aunt and uncle owned a shack in a Negro neighborhood that G.R. describes as "rough." The economic status was on a subsistence level: "He would make enough to live on from week to week but he didn't save none. I had enough to eat but I didn't have enough clothes nor like Christmas time I didn't have any toys and things kids like, the things that made other kids happy. All I had was some fruit and maybe a new pair of overalls. The other kids had tricycles and played with their toys and I didn't have anything. I was kind of ashamed to make with the other kids too much because I never had what I wanted—nice things. I hated to go to school with overalls on. That's why I always felt when I was small I'd been better off if I'd had at least a father when my mother died, but he left right after I was born." The uncle never failed to let G.R. know that he wasn't wanted: "He always threw up to my aunt that he had to take care of my sister and me. That's what they always quarreled about. We was young, but we heard, and as we growed up, it growed in us, and we still thinks about it. He would start arguing and cussing. He wanted me to get out of school and work." Discipline was rather strict and G.R. was frequently beaten, almost always by the uncle: "The least little thing you do wrong he told you not to do he'd whip you. He was pretty cruel." In return for their keep, G.R. and his sister were required to do the housework. Both took turns at cleaning and cooking. Religion was not an important issue. Sex was never mentioned in the household, but neither was there any intimidation.

He entered school at 6 and attended regularly until ten. He did poorly scholastically. He attributes his poor grades to two factors: "I didn't do so well because I never had no one to help me study. I never got further than the fourth grade. My uncle didn't pay no attention to us. Even when I tried to get him to help me with my lesson, he would say he was tired and start cussing me. Then, after school I would have to go around to people's houses and sweep the yard or mow the lawn. If I didn't do that, I would have to go home and work there." At ten, the uncle took him out of school and put him to work in a peanut oil company. Here, G.R. labored twelve hours a day, shoveling peanuts and coal. For this he was paid $1.20 a day. He finally became twelve years old, and true to his earlier promise, he left his aunt and uncle and struck out for himself: "I had told him when I was 8 and he beat me so bad I swolled up for weeks that I would leave when I was twelve. So I was twelve—and I put on two pairs of shirts, two pairs of pants, two pairs of socks, and I hit the road."

For the next several years G.R. traveled throughout the South and worked at many jobs. He shined shoes and he picked fruit. He was a bellhop and a bus boy and a porter. He washed dishes and he cooked. There was hardly a form of unskilled labor at which he didn't try his hand. He spent whatever he earned: "Clothes, soft lights, wine, womens, and music. I always lived good and had a good time."

At twenty-two, he met and married his first wife. He acted on this new responsibility by taking a permanent job as attendant in the shoe-shine parlor and men's room of a railroad station. Immediately, however, the newly married couple was beset by "in-law trouble." The wife's relatives interfered in their affairs and there was one fight after another. Nevertheless, G.R. held on to his job and became the father of two children. Finally, after two years of endless bickering, he decided to come to New York to get his wife away from the family. He would go first, get a job, and then send for her and the children. This he did, but when the time came, his wife refused to leave her parents. They had a lengthy correspondence and then she stopped answering his letters. He let it go at that and considered his marriage ended. They have not seen each other since, although he has been required by court order to contribute to the support of the children. Shortly thereafter he took up with another woman with whom he lived as man and wife. He had two more children by her. One day he came home to find his "wife" unfaithful. She proclaimed their association at an end because she no longer felt herself in love with him. Again he was ordered to provide for the children. Further, in order not to deprive the children of their home, he agreed to continue payments on the furniture which had been bought in his name. He found himself hard-pressed financially. To alleviate matters, he drew welfare funds while still employed. This, of course, is illegal. He was arrested, tried, and sentenced to thirty days. His employers advanced him the money for attorney's fees and now he is more in debt than ever. This is the point at which we find G.R. in the interviews. He has recently been released from jail and is engaged in a desperate effort to earn the money to pay off all his obligations. He is now thoroughly disillusioned with women. He lives alone in a furnished room, limits his contacts to casual girl friends, and has no intention of marrying ever again.

G.R.'s current preoccupation, therefore, is with making money and holding on to it. This is not to say he wasn't concerned with earning money in the past. He was, but the need for saving it was never so pressing. He now has a regular job as a porter. On the side, in the mornings and evenings, before and after work, he shines shoes for the various employees of his firm. Week ends he spends doing domestic work and gardening at the homes of his employers. Thus, G.R. works hard, and it is a seven-days-a-week proposition. Just how hard he works is revealed by the following dream:

I was walking in the woods and came to a parked car. It belonged to one of my bosses. He had his two kids with him. He said to me, 'Get in the back seat there and eat. There's plenty of food in there.' So I got in there and he had some ham and some kind of sweet muffins. So I was sitting there in the back seat eating. He drove back to the house and I ate all the way. Then we got to the house. I saw two large colored men working around the garage. I went to sit down on what looked like a rose bush only it had some kind of heavy stickles on it. I was still eating and one of those heavy stickles fell around my neck and it was sticking me and I was hollering, so my boss was telling these colored fellows, 'Come here and get it off him!' I was still eating and I was still hurting and that's when I woke up.

The dream followed a killing day's work at the country estate of his boss: "Last Saturday I like to die! I worked from 9:30 in the morning and ended up 9:15 at night. I planted grass, carried dirt, and painted the garage. I carried dirt all day. Sunday I couldn't get out of bed I was so tired." He also comments: "Maybe the dream means it hurt my pocket. I'm always broke. I have a hard time, believe me!" Put simply, the dream states, "It hurts to eat." By this G.R. means it is a backbreaking task earning enough money to retire his debts and support two wives and four children, as well as himself. In fact, he is doing the work of three men. That is why he can be relieved of his pain only through the aid of two other Negroes, both large and, therefore, strong enough to carry a full share of the work-load.

G.R. does not depend only on hard work. He lives also by his wits. He is a master psychologist and makes use of highly polished techniques of ingratiation to disarm and then exploit his victims—the affluent whites. That is why, in many ways, even with its discrimination, he prefers the South to the North. The Southerner, into whose motivations G.R. has acute insight, is much the more susceptible to his approach. Let us listen to his own account of his behavior: "Peoples say the South is much different from the North but I'd just as soon live in the South as I would in the North. I never had no trouble with the whites. I treat them with respect and they treat me with respect. I mind my own business and they mind theirs. The peoples I worked around, they never did call me 'nigger.' Mostly they treated me pretty swell. I never had no trouble in the South, even in the roughest towns, and I made a pretty good living. One time I was assistant manager in this pay toilet. I could make $25 to $30 a day. To make money on personality like that you got to laugh with them—jokes—tell something funny. As long as you seem regular and nice, they won't bother you, but if you figure you're a wise guy, they'll always try to put the hook on you—treat you pretty rough. The Southern peoples are not as civilized as the Northern peoples. I calls them the hill-billy type. Most of them you can't talk sense to. I've had drunks come in and maybe wanting a colored guy. That's what they always do—start picking on a colored guy. That's the first thing these hill-billies do when they get drunk. Well, I tries to take them back to the wash basin and get them to clean up. I tells them, 'Come on back here and freshen up.' Then I tries to get them to take a towel. They says, 'How much is it worth?' Well, it's worth five cents, but I smiles at them and says, 'Whatever you feel it's worth, boss.' I shame him out. It's better that way. You understand?" (You put yourself in the lower position.) "Yes, I do that." (How does this make you feel?) "Well, you just say words ain't going to hurt you, especially when you know you get paid for it. I had a Captain came in one Christmas time. He gave me five dollars to shine his shoes five times. He was drunk and had his bottle with him. He said, 'I'm going to give you a dollar every time you shine my shoes and I'm going to call you old nigger!' And he did." Here, G.R. laughs. He goes on: "It hurt me, sure, but it was the only way to get his money and get rid of this guy. So let him talk! He seemed like a pretty nice guy when he first came in, but what was in him had to come out. He was hill-billy before he came into the Army. He was born that way. And he'd probably been away in the North and hadn't said that word for a long time. It just makes him feel he is much more important than you are. It must give him a kick, a thrill, so he was willing to pay me to get to say it. I figure he's the one who's stupid, not me. So let him say it! It hurt a little, but it didn't kill me." Again G.R. laughs. "So let it hurt." After a pause, he laughs once more and concludes: "We could go on like this for hours. That's why I say—it don't make no difference where I live—in the North or the South. I always studies the peoples—whites and colored. Mostly you can tell what kind of peoples they are—right away. That's how I've always made my money. The Southerners are much bigger suckers with money than the Northerners. If you are a good talker and a fast talker you can sell them anything."

The advantages G.R. gains are obvious, but what are the psychological costs of such behavior? First, it can be perpetuated only through an inhibition of overt aggression. Second, the deflation of the self-esteem must be tremendous. The victory gained over the white man must fall far short of adequate compensation for the repeated humiliation and degradation. Let us take up the aggression first. We are not dealing here with repression, but rather with willful suppression at the cortical level. In repression the emotion is either poorly felt or not felt at all and the capacity for its activation is markedly limited or absent. This is not the case with G.R. He is both aware of the anger and capable of expressing it, but only under conditions favorable to him and in a manner of his own choosing. This means that he is engaged in a constant process of control. He must be ever vigilant and he dare not act or speak on impulse. Control, however, can never be perfect, and, on occasion, overt aggression inadvertently slips out. G.R. then evokes a secondary defense—the mechanism of denial. Laughter is the primary prop for this mechanism, and simultaneously, it serves as a vent for tension, which, if allowed to accumulate, would soon become unbearable. Protected by these devices, the aggression finally released by G.R. is further camouflaged by a cloak of ingratiation, and as we have seen, is most devious in its character.

These mechanisms can all be demonstrated in the relation between the subject and the interviewer. Midway through the study G.R. lacked money to pay his monthly furniture bill. He asked the interviewer to pay his bonus in advance, rather than at the end of the final session. This was acceptable to the interviewer and the loan was granted. The next month, when the installment again came due, he asked for a loan of $100. This was unacceptable and the loan was denied. That night he had the following dream:

You and I was talking and every time I came over here you would give me ten cents. It seems I was very happy about it. There was plenty more happened but I can't remember. All through the dream I was thinking about you. I was very pleased about the ten cents. It seems like you was giving me a dime every time I come here and that's all. The $1.50 didn't enter into it at all. The ten cents seemed like a lot of money and I was very happy when you give it to me. I would be laughing. I was thinking at least I got my carfare back.

The meaning of the dream, of course, is obvious. He resents the refusal of the loan and derogates the interviewer as a cheat who underpays him. He hides his true feeling by denial and disguises the anger by laughter. After relating the dream, he claims he has no associations. He is silent for a few minutes, then insists his mind is blank. Such blocking is a sure sign that he fears exposure of the underlying aggression in the dream. In order to draw him out, the interviewer began to press him. His resultant behavior is so remarkable and so revealing that it is reported in full: (Why are you so happy about the dime? That's not much.) "No, but I was happy for anything and grateful to have a dime." (How would you really feel if all I gave you each time was a dime?) Laughs and wriggles uncomfortably. "Well, I don't know. . . . That's a pretty stiff proposition. . . . Well, if it meant that much to you, and you didn't have no more, I wouldn't mind helping you—if you didn't have no more than a dime, my carfare. I would consider myself doing you a favor." (How would you *really* feel?) "How would I *really* feel? Well . . . I would *really* feel . . . laughs . . . If you couldn't afford it I would feel happy to help you, but if you could afford it, I wouldn't do it." (You're dodging the question.) Laughs. "I'm not answering the question right yet. I would feel I'm doing you a great favor." (I don't feel you'd be so pleased.) "At ten cents . . . laughs . . . No, at ten cents I wouldn't be very pleased— There ain't no sense me saying that." (Would you be angry?) "No-o-o-o-o! I wouldn't be angry. I wouldn't say that, because I wouldn't do it at all then. If I felt sarcastic that way I wouldn't come around at all. I wouldn't bother. This is something I do because it comes from my heart." (Why are you so happy in this dream? Even if you are willing to come, there is no reason you should get so happy about a dime.) Shakes head and grins. "No, it don't seem possible, really." (Maybe you are trying to hide your real feelings in the dream. Maybe you are really angry.) "No, I'm not angry because I like you. Even when people mention your name I tell them you're a swell fellow." (Even when I only give you a dime?) Laughs. "Even from the first time I met you, I liked you, but why I am so happy at the ten cents in the dream I don't know." (What caused the dream?) "Well, I don't know. I was in a tight jam. I needed $100. I could have asked my boss, but he just lent me $200. I finally got it from him." (How is that related to the dream?) Laughs. "Well, I guess I felt happy no matter what you gave me . . . but I'd felt happier if you'd given me half . . ." Pause. (Half?) Laughs. "Half the hundred . . . laughs . . . but I was thankful for anything you would give me." (I think this dream means you were mad because I wouldn't give you the $100 and you're covering up by laughing.) Roars with laughter. "Mad! Naw, I ain't mad!" (You're saying in this dream, "Dr. Ovesey is a cheap bastard," but you're covering up with laughter.) Laughs almost hysterically, slapping his thighs with his hands. "No, it's like this: A $100 is a lot of money. You just don't walk up to a man and ask him for a $100. No, I wasn't mad. If I was that mad, it would have come out and I would tell you." (You did tell me. It came out in the dream.) Laughs uproariously. "That ain't the way I feel. I don't see it in my mind." Laughs and laughs and laughs. (You don't like to tell me.) "You know if it was there, Doc, I would tell you. I couldn't walk around with it on my chest. It would have to come out." (The normal reaction to the refusal of a loan is to get angry. That doesn't mean you think I'm a bastard in general, but in relation to the loan, I'm a bastard in particular. You were mad but you were afraid to express it, so it came out in the dream in a subtle way.) "But I wasn't mad because I had no right to ask for the money. I just felt pretty low because I knew I would have to go and ask the bosses and I didn't want to get involved with them again. That's why I asked you." The interview ended here, and on his way out, G.R. said, "Could I have the rest of my appointments this week so we could finish up? We have five new salesmen and I want to get my shoe-shine business in full swing. I can make $15 a week extra that way." This concluding remark means simply that the interviewer has found him out and the situation has become too dangerous. Now, his only defense is escape.

Prior to this episode, G.R. had only praise for his employers and his fellow employees. He spoke of them several times in a rather ecstatic vein. Now, however, in the final two sessions, pushed by the recent unhappy experience with the interviewer, for the first time he allows his grievances to come out. He complains bitterly that his bosses exploit him and his co-workers deride him. He is expected to work longer and for less pay. Further, he is supposed to be a fool, simply because he is colored. He cannot meet expenses on the small salary he is paid and he is thinking of getting a new job. Frightened by this outburst, he promptly has an anxiety dream, in which he expresses his hostility toward the whites, but fortifies himself against retaliation by attributing his feelings to other, more powerful Negroes, who are better able to defend themselves:

It concerned the office. A colored fellow brought in a package. It was collect and he handed me the bill. I went in to the secretary's office to get it signed. So I was standing near the secretary, a white girl. There was a colored girl just outside the office. The secretary said to me, 'Those niggers really don't know how to dress, do they?' So I said to her, in a nice sarcastic way, 'What did you say?' So she repeated the same thing over again. So I said, 'You better be glad you're saying that to me, because I can ignore your stupidness, but you'd better not say it to one of them because they'll hit you right across the face.' So it wasn't any more said, but when I woke up I was very mad about it and nervous, too, because if any one of those other colored people had heard it, they would have fought. They would have been fighting mad. Right there in the office. If she said it to me I would ignore it, because I would know she didn't know no better and didn't have no intelligence.

The immediate stimulus for the dream was a minor incident in the office. The secretary accidentally struck her leg against his water pail and angrily accused him of being careless. He comments, "She wasn't looking where she was going and then she blames me. Then she blows up and I'm supposed to be stupid because I'm colored."

We have already stated that one of the end products of G.R.'s self-debasement before the whites is, of necessity, a lowering of the self-esteem. However, this alone is not the sole reason for the deflation. There are plenty of others. One of the more important is his failure to achieve ambitious goals. He has attained none of his aspirations. These are quite modest. His daydreams deal mostly with material comfort and security: "I never did want no lot of money, but I do want a nice living where I don't have to worry. I just want enough money to have enough to eat, enough clothes, and when I get older so I won't have to stand on the corner with a cigar box or apples. I'd like to get a house, too, and I always wanted to be able to hit a sweepstake ticket and stack that money away and have it waiting there 'til I was ready to retire. Then I would have something to look forward for in the days to come. I always studies peoples on the street and when I sees the blind or the crippled or some bums selling pencils—I always wonders if I'll be like that. I figure now is the only time if I figure right to *don't* be that way, but if I don't do right and don't get the opportunity, I don't know what will happen. I notice mostly every time I get a chance to start saving some money something usually happen."

There is a hopelessness and a futility about G.R. as he describes the repetitive frustration of his ambitions. No matter what he does, nothing works out the way he wants it, nothing seems to go right. Everything ends in failure. People are always taking advantage of him. They cheat him, make a fool of him, reject him, and derogate him. All of these attitudes are reflected in his dreams. He reports hardly a one that does not contain several of these elements in various combinations. The interviewer finally pointed out the constancy of this theme in his dreams. G.R. morosely shook his head, "That's right. The dreams show it truly. Nothing never works out as you plan, so what's the use of planning."

His self-esteem is further depressed by the caste system which relegates him to a position of inferiority. The operation of this factor is illustrated by the following dream:

It was a big house with two stories but only two peoples living in it. This fellow and a woman was watering the lawn. They was both white and they lived in the house. All of a sudden, all three of us was colored. The man said, 'Let's go in the house and have something to eat and drink.' So we walked up on the porch. There was a lot of mud on the sidewalk. They wiped their feet and walked on in the house. I was still trying to wipe my feet. I had a pair of rubbers on. So I couldn't get the mud off my feet. So I said I'd pull my rubbers off, but the dream ended, and I didn't get into the house.

The day of the dream he had tended the lawn of his employer's suburban estate. The white man and the white woman are the employer and his wife. The dream represents a miscarried wish for social equality. He transforms the whites into Negroes, but in the end they are still white and he is still colored. He can't be one of them after all. They do not let him into their house because he is black, dirty, and inferior. Thus, in classical psychoanalytic terms, the final identification is with feces.

G.R.'s main compensatory devices for the inflation of his self-esteem are clothes and women: "In the colored race the peoples usually figure you on how you dress. Even if you ain't got a dime in the world, if you dress nice you can make with some of the biggest ones. I always likes to wear something nice. I always did since I was a kid. Even as a kid I never liked to wear the same thing twice. I always liked to wear different things every day. As long as I had two pairs of pants, then I could change them; if I didn't, then I would clean them and press them every night and they would look new. As long as I can wear a clean shirt and clean socks and everything new every day, then I feel as good as the next person. If I'm nasty and dirty and smelling loud I don't like to be with peoples. You can mostly tell what kind of a person you are by your clothes and your personality. You can tell whether you been around, got intelligence and sense, and whether you're a good mixer."

Some of his women G.R. uses in the same way he uses clothes—for "flash." These women are casual dates, who accompany him to night clubs where he can show them off and receive the envy and admiration of other men. He may not even be particularly interested in them sexually, using them primarily for purposes of prestige. One day, after such a date, he explains to the interviewer why he took the girl out, even though he didn't sleep with her: "I never did lay her. I take her out, number one, because she's a good mixer, and number two, because she's a good looker, a beautiful flash. Those kind of women you don't care much about laying, at least I don't. They're too independent. I figure what's the use of playing with fire when you know you'll be burnt. You mostly use them as flash. You know what I mean as a flash? You're out cabareting and you want somebody with you that don't look beat-up, that looks sophisticated; someone who knows how to hold an interesting conversation with anybody, anytime, anywhere; someone who ain't going to make you ashamed."

Most of G.R.'s relationships with women, however, are not of this variety. He is currently involved with several different women, all of whom he uses essentially as bed mates, and for little else. His two marital failures, at least for the time being, have completely soured him on further ventures with more affectionate overtones. His distrust of all women is a frequent theme during the interviews: "I live alone, I walk alone, I stay alone. I don't have no confidence in womens. I don't trust them no more. As you said, it shows in my dreams. I'm always disappointed. Nothing goes my way. No matter how many womens I get—beautiful or not beautiful—I'm still afraid to take a chance on them. All you get from womens is razzin'. Your misery just grows deeper, deeper, deeper. I don't care if I don't see them again. There's no love lost on my part." Nevertheless, his affectivity, what there is of it, is limited to women. The relative kindness of the women in his earlier years—his sister and his aunt—managed to salvage some capacity for affection. From his descriptions, his two marriages were not entirely devoid of warmth.

His sexual behavior appears to be within normal limits. He has had regular intercourse since the age of seven. Masturbation has been infrequent and did not begin until thirteen because "I didn't have to. I always had girls." There are no disorders of potency.

His attitudes toward men are predetermined by the traumatic experiences with his uncle and his cousin. We would not expect his subsequent relationships to be very effective and, in fact, they are not. He introduces this subject early in the interviews with the remark, "Sometimes I feel lost—like I ain't got a friend in the world." He then goes on to elaborate his social and emotional isolation from his fellows: "What I mean is when I'm home and alone I'll hardly ever mix with peoples—except when I'm out with a girl—but during the day, Oh, I'll laugh and talk with peoples, but I'll hardly ever mix with other mens. Do you understand? I ain't got no friends—just the girls I go with and the bosses down at the office, but colored friends to go with I ain't got any. The last four years I ain't really been happy. I only been kidding myself."

Later, he explains this lack of friends: "Number one, I just don't trust them too well. I know if I stay around them I'll only get into trouble; and, number two, a lot of fellows ain't honest and I know they'll steal the shirt off your back if you turn your head. I know if I go anywhere, like to a night club, I go alone because I know I won't get myself in trouble. I had a man friend once and we had a misunderstanding. He was the only man friend I ever had. He was a very nice fellow. I took him mostly as a brother and he took me like that. Then we had a big argument." Here, he gives the details of a knife fight over a woman. He and his friend slashed each other thoroughly and both were taken to jail. He concludes, "And that's what made me afraid to have a boy friend again. I never trust nobody and I live by myself. I never had a roommate again." This attitude prevents him from joining any of the social clubs in which Harlem abounds. He reasons that he would only be "gypped in the deal" so why join?

This is the story of a man who is completely frustrated. He has lost out in every area of activity. The final result is an underlying chronic depression and an explosive kind of hedonism. The latter accounts for G.R.'s failure to show more for his efforts. The internal pressure for escape is too great. He no sooner accumulates some money, than he is impelled to spend it: "I have never been able to work up a budget. I just can't do it. As soon as I save a little money I get in one of those spells and I cabaret a little more than I should. At times I think I have a mind of a kid. I get foolish and I just say, 'The devil with it!' I work and work trying to get ahead and I never get anywhere and suddenly it comes into my mind, 'I want to spend this! I want to spend that!' So I spend it, and then I never stop punishing myself."

G.R. no longer has confidence in himself or anyone else. The treadmill on which he finds himself describes quite fully how many of the Negro males come to the pass of "not caring" about anything. It is an endless cycle of contracting obligations, paying them off, getting tired, trying to have a little fun, frantic efforts to recapture lost ground, then ultimately giving up altogether. Momentary satisfactions are gained through clothes and conquests over women, for whom he can assume no responsibility. He can afford only to live for the moment, casting about opportunistically for the satisfaction of immediate wants. To this end, G.R. displays an extraordinary adaptability, and did so from childhood on. His adaptation to the hostile environment in which he is forced to live must be classified as highly successful—at a price, of course, in comparison with white standards.

W.L.

This subject is a dark brown, 38-year-old chauffeur. He shares a small apartment with his wife in the heart of Harlem. They have no children, although they have been married for nine years. He appears for the interviews dressed either in a chauffeur's uniform or in business suits, but with flamboyant, open-collared sport shirts. He smokes a cigar and his demeanor is a caricature of Rotary Club, Babbitt-like affluence.

W.L. is a patient in psychotherapy. His presenting complaint is impotence of sudden onset, but only with his wife. He continues to be perfectly potent with other women. His symptom began six months ago and he is completely unable to explain its appearance. It is particularly baffling to him because he has never had potency trouble before. He has spent all his savings, going from physician to physician, each of whom treated him with "injections," but to no avail. Finally, his money gone, he applied for help at a large hospital, where it was suggested his difficulty was psychological in nature, and he was referred for psychiatric treatment.

W.L. was born and raised in poverty on a farm in the Deep South. His environment was persistently hostile, traumatic, and devoid of affection. His mother died from unknown causes when he was only eighteen months old. His father, an uneducated sharecropper, was a violent-tempered disciplinarian, who beat W.L. mercilessly at the slightest provocation. The mother's death left him with three small children, but the two older siblings—a brother and a sister—died within a year, leaving only the subject. The father remarried when W.L. was three. If anything, the step-mother—an illiterate housewife—was even worse than the father. W.L. gives rather harrowing details of her ferocious behavior toward him: "She was very cruel. When I was three she beat me and I crapped all over myself. Once she put me in ice cold water in January and left me there for a couple of hours until my aunt found me." The step-mother brought three children with her, all boys. One was W.L.'s age, the other two were slightly younger. They were favored by the step-mother, and all three followed her example, ganging up on W.L. and treating him with great brutality: "They were devilish. My step-mother brought them up like that. They always were out to play and she kept me in the house to work. She was the type of person just because my father married to her I didn't mean anything to her at all. Her kids would go out and do devilment and then when my father came home she would tell him and he would take all the bad things out on me. She was good to her kids—but I didn't get so much affection. Even after I was grown I was threatened by them. My oldest step-brother was looking for me to kill me. After my uncle told me, I just stayed out of his way. His mother taught him to be like that to me. A kid never learns that alone. She thought my father gave me things he wouldn't give them. I dislike her so much, it ain't funny." The only bit of kindness he knew in these early years was from his maternal grandmother, who lived near by and was quite fond of him. Both the father and the step-mother were very religious—a somewhat incongruous note in the midst of all the violence. The whole family, including W.L., attended church almost daily. Grace was said at every meal, and family prayers were offered in the morning and in the evening. Discussion of sex was forbidden. The father beat the boys whenever he caught them talking about it.

He began school at six, and here he behaved in accordance with his training at home. His experience had already destroyed his capacity to be aggressive; the fear of retaliation was too strong. Thus, he was submissive both with the teachers and with his fellows: "I've always been afraid of a beatin'—never liked to get a beatin'. So I behaved well. I never liked for nobody to hit me. Don't like to today. . . . I only had two fights while going to school because I was a coward—I never would fight." He didn't attend school very long. He left at the age of eight to work as a delivery boy for a fish market.

As time passed he began to think of escape from his family and their cruelty. He made an attempt at ten: "Things got so bad I left home. I went to my grandmother's to live. My father came and got me and took me home. He whipped me. He whipped me so much I was afraid of it. He would make me take my clothes off to whip me. In January—snow and ice—I ran out without clothes and stayed out two or three hours. He didn't catch me. I got across a big ditch. He fell into it. I ran under a church and stayed there until morning. Across from that church some people were fond of my mother, so I went there. I stayed and got warm. So my father came there and asked if I was there. They refused to tell him. That's the only fault people had against my father—the way he treated me. Finally, two weeks later he got me."

Some months later, at eleven, W.L. tried again. He made the attempt in a fit of desperation precipitated by the following incident: "The man I worked for, he like me so much he bought me a bike and took so much each week from my salary because I was so crazy about a bike. I would do anything for him after that, I was so crazy for a bike. He was paying me $11.00 a week and took out $1.50 for the bike. When I go home, dad would take all my money. I never had no money for candy like the other kids. I went home with my bike. The kids took it out and broke it up. My dad had warned them about it—not to bother it. They took it out to ride it and ran it right into a car and the car ran over it and tore it up. Naturally, you know, you get very angry about those things. So that Sunday was the last Sunday I ever stayed home. I was so angry I chased them and began to fight. She saw us and grabbed me. She was very fat—very fat, and she put my head between her thighs and whipped my rump. I bit a plug out of her leg and ran off. She called my father. He broke off a broomstick and began to hit me. I said if he hit me again both of us was going to die. He thought I was crazy and hit me again. So that night I pulled out."

Somehow he made his way to a large Northern city. For the first year he sold papers and worked sporadically at odd jobs. He made enough money to eat, but not enough for a place to live. He slept anywhere he could—in cars, hallways, parks. Finally, he got a regular job delivering for a tailor shop. This enabled him to save enough money to rent a room. At fifteen he had his first sexual experiences with a woman, thirty-five, who lived in the same house. It was at this time, too, that he first began masturbation. He gives as his reason for such a late beginning that he didn't know about it until after he had intercourse with this older woman. His employer taught him how to press clothes and he became quite expert at this trade. He became dissatisfied with his salary and decided to come to New York in search of greater opportunity. He was now sixteen. He secured immediate employment as a presser and held this job for five years. He also attended night school and managed to complete the eighth grade, for which he received his diploma. A friend taught him how to play the saxophone. He became so adept that a jazz band hired him. He quit his job with the tailor and for several years traveled throughout the United States playing with the band. On one of these tours he met his wife, a very pretty young Negro girl, almost light enough to pass for white. During the war years he held an essential job as a Pullman porter and so was not subject to the draft. Since the war he has worked as a chauffeur.

The reason's for W.L.'s impotence came out early in therapy. He related that he had been away from home for three months on a cross-country tour with his employer. Upon his return he was greeted by his wife and her girl friend. He was in the bathroom washing when his wife's friend answered the telephone just outside the bathroom door. He overheard her remark, "I'm sorry, Jack, you can't talk to her now. Her husband's home. I'll have her call you tomorrow." Another man, his suspicions aroused, would have confronted his wife immediately, but not W.L. Let us listen to his own account of his behavior: "I didn't say anything at all. I went and finished what I was doing and went out and continued as though I hadn't heard a thing at all. Knowing the circumstances, I didn't feel so good about it, but I didn't say nothing. I tried to pay no attention. It made me very unhappy to think about it." That night he could not get an erection and he has remained impotent with his wife ever since. Subsequent events served only to confirm his worst suspicions: "I answered the 'phone several times when she wasn't home and he answered it, not knowing it was me, as Jack. Another time he was drunk and give out his full name. For about two weeks after that she would get calls from different ones and some would leave names and then all of a sudden it stopped." Still, W.L. kept quiet. In fact, it was not until three months later that he dared make a reference to Jack and then in a most oblique, apologetic way. His wife angrily denied it, and from then on, W.L. kept quiet for good.

How can we explain W.L.'s behavior? We must not be fooled by the sexual façade of the problem. The trouble here is not sex, it is aggression. The impotence is simply the end product of W.L.'s failure to assert himself. Only an understanding of this failure will explain the sexual symptom. We saw in the description of W.L.'s developmental years that he had no chance to integrate adequate patterns of aggression. As a child he was much too weak to stand up against the combined onslaught of his father, step-mother, and step-siblings. The retaliation was too swift and certain. Instead of resistance, W.L. developed techniques of avoidance. He then expanded these techniques to include all forms of self-assertion, not just those limited to physical violence. Unfortunately, however, in his unconscious mind, he drew no distinctions: assertion equals violence, no matter what its form. The expected and inevitable retaliation is equally violent. The result is a submissive individual, literally afraid of his own shadow, who will do anything to avoid conflict.

These are the reasons why W.L. has been unable to accuse his wife. The fault lies in his basic inhibition of aggression. In the immediate situation, if he speaks up, he is fearful of attack from two directions: from his wife and from his male competitors, her lovers. Let us consider the fear of his wife first. This stems from the original relationship with his step-mother. He has never been able to overcome his earliest impression of a woman as a punitive figure, who gives no affection, and against whom there is no recourse. His description of his marital life shows that he has been no more able to stand up against his wife than he was able to stand up against his step-mother. Her intimidation has him thoroughly cowed: "She's all right sometimes, but sometimes she is very cross—very, very cross. Whenever I see her in that mood, I try to say less about things to her. She raises a lot of noise, so I don't say anything. In some cases, I feel bad and walk away. I don't pay it no mind, but I hate to see it. It don't make me feel good. I do a lot of thinking, but not much talking. I been like that most of my life. I never was a big talker. When I am around the house I talk a little bit, but I don't have much to say. Lots of times she don't feel like talking, being bothered, so I don't bother her. I feel she shouldn't be that way. If I say something to her and don't get an answer, I know she don't feel like talking, so I don't bother. It happens quite often. If I ask something important: Yes or no, that's all. If I want to go to a show and ask her and she don't want to go, I don't bother. She keeps telling me I don't make enough money for her. There is nothing I can buy her that she appreciates. I can't afford to live above my means. It don't make sense. I can't walk around with my head in the lion's mouth. There's no use working if I have to do that."

Following the above discourse, he had two dreams which shed light on his unconscious representation of women:

About some rabbits. I was out in some sort of an open field, sleeping. I went through a place there and it looked like lions. I was very much afraid and didn't know whether to go past them or not. But when I got there they was rabbits.

His immediate association was to his employer's wife, another aggressive and dominating woman, to whom he is forced to submit: "Well, the only thing I can put it on when I went to work yesterday the boss-lady was so cross I was waiting for her to argue, but she was cool and calm and collected, and didn't. She just has to fuss. After, she don't mean a thing by it. When I came in I spoke to the cook. She said, 'Her and I had it this morning.' So I kind of expected it. She always is arguing over nothing and don't wait for you to tell her anything before she breaks in." Thus, he says in the dream that something he expected to be dangerous turned out to be harmless. The dangerous object is the boss-lady. He expected her to attack him like a lion, but instead she acted as meek as a rabbit. The important point here is the equation between women and dangerous beasts. W.L.'s remark of the previous day—"I can't walk around with my head in the lion's mouth"—is no accident.

The same equation is drawn in the next dream, this time more directly concerned with his wife:

Horses. They was in a store. Some was loose. They was wild horses. They was running after me. So I ran into a cover—a sort of a stall—but instead of it cutting off it went all around (a maze). So every one of those ends I would get to I would look for an out, but I couldn't find any. So I went into one and ran into a horse. I turned and ran out. I ran in the other direction. It led me out to a place. I couldn't get out. So I climbed over a fence and jumped into a bunch of something, I don't know what, but I had to get back over the fence. So I jumped back over it. I got away, but how I don't know.

His associations deal with his wife's intimidation and her refusal to help him settle the discord between them. She constantly berates him for his impotence and makes sarcastic references to his manliness. Unless he improves, she threatens to leave him. He feels trapped and there is no escape from her pressure, which in the dream he represents as a violent attack upon him. No wonder W.L. has potency trouble. Images of the woman as a wild and dangerous animal are hardly conducive to a good sexual performance. Again, it must be emphasized that the problem is not primarily sexual. Rather, W. L. is incapable of having intercourse with a woman while he harbors suppressed hostility toward her. He is too fearful that if he provokes her during the sexual act, retaliatory violence will be unleashed against him and it will be aimed at his genital, the symbol of masculine assertion. That is why, at present, W.L. is potent with other women, but not with his wife. He has no ill will toward the former, but is filled with rage at the latter—a rage he is utterly unable to release.

The other source of his impotence stems from his fear of social and sexual competition with men. This is a direct result of his conditioning at the hands of his father and his step-brothers. Automatically, he assumes a submissive role. Thus, confronted with his wife's infidelity, he dare not compete with her lover. Instead, he relinquishes his masculinity in advance by surrendering his male prerogatives. He saves his life, but at the cost of his penis.

An individual with W.L.'s familial background and developmental history can hardly be expected to have a satisfactory self-esteem system. His family made him feel worthless and unlovable. Furthermore, no one with such a marked inhibition of aggression can possibly think well of himself. He proved this to us by derogating himself as a coward because he did not fight back in school when provoked by the other children. Add to these individual factors the social stigma of being a Negro and W.L.'s self-esteem doesn't have a chance. He gains some satisfaction from being a self-made man, a fact to which he proudly calls attention many times during the interviews. And he has every reason to be proud, his adaptability having been well-nigh incredible. Unfortunately, this compensation is just not enough, and he is engaged in a constant struggle for status. His descriptions of his attempts are almost pathetic: "I tried to educate myself, you know, but my work interfered. I went to the eighth grade; that's as high as I got. Then sometimes I'd sit around and read books and mess around with figures. I tried to keep myself occupied, you know. I got a library card and I go there. History and things, you know. Sometimes I sit down and write twenty pages out of the book. You get more contact that way, you know. Of course, I'm not such a hot writer. The main issues I wanted to learn in life was to read and count. Writing, too, but just enough to protect myself."

Thus, W.L. does not seek education for its intrinsic value, but as a badge of higher status. His account of his social aspirations is shot through with wishful and transparent boasting: "I belong to the Masons. Then I belong to the Bugs Club. That's one of the greatest clubs going in New York. There is 500 members in the Bugs. Brother, when they give a dance you can't get in the door unless you got an invitation because there's so many of them! You can't buy a ticket at the door. As soon as the dance is announced, it's sold out, even without the tickets printed. I would love to get as high as I could in the Masons. It's like going to school—you have to study the codes of the organization and you have to know the codes by heart because you don't know when you'll have to recite them. Some big fellow may come to see how your organization is climbing, progressing, and you got to be able to recite. You got to know the book by heart and the book isn't written in English. I know lots of doctors and lawyers and all that, you know, who belong and they got to study the book, too. I had a chance to belong to the Grand Street Boys. That's an old social club in New York. Jimmy Walker belonged to it. This is the oldest and most populous organization in New York. There is no discrimination as long as you have a nice background, a nice record. Nobody bothers you as long as you act in a decent way. Why, millionaires belong to it, and poor guys can, too. I'm going to join, once I get some money together."

W.L. has few, if any, affectionate relationships that are intimate, warm, and meaningful. At least, no such relationships ever became apparent during the interviews. The union with his wife is based almost entirely on dominance and submission with W.L. always in the lesser role. Contacts he describes with other women are purely sensual and seem to be divorced from any tender affectivity. Neither does he have any close male friends. His relations with men are quite superficial and consist of associations through common interests, such as lodges or clubs. These are used as status implements or for purposes of recreation, but in either case, they are devoid of close emotional ties. It appears, then, that W.L. simply cannot connect emotionally with an object, or put in another way, his potential for loving people is very low. He was born with that potential just like everybody else, but his early environment gave him no opportunity to establish meaningful relationships. His capacity to love was killed at the source. As a result, W.L. just never learned how.

The psychological picture here is of a person easily abused in our society—for he lacks every implement of self-defense. Still, notwithstanding the scarring effect of his struggle with aggression, he has made a most strenuous and effective effort to surmount his hostile environment and his personal handicaps. He unquestionably would have gone much further had society let him. The external obstacles were simply too great. This case is an excellent example of the human loss incident to oppression. In addition, it makes still another point. It demonstrates that premature independence hurts adaptability in the long run, because it is based on mistrust of others. That is where it begins.

H.N.

H.N. is a 28-year-old, medium brown, paid subject who comes for study quite by accident. G.R., another paid subject, had been offered five dollars if he could induce a lower-class Negro male to participate in the project. One morning, at eight o'clock, G.R. appeared in the interviewer's office with a most disreputable-looking character in tow. This was H.N. His appearance indicated he had spent the night in the streets on some kind of a bat. He was unwashed and unkempt, his face bore several abrasions covered with freshly clotted blood, and his clothing was dirty and torn. G.R. explained: "I don't know who he is. I never seen him before. He was standing on the corner and he looked hungry, so I asked him if he wanted a job. He said he did and I brought him up here quick-like before he could change his mind."

It turned out that H.N. was an ex-convict and a drug addict with a long history of criminal activity. He got out of jail only a month ago. He is now looking for honest work, but with no success. However, he admits he is not looking too hard. So far, since his release, he has stayed away from narcotics, but once again is beginning to feel the urge. He combats this desire by resorting to alcohol. That is how he accounts for his initial appearance. He had been out on an all-night drunk. He vouches for the truth of his story by baring his arms and displaying the telltale scars of innumerable heroin injections.

H.N. was born and raised in Harlem. The family consisted of the father, the mother, the maternal grandmother and six children—two older sisters and four younger brothers. H.N. is the oldest son. The economic status was always marginal. The household was organized in a matriarchal fashion with the mother and the grandmother dividing the authority equally between them. The mother was an uneducated but literate housewife who worked occasionally as a domestic. She provided for the children's needs as best she could but showed them little warmth. The grandmother was of the same ilk—severe and unaffectionate. The father played an entirely subordinate role. He, too, was uneducated but literate. He worked as a night porter.

He tried to protect the children from the wrath of the mother and the grandmother. However, he was no match for them and the protection he offered was sparse. H.N. remembers him with kindness. Unfortunately, he died when H.N. was only eight. H.N. also remembers his paternal grandmother with kindness. She was the only person in his early life who was really positive in her affection toward him: "She was very nice, very nice. She was a combination of this nurse, Florence Nightingale, and Santa Claus. She was the nicest grandmother anybody could have. She was always doing things for the kids—giving us presents all the time." Discipline was maintained by the women and beatings were an almost daily occurrence. Religion was of no importance in the household and sex was never openly discussed.

After the father's death the economic situation became desperate: "The Welfare Board sent my mother some money but it was never enough. After we come of age, everybody got out and worked. Oh, it was pretty tough! A lot of times we'd see things we'd want and we'd tell mother about it and she'd tell us we couldn't have it because there was no money. A lot of times we'd come home from school and all there'd be to eat was a piece of bread and water with sugar in it. I'd fly up in a tantrum and she'd say, 'That's better than nothing.' "

There were no behavior disorders of any significance during H.N.'s early childhood. His scholastic record was excellent and he even skipped two grades. At the age of twelve a decided change took place. He became a behavior problem in his classes and he repeatedly flaunted the authority of his teachers. Simultaneously, he stopped studying and began to play hookey: "I wouldn't study. I used to hang out behind the Apollo Theater there with the sporting element—stage people, sporting girls, pimps. Those are the ones always seemed to have money, always seemed to have a good time. All the things the others were doing and getting a kick out of, I wanted to do it—and I done it, see. I guess in my life I've just about done everything wrong. I've drunk, stole, smoked reefers, and used all kinds of drugs—heroin, cocaine, morphine, opium."

At fifteen he gave up all pretense of going to school and quit for good. He devoted full time to delinquent activities. Finally, he was caught stealing and sent to a training school for boys where he remained for a year and a half. Upon his release, he simply picked up where he left off. At nineteen he was arrested again and placed in a reformatory for older boys. He stayed there for ten months. Then he really got into trouble. He attempted robbery with a gun, was chased by the police, and shot in the leg. He drew five years in Sing Sing and this is the sentence he has just completed. In between jail terms, he has twice been hospitalized for heroin addiction, once at seventeen and again at twenty.

Several times as he related his history, H.N. appeared conscience-stricken. For example, while describing his induction into criminality, he suddenly stopped and asked, "Am I the worsest person you ever met? The reason I ask is because when we first started I didn't tell you this, but I'm kind of loosening up now. I'm not proud of it." Throughout the interviews, he repeatedly complained that he felt he was being "judged": "You looking at me like that. . . . Maybe it's because I been so bad. . . . I don't like people staring at me. That's one of my pet peeves and I can't look at people either when I talk. That hurts me—and it makes them feel bad, too—but I can't help it."

One day H.N. described his struggle against the drug: "I have to drink to keep from taking the other stuff. I ain't strong enough to do it yet without drinking. And I want to stop real bad. It causes too many heartaches. My mother, my family, my uncle never let up on me, never! Why don't I leave it alone? I don't have to do that! I've been staying at my aunt's. I don't go up to my mother so much. I can't face her any more. Each time I would go there I'd tell her I would stop. Then I would start again. That's why I want a job now. I really want to stop." That night he had a dream, the only one he reported during the entire course of interviews. Luckily, it clearly reveals the framework of the basic psychological system within which he functions:

> Me and my aunt. She wanted to buy something—I don't know what—and we met two guys on the corner and they had something in two baby carriages, but they was covered with a bedspread—each of them—pretty ones—and I was wondering what they was doing with them. Then they showed my aunt some pillows in the carriages. Then I was sleeping in a chair and it seems I wanted a shirt and I went back into my house into a big closet and there was a guy there I'd never seen and he was selling shirts. So I takes off my blue shirt and I bought a pink one

from him. Then suddenly he took the blue shirt. No explanation or nothing. I was amazed he do that.

He spontaneously associates to the dream: "This closet has a lot of clothes in it. They used to belong to my grandmother, the one I liked. I couldn't tell if this guy was white or colored. He had one of those visors on that you keep the sun out of your eyes. Why'd he take my shirt? Only thing I can figure, I been wanting to buy some shirts. I been wanting to buy a lot of things since I come home last. You know, all these other guys on the street looking good. I want to, too. This guy is taking something from me. He gave me a shirt, but I paid for it. He gives me a bright-colored one back, a bright-colored one! I likes them bright-colored ones. Who is this guy? Those old gamblers always had them visors. In a way he could be anybody—guys who take things from me. In one extreme he takes from me, in the other he gives me something. So maybe he could have been my friend or my enemy, or something I want but I can't get. I been daydreaming about gambling. I been thinking of trying to get some money. I been thinking I'd be lucky. I been thinking maybe this time I'd make a big pile, but I been worried I'd lose." (You seem to say in the dream: "If I gamble to get money for clothes, I may end up by losing the shirt off my back.") "If that's so, then I know the first part of the dream, too. I can explain that dream fully. Also, besides this gambling, I been thinking of stealing, too. After all, that was part of my life. Now, these two guys, the bedspreads was pretty, they was fine silk. I figure they was hot stuff, stolen goods, the kind of stuff I never had unless I stole. The pillow is hot, too. I used to do that, I used to steal and sell the stuff. Now when she wanted to buy that stuff in the dream, I didn't want her to. I wanted to protect her. She's the one I don't want to hurt by stealing. So this dream is my urge to steal, but I don't want to hurt my family by it, especially my aunt." (So you say: "I need money for clothes. One way to get it would be to steal it, but I don't want to hurt my family. Another way to get it would be to gamble, but I might lose the shirt off my back." That is your quandry—how to get what you want. Should you steal, gamble, or work?) "So there's a fight going on—a fight inside me."

Superficially, the dream depicts the current situation in which H.N. finds himself. It is a situation that has repeated itself many times throughout his life. He has many needs which he cannot satisfy. Should he rely on fair means—with almost certain disappointment—or should he resort to foul? The dream also has a deeper meaning. It has genetic significance. He turns to his paternal grandmother, the combination of Florence Nightingale and Santa Claus, to get his shirt. This is at one and the same time an admission of helplessness and a plea for magical relief. Evidently, H.N. does not place a high value on his own capacity to satisfy his needs. However, a magical adaptation cannot succeed, and when it fails, there is little doubt in which direction he will move. It is at this point, when the cumulative tension of many frustrations has reached an unbearable pitch, that he attempts to resolve the conflict by turning to crime and narcotics. The operation of this dynamic sequence can be demonstrated in the interviews immediately following the dream.

He began the next hour with a description of his ambitious goals and his lifelong failure to achieve them: "I guess I just don't have the initiative to get out there and do anything. I always had ambition to be a writer. I used to get good marks in English. I read a lot, but something is keeping me back. I don't do nothing. Maybe its because I daydream too much. Then I wake up to reality. I think about time. It'll take too long. I'm twenty-eight now. When will I be famous? When will I amount to something? Ten years? Twenty years? It's too long, too hard, too tough. Maybe I'll only be a failure. So I dream. Oh, I dream I'll be the biggest guy in the world. But me, I'm hopeless, just hopeless. But yet I know all those things, I know all those things but I take a defeatist attitude. I don't do nothing."

He defines the acme of his ambitions: "Oh, I would dream of getting to the top, to the top! I would start excelling in everything I do. If it was baseball I would start making impossible catches. If I was a writer I would have five hit plays on Broadway in a row. I tell you, when I dreamed, I went whole hog! I never gave myself the worst of it. Always the success! Always fighting! I used to think of fighting, being in the ring, and all that. I used to dream that stuff. I used to dream it all the time. And in those dreams I had girls. They was just idolizing me. My favorite dream was to be a great author, have a beautiful wife, not too possessive, a good companion, people commented as we went down the street, we had beautiful kids, the finest kids in the whole town. Always that wife! And I never even been married. Maybe underneath I'm scared I will never get married. Maybe being a success ain't really the important thing. Maybe it's a wife, a wife, who underneath I'm really craving. . . . I'm slowly getting to understand myself better." Unfortunately, understanding that is only a recital of one's failures hardly works to one's advantage. It boomerangs, and by the end of the interview H.N. was visibly depressed. His attempted repair was strictly according to Hoyle: he fell back on heroin.

He arrived two days later, forty minutes late for his appointment, and under the influence of the drug. He was bathed in perspiration, appeared drowsy but excited, and spoke under a great pressure of speech. His associations are revealing. First, he establishes his mood: "The weather is stifling and very depressing. Not that I feel depressed, but the weather is depressing." Next, he remarks on a magical attempt at inflation. He attended a movie and in fantasy identified himself with the hero: "I went yesterday to see a very good picture—'The Champion.' It was about the prize fight racket, but essentially it was a story of one man's rise to the top. It was a story of how he didn't care for nobody and was willing to hurt anybody in order to reach his goal. It was a masterful characterization. I enjoyed it immensely. All sorts of emotional crises, romance, comedy. The photography stands most vividly in my mind. It was excellent. It was quite a picture." Here, he suddenly catches sight of a book in the bookcase. He is reminded of his own wish to be a writer: "I've read a review, a synopsis of this book. I wish I could be a writer or an actor. I love it. My secret passion is to be that." This reflection brings him up short. It defines all too acutely his many failures. He blocks, and there is a long pause. He concludes on a final note of despair: "Boy, I'm tired! I haven't been asleep for two nights. I stayed in the street all last night. What school did you go to, Doc? Did you find it hard, Doc? Did you have to struggle or did your family help you? Did you enjoy every minute or did you find it pretty bleak? I guess you had determination. If a person has determination, everything becomes easy. I have a jag on. I'm sorry. I was weak. A guy offered it to me and I accepted. I'm sorry I was so weak, Doc. I apologize."

H.N. presents the usual clinical picture of the drug addict. These people have a peculiarly low threshold for frustration-tolerance. At the same time their demands from life are exorbitant and mostly unattainable. It is the interaction between these factors that so thoroughly deflates the self-esteem and produces a "tense depression."[1] Recourse to the drug is a reparative measure. Its purpose is to dispel the tension, lift the depression, and enhance the self-esteem. This it accomplishes by blunting the sense of reality and deadening the psychological pain that accompanies failure. Simultaneously, it stimulates grandiose fantasies through which the addict can at least momentarily satisfy his frustrated needs. H.N. confirms this action for us: "When I take heroin I don't care whether I am a success or a failure. I don't care how I dress or what my financial standing is. When I take heroin everything is all right."

This clinical picture will be the same regardless of the race of the addict, be he Negro or white. However, the facility with which an innately predisposed individual will resort to narcotics will depend upon the extent to which realistic channels of expression are closed to him. The same is also true for crime as an answer to frustration. For this reason we would expect that the incidence of narcotic addiction and crime in the Negro, who is confronted with far greater social obstacles, will be higher than in the white. In subsequent interviews, H.N. discusses this added pressure upon the Negro and describes the role it played in the development of his own life.

The next session was on the following day. The affects of the drug had worn off and once more H.N. was depressed. In addition, he was sullen and testy. He talked about the social role of the Negro: "Any person who has any intelligence knows a colored person don't get many breaks. There's a few who made a success of themselves. Then there are some who are contented. Then there are a whole lot of them who don't know what they are. That's the most of them. You can put me in the latter. Just like I told you the other day, a young kid growing up in Harlem, the only people he sees who have money are the pimps, the prostitutes, the people in the sporting world. So then maybe he go home and maybe his mother ain't working and he asks her for money and she ain't got none and maybe sometimes there ain't even no food. Then he grows up and gets a job and all his money goes for rent and food and clothes. Maybe if you want a suit made it takes two week's work. You ain't got nothing. Then you see the sporting people and they seem always to have it, right in their pockets. A man got to be pretty strong to

[1] Rado, Sandor, "The Psychoanalysis of Pharmacothymia (Drug Addiction) I. The Clinical Picture," *The Psychoanalytic Quarterly*, Vol. II, No. 1, January, 1933.

resist that temptation. Even if sometimes you find they got in jail, that don't mean nothing to you, you don't care, as long as maybe you can get something for yourself. All right, so I been in jail and my brothers haven't, but I don't see where they accomplished nothing either. They stay on the job but they're broke all the time." As he talked, he became more and more depressed. Finally, he stopped, and after a silence, remarked, "I can't get my thoughts together today. Sometimes I feel like talking about things, and I think I can express myself, but I can't do it right now. I just feel beat, that's all."

He failed to appear for his next interview. Later, he called and asked for another appointment. Again he came while under the influence of heroin. The following remarks illustrate the intensity of this man's suffering: "Oh, gee! I'm sorry. I have no dreams for you. I'm sorry. Tell me, is that bad, does that show signs of a sluggish mind, a mind of total unevenness, a mind on the brink of disaster? All the patients aren't alike. You've seen all kinds of insanity. Have you seen violently insane people? I have a friend in the State Hospital for the Criminally Insane. I was told he eats the waste from his bowels. Oh, God, what despair! What torture! How he must suffer! How these insane must suffer! One time I was bad while I was incarcerated. I got in trouble with the authority and I was put in solitude. I was there for two months. Once, all of a sudden, I had a roaring in my head and I thought I was going crazy. So I called to the guard and asked if I could go see the Principal Keeper. He let me see him and I told him I was sorry for what I had done and wouldn't he let me out because I was afraid I was blowing my top. He let me out, but for a long time after that I would have that funny sensation in my head and I would be afraid I was going crazy, but it went away. I'm a little high today, Doctor. I've been taking the drug. So I've been weak again, very weak. I'm just a total loss, no good, but when I take that, it makes everything seem gay."

He missed the next two interviews. Finally, he came again, sober this time, and delivered with great fire an eloquent discourse on the evil effects of prejudice: "Prejudice is the scourge of this nation. It's one thing the U.S. can't laugh off. This is one of the richest countries in the world but it could be still richer if it gave equality to every citizen, every citizen, equal opportunity. There's a lot of colored children—maybe some of them are potential geniuses, potential geniuses, but they got to try to raise themselves by their bootstraps.

They end in the mire, in the mire—no sense, stupid, and they start stealing, or something like that. I remember one time when I was in a little kids reformatory I told the officer I wanted to take up acting. We gave a lot of shows there and they praised me for my performance. So after I got out they sent me to this school for acting. They gave me a letter there and I remember—I'll never forget this—I gave the lady in charge the letter and she said they couldn't take me because I was colored. After that I went around to no place again to try to be a performer. Unconsciously, maybe that's why I gave it up, because I felt there was no chance because I was colored. My ears kinda burned when she said, 'No colored children.' I remember this one incident so well because it affected me so direct, because it was a moment in my life I might have amounted to something—and that happened to me. Every once in a while I'll just be sitting down and that moment will come back to me. There were probably other incidents, but that was the bitterest. You know, how sometimes it takes a few years before you know what really happened. It's like a bruise. You don't know 'til later how much it hurted you."

He concluded in a burst of passion: "Down South the white men sleep with colored women. I heard from people who seen with their own eyes white men mating with colored. Sometimes down there white men will kill a colored man to keep him from colored women they like. They got all these artificial barriers down South. They take a colored woman and have her nurse their babies, suck the milk right out of her body; then when he grows up he can't even sit next to her. Or take a colored porter—he can go through a car with his uniform on and nobody will say nothing, but take off his uniform and he puts on civilian clothes and he can't get into the car. Why? It's the same man! The South! Huh! And all because we was the last race to come out of slavery. Every race on this earth was in slavery at one time or another. It's just that our race was the last, our race was the last! They started discrimination in the Reconstruction Period because they let the South get out of hand. There were forces in the North in sympathy with the South and they got their way. The South got out from under and made their phony laws to keep Negroes down and ever since then it's been like that, right through the ages. Nobody tried to make it so that Negroes and whites would learn to be friends. Then the North put uneducated Negroes in high positions—senator, governor—naturally the South wouldn't put up with that. So the South went wild and they made these laws. Father tell son . . . son tell son . . . and so it went on."

He failed to appear for his next interview and was never seen again. Attempts to trace him were unsuccessful.

This biography has afforded us a rare opportunity to look into the psychological make-up of a thoroughly crushed individual, one reduced to a kind of half-existence on the lowest level of the social scale. The chief configurations here are the overweening ambition, the inflation of the ideal self, and the catastrophic comparison with the real self. As we saw, these are the tensions that lead him to narcotics. His hopelessness is genuine, but it is a hopelessness engendered by the complete absence of time-sense, by the poor adjustment of fantasy to opportunity, and by the inability to apply himself to anything. He possesses high intelligence, but is without emotional anchorage in any human relationship. In short, the story of H.N. is the story of human wastage. He is a total loss, to himself and to society. The fact that he is a Negro and subject to discrimination makes it possible for him to make all the necessary excuses for his lack of effort and his abandoned flight into fantasy. But nevertheless, it is likewise true that being a Negro has also been instrumental in bringing him to his tragic fate. H.N. is a fallen "genius."

II. FEMALE

A.F.

A.F. is a 33-year-old housewife of medium brown complexion. She appears several years older than her stated age. She is a small, wiry, wooly-haired woman who dresses very shabbily. During the initial interviews she is in the final month of a pregnancy and wears a sacklike, one-piece "Mother Hubbard." Later, she frequently appears in very mannish shirt and slacks. She is separated from her second husband and lives with her two small boys, aged four and two, in a three-room railroad flat in an East Harlem slum. Her building is so markedly deteriorated it has been condemned and soon will be demolished. She is maintained by the city on relief, but picks up extra change by occasional prostitution. The current pregnancy is the result of this latter activity.

A.F. is a paid subject. She was first seen in consultation at the Psychiatric Clinic of a large hospital. She had sought aid for her two children, who were behavior problems. They cried, screamed, and demanded constant attention. As a result, she had become increasingly nervous and irritable. She told a story of economic harrassment. Single-handed, she took care of herself and the two children twenty-four hours a day. The problem appeared to be more a socioeconomic one, than psychiatric. It was felt she stood to gain more from a financial reward, than from psychotherapy. On this basis, she was frankly told the nature of the research project and asked if she would cooperate. Her response was, "If by telling you the story of my life, I can help other girls keep from doing what I did, I will be glad to work with you."

She was born and raised in a large Southern city. The family unit consisted of her mother, herself, and a younger sister. Both children were illegitimate, but had the same father. The mother had several other children, either by A.F.'s father or by other men. All were born prematurely or died shortly after birth. The father never lived with the mother and A.F. did not even see him until she was five. She remembers him during her childhood only as a "casual visitor." Economic circumstances were always marginal. The mother was the sole support, the father contributing nothing. She worked as a domestic from eight in the morning until eight at night every day in the week including Sunday. Frequently, when A.F. and her sister were small, no one could be found to watch them while the mother worked. On such occasions the mother simply locked them in the apartment and there they stayed until she returned. At the age of five A.F. was given a key and became responsible for the care of herself and her sister in the mother's absence.

The mother had no formal education and was barely literate. She tried to provide for the children's material needs, but offered them no affection. A.F. remembers that her attempts to kiss her mother were rebuffed with the accusation: "You deceitful wench! What do you want now?" The mother had a violent temper and beatings were frequent. She struck out with whatever was at hand—straps, shoes, sticks—or if nothing were available, she used her fists. Once she even beat A.F. with a shovel, almost knocking her senseless. Sometimes, when beatings failed to produce the desired result, she would cut off A.F.'s hair and dress her in long petticoats. A.F. would then be held up to public ridicule for "looking like a clown." The father was very black—"pure African Negro." He had some grammar school education and could read and write. He worked as a jazz musician. He was thoroughly irresponsible and, like the mother, had a violent temper. A.F.'s overtures toward him were either ignored or answered with beatings. She remembers him only with hatred: "If I described him in my words, you wouldn't be able to write it down. It wouldn't be fit to print." Neither does she think of her sister with kindness. Their relationship has always been one of mutual antagonism, and for many years they have had nothing to do with one another. As children, A.F. always had to take care of her. She remarks, "I was more like a mother to her rather than a sister."

A.F. was a tomboy and played mostly with boys. She did everything they did and tried to do it better. She had many fights with them which she usually won. She became a leader of boys' gangs and captained their athletic teams. After school she cleaned the house, cooked dinner, and looked out for her sister. Occasionally, she got out to play. She had nightmares two or three times a week. The dreams were always the same:

> A witch would tickle me so much I couldn't do anything. Then an elephant would chase me. This fellow—a nice young fellow—with a red cape with a blue lining would always save me. I would fall at his feet and he would save me. He was always a white man. I would wake up perspiring and scared to death.

The failure of her mother (the witch) and her father (the elephant) to provide for her is represented as an attack upon her. Her romantic savior is the affluent white man, the direct antithesis of the black father, who rejects her. As she grew older she began to have another characteristic nightmare, which has continued to the present:

> I always see this white house I want to go to, but I can never get there. Then, suddenly, the world is destroyed. It's destroyed in many ways. Sometimes the sun falls apart, sometimes it's a flood or a fire.

Again, in this second dream, she associates security with the color white. Both dreams represent an anxiety concerning survival. They are the hallmarks of an individual, who is exposed to overwhelming pressures but lacks the resources to protect herself.

When A.F. was eleven her mother died. The sister was shipped to an aunt in another city and A.F. went to stay with her father. He frequently beat her with a cowhide whip until her skin was raw. After a few months, while she was in the sixth grade, he took her out of school, and apprenticed her to a madame, who ran a local house of prostitution. She was required to turn most of her earnings over to her father, but he allowed her to keep a small sum for spending money and clothing. At twelve she acquired a pimp, who provided her with a four-room house in which she set up her own business. She catered to a select clientele of only three or four men and she was quite happy. As she puts it, "I had everything a poor girl could want." Her business venture did not last long. She had an argument with her father about finances and refused to give him any more money. He notified the police of her activities and she was arrested as a juvenile delinquent. The court placed her in a Catholic institution for wayward girls.

She remained with the nuns until she was twenty-one. She learned laundry work, sewing, and crocheting. She was indoctrinated in Catholicism and finally was confirmed. She left the institution for a sleep-in domestic job. The depression was at its height, her work was arduous, and her pay was low. She decided there was more opportunity in the North and she came to New York where she has been ever since. At first she worked as a domestic on the Bronx "slave market." During this period she "went" with several men and finally established a liaison with one of them. He turned out to be a drunkard and they had repeated fights. One cold, wintry night, after he had slapped her, she took her revenge. She stretched him on the bed drunk, took off his clothes, and opened all the windows. She never heard from him again.

Life was hard. She was exploited on the "slave market." The only women in Harlem who appeared well-dressed and comfortable were the prostitutes. She decided to return to her former profession. For a time she worked for a professional gambler, who also provided girls for white men. She wanted her own man and soon established a relationship with a building superintendent, who hustled on the side. They lived together and she prostituted. She gave it up when the War started and went to work in a factory. She and her man gradually drifted apart and finally separated. She "fell in love" and married her only legal husband. She soon discovered she had been tricked. He was a pimp who needed a legal wife as a shield for his

16-year-old prostitute. This girl continued to live with him and all three slept in the same bed. Nevertheless, A.F. stayed on for four years and had her two children by this man. Again, there were many fights and she was frequently beaten up. Finally, she threw a can of lye in his face. He left and didn't come back. This was two years ago and since then she has been on her own. Her husband has disappeared and does not contribute to her support.

Her present life is concerned entirely with the children. She cannot afford help and must take care of them herself, day and night. She sacrifices her needs to their benefit. She buys no clothing for herself, so that they may be properly dressed. She goes without meat and milk, giving it to them, so that their diet may be adequate. She has no recreation and has let her personal appearance deteriorate. In spite of these efforts she cannot make ends meet: "I struggle along from hand to mouth on relief and borrow, borrow, borrow, but you can't live on what you get on relief, so naturally, when I get a chance to make $2, I make it. The kids got to eat. That's how I became pregnant with this one." The third child will only multiply her difficulties.

The end results of such unbearable pressures can be predicted. They are constant worry, anxiety, irritability, depression, and psychosomatic disturbances. She herself is well aware of these effects: "I get so worried and depressed. It seems I have no ambition for anything. I think I'm reconciled to the conditions I'm living in, but at times, I guess that's what's causing it. I never get to go nowhere. I'm always looking like a hag. I'm a person who likes nice things and I don't have any. Then I guess it causes my physical condition. I'm always aching and complaining, yet they can't find anything wrong. I usually manage the best I can, but I am very nervous. It doesn't take much to make me cry. The kids work me up so I feel if I hit them I'll kill them."

She is constantly preoccupied with impending disaster. She complains of morbid thoughts. In the subway she fears the train won't get to its destination. In an elevator she fears the car will get stuck. She worries that something will happen to her children or that she will die and they will be left alone. She has repetitive dreams that are merely symbolic reflections of these conscious thoughts. The following dream is typical. It expresses her anxiety for the welfare of her children as well as the unconscious wish to be rid of them:

I saw my oldest son on the running board of a truck. A couple of other kids were on the truck, too. They jumped off when the truck started to move. My son hung on. I yelled, 'Jump off! Jump off!' But he didn't pay any attention. The fellow drove off and I ran after him. I cut through a lot to intercept them. I caught the truck, but my son wasn't on it. I woke up. I was hysterical that I couldn't find him.

The next dream was precipitated by a realistic fear that her decrepit building would collapse. It, too, carries out the never-ending theme of impending doom:

My house was falling down. I didn't get hurt or nothing. I just got out of there. It happened just as I was putting the kids to bed. I heard a crack and somebody yelled, 'The house is falling down!' I grabbed the 3 kids under my arms and rushed out. We just got across the street when, brrrrooom! Everything collapsed.

The endless, solitary struggle for survival produces agonizing despair:

I dreamt I was on a long road and the sun was shining real bright and there were no trees. It was like a sand road. I staggered down it and there seemed to be no end to it. There was no houses around. I finally fell down. I was all by myself and I lay there crying. I felt if I drew another breath my heart would burst. My heart was just swelling. I was crying and that's how I woke up—crying hysterically.

She strives hard to achieve respectability. She is really quite conscience-stricken by the sordid details of her life. She angrily justifies her behavior by pleading necessity: "I was a prostitute only out of need. I loathed it. I didn't do it because I liked it, but only because I had to keep body and soul together." The following dream shows a painful awareness of her neighbors' scorn:

A neighbor came into my apartment and said, 'Everybody is jealous of my Larry.' I said, 'Why should I be jealous? I have two beautiful boys and I don't have no cause to be jealous.' She said, 'At least Larry knows his father.' I said, 'My children know theirs, too. And if you are referring to the one in my belly, I'm very proud of him, too!'

Her associations to the dream elaborate her shame: "Maybe I just resent this child being born out of wedlock. Maybe in my subconscious mind I resent people looking down on me. My life is such an open book, naturally people will look down on me. I don't care what people think, but I have always had a resentment at being born a bastard and I don't want my children to be like that. When I went to school the other kids called me a bastard and said I didn't know my father. So I didn't want it for my children, but it's one of those things that happened, so I'll have to make the best of it. A lot of my neighbors have gotten nosey and want to know who the father is. I told them it was none of their concern, but it sort of galls me, I guess."

She attempts to compensate for her low status through social and intellectual snobbishness. She holds herself above her neighbors, whom she variously describes as "drunkards, bums, and illiterates." She finds no one in her milieu suitable for companionship. She complains: "The class of people I live around, there's no one I can talk to. That's one of my troubles. I have no outlet. My brain is stagnating. Even if I do start a conversation about a movie or a book, these people don't know what I'm talking about. They don't know nothing about a moral of the picture. All they go to a movie for is the love-making or the fighting."

She cultivates intellectual pursuits in order to accentuate the difference between her and the people she lives with. She embellishes her speech with complicated terms which she frequently mispronounces and uses out of context. She disparages popular forms of entertainment such as jazz and the comic strips; instead, her interests run to "good radio programs, the plays, and symphonies." Yet, though she rejects her neighbors, neither is she comfortable in the more affluent circles to which she aspires: "I am associated all day with people beneath me, and when I get with superior people, I get self-conscious. I don't know how to act and I'm never dressed well." Ill-at-ease in either group, she usually refuses the rare social invitations that come her way. She ends up, for all practical purposes, a social recluse.

A.F. is quite color-conscious. At first she denied she drew distinctions, but later, in the face of dream material to the contrary, she admitted her prejudice in favor of lightness. Her attitudes toward color are derived from two sources: the painful relationship with her father and the social conventions. She equates her hated father's blackness with evil. This attitude is brought out in a dream which expresses her current distress in terms of the infantile fear of the father:

I was in a schoolroom in charge of several small children. Somebody was trying to harm them. I locked the kids in a room and started running to get help. There was a deep snow. It was a man chasing me and it was an extra big man. Oh, he was about seven feet tall and everything he had on was black, including his hat. I hid behind a statue of a guardian angel. He went right by without seeing me. Then I struggled through the snow and went to get the children. I went into the wrong building and that's where I got lost, trying to find the room where I had put them. It was like a maze. I went upstairs and downstairs and upstairs and then I got to a place where the steps were like cut-off. It was a little chasm, and I wondered, 'Now how am I going to get over that?' So I decided to jump over it. I jumped but the steps folded up like escalator steps and I started falling into the chasm. I don't know if I ever hit bottom because I woke up.

She spontaneously associated the black giant with her father: "He seemed like a big gorilla to me. The only man I ever saw who looked like that was my father when he came for me once in a dark alley. He looked just like an ape then." She went on to clarify the equation between black and evil: "I don't care for anything dark. My second child is dark. I've noticed when he does something I act as though it's very bad, but if my first child, who is light, does the same thing, it hardly aggravates me. Maybe I associate my second child with my father."

She also uses color for status purposes. One day, during her pregnancy, she was irritated by a neighbor, who boasted of a light grandson. She promptly had a dream:

All I remember is seeing my new baby. I saw him as he looked when he was born. He was very light. He looked white.

She rejected the obvious wishful quality of the dream. She insisted she had no preferences. However, in the first interview after the delivery, she triumphantly proclaimed, with evident satisfaction, "Remember I told you I was going to have a white baby? Well, he came out pure white!"

Her childhood conditioning at the hands of her parents is hardly conducive to close relationships with either sex. One is struck in the interviews by the absence of intimate human ties. Her only affectionate contacts are with her children. In her own words, A.F. is a "loner." Yet, the warmth she gives her children demonstrates some capacity to love. The trouble lies in the inhibition of this capacity through the expectation of attack and rejection. Her relations with men have always been violent. A nightmare involving her ex-husband is typical:

> I was on a bus and got into a fight with a heavy man. He was very dark. It must have been my husband. He cut me with a razor. The people there separated us. I asked them to get me a doctor but nobody would. I started to cry and I was miserable. Then he come at me again. I took off my shoe and hit him with the heel. I woke up in a sweat.

Her antagonism toward men is further intensified by her own masculine identification which throws her into competition with them. We saw early evidence of this masculine trend in the tomboy behavior of her childhood. A.F. equates masculinity with power and adequacy; in contrast, femininity is weakness and inferiority: "I was never interested in things girls were interested in. I wanted to do the things boys did. And as I grew up it settled in me. I am masculine in my walk and I think like a man. Women look at me and think I'm a Lesbian just on general principles. Things that interest men in talking, those are my topics of conversation. I fight like a man. I swing my fists. I don't scratch. I would rather be with a man than with a woman. I enjoy their talk more. Men seem to be more intelligent. And those frilly clothes that women wear, I don't care for them. I like the slacks I'm wearing now. I can sit and sprawl like a man and I'm comfortable." This constellation undermines her relations with women and she has never had any close women friends. The masculine identification is enhanced by her need for complete self-sufficiency. Its primary roots are undoubtedly sexual but these are not discernible from the available data.

A.F. was raised in an environment that appears relatively free from sexual intimidation. However, this must be an artefact as her masculine strivings, excursions into homosexuality, and relative frigidity are inescapable evidence of sexual psychopathology. She began masturbation at the age of six and this continued into early adulthood. First intercourse occurred at eleven when she became a prostitute at the instigation of her father. Heterosexual contacts were cut off when she entered the House of Correction. Here she began regular homosexual activity. She is attracted to girls who are especially feminine—"small, nice, and cute." She engages in simulated intercourse in which she always plays the masculine role. She usually achieves orgasm through this activity. She has had half a dozen homosexual affairs over the years since leaving the institution. Her sexual experiences with men do not appear to have been as satisfactory as those with women. She rarely achieves orgasm during intercourse, and then only if she is "on top" in the masculine position. In recent years she has been almost completely frigid and has had little sexual desire.

She has continued to practice Catholicism and religion plays an important role in her life. She goes to Mass and Holy Communion regularly. It gives her comfort in her trials: "I get consolation from my religion. I know some day God will make it all right—but I don't know how or in what way." She has no doubt her "sins" will be forgiven: "Some day I'll go to the Lord and I'll tell Him and He'll understand better than any man would. He'll know what I did was a necessity and He'll forgive me, like the Prodigal Child."

This woman's psychological picture shows an extraordinary adaptability in the face of unremitting hardship. There are neurotic configurations, to be sure, but the significance does not lie in these. Her neurosis is orderly and consistent with the provocations. To this belongs her homosexuality, which is a rational retreat from femininity, a role which meant nothing but abuse and hardship and degradation. She uses her femininity simply as a means to an end: for sale—cheap. But this does not phase her, any more than does any other form of work. In homosexuality, she regains momentarily a dominant mastery and with it she can get orgastic expression.

Otherwise, her life is one endless conflict with a hard and unyielding world. Her inner anxiety and discomfort are difficult to equal except in the war neurosis, where, as in her case, the world has withdrawn its hospitality. Notwithstanding all this, she stands up and takes the blows that fall upon her. The best proof of her stamina is the emergence of her maternal feeling in the face of these insuperable odds. The rest is complete loneliness, cynicism, hopelessness, and a deep inner fatigue. Her emotions move heavily; there is no lightness, humor, or relief. But she has enough to feel shame—of which she is not ashamed. How confident she is that she will be forgiven! And yet she cannot retreat completely into apathy. The horrible experiences of her childhood have lost their sting, and she has almost accepted the idea that all people live that way.

E.J.

E.J. is a dark brown, 42-year-old, paid subject who works as a chambermaid in a large, exclusive apartment hotel. She is most anxious to cooperate with the interviewer as a favor to her employer, who recommended her for the study as one of the more steady and reliable employees in the hotel. Furthermore, she can use the money, especially at this time, as she is separated from her husband and must support herself and her 24-year-old son, a sickly young man with rheumatic heart disease, who lives with her.

She was born and raised by her grandparents on her maternal grandfather's farm in the South. Her mother was an uneducated farm worker, who died at the age of eighteen from post partum complications two weeks after E.J. was born. The father was a barely literate, irresponsible laborer, who went his own way and showed no interest in the subject. Her attitude toward him is expressed in some remarks concerning his death a few years ago: "Truthfully, I don't really know what he died from. I didn't even go to the funeral, 'cause he was no good to me. All I knowed was my grandmother and grandfather." The grandmother was an illiterate housewife, whom E.J. does not remember with kindness: "Well, I'd like to tell the truth, you know. She was a very evil person. She wasn't any good at all. She wouldn't let you do nothing you wanted and she was beatin' on you all the time. Every little thing she'd hit you. Maybe she didn't know no better but that's what I call evil." Her grandfather also had no education, but he was sufficiently literate so that he could read the Bible, the only book he ever read. She was treated much better by him: "All I can say, he was good to me. He'd take me everywhere he went. Him and I were great old pals. He used to have a little old mule and a wagon and he used to take all of us grandchildren with him. He had a lot of grandchildren and he had a good time with them." E.J. was her mother's only child, so there were no siblings, but innumerable grandchildren occupied adjacent plots, and she worked and played with them.

The grandfather's farm was very small and quite poverty-stricken. Life was hard and at times there was scarcely enough to eat. E.J. was inducted into work at the age of five: "I could never do what I wanted. I always had to be working. The sun never went down on my grandfather's children or grandchildren. From early morning to night we had to work in the fields. I'm telling you the truth—I been working since I was five. I started then picking cotton and potatoes and hoeing, and I been working ever since." The atmosphere was long on discipline, but short on tenderness: "No, those kind of people don't give you no love or affection. From the time you're old enough to walk, they talk to you just like you was a grown person. Oh, no, I never knew what it was for anybody to baby me up." In this respect, even the grandfather let her down: "No, he didn't show me no love either. He was a good person and he treated me good. He wouldn't hit me like my grandmother—any little thing and she would hit me—but love, no." The church was practically her single escape from the routine of school and work: "My grandmother was pretty religious. We went to church every Sunday, and all during the week she would take us to revivals when they was around. That's the onliest place we did go was the church." Her religious training was further enhanced by her grandfather, who regularly read his Bible to her. Sex was never discussed: "No, sir. She'd never tell us those things, never did, never told us nothing. When I was a little girl I would see a baby and I would ask where it came from and she would say from a tree. There was an old stump there and she said they came out of that. So I was always hanging around that because I wanted a brother or a sister to play with. No, she never told me nothing. I had to learn things from other children, the children who had mothers. That's how I learned—from other children." This is a telling statement which goes far beyond mere sexual information. It reveals clearly some end products of affect-deprivation: a persistent longing for the "good mother" upon whom she could be dependent, and a wish for more intimate familial ties with parents and siblings of her own.

E.J.'s developmental history shows symptomatic evidences of dependency frustration and early inhibition of aggressive impulses. She sucked her thumb until she was ten and to this day she habitually sucks her tongue. She has tried to stop several times because of unfavorable comments by observers, but as she puts it, "I ain't stopped none too good." Toilet training was accomplished primarily by herself, and so was without severity: "As far back as I can remember I was going to the bathroom myself, 'cause, you know, in the South, in the country, little children just go off to the side in the bushes." She is fortunate that in this matter she was allowed to go her own way instead of coming under the aegis of her grandmother's discipline; however, she sees it as further evidence of her elders' neglect and critically adds, "To tell you the truth, I don't even know why I'm living, the way I was brought up." She feared to display hostility toward her grandmother. She remarks about temper tantrums: "Those things you couldn't have around her no ways." A probable devious expression of her resentment was bed-wetting, which finally stopped at seven. Here, again, she was subject to her grandmother's wrath: "I can remember that good as though it happened only yesterday because she used to give me beatings for it. If you got the right kind of beating, you stopped all right!" Throughout childhood she was afraid of thunder and lightning. This undoubtedly was a symbolic displacement of her fear of the grandmother.

She began school in a one-room schoolhouse at six. She got along well with both the teachers and the other children; in fact, she got along well with everybody: "I never had no trouble with nobody. I never bothered no one and no one bothered me. I never liked to fight. I had gotten so many licks myself I didn't like to give anybody else none. I was a quiet little girl. I didn't say much." After school she went into the fields and worked every day until dark. At fifteen, while in the fifth grade, she suddenly got married to a nineteen-year-old farm hand and simultaneously left school.

The marriage was primarily an effort at escape: "I met a little fellow and he liked me and he asked me to marry him and I wanted to get away from my grandmother—she was so evil—so I did." It ended in failure: "He wasn't any good at all. We didn't live together quite two years. He just wouldn't work. I never had nothing to eat. It was worse than it was before, so we had to go live with my grandmother, but he wouldn't work and finally my grandfather run him off." So E.J. was right back where she started, but now she had the additional responsibility of a one-year-old son. She earned a few dollars a week through part-time domestic work for a white lady; the rest of the time she worked on the farm. Within a few years, the grandmother, the grandfather, and finally the white lady died. Destitute, E.J. left her son with friends and came to New York to seek work. She obtained a job as a domestic, saved her money, and a year later her boy was able to rejoin her. She has remained in New York ever since, and because of her diligence has never lacked for work.

She remarried in 1938 to her present husband, an uneducated, but skilled carpenter. It turned out he was a drinker and three years ago she reluctantly decided to leave him: "I left him because he drink so bad. All I can say about him is that he's a very good man but he just drinks and throws his money away. Otherwise, he's as good as he can be." Currently, her husband claims he has stopped drinking and he is negotiating his return. She is giving his plea serious consideration, not because of love, but on the purely practical ground that it would ease the burden of providing for herself and her semi-invalided son: "The only thing that is on my mind now is trying this husband out again. I'm not getting no younger and I really need his help. I been keeping the place going myself and it's not easy at all."

E.J.'s main preoccupation during the interviews is with the mechanics of material existence. All other pursuits are subordinated to this primary goal and revolve around it. As a matter of fact, her present life is essentially a continuation of her childhood struggles, but without the restrictive disciplines of her grandmother, and projected on an adult level. The mainstays continue to be work and the church, to which, as recreational outlets, she has added the movies and the radio. Affectionate relationships with other human beings are mostly absent. The only exceptions are with her son, whom she overprotects, and with small children, whom she adores and for whom she is forever doing things. She showers them with gifts and attention. This interest stems from her own frustrations as a child. Now she does for other children what she wishes her elders had done for her. The relation with her husband is mainly utilitarian, and the same is true with her so-called "friends." They are merely the vehicles which enable her to engage in group activities that give her pleasure. There are such things as the various church functions, card-playing, trips to Coney Island, etc. She is much better able to relate emotionally to her dog than she is to humans. Her low affectivity and her limited capacity to form strong attachments are directly traceable to the absence of affection during her formative years.

Let us listen to E.J.'s own account of her life: "I never did like to be around a lot of people. I would rather be in a place where there's a few people. I only likes to go to work, the church, and back home. That's my life. I likes the movies, too. I goes once or twice a week.

I don't even look at the names of the pictures 'cause I likes them all. It don't make no difference. I have a little dog, and I'm very crazy about my little dog. I takes him out for long walks, day and night. I have friends come to see me; they don't like my dog so they don't come back. I had a roomer and she left 'cause she didn't like the dog. I don't have many friends because I don't have the nice things they have so I don't go around to see too many people and they don't come to me. So I stays alone most the time. I likes to cook and eat and listen to the radio—that's my pleasure, too. I likes that. I do all my laundry, washes my walls and things because nowadays you don't get the painter unless you pays more rent." The reason she gives for her lack of friends is, of course, a rationalization. The true reasons, as we have seen, lie within her and are not tied to external factors.

Her endless struggle for security perpetuates infantile dependency cravings. These find their simplest expression in repetitive dreams concerning food. The following is a dream prompted by a discussion of her youth in the South:

I was in the South in the woods picking berries. I picked a big pail full. It sure was a big pail—about three feet high. I sat down and ate them all. I was enjoying eating all them berries. My grandmother and my family was there. They thought I'd get sick.

This dream is a simple wish-fulfillment in which she denies the realities of her childhood. The size of the pail and her greedy gorging are telltale measures of the affect-hunger that was imposed upon her.

A somewhat similar dream, but one that revives the grandmother's nefarious role, was stimulated by a visit to her grocer's. She was unable to buy the fruit she wanted because it was too expensive; instead she had to content herself with an inferior batch. Her dissatisfaction led to a latent impulse to steal the desired fruit and resulted in the following dream:

We was going to school in the country. We was walking on the highway and on each side there was a lot of orchards with a lot of trees and a lot of fruit hanging from the trees. So every tree that we could get to we'd take some off. We couldn't eat it all so we put it on the ground and piled it up to see how high we could get it. So some of the kids said, 'A man is coming who all the fruit belongs to!' He said, 'I'm going to hold you all and tell your mother and father to come and get you. I could put you in jail but I won't.' So my grandmother come and got me and she was giving me a good licking. I woke up hollering, and my son said, 'Why are you hollering?' And I said, 'I'm hollering because my grandma is giving me a beating!' He said, 'No one is beating you.' So I woke up all excited.

Here, the grandmother's denial of her dependency needs is negatively represented as an attack upon her. The dream, among other things, also underlines the extent to which she dreaded her grandmother's restrictive disciplines.

Other dreams express her unconscious search for the good mother she never had, who magically performs for her:

I was on my way to visit some friends. It was at a place in the South, it looked like, and the rain caught me. So I stopped in at this little old house in the rain. So I was looking around for something to sit on but I didn't see nothing in the little old house so I walked to the door. Then I looked back and it looked like somebody had set a box right in the middle of the floor and said to me, 'Sit down.' I looked around but I didn't see nobody. So it was getting kind of dark and I was wondering, 'What is going to happen to me? It's raining so hard.' So I sat down 'cause I couldn't get out of there. Then someone said to me, 'Aren't you hungry? Do you want something to eat?' Then I spoke, and I said, 'Who are you and where are you?' Out walks a lady and she says, 'I'm your mother.' Then she fed me good and I woke up.

Her associations verbalize the dream-wish: "I always wish for a mother. That's the way I feel all the time. My mother never had a chance to do nothing for me, so she makes it up in the dream. I don't believe in ghosts because if the dead really came back then all the mothers who died would come back and do something for the children they left."

Her daytime fantasies are about what we would expect: "Daydreams? Oh, I have those. I've had them all my life. I've never wanted real expensive things because that I know I could never get, but I always wanted nice clothes and a nice apartment and nice furniture and a good husband, who don't drink. I don't care if he drinks as long as he don't get drunk and throw away all his money and forget about the food and rent and all that. I always wanted to be out in the country. I likes to be alone. I likes a nice country home in a small town. I likes a lot of flowers in my yard and chickens and lots of cats and dogs. That's my wish—those things."

Many of her dreams are simple mirror images of this fantasy. A single example is characteristic of all:

I was in the country and I had a nice home out there—a garden, chickens—everything I wanted. So it was like I had lots of chickens and it looked like everywhere I looked they was laying eggs. And there was lots of flowers and things in my yard. I told my husband, 'It looks like I have everything I wanted—cats and dogs and lots of chickens and the yard is full of everything.'

She is hesitant and uneasy during the discussion of sexual topics throughout the interviews and repeatedly changes the subject. However, she reveals enough to disclose considerable sexual inhibition. She has never masturbated, classifying it vaguely as a bad habit, and has had intercourse only with her two husbands. She correctly designates her grandmother as the prime mover in shaping her sexual attitudes: "My first husband was the first man. I'd had to get out of the United States if I slept with a man—the grandmother I had! I didn't go out with mens. There's not many people stick to their raising like I did. I did everything my grandmother said to. She didn't want us to get a bad name, so I didn't get one." She has no idea what an orgasm is and one can safely surmise she has never had one. She claims she enjoyed sex more when she was younger but in recent years has lost interest. She excuses herself with a convenient rationalization: "A woman my age, she's tired all the time, she works hard, she don't want to be bothered." We can conclude that E.J. in all probability is a frigid woman, who tries to avoid sex, submitting to it as a "duty," but never playing the role of an active participant.

Her self-esteem is undoubtedly depressed, but she does not seem unduly preoccupied with its inflation. This relative self-satisfaction can be explained by a number of factors. Two of these—the preponderant importance of the struggle for material existence and the low aspiration level—combine to reduce the intensity of the status conflict. The third, and the most significant lies in the tether of her conscience. Her self-esteem is primarily tied to "respectability," and its achievement is guaranteed by the ease with which she is able to respond with automatic obedience to the internalized grandmother.

Her aggressive patterns are exactly what they were in childhood: she still "don't bother nobody." Any awareness of hostility either within herself or in others produces immediate anxiety. Thus, she describes her feelings upon observing a fight: "I seen these two women fighting and one of them grabbed the other by the hair and got her head on the sidewalk and was beatin' it and beatin' it. It was so bad that whenever I see anything like that I just go to pieces because I never like to see nobody hit nobody never no time." In consequence of such a reaction, her technique for handling aggression is strict avoidance.

This defense is the major determinant in her attitudes toward the race problem. She is too fearful even to question the status quo, much less do anything about it. Her description of the Negro's position in the South fits into this framework: "To tell you the truth, I never had no trouble down there. I heard of people being treated bad but it never happened to me. The people I worked for, we got along fine. When you live there you know where you're supposed to go and what you're supposed to do and if you mind your own business you won't have any trouble. It's like that wherever you be. The world is like a bunch of bees. If you stir them up you get into trouble. If you just let things be you won't have no trouble, but if you go looking for trouble, you'll get it."

This subject is severely constricted in aspiration, participation, and affectivity. She is much too frightened to want anything above subsistence. She is burned out and has no emotion left to expend on any relationship. She has no expectations from anyone and lives in withdrawn resignation. Most of her aspirations, like those expressed in her dreams, are empty and vague, attached to childish images of the good, kind mother rescuing her from distress. She avoids aggression as she avoids everything else in life. She is not so much humble, as she is non-participating. She has an incredible emptiness that can only come from life-long frustration. Her only ties to life are her dog and her son. She has a vicarious enjoyment of mother love through her kind but impersonal behavior to other children. She is too frozen even to know whether she does or does not enjoy sex. She is a completely isolated human being. She is among people, but not with them.

This is about as empty a psychological picture as it is possible to find in our culture. It borders on complete apathy. Such a person is no longer capable of much protest; neither is she capable of any more participation than is permissible through the functions of fear and the repressed rage, which she no longer feels. One can truly say of E.J. that she "knows her place." This characterization is the complete indictment of the conditions which permit such human degradation—the all but desensitized human automaton or robot, who no longer has any vested interest in herself. E.J. is the perfect slave.

V.P.

V.P. is a medium brown, 28-year-old, unmarried woman, who is a patient in the Psychosomatic Clinic of a large hospital. She has a rather pretty face that is marred by a perpetual expression of sullenness and anger. She is employed as a domestic and lives in a women's residential club where she shares a room with her older sister and a community kitchen with sixty-eight other tenants. For years she has suffered from severe headaches associated with gastric distress consisting of pain, nausea, and vomiting. Usually both the headaches and the gastric symptoms occur together, but on occasion, one or the other may appear separately. She also complains of lifelong dysmenorrhea, so intense that she is almost completely incapacitated during the duration of the flow. She has gone from clinic to clinic seeking relief but no organic basis for her complaints was found and medical treatment was of no avail. Finally, an emotional etiology for her distress was suggested and hence, she was referred for psychotherapy.

V.P. was born and raised on a "tremendous big farm" in the South where her father was a tenant farmer. Their house was a four-room "broken-down, old shack." The family consisted of eleven people: the father, the mother, and nine children—five daughters and four sons, all within twelve years of each other. V.P. is third from the youngest. Originally, there had been fourteen children, but five died before V.P. was born. The economic status was on a subsistence level. Both parents were uneducated and practically illiterate. The father was a seclusive, taciturn, violent-tempered man, who showed little interest in the children and apparently gave them no warmth or affection whatsoever. V.P. describes him solely in punitive terms: "I never could understand him. I was always frightened of him. He was quiet, never talked much, and when he said something, he meant just what he said. He never said he would whip us; instead, he would threaten to shoot us with a gun to frighten us." The mother, however, was quite the opposite. She was loving and kind and protected the children as best she could from the wrath of the father. It was primarily she who brought them up. She set the behavioral standards and insisted on obedience, but in an atmosphere of kindness. Religious training was not strict. The children usually went to church, but if they didn't feel like it, they weren't forced. Sexual morality was stressed by the mother and the girls were expected to be virtuous until marriage.

V.P. shows evidence of an early difficulty in handling aggression. Thus, although she had no temper tantrums, it was not because the temper wasn't there: "I could have done it, but I didn't. I felt like doing it, but instead of doing it, I wouldn't." She stammered when she first started school. She denies convulsions, but remarks "I never had them, but they used to call me 'Fitty,' why I don't know." The reason is obvious. The other children must have been well aware of her propensity for temper-display.

She began school at seven and immediately identified the schoolmaster with her father: "I only had a man teacher that I hated. He was cruel. He reminded me of my father. I always said that and that's the way I feel up until today toward any man." After school she came home, did her chores, and then attempted to study, but her father always interfered with the latter activity: "I would study my lesson, but father would yell we were staying up too late and making too much noise. Then he would start fussing and I would get nervous and couldn't study any more. I was always thinking of what he was saying." It is significant that she associates the onset of headaches and gastric distress with these initial attempts to study. She has developed some insight into the relationship between these psychosomatic disturbances and anger: "If I get mad—not while I'm mad, but after I'm through—I get this nausea, hurtin', and headaches."

She finished the sixth grade at sixteen and then quit school. For reasons that are not quite clear she decided to go away and work. She obtained her mother's permission and came to New York where she joined her next older sister, who had preceded her. The two have lived together ever since, both earning their livings as domestics. Their relationship is anything but an amicable one. Like the subject, the sister also has a quick temper, and they quarrel constantly. The sister is most often triumphant: "My sister always wants to have her way about everything. We quarrel a lot, but I've gotten so I just don't say anything any more." The main issue between them is men. V.P. rarely goes out while her sister is immensely popular and has constant dates. The difference has to do with their sexual attitudes: the sister evidently sleeps with men and V.P. refuses. Concerning this difference, V.P. remarks, "We talk and are very close together, but we doesn't agree on much, especially when it comes to a man. She doesn't understand what I say and I don't understand what she says."

In consequence, V.P.'s present social life is not very gratifying. She spends time either by herself or with similarly minded girl friends: "I don't have no social life. I go to a movie sometime. I have lots of girl friends, but I don't go out with men. The other girls go out all the time. If you go out with men you have to go to bed with them. There are a couple of girls there who don't go out because they don't want to go to bed with fellows. We talk together but I don't call that very much fun. I don't have no fun. I work, come home, cook supper, and go to bed. I don't know what kind of fun I would like to have. I don't call going to hotels and drinking a good time either."

Her sex life has been equally as barren as her social life. She has had intercourse only one time and it ended disastrously: "I've had intercourse with one boy friend in my whole life. It was just one time. It happened five years ago and I got pregnant. I went to a doctor and had an abortion. After that I was so disgusted I wouldn't go out any more. I always thought it would be disgusting anyhow. I never could understand my father and I never could understand any man." The spontaneous association between sex and her father is, of course, very significant.

V.P.'s life represents a ceaseless effort to hold in check her sexual impulses, which for a variety of reasons she sees as threatening to her. Her behavior on any level—be it physical or social—can only be understood within the framework of this sexual conflict. We can safely assume that she has the same sexual desires as everybody else. As a matter of fact, she frequently reports spontaneous orgasm in connection with dreams of sexual content. This is evidence that she is not lacking either in sexual drive or in the capacity for its gratification. Our task is to explain why it is so necessary for her to prevent its expression. The answer lies in the inhibiting influence of fear upon the sexual function.

What are the sources of V.P.'s sexual fears? The main difficulty has its roots in the relationship with her father. She sees all men through childhood eyes. She is completely incapable of discrimination, but identifies each and every one of them with paternal cruelty, rejection, and violence. She now expects from all men the same treatment she originally got from her father. This much of the problem she herself is aware of: "It all started with my father. What I am thinking about all the time is why I hate men so much. I always like to be with them but when I get near them I choke and feel mean and bitter. I can't even sit near them then. I never seen any man I liked. I don't understand them the least bit. I don't even think they're human. I hates them like poison. I don't think they have any feeling. My father was the only example of a man I know. He just never cared and I never found anybody else different. My father was cruel and I feel they're all cruel. All I met were like that." She reiterates this theme over and over again. If she says it once, she says it literally thousands of times. What V.P. does not know is that her sexual feelings are now conditioned by this image of her father and, therefore, represented in her mind in terms of violence. She conceives of the sexual embrace not as an act of love, but as a danger situation in which the woman, through submission, exposes herself to damage from the more powerful and potentially violent male. An unresolved oedipal involvement, wherein the initial object of her sexual needs was the father, continually strengthens this idea. Under such circumstances she can hardly anticipate sex with any pleasure nor can she see men as other than dangerous aggressors. Unfortunately, this does not put a stop to her sexual desires, and herein, as we shall see, lies her dilemma.

This dynamic sequence is verified for us in her dreams. She is a prolific dreamer and rarely does a night pass that she doesn't have a nightmare. They are all stimulated by her unsatisfied sexual cravings and in them she expresses a repetitive constellation of ideas. These invariably deal, in symbolic terms, with the oedipal prototype: the wish for sexual gratification from the father represented as a violent attack (rape) upon her. The remark that to her men are not even human is no joke. In her dreams they are rarely men, as such; more often, they are bulls, horses, snakes, dogs, bears, lions, or jackals. A typical dream is the following:

I was in the country in the South. There's a barn there where my father goes all the time. Suddenly I saw a black stud horse. My father wanted to put him up in the barn. The horse, though, was running-mad. He was in that mood-like, as though he wanted to go with a woman horse. He was the most frightening looking thing I ever saw in my life. I climbed up the ladder in the barn and tried to get away from him. I went up into the loft. I woke up very scared because I didn't know whether I climbed up the ladder or not.

The black stud horse, of course, is her father. It is not simply sex that she fears here, but the violent connotation of the sexual act. She even tells us as much in her spontaneous associations to the dream: "I wasn't afraid of the horse sexually. I was just afraid he would stamp me to death. I feel I'm afraid of men in the same way. They're mean. But I'm not afraid of them sexually. I know sexual intercourse isn't dangerous." Here we have a typical example of neurotic behavior: the existence side by side of contradictory emotional and logical attitudes. In such a situation, the emotion invariably wins out as the primary adaptive determinant.

The recapitulation of these infantile attitudes in current relationships with men is well illustrated by a transference dream. Here, impelled by sexual feelings toward the therapist, she reproduces in almost identical terms the original fear of her father:

It was somewhere in the country. I thought I heard a noise and something was running. Then I saw a very big white stud horse. I was in this big open field and there was just grass but it was tall grass like hay when it grows and there was no place I could hide but then I thought I would stand in the grass and hide there but then I thought he would run over me there and he ran right close to me but he didn't run over me. I woke up because of being so frightened in my sleep when he was running so close to me. Of course, I had an awful headache.

The only essential difference between this dream and the preceding one is in the color of the stud horse. The first one was black, the color of her father; this one is white, the color of the therapist, a white man.

Another aspect of her sexual conflict stems from the relation with her mother. The mother's sexual mores are incorporated in her conscience. The inhibiting effect of their operation is indicated in the following dream:

Oh, this was an awful dream! I was having intercourse with some man. Then it looked like it wasn't a real man. It was just a douche bag. I said, 'Mother wouldn't want me to do a thing like that.' I was trying to keep her from knowing what I was doing. It was awful miserable. It was at home, too. I was wondering if mother could see me.

This dream was prompted by sexual sensations while douching. It reveals her guilt both for childhood masturbatory activities and heterosexual desires. She verbalizes this guilt in her associations: "I wouldn't want mother to know I was a bad girl and do anything not nice. I would only want to do that whenever I get married. I want children and marriage, but I have no sex feelings for a man. I don't know why I don't have it exactly. Maybe it's just because I haven't had much experience. Yet, I don't want to do it 'til I get married. I want to do what my mother said because I feel she was right."

We see, then, that V.P.'s sexual inhibition is an important prop in her self-esteem system. As long as she meets her mother's standards for virtue, she is entitled to think well of herself. But self-esteem is not the only gain; she also protects herself from maternal punishment. As a child, she feared the loss of love and protection if she violated her mother's sexual dictates. Now, as an adult, even with the mother dead for many years, she continues to respond in the same way: sexual transgression reawakens the childhood anxiety that dependency needs will be denied. The following dream, one of many that are similar, illustrates this point:

> I dreamt about a man. No, not a man—a bull. Yes, it acted just like a bull. He was chasing not only me but a lot of people. It was in the South again. I was wishing he would run into a barn because there was quicksand there and he couldn't see it. I ran straight to the barn. I was going to jump out of the way and let him go into the quicksand. I saw him sink. Then we were all buying these dishes and things to eat and we were all very happy, sitting around eating. Everything was comfortable and I felt relieved.

Here, she disposes of the bull, thus denying her sexual impulses toward her father, and insuring dependency gratification (food) from her mother.

We can now define V.P.'s dilemma: she continues to have sexual desires, but she dares not gratify them because of her fears of injury and punishment. Her solution is a typical neurotic one. Instead of facing the problem, she takes refuge in her hysterical symptoms and thus manages to skirt the basic conflict. A number of rationalizations then strengthens her defenses. The first of these makes use of the symptoms to explain her difficulties. Thus, she insists, if it were not for the symptoms she would be able to do everything she now cannot do: it is the symptom that holds her back. This, of course, is simply putting the cart before the horse. Other rationalizations have to do with her social behavior. Actually, her social withdrawal is a defense against sexual involvement. If she does not go out she can hardly succumb to sexual temptation. Rather than run the risk, she almost completely cuts herself off from people. This is the true reason for her social isolation. Her rationalizations, however, evoke anti-Negro stereotypes: "There's only one special kind of man I don't get along with—the drunk that's always standing around corners. What's the use of taking up with such a man? That's the only type of man I come in contact with. I'm colored and I know my color. Those men are in the majority. There are some decent colored people and I know it, but it's like trying to find a needle in a haystack. They expect women to live with them not married. They don't know what to think of you if you don't go to bed with them. A human being has short patience when a thing happens and happens and there is no other way. I want marriage and children, but not a drunkard. As you walk through the block those people are always standing and talking—drunk. They don't know what they're doing. They are swarming on the corner like bees. If you talk to them they might fight and curse you in the most awful language. Nobody wants to be embarrassed like that. It happens to everybody that passes almost all the time. They stand there spitting; they practically spit in your face. What worries me so much is that I hate drunken men so badly. I could vomit when I think of that. If I could only get over that feeling I could go in the street and notice them. It just leaves me cold and nauseated. I can't have no other feeling for a man."

It is no wonder, with ideas like this, that she cannot form an effective relation with a man. Every social contact with a man is seen from the same vantage point. Thus, she describes a party: "I went with a girl friend to a private party. I talked to a couple of men. I tried to dance. But the men only talked a lot of nonsense, crap, and foolishness. The bar was the most important thing to them. They just love that sort of thing—the bottle and talking nonsense. They say if you don't want to go to bed why come to the party." Even going to church is placed in the same framework: "I go to church sometimes but I don't think you have to pray all of the time. There are men there, too. They get fresh right in church. They have their bottle of whiskey in their pocket. They do the same things in church as on the street."

Her relations with women are only slightly better: "My girl friends make me sick. They are all prostituting around and sleeping with men. We aren't even company for each other. They have their boy friends and they all go to bed with them before they get married. There is only one girl in the house like me and she has no fun either." She insists that it is impossible for a person with her moral code to make a satisfactory adjustment to the social circle within which she must move: "It's impossible to make it. I know it is. I understand perfectly what you mean. I think you are saying that if I want to get better I will have to go out and associate with people. I know that. I could have told you that before. It didn't take all these dreams to figure that out for me. But I don't think there is much for me to do where I live—not with my standards. With my background it's hard to meet anybody other than the people I meet. I am one of those little people living from hand to mouth. I have nothing else but to be decent. I'm big, fat, ugly—but I'm decent."

This inflation of her self-esteem is the only reality gain of her neurotic conflict—and it is derived at the expense of alienation from her own kind. The other two gains—the safeguarding of a magical dependency and the escape from injury—are purely illusory.

V.P.'s handling of aggression presents her with a constant problem. She equates hostility with violence and she must hold it back at all costs: "You don't know me, what I'm like when I get angry. They would have to put me in an asylum—a crazy house. I don't care what I do or what happens when I get mad." As we have seen, V.P. feels she has plenty of reason to be mad. The repression is only partly successful, and then it results in a headache. The rest of the time she is like a boiling teakettle. She is liable to explode any minute.

T.G.

T.G. is a 34-year-old, paid subject who works as a cook in a hospital kitchen. She is married, but her husband is an invalid confined for years to an out-of-town convalescent home. She and their eight-year-old son have remained in New York. She is a large, heavy, motherly-looking woman of medium brown complexion, dressed plainly but neatly in very clean clothing. At first glance she appears depressed, but it soon becomes apparent that this is not so much depression as it is resignation. There is a constant aura of sadness about her and she rarely smiles. Life for T.G. is a chore, a burden from which there is no escape.

She was born in a large Southern city and raised there in squalor: "We lived in a small house on a side street. We had no backyard—just the front steps. My father would bring home broken crackers the grocer would give him. I know we had mice because mother would get up on a chair. The house was very poor. We had no bathroom and no tubs, just a laundry sink. The three of us children slept in one bed." The mother worked occasionally as a domestic. The father, when employed, earned his livelihood as a truck driver. There were two siblings, an older sister and a younger sister, who died at the age of three. T.G.'s account of her sister's death is to the point and bleak: "My aunt took care of her while my mother worked and just didn't give her enough to eat. She just died of starvation." Both parents were kindly people, not very strict, who showed the children "lots of love." They fell ill and died within a month of each other when T.G. was only six.

The two children were separated. The sister was sent to relatives in the country while T.G. moved in with friends in the city. Her new family consisted of the step-mother, a domestic worker; the step-father, a laborer; Cousin Wally and Aunt Jackie, aged relatives who did not work; and from time to time a boarding couple. T.G. was the only child in the household. She shared a room with Aunt Jackie and slept in the same bed with her.

The foster family took good care of the child. Their economic circumstances were better than those in which T.G. had lived. All the members showed affection toward her. The items she chooses to describe them are significant: she focuses on their ability to gratify infantile needs. Thus, of her step-father, she says, "He was very kindhearted. He would buy me two pairs of shoes at a time." And again, of Cousin Wally: "He used to take me to the park and zoo and buy me candy." As we shall see, her oral strivings persist to this day. During this period it was Cousin Wally who introduced her to the color hierarchy: "He was fair and didn't seem to like dark people very much. He would give me a quarter every Saturday night and tell me to buy a cake, but not a chocolate cake because it would make me dark. So to please him I would always buy a cocoanut cake." The foster parents sent T.G. regularly to church and to Sunday school. Sex was never discussed.

The step-mother died when T.G. was twelve and the home broke up. T.G. went to live with two maiden aunts, sisters of her mother. The new household consisted of just the three of them. The two aunts allowed her to attend school until she finished the sixth grade; then they forced her to take a job as a nursemaid and turn over her salary to them. Soon she began to resent her aunts' exploitation of her, and at eighteen she suddenly eloped with the owner of a traveling medicine show, a dark-skinned Asiatic Indian who was twice her age. An uncle followed them and had the marriage annulled. The medicine man put up no fight, and T.G. was shipped to friends in New York. For several years she did sleep-in domestic work. She knew no one and her social life was very meager. Occasionally, a girl friend would arrange a date for her. In this way she met and married her present husband, a dark-skinned Porto Rican laborer. Their only child was born within a year. A few months later the father entered an up-state sanatorium as a chronic invalid and T.G. became solely responsible for herself and the baby.

The period that followed was one of great trial: "I went on relief but it just wasn't enough money to manage. Of course, the baby had everything he needed, but there wasn't enough food for me. I had to eat cereal or potatoes, stuff like that, to fill me up. If the baby left food on its plate, I would eat that, too, because I was hungry most of the time. He had the best cod liver oil, and everything the doctor said should be added to his diet, he would get it, but sometimes I didn't even have stockings. It was several years before I could buy clothes or shoes." She refused to give up the baby. This meant she could not go to work because the child was too young to leave in a day nursery. She became more and more desperate: "I got very moody and I had crying spells. The baby was getting old enough to understand, and I started talking to him, telling him how unhappy I was. I used to think of ways of smothering him with a pillow. Once I drew a bathtub full of cold water and I thought I would put him in there and he would catch pneumonia. I started to, but he began to cry and I knew then I could never hurt him. So I decided if we starved we would have to starve together because if I did away with him I would have to do away with myself. I loved him so much I just wouldn't have been able to live without him if I had done that."

The extent of her guilt for wanting to desert the child is illustrated by a dream. She introduces it with the following remark: "I had a dream ten years ago. I read in the paper that somone in Germany was going to be beheaded because she had gone out and left her children alone without food in the house. So I dreamt I was so sorry for her that I would take her place and be beheaded instead." Evidently, for her the punishment for denying a child's oral needs is death. This unconscious perception is, of course, conditioned by her own hostility for a similar deprivation during her childhood and is a measure of the intensity of her infantile rage.

Her baby was finally accepted in a nursery for day care when he was three and she secured a job as a cook. Gradually, things improved. She received some raises in salary and eventually managed to secure a small apartment in an interracial housing project where she currently lives. During all this time she communicated with her husband only through the mails; she could not visit him because she did not have enough money for travel. Today she and the child are able to visit him every week end.

Although she now has a degree of economic security, the never-ending routine of job and home leads to chronic dissatisfaction: "Now I work all day and I don't have much time for brooding and loneliness. And I have lots of fun with the child. He's old enough now. Then there's four of us where I work and we've been there for years, and we have lots of fun, and it takes our minds off the monotony, doing the same thing every day. Still, somehow I'm not satisfied. Sometimes, I feel I should be satisfied, but I'm not. I wish sometimes I could go away somewhere, far, far, away." This escape motif recurs constantly in her thinking as well as in her dreams. Throughout the interviews she comes back repeatedly to the subject of travel. She has many fantasies of visits to foreign lands. This wish to escape has its roots in primitive oral strivings. T.G. is still searching for the good mother she never had, one who will love her and provide magically for all her needs. In her unconscious mind, this is the ultimate solution to her major problem—the necessity of providing for herself. Her preoccupation with travel is simply a projection of this search, a symbolic representation of the desired end. She hasn't found it in America; perhaps elsewhere there is the promised land.

Several dreams reveal this underlying meaning of her desire to travel. The following is a typical example. The wish for dependency is expressed on the infantile level of gaining the breast:

It was a very bright and sunny day. It was green grass and trees everywhere, but it didn't seem to be in America. I was on a very high hill and very happy. I could see the people. They were picking grapes and they had something like a bag around their waists to put the grapes in and I was eating grapes but I wasn't near them. I was at a distance and I've never seen such large grapes. They seemed to be about the size of an egg. They were very sweet. I remember the taste and I was very happy eating these grapes.

Other dreams express the same theme but in terms of more adult material needs:

I was on this large ocean liner. It didn't seem to be going anywhere; it was just in port. It didn't seem to be in New York but it could have been. I went downstairs on this liner and I had so many beautiful clothes —all kinds—coats, dresses, shoes, hats—just like in a store. I knew they all belonged to me and I was very happy.

Her social life consists primarily of club activities. She belongs to one social club and her membership in this is determined by her color conflict. The members are all Negroes, who refer to themselves as "Afro-Americans." They consider the designation "Negro" a derogatory term equivalent to "nigger." She points out that Americans of Italian ancestry are Italian-Americans; those of Japanese ancestry are Japanese-Americans, and so on. In the same way, since she is of African ancestry, she is Afro-American. She rejects Negroes, who are willing to be called "Negro" and associates with them only as "acquaintances"; this, of course, drastically limits the number of her friends, and the few she does have are also members of her club. This attitude toward color was the determining factor in her two marriages to dark-skinned white men. She says, "I decided at an early age I would never marry anyone who considered himself a Negro. It didn't make any difference what his color was, how dark he was, as long as he didn't consider himself a Negro." Unable to find such a Negro, who was also sufficiently personable, she compromised with marriages to white men of dark color.

T.G. has difficulty in expressing aggression. Her inhibition finds symptomatic expression in migrainous headaches and high blood pressure. She is aware of the emotional background of these headaches: "If I get too emotional, I get them. Once a woman that works with me was sick and I heard she couldn't come back to work. The idea she has two children and wouldn't be able to work just stayed in my mind. I got so upset I got sick. I started getting headaches right away and I couldn't sleep at night." Associations with violence lead to headaches: "If I go to movies with lots of excitement, next morning I'm sick, if there's a killing or things like that, or if there's various sad movies, like if someone dies, or something. And I don't like to hear a fight on the radio, either. I never listen."

It is difficult to evaluate her sexual adjustment. She claims she achieves orgasm, but one would be inclined to doubt this from her attitude toward sex. She looks upon it as a "bother" and expresses the opinion that the nights were made primarily for sleep. She denies masturbation at any time in her life and believes not only that it is wrong, but also that it is dangerous, leading to such things as "weight loss, poor appetite, and a sallow complexion." She has had sexual experiences with no other men but her two husbands.

T.G. has shown the usual history of an early broken home with a changing and unstable environment. Her predominant patterns of adaptation are based on a variety of escape devices. The most important of these is denial. Thus, she insists that she is not Negro, but Afro-American, indicating how deeply vulnerable she is on the subject of color. This means that her predominant trait is self-hatred, which she deflects from herself by denying the existence of color, one of her attributes as a Negro. For the rest, she is always wishing to be elsewhere, to get away from herself, or to be compensated by food (the good mother) for her many frustrations in life. She is quite affectless, but disguises it in a feigned sociability which she really does not feel. Like so many of our other subjects, T.G. is one of "the lonely ones."

M.K.

M.K. is a paid subject. She is a medium brown housewife, twenty-five years of age. She was born and raised in Harlem. The family unit consisted of the parents, a brother, and herself. The father is an unskilled laborer. He is a chronic alcoholic and has always been completely irresponsible. There is no love lost between him and M.K. He openly declares his dislike of her and treats her with considerable brutality. The mother is exactly the opposite. M.K. thinks very kindly of her: "She's very friendly. She's just nice. She's good. She doesn't drink often, just once in a while. She's goodhearted.

That's all." The brother is a year older than she is and their relations have always been friendly.

Economic circumstances were hard. The father was never able to hold a steady job. To help out financially, the mother took in washing and there were always one or two roomers living in the house. The home atmosphere was a discordant one. The father was drunk a good deal of the time, quarreled constantly with the mother, and expended his drunken wrath on the two children, particularly on M.K., whom he disliked the most. He was solely a punitive figure, and nothing more. It was the mother who held the home together and she was the only source of love and protection. She set reasonable standards and discipline was quite lenient. M.K. attended Sunday school regularly, but beyond this religion was not important. Sex was never a topic for general discussion but the mother did impart sexual information.

There are several items in M.K.'s developmental history that are of interest. At six she began to have nightmares and still has them occasionally today. She dreams of falling or of being chased by snakes or the devil. She had a number of childhood phobias, some of which continue in an attenuated form. From the age of six to eleven she was afraid to sleep alone. She was also afraid of men and thunder and lightning. These are derivatives of her father's wrath: "A lot of time I was scared of men. I was scared they was going to beat me like my father did. I was always afraid of thunder and lightning and I still am."

She always mixed easily with other children. As she grew older she became very popular with the boys and by the time she was thirteen she was dating frequently. She began having regular intercourse with one boy at seventeen and this affair continued until she married someone else. She left high school at eighteen after completing three years and went to work: "I had to leave because I had to start helping my mother because my father wasn't bringing no money in."

Her first job was as a domestic and lasted a year. During this period, in an effort to escape her father, she suddenly eloped with a young man of brief acquaintance, who was employed as a porter: "My father—you know how he fights so much. I was so tired of listening to him I thought I'd get married." Her mother had the marriage annulled within three weeks. The husband entered the

Army and has not been heard from since. She secured a job as an operator on ladies' coats and worked steadily for two years. She met her second husband when she was twenty, and after a brief courtship of only two weeks, they were married. He was a 22-year-old, semi-skilled electrical worker. A few months later he departed for the Service and she moved back to her mother and father. She stopped work when the baby was born. After her husband's return, due to the housing shortage, they stayed on with her parents and are living there at the present time.

The responsibilities of the household are divided. The husband is the chief breadwinner and the nominal head of the family. Additional money is provided by the mother who works occasionally as a domestic. The subject does the housework, cooks the meals, and takes care of the child. In these tasks she is aided by the mother. The father is drunk most of the time and serves no useful purpose, whatsoever. The life they lead is as close to a hedonistic existence as they can make it. Each day consists of gossip with countless friends, neighbors, and relatives who wander in and out of the house at will, round after round of drinks, continuous card-playing, and general carousing. These activities are implemented by similar goings-on at the homes of others, visits to local bars, night clubs, and dance halls, and frequent attendance at the movies. The aim of living appears to be immediate pleasure and except during periods of crisis the future is never too seriously considered. It is within this framework that household responsibilities are carried out and the inevitable interpersonal clashes occur.

Most of M.K.'s interviews are a diarylike recording of these day-to-day activities. A typical example follows: "Let's see, what happened lately? Oh, yes, my uncle and my cousin came over and I was ironing and they said, 'Let's play some poker,' so we played it. Then a friend of mine from next door came in. He brought something to drink. I didn't want nothing but beer. I had lost a dollar so I quit. They played and I finished ironing. Then I cooked. My husband came home. He made me mad. I asked him to loan me a dollar. For one dollar him and I get mad. Seems like when he agitates me suddenly I lose my temper. I just slammed out the house. I don't know why he makes me drink when I get mad. I like beer but when he makes me mad I drink whiskey and I don't even like it. I go out and get just two highballs and I'm floating. And the same thing like

Thursday. My uncle came again and we played poker again. Now when I lose, my husband won't give it to me, but when I win, he wants part of it, and he gets mad if I don't give it to him. I don't like gambling anyway but I do it to pass time away. Then the baby and I went out and I came back. I asked him if he wanted me to cook and he said, 'No'; then we were playing cards at one o'clock at night, and in the night he tells me he wants me to cook and I said, 'No.' I handed him two raw frankfurters and there was another argument. Then I went to bed and stuffed a pillow on my head so I wouldn't hear his mouth. Seems like most the things I'm thinking is about the arguments. Friday night my cousin Bill and his wife came and we decided we'd play poker. We played for a while. Then my husband had to get some change and he wanted me to go and I didn't want to go and finally he gave me an evil look and went downstairs. After Bill left, my husband and I had an argument. He said if I'd gone he could have played longer. He said I was stupid for not going. I got mad and went in my room and took off my clothes and went to bed. He went out for a while and when he come back and got into bed I didn't say nothing. I was too mad. My daughter was sick Saturday so I took her down in front of the door. I thought maybe the air would settle her stomach. About three o'clock my husband and my Uncle John came in. I fixed some highballs. We talked for a while. Then we played some poker. Then Bill and his wife came, too. We anted up a nickel each to buy some beer. I went down and bought some beer. Then Grace went down later and bought some more beer. Then my Uncle Hodge came over. Boy, is he a miser! He holds on to that buffalo 'til it jumps right out at him. He said to me, 'Why you so stingy? Why don't you go buy me some beer?' I told him I had no money. He said, 'You're a fibber and tell lies.' So he had to go buy the beer himself. Before Hodge and them came, my husband and I had been drinking and having a little party of our own, drinking and dancing around a little. I like that, our own little party sometimes, when nobody else is there. So then we all drank and danced and my father came in that night staggering and I put him to bed. Then after they all left my husband and I talked about how we wished we had our own apartment. Then my daughter got sick again and we lost all interest in drinking. I changed her and we went to bed. That's all that happened that night."

The various facets of M.K.'s personality can best be demonstrated by focusing on her relationships with the many people that surround her. Let us begin first with her father. This relationship continues to be one of mutual antagonism and periodically flares into overt violence. Her descriptions of their battles are somewhat harrowing: "Last year I got pregnant. Then my father and I had a bad fight. He was drunk and didn't know I was pregnant. He knocked me down and kicked me. I got some boiling hot water and scalded him and then he scalded me. I was about two months gone. After he kicked me I started getting pains that night and I passed some clots and then I flowed hard. My husband called the doctor. I didn't tell the doctor what happened because he could have put my father in jail. He told me I lost the baby."

One morning, an hour before her appointment, she phoned and said, "My father got drunk yesterday and beat me up. My face is all swollen. Should I come anyway?" The interviewer was agreeable and she appeared for the appointment dragging her daughter in tow. She was quite drunk on arrival, and although she could walk steadily, her speech was slurred. Her dress and stockings were ripped and torn and on her face, neck, shoulders, chest, arms, and legs were numerous scratches and bruises. She opened the session with an apology: "I got to apologize to you. I've had some beers and you might smell liquor on my breath. Look, I want to show you." Here she demonstrates her many bruises. "It's from my father. Yesterday was my mother's day off. A friend of mine invited us over for drinks. When we got home my father hit my mother. He was kind of jealous she had been gone. Well, naturally, I'm her daughter, so I hit him back and we started to fight. I wouldn't have gotten hurt if I hadn't been drinking myself. He bit me here." She shows the teeth marks on her arm. "Then he kicked me here." She displays a large bruise on her leg. "Then he tried to strangle me. And he called me . . . Oh, I've got to tell you the words! I'm going to say it." She claps her hands over her daughter's ears. "I don't want her to hear it. He called me a g-o-d-d-a-m b-i-t-c-h. I'm spelling it just the way he pronounced it. I've got to spell it because of this here loudmouth here." She points to her child. "We had two fights. Then my husband came home. I told him he had to get me out of the house or I would kill my father. I'd kill him! Yet I love him in a way because he's my father; yet I hate him! I hate him! I never hated anybody so much!" At this point she begins to sob, and groans with pain. Finally, she quiets down and concludes her story: "This morning my father apologized. He said, 'Oh, M., I love you. I'm sorry.' Then he brought some beer and whiskey. So I had one drink of whiskey and two cans of beer with him. You know, it's still on me now. Then my uncle came up to the house. Then we played a little poker—my uncle, and me, and my cousin. Then my father came in and cussed my uncle out 'cause he doesn't give him no money to buy drinks. He buys King Kong—bathtub gin So then my uncle and cousin got me dressed and got my daughter dressed and told us to come down here. That's how it ended."

The relationship with the father is almost entirely of the order just described. Nevertheless, behind all the hostility, she has in truth a soft spot for him. This is evident not only in the facility with which she forgives his maltreatment of her, but also in the solicitude she repeatedly shows him. The following incident which occurred during a poker game illustrates this point: "Tillie went down and bought some beer. She said she got ten cans. I went in the kitchen and there was only nine. I went to my father and I said, 'Dad, did you take any beer?' He said, 'No.' I looked under his table and there was that can of beer. I said, 'I know that beer didn't jump there by itself.' He said, 'I was just kidding.' I said, 'I don't care if you take it. It's just that you lied about it. If you wanted beer all you had to do was say, 'M., I want some beer,' and I would have given you some. I told him he could have a can. Then I went back to play cards. Whenever we play cards we always give him some beer or food and sometime we even ante up and give him a quarter or so."

M.K.'s unconscious expectations from men are conditioned by the brutality of her father. This is demonstrated within the transference by a dream with which she opened the first session of free association following the initial history-taking interviews:

I dreamt I was being chased. It was like a devil. Then I was in the kitchen with my mother. I was eating.

This dream represents the first impact of the interview situation upon her. She identifies the interviewer with the devil—the father —and fears that he will attack her. It is not clear whether the expected attack is sexual or non-sexual, but it could well be a combination of both. She escapes and finds safety at the breast (food) of her mother, unconsciously verifying for us the true source of her infantile security.

Her relationship with her husband in some respects parallels that with her father. He is not a chronic alcoholic but he has another curse almost equally as bad. He is a gambler and practically all his free time outside of work is spent at the card table. This is a never-ending bone of contention between them. Outside of bed they have very little life together. Their conversations are limited mostly to arguments and he rarely takes her anywhere. Also, they are always short of money because of his losses. Another similarity with the father is the violence with which he treats her. The main difference here is in the frequency. The husband does not beat her up as often as does the father.

One day she called in tears. She had just been beaten up by the husband: "My face is still swollen, my arm is in a sling, and I can't hear out of one ear. I don't think I better make an appointment with you 'til my head clears up more." It was more than a week before she was sufficiently recovered to come to the next interview. She described the fight with her husband. Both had been drunk and he became furious when she criticized his gambling. She begins to cry and sob at the end of her story: "He's been gambling ever since . . . No way to stop him except death. . . . He'll never stop. . . . He's a gambler. . . . He'll come home with money and gamble it away. Now he wants to sell all our dishes and furniture to get money. He beats me up whenever he's mad because he's jealous or because he's lost in gambling. The last time he took me to a show was six months ago and he always hollers at me, 'If you want me you know where to find me.' He's always downstairs in the candy shop gambling. But if I call him, he never comes."

Just as with her father, she quickly dissipated this resentment toward her husband, and in a few days had recovered her good humor. In spite of the treatment she receives, she continues to profess her love for him. She frequently contemplates divorce but in the end inevitably decides against it. He is extremely jealous and often accuses her of infidelity. She insists to the interviewer that she is faithful and has had intercourse with only three men in her life: her first lover, her first husband, and her present husband. She has plenty of opportunities but always turns them down for two reasons, one practical, the other moral. The practical reason is her fear of being caught. The moral reason is derived from her mother's dictates: "I used to see kids under the stoop. The boy would be on top the girl, but I never did it. It disgusted me. Then it seemed to me they stunk. I don't know why but it always seemed to me those that did it smelled afterwards and you could tell who did it. After my mother explained things to me I used to feel that those who did it had no pride. She said, 'You have to love somebody,' and if you loved them you gave in to them. That's why I guess I wasn't too ashamed with my first boy friend, because I loved him. Yet, in my heart, I was still somewhat ashamed." She denies masturbation at any time. She has orgasm irregularly, but achieves it more often than not. She has severe menstrual cramps and is quite incapacitated during her periods. All of this information points to a partial sexual inhibition based on guilt toward maternal restrictions and on fear of injury, the latter in the form of punishment from the mother and violence from the male (her father).

M.K.'s closest ties are with her mother and daughter. The former relationship is founded on mutual affection, respect and loyalty. The two like each other's company and frequently go out together. As M.K. herself points out, they are more like two sisters than like mother and daughter. She is also capable of a great deal of affectivity in the relationship with her own daughter. This is patterned after her mother's behavior toward her. She resents the responsibility, but does a good job nevertheless. Toward the child she is patient, loving, and kind. Her concern comes out several times during the interviews in her dreams, of which the following, prompted by a roof picnic, is a typical example:

I dreamt I was falling. We were up on a roof having a picnic. Mary's three children were up there and my daughter was there. My daughter went up on the edge. It's not big enough for a grown person but a kid could fall through. I went up to catch her and I caught her and threw her back but I lost my balance and screamed and fell off the roof.

This is an accurate representation of the responsibility she feels toward her daughter, as well as her latent hostility, for which she pays in the dream.

M.K. differs from many of the other subjects who came for study particularly in her capacity for affectivity and in the fluidity of its expression. She is relatively without inhibition, emotionally speaking, and gives full play to all the affect of which she is capable. Her capacity for warmth has already been documented. Her emergency functions are equally able. The following incident is an example of the readiness and ease with which she mobilizes and activates aggression: She describes a party at which her friend, Betty, became so drunk she passed out on the floor. Betty's husband was so disgusted he just let her lie there. The subject, as is customary for her, was more solicitous: "I picked her up and took her in the bathroom. The next day she spread a big lie about me. She said that I was running around with her husband. She kept telling that story and everybody started talking to me about it. Finally, I got mad and I went over to her house and I said, 'Now, Betty, what's all this you're saying about me?' She jumped up in my face so I hit her on the chin and knocked her down. She was afraid to hit me back. All she did was cry." True to form, she did not hold her grudge very long, and in a couple of months she and Betty were friends again.

Her aspirations are quite modest. Her fantasies run to "a white house with a picket fence with a garden with vegetables and flowers." At times, she is rather pessimistic about her chances for the ultimate realization of this dream: "I guess my whole ambition right now is just to get a home. But in my heart I don't think I'll ever have one. I couldn't be no worse off than I am right now. I can't find a place. I ain't got no money. All I do is eat and sleep. It wouldn't take much to make me happy. Just give me my own apartment, my own home, and I would be happy."

In spite of her frustrations, however, she is not unduly preoccupied with status strivings. She appears to maintain her self-esteem at a fairly respectable level and it does not pose a particularly crucial problem for her. This is due to a combination of several factors: the capacity to idealize her mother, the relatively easy acceptance of Negro-identification, the low-aspiration level, and the major significance of the material and pleasure aspects of living.

This subject illustrates the device of scotomization better than any other so far recorded. As we have seen, she leads strictly a day-to-day existence. There is no planning nor retrospect or remorse. She is able to maintain psychic equilibrium by circumscribing each event and depriving it of continuity with both past and future. This property accounts for her ability to enter into drinking and card-playing irrespective of her previous mood. She accepts the inevitable, without too much protest and without stoicism. Her capacity to isolate and deny reality aids her stability in still another way. It makes it easier to control her aggressions, which would otherwise be in a constant state of turmoil. At the basis of all of this is a lively affectivity, shown chiefly in her strong attachment to her mother, less so to her daughter. All together, these personality traits add up to a very effective adaptation to an environment which would quickly demolish a less adaptable person.

CHAPTER SIX
The Middle and Upper Classes

I. MALE

W.S.

W.S. IS a dark brown, 27-year-old, government clerk. He is meticulously dressed in clothing far more expensive than his white-collar status would warrant. His emotional tone is a constant sullenness. The expression on his face is fixed—a dead pan—and is emotionally flat. He rarely smiles and when he does, it is forced. He speaks in a monotone, but is verbose and pretentious, and over-intellectualizes everything. He is irritable, has little control, and is constantly wearing a chip on his shoulder. He is especially sensitive to aggression and fears being dominated. He feels that his chief problem of adaptation is his difficulty in sustaining interest in any activity for any length of time. He complains that three or four hobbies held his attention, only to vanish completely after a while. Though easily fascinated, he has no staying power or persistence. W.S. is a rolling stone.

He has just left his wife and child and currently lives alone in a small Harlem apartment. The separation has caused him to have great misgivings about himself. He feels he has made a failure of everything. He has achieved neither marital nor vocational success. He wonders who is to blame. He has habitually blamed everyone but himself, but now he is consumed by doubt. Could the fault really be his? Recently, he read a popular book on psychiatry and the subject matter caught his fancy. He comes to psychotherapy in the hope of finding his answer.

W.S. was born and raised in Harlem. He is the youngest of four children. He has two older brothers, 38 and 35, and an older sister, 32. The father was a common laborer, uneducated but literate. The mother was a high school graduate who worked sporadically as a secretary. The early environment was that of a woman-dominated home. There was considerable discord between the mother and the father, the home breaking up several times. W.S. nominally stayed with the mother, but she frequently farmed him out to an aunt, who cared for him a good deal of the time. He received little affection either from her or his parents. Both the mother and the aunt were strict disciplinarians, especially the latter who tended to be tyrannical. She was a stickler for small details and insisted on immediate obedience. Failure to conform brought a walloping in its wake. This, W.S. recollects, he resented bitterly, but there was nothing much he could do about it. He states very laconically, "I conformed." His lot was made still worse by the oldest brother, who was a bully, and took it upon himself to see that W.S. did what he was told. The children attended Sunday school, but religion was not particularly stressed. Morality was middle class and sex was never discussed.

He at first did well in school, but at fourteen he began to fall behind. He ascribes his difficulties to a sensitivity which seems pathological. His parents were too poor to buy him clothes of his own and he was forced to wear the castoff clothing of his two older brothers. He was so ashamed of these shabby clothes that his working capacity in school flagged. When his clothes were poor, he played hookey. As they improved, his capacity for study increased. In the years between twelve and fifteen he went around with boys five years older. This piece of behavior stems directly from his position in the sibling hierarchy. It reflects his refusal to be an underdog and his frantic aspiration to be big. Finally, he lost all interest in his studies and in the third year of high school dropped out. This naturally curtailed his opportunities to find a skill and he had to take random jobs. First he was a messenger boy, then an orderly in a hospital. During the war he served in the Army. He became a sergeant, but lost rank because of minor insubordinations. After his discharge, he took the clerical job he now has. A year later he married his wife, a light brown salesgirl.

His description of what broke up his marriage is very significant. His wife was very devoted to her mother. He wanted to build a family of his own, but found himself forced to become a part of his wife's family. She insisted they live in her home. She spent most of her time with her mother and he could never be alone with her. He complained bitterly but the two women paid little attention to him. The birth of his child further aggravated the situation. The mother-in-law pre-empted all maternal functions and his wife practically took no part. The matriarchal pattern prevailed to such an extent in his wife's family, that he felt he had no home. If he protested against this state of affairs, he was told he could get out. Finally, he rented an apartment of his own. His wife followed him, but, not being used to running a household, she tired of the situation and quarreling was incessant. Then his wife began returning to her mother. Their difficulties were aired in the domestic relations court, but no peace could be effected. In the end they separated, after he beat her up.

He is driven by a dominant passion to be on top, to get distinction, to make money, to be concerned with big things, to manage people. But he has no judgment and cannot accommodate himself to any opposition. He then becomes dogged, never changes his mind, and merely succeeds in getting himself disliked. He is resentful of his inadequacy and his persistent failure. In his social role he is decidedly limited. To make up for this he undertakes big-time enterprise within his own group, where he wants to be a leader. When he fails, he complains that people do not trust him, that they do not value him but instead suspect him of incompetency. The entire cycle ends in his feeling miserable.

The manner in which he persistently and habitually anticipates opposition is illustrated by the first dream he reported. This is a transference dream which occurred on the night of the first interview. It expresses his discomfort and resentment at the questions asked him. He reacts to his fear of exposure with an attack on the intelligence of the interviewer:

Someone asks me if a little toy shoe is my son's first shoe. I say, 'No!'

This knickknack he picked up during his honeymoon, a souvenir of Niagara Falls. He remarks, "People are always asking stupid questions. I think it is stupid for people to ask me whether it is his first shoe. It irks me that people use it as an ashtray." The implication, of course, is that the interviewer has asked him stupid questions.

The dream is filled with sullen rage, with disparagement. His associations led to a failure in a business enterprise he initiated. Everyone opposed his ideas. The original plan had some merits. But when it came to procedure, instead of consulting with the others concerning the most desirable steps to be taken, he was too busy entertaining ideas in opposition to theirs. He feared if someone else's were accepted, his prestige as "president" of the organization would suffer. His idea prevailed and the enterprise failed.

This particular enterprise highlights some of the social activities of Harlem. It consisted of the formation of a club with either a high-sounding or an absurd name, such as "The Cavaliers" or "The Hot Rocks," to give dinners, run contests or hold dances. W.S.'s motives were to be "president" of something, to gain happiness, and if possible to make a little money to get some luxuries. His efforts to be "president" are closely related to his sufferings as a subordinate on his job, where he must obey "petty rules and regulations." This he cannot tolerate. But when he is in a position of some authority, he is more arbitrary and dictatorial than his official superiors. He is in a constant gripe about "injustices" he suffers, and he worries over the fact that no one sides with him.

His relations with his wife were dominated by the same constellations as his relations with others. Any opposition or even difference of opinion was greeted with violent aggression and hatred. When divorce was discussed, his wife wanted custody of the child. This claim was exaggerated into the conviction that his wife would never allow him to see the child, or that this was an indication of complete mistrust. He is vaguely aware that all of this is due to his feelings of inferiority and his compensatory efforts.

Two of his difficulties are his bad judgment and unreasonable expectations from activities which cannot possibly yield him the satisfaction he seeks. On the other hand, he fears taking high position. In the Army he was offered a chance to attend Officers' Candidate School. He refused. He rationalized that "a Second Lieutenant is a little shavetail" and besides he wanted to stay with his buddies. The fact is that he feared advancement, though he was constantly striving for it.

The polarities of agitation and quiescence exist side by side without serious incompatibility. Thus, he related a dream in which the bed was rumpled but the blanket was neatly folded. In association to it he says that he stayed in bed one day "taking it easy." He goes on to narrate an argument with a radio salesman about the high price of radios. He felt the white man had wanted to cheat him. He reproaches himself for not having kept his mouth shut. He then proceeds to discourse on the unfairness of racial discrimination and recognizes that the argument with the salesman was his aggression against discrimination, or what he perceived as such. So deeply rooted is his conviction that he is no good that he reads this interpretation into everything the white man says or does. On another occasion he was expatiating on the subject of discrimination to a Jewish girl, who sympathized with his point of view. This overt token of affection was rejected by him as a piece of aggression. In other words, he perceives what is predetermined by his inner needs, not what the external reality warrants. He is torn with doubt about what he should do: to react aggressively or to remain quiescent. This is the symbolic meaning of his dream. If he does the first, he incurs more hostility. If he does the second, his self-esteem falls. It is a choice between fear of retaliation or depression. And this in turn leads only to efforts at flight.

Following a discussion of the above material with the interviewer, W.S. suggested that perhaps he ought to give up his job, buy a farm, and take to raising chickens—in other words, a complete retreat from human contacts. This is the logical outcome of the inability to consummate any successful emotional release from his relations with human beings.

W.S.'s failure in adjusting to demands made on him began very early in life. The chief disciplinarians, his aunt and his older brother, inducted him first into orderliness about toys and clothes. Later, this concept was generalized to include every task he had to perform. He could never understand the meaning of such attention to detail. Instead of incorporating the precision as a reasonable adjustment to reality, he resented it but obeyed it compulsively. This means that it was never made a part of his ego-ideal but remained a part of his obedience-resentment constellation. He never fought back against these demands. The resentment occupies only the façade of this constellation. In back of it was the fact that these disciplines were arbitrarily imposed. This was the consequence of his loveless early environment. He is not a coward; he often settled his disputes with a fist fight, but he would rather avoid violence. He prefers intellectualization and abstract talk that has no bearing on the issue at hand.

This group of mechanisms has a specific relation to his being a Negro. The original conditions which gave them origin have nothing to do with his color; but they were all accentuated at puberty when his efforts at social mastery fell through and opportunities for expression failed to materialize again and again. His ideal of success is the man who works against obstacles and wins wealth and social acclaim. He professes not to entertain such lofty ambitions, but claims instead that his social goals are a well-furnished home, a few luxuries, to be appreciated and respected by his fellows. Lack of this appreciation deprives him of incentive which in turn depresses his self-esteem. This is a very important point; for his interest has shifted from the intrinsic enjoyment of a task performed to a means to the end of gaining recognition. This is, incidentally, the reason he abandons enterprises so easily, for the intrinsic enjoyment is lacking. He, therefore, spends his time, in spite of intellectual equipment which could give him great enjoyment, listening to the radio in solitude. Human contacts bring no rewards. "This," he says, "is like trying to fill a bathtub in which the water runs out faster than it flows in." So unrewarding are social contacts to him that he avoids even women for purposes of sexual satisfaction: "Just don't bother." Thus, his efforts to avoid the dangers of social relations leave him lonely and depressed.

It would be unreasonable to expect that this man could have much in the way of tender relations with a woman. They are mainly utilitarian. He has a determined rigid front to women and defends himself against any tender sentiment by calling it "malarky." If he wins a woman easily, he finds that she isn't worth while. If the woman is too hard to get, that isn't worth while, either. He complains, "I don't seem to be able to form any affectionate relationships." At least he knows the possibility exists. This incapacity is equally true with men or women. He thinks this is due to the high standards he has of himself and the great expectations he has of others. Since he can't realize either, he abandons all feeling for human beings. His fantasies run on a well-decorated apartment and on the merits of the new-model cars, both of which he wants but doesn't have. He turns from people to things and cannot reach either of them. He blocks on emotion and on ambition, the latter being much exaggerated because it is a means to lifting his self-esteem. Hence, he has a great feeling of guilt about his ambitions and the competitiveness they involve. The latter evokes an unpleasant fear of retaliation. This is the chief reason why he can't accomplish his ends. Everything in his life ends in blocked emotion, abandonment of goals, guilt, fear of retaliation, apathy, or depression.

His apathy is quite remarkable. It is not the kind we observe in deteriorated schizophrenics. He is aware of it, and knows he doesn't react as other people do, for example, to the death of a friend. It is almost a conscious withholding of feeling. Just as he characterizes "love" as "malarky," he regards all feeling as "foolishness" and those who display it as insincere. He thinks "people show emotion because they are expected to do so." This is an indication of how far he has grown from feeling. He tries to "intellectualize," not to feel anything. This, in turn, robs him of any spontaneity.

At one time during his interviews Christmas was approaching and he was turning over in his mind the advisability of sending out season cards. The year previous he had sent out four hundred and received acknowledgments from only forty. On this ground he decided he wouldn't bother sending any this year. In response to this day stimulus, he had the following dream:

I saw standing in front of a big window of a home two little boys, who were supposed to be singing Christmas carols. They presented the conventional thing you see on Christmas cards. Although the boys were standing between me and the window, and the boys should have been more prominent, it seemed the window showed up more than the two boys. I began to cry, and then I woke up laughing and asking myself, "What the hell are you crying about?"

This revealing dream, and the additional information supplied by his associations, gives us a complete portrait of our subject. The window is more prominent than the boys. He equates the window and its contents with his ambitious goals. But two boys stand between him and the window. He is definitely on the outside looking in. No doubt they are his sibling brothers, who always stood between him and the good things in life. Thus, he defines his adult frustrations in the light of his "younger brother complex." His emotion betrays itself in open crying, an emotion he is eager to deny at once.

This is obviously the dream of an embittered person, who longs for much, but knowing he cannot have it, disqualifies the objective and does not allow it to enter his awareness. On the previous day, in addition to the thought of sending out Christmas cards, he had the idea of buying a beautiful holly and putting it into the window. The answer to the thought was immediately, "What for?" The laughter followed on the crying within the dream, itself. That this laughter is a form of protection showed itself clearly in his statement that when he allows himself to feel anything, it is the equivalent of "getting kicked in the pants." From this point on, his associations were about one frustration after another: the Army, marriage, work, etc., all of which he characterized as a "raw deal." He concluded with a bitter denunciation of Jim Crowism and indulged in several aggressive fantasies about how to fight it. This particular material contained in the dream led to two broken appointments. The reason given was that he couldn't think of anything to say. It was obviously too distressing to discuss the matter any further.

However, the discussion did have a beneficial effect. Having digested the content for some time, he returned and volunteered the information that he was feeling more relaxed about the circumstances of his life. He said he had resolved to "make the most of what he had," even though the world was not rosy. He tried in several ways to implement his new resolution. Instead of the flat, dead-pan expression on his face, he began to smile and tried to laugh more often. He also began to redecorate his room. But the new mood was short-lived; he soon lapsed into more depressions, which seemed to be caused by the cumulative effect of aggressive impulses which were suppressed. He put this suppression under the general name of "shyness" and tracked it down to the disciplines of childhood, when he was constantly made to feel insignificant in the presence of elders. This may well have been its origin; but it has received innumerable reinforcements from his social role as a Negro and the many limitations this brings with it. It is interesting to note that when he was talking of his so-called "shyness," his associations led to his fear of death. This is the direct result of aggressions intended for objects in the outer world which ricochet back on him. His thoughts wandered on to a movie about Abraham Lincoln, who had a premonition of his own death in a dream. He, himself, had had a dream in which he saw himself dead and was mourned by many women. Lincoln struck out against injustice and was killed. The same may happen to him.

The interviews had given him insight into the fact that his aggressions had gotten him into trouble with people and alienated their affection. He therefore began suppressing these minor aggressions, with the resultant effect of increasing his depressions. As a matter of fact, he really did not get the point. He was passive in the major situations of his life and permitted himself aggressions mainly with his equals or subordinates. These latter displacements were the aggressions he was now suppressing, which only made him more uncomfortable and did not alter the more important situations. However, these displaced aggressions upon his equals or inferiors had some expressive and tension-releasing function. He sought compensation for these suppressed aggressions in a dream in which Joe Louis was looking for keys in a coat and couldn't find them. Finally, he hands the coat to our subject. His associations were: "I can do something Joe Louis can't." Naturally, Joe Louis represents the highest achievement a Negro can accomplish. In the dream he bests the racial idol. Besides, he represents overt and successful pugnacity. Further associations were about how much better he is than other Negroes.

In other words, the frustrations the Negro has in his social role relative to whites increases the hostility and competitiveness between Negro and Negro. Another reason for his failure in his social relations with Negroes is that in every Negro he encounters his own projected self-contempt. As he puts it: "I can't get along with people because of the high standards I set. I know that prevents me from feeling an attachment to anyone else." He feels free to be criticizing and exacting about every other Negro. It is as though he says: You are no better than I am. You should be all that I want to be. If you were I could respect you! But this is an expression not of a true self-assertion, but only of a projected self-hatred. That is why he is so much afraid of retaliation, and why he goes to such lengths to protect his feeble self-esteem. This system of defense is, however, a costly device. It is based entirely on dominance-submission polarities and hence by-passes all affectionate relationships. Further, the defensive measures give him no real outlet and he must labor under a constant feeling of restraint which he projects into a mild claustrophobic perception. This is a sure indication of being in an emotional "cul-de-sac" out of which he cannot move: "My needs are too much out of proportion to my station. This life is not to my liking, but the things that are my needs are too high. It's no use thinking about them. If you (the interviewer) were a fairy godmother, I might ask for a million dollars and an auto." Instead, he tries fixing his apartment to look better. But this effort, like all the others, leaves him completely unsatisfied and reinforces his sense of inadequacy and the resultant depression.

This is a highly instructive personal history of a white-collar, lower middle-class Negro. His adaptation is eminently unsuccessful. He is constantly occupied with status and all his efforts at achieving some contentment have ended in distortions of character terminating in blind alleys that have no expressive possibilities and only leave him emotionally isolated. The chief disturbance lies in his self-esteem system. The dynamic interconnections are indicated in the accompanying chart:

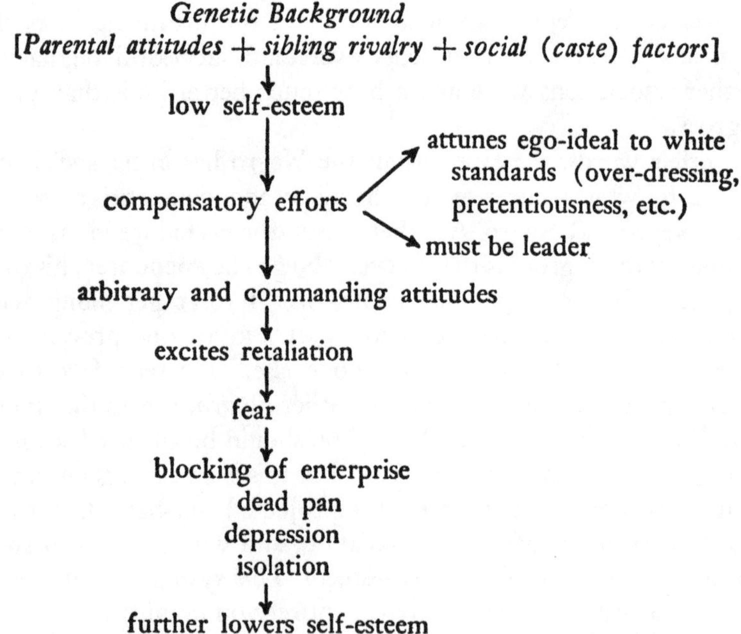

He begins and ends with low self-esteem. All compensatory efforts fail and terminate in a reinforcement of the originally low self-esteem with which he started. It is apparent from the diagram that no course of compensation leads to any adequate outcome. All lead to blocked action or to aggression of which he himself ultimately becomes the victim. One might ask in what way this particular personality scheme differs from that of a white man. It differs in only one respect. It is possible to find a white man with the same psychological constellations, but it would be hard to find one in whom the social opportunities are so completely blocked. Our subject's low self-esteem is not due to his persistent incompetence, but to a situation for which he is blameless—the caste system.

R.R.

R.R. is an unpaid subject, a 26-year-old married veteran. He heard about the research study of the Negro personality and volunteered his services. At the present time he is a student in college where he is seeking a technological training. In addition he has a part-time job as an office boy. He is moderately tall, athletically built, and quite handsome. He has distinctly Negroid features, a very light tan skin, and characteristic kinky hair. He is neatly and tastefully dressed in the best of collegiate fashion. Superficially, he appears well-poised. He has a fine speaking voice, but as he talks he does not look at the interviewer. Rather, he keeps his gaze averted.

R.R. was born in Harlem. He stayed there only until he was two. Then his parents made a series of moves, first to different neighborhoods in New York City, and finally when R.R. was ten, to a suburban community where they settled permanently. He explains these moves as follows: "My mother and father spent most of their time moving out of Negro neighborhoods. As soon as too many Negroes moved into a neighborhood, they would move out where there were less of them." The father is a semi-skilled technician with only a grammar school education. His skin color is practically white and he has Caucasian features. He can easily pass for white and frequently does. He is an embittered man of enormous, but frustrated ambition. His temper is violent, extremely labile, and when he is aroused he becomes absolutely uncontrollable. At such times no one can reason with him. He has never been a responsible breadwinner and has failed utterly to provide his family with sustained material comfort. The mother is a high school graduate and has always worked as a government clerk. She is light tan in color and unquestionably Negro in appearance. She is somewhat timid, but nevertheless independent. She has done her best to stand up to the father's rages and shield the children from him. She is kindly and warm and whatever free time she had she devoted to her children. There is one sister, a year younger, who is the subject's color. She is a high school graduate and currently does office work during the day while attending college at night.

The parents always managed to maintain an "adequate" lower middle-class apartment, but financial worries were a constant irritation. The family wanted for clothing and at times lacked sufficient food. The mother and father seemed to get along fairly well during the first few years of their marriage. Then, gradually, as the economic pressure increased, they began to quarrel and fight with increasing intensity. R.R. describes the deterioration of their relationship: "He beat her unmercifully. She would beg him not to hit her any more. They were always arguing about money. He was always screaming she spent too much." As the years passed, the father's temper outbursts became more and more violent, going as far as breaking furniture and throwing dishes. The mother and the two children out of fear of the father banded together and tried to live their life apart from him. Thus, the home became divided into "two camps." The mother and the children enjoyed each other's company when they were alone, but as soon as the father came home everybody fell silent. The children rarely talked to him except on his insistence that they say, "Hello, dad," when he returned each evening. Even this, however, ceased when R.R. was thirteen. The father became so resentful at hearing the trio talking and laughing without him in the kitchen that one day he informed the mother, "Tell those two black bastards to call me Mr. R. from now on or stop talking to me altogether." They stopped. The father often beat the children, but for "trivial" things. R.R. insists, "We weren't bad children." Discipline in the household, therefore, was rigid and enforced through fear. Neither parent went to church and religion was never discussed. The general attitude toward sex was characteristically middle class.

He began school at five and at first did well scholastically. His father beat him if his grades were poor. One time at seven, while running from his father in the dark, he fell down a staircase and broke his leg. Thereafter, until he was sixteen, he was afraid of the dark: 'I was afraid to go into the halls. I would think people were behind the staircase. I would tear upstairs if it was dark. I kept the lights on if I were alone. There was some actual danger. There were a lot of drunks. I feared my father terribly." He and his sister formed a twosome and were always together throughout their childhood. They ran around with the same gang. The two were constantly compared to his disadvantage: "My sister was a tomboy. She was better in all sports. I could never catch a ball. I was meticulous about my clothes. Everybody called me sissy. I tried my best to convince the gang and myself that I wasn't. I never got along too well with the gang, but I was accepted. I had no close friends."

In high school he stopped participating in sports altogether, but he tried to be quite active socially. He and his sister went to many parties and dances given by social clubs and churches. However, he gradually became increasingly ill-at-ease in group functions. He began to hold himself aloof and put on airs. The other children came to look on him as a snob. He began to date at sixteen and never lacked for girls. His grades changed for the worse. He failed some courses and had to stay in high school for an extra year. He finally graduated, but with a very low average. His sister, on the other hand, did exceedingly well.

After graduation he had various jobs as an office boy, salesman, or clerk. He invariably got into trouble. Either he felt he was being discriminated against or he did not receive proper recognition: "I like to get a raise or a pat on the back after I have been on a job for a few months. I want recognition. I feel I should have compensation. It's a sore point with me on any job I have had. The same today. I haven't had a raise yet and my feelings about the job have changed." He lost several jobs because of clashes with his supervisors. During the war he served with supply troops. Here, he got the recognition he sought. His performance was excellent and he was promoted regularly. He was discharged a master sergeant. He made up some poor grades in night school and thus was enabled to enter college. He met his wife a light-colored stenographer with a college education. She can pass as white. They are pretty much two of a kind. They both consider themselves well above the others in their group and do not hesitate to show it. They have a well-earned reputation for their arrogant and haughty ways.

R.R. has many problems but in terms of observable behavior they are all reflected in a perpetual struggle for status. Everything he does, every move he makes, has for its ultimate goal the elevation of his self-esteem. This is a major reason for his social behavior. He has perfected techniques for belittling and ignoring his associates. In this way, he can inflate himself at their expense. He very neatly sums up his behavior for us in the following declaration of social policy: "I feel I have to compete with the world. I have to fight all the time and it could be I just apply the whole idea to my immediate surroundings. *I feel I must compete with people rather than live with them.* My impression is that everybody thinks I am hot stuff and wants to knock me down. Most of my conversations with my wife are concerned with what I am going to do next to show the crowd. Any little thing that is different that they haven't got, I gloat." It seems, then, that life for R.R. is one of ceaseless combat with his fellows.

This behavior has both familial and societal origins. Let us take first things first and start with the former. As far as R.R. is concerned the world is peopled entirely with his father and sister. He now reacts to everybody in terms of the original competitive hostility he felt toward them. Of the two, his father was by far the more frightening figure. His intimidation of R.R. was both violent and deprecatory. Under its impact R.R. could not help but lay down the conviction that the world was a threatening and dangerous place. Potential violence lurked everywhere. At the same time, as a child he was not equipped to defend himself. He realistically was the weaker and his only choice was submission. The father's deprecation of him further consolidated his feelings of inferiority and worthlessness. Such a one-sided power struggle has a devastating effect on the self-esteem of its victim. His tremendous rage is forestalled by even greater fear. The end result is a feeling of impotence, so intolerable, that intrapsychic comfort becomes impossible. It is this pressure that forces R.R. to engage in ceaseless efforts to elevate his status and retrieve the deflation of his self-esteem.

The extent to which the childhood relationship with his father colors his present-day adaptation is well illustrated in the following transference dream. Here, his perception of the interview situation is predetermined. He must automatically identify the interviewer with his father and react to him accordingly:

I was coming down the street. I walked into an office. My father was sitting in a chair. I was afraid and didn't know how he would accept me. I went up to shake his hand. He smiled and shook hands with me. My wife came up and said, 'No, that's not your father. There he is over there.' I saw a great big man, twice the size of the other one. He was huge. It was my father. I understood that the smaller man was George, my father's brother—only my father has no brother. I was afraid to go to the huge man, but he held out his hand and as soon as I saw that he was going to be friendly, everything was o.k. and I felt o.k.

He associates: "I see my father as two people, one small and one big. This fellow, George, sat quietly and smiling. I suspect it was you (the interviewer). He just watched what was going on. My real father was tremendous in the dream. If I take this George to be you—the two authorities, the two people who have a bearing on my actions—George is smaller because in the end my father would have the stronger influence on anything I might do. My feeling in the dream was: I'll be friendly if he is friendly. I went up to George and shook hands and waited for him to blow up. When he didn't, I felt better." This dream typifies R.R.'s reactions to any figure in authority. He is beset by the same qualms he originally felt toward his father. He represents him as a giant. This is a clue to the omnipotence with which R.R., as a child, endowed him. Evidently, he still sees him in the same light.

His inability clearly to distinguish between his father and other authorities keeps him in hot water: "I'm always touchy on a job. Right now I'm having a battle of wits with the supervisor. I like to talk a lot. I guess since I couldn't open my mouth at home I carried it to school and society. I would gloat if I could outwit my supervisor. I never could outwit my father. He always said if I didn't like it I could get out. So now I try to take it out on others. I try to get the last word. I try to make an adventure out of seeing how far I can go before getting fired or thrown out of school. Authority doesn't like talking. I guess that's why I talk so much. At first I am shy and quiet with people, but after I get to know them I change completely. I become a nuisance and try to be irritating." This is hardly a formula for successful interpersonal relations.

A week rarely passes that R.R. does not have a nightmare involving his father. The following is a typical example:

I had a violent dream last night. I have been having them often, every three days or so. I always meet my father some place. We fight violently. Usually, I punch at him, but he is not there, but last night I punched and hit him. I felt I won this fight. I felt satisfied and went back to sleep.

This dream was prompted by a quarrel with his landlord: "I was excited when I went to bed yesterday because I had a fight with the landlord about the rent. He made a mistake and thought we were behind when we weren't. I talk in my sleep sometimes. Sometimes I swing. My wife says I hollered out last night: 'I hate you! Why the hell don't you get out of here!' I was talking to my father. Whenever I'm upset I get these dreams. The past weeks I have been doing poorly in exams. I want to show antagonism to somebody, so I take it out on my father. I used to be punished in school when I didn't do well. I often used to wake up at night and hear my mother and father arguing. He would smack her. I saw him strike her last summer. I went to her defense. He decided either he or I would have to leave. My mother said she was paying the rent and I would stay. We had a terrible fight. He broke a table over my head. There was a lot of furniture broken. He left after that. Now, he comes by the house and hangs around. He wants to get the family back together again. That would be bad for everybody. I don't fear for myself as much as I do for my mother. I have a terrified fear that something will happen to her. He was always beating her up."

R.R. is not being quite truthful. Actually, it is not his mother he is so worried about, but himself. He is in mortal fear of a final showdown with his father: "I feel directly responsible for my mother and father splitting up. I feel guilty about it. In spite of the way he treated her, she must have loved him. I feel if I had stepped out quietly they would still be together. During the fight I finally began to tell him all the things I'd held back in all these years. He said that if he thought I were serious talking to my father that way, he'd kill me rather than let me carry on like that. It scared the hell out of me and I shut up. He has always put a barrier in front of me. I have always wanted to get even with him. Now I fear if he decides to visit me and forces his way into the house, what will I do then? I have always felt there can be no peace between us. One of us will have to kill the other." His anxiety in this connection reflects the sexual competition of an unresolved oedipal complex. At the moment, he has won his mother from his father. The punishment he expects is the classical one of death (and undoubtedly castration).

This conception of the father as the superior male is unconsciously represented in organ symbols. R.R. equates masculine power and strength with the possession of a large penis. His father, of course, had the largest of all. His in contrast was much smaller. Originally, this concept referred mainly to sexual supremacy, but as he grew older it was generalized to include paternal dominance in all areas of competitive behavior, be they sexual, social, or vocational. Now he applies this standard to everybody. For many years, in order to evaluate masculine adequacy, he has had a compulsion to glance down and judge the size of the penis in every man he meets. This act is directly derived from the infantile comparison of his father's penis with his own. The fact that his sister was considered superior to him didn't help matters any. It simply fused her image with that of his father and further consolidated his feelings of inadequacy.

His subjugation at the hands of his father gives him a dim view of his own masculinity. This is true in spite of the fact that he has no potency trouble whatsoever. The result is an unconscious homosexual conflict. He fears his failure in masculine assertion will be interpreted as femininity. This means that in any competitive defeat he will be exposed to anal rape. He will be used as a woman by the victorious male. He finds such a prospect most humiliating and reacts to it with tremendous rage. However, in actuality, he harbors a wish for the very act he finds so abhorrent. This wish is based on his infantile illusion that he is not a man because his penis is so small. He believes, in fantasy, that he can secure an adequate penis (his father's) through anal (or oral) incorporation. This is simply another way of saying that he would like to admit his weakness and assume a passive feminine position in order to get the boons of a stronger man's power. The unconscious awareness of this desire is so painful that he must react with even greater rage at the possibility that it may be consummated. This, as we shall see, is the taking-off point for a paranoid development. R.R. is so fearful that his desire for a homosexual act will become apparent that he attempts to deny it through the mechanism of projection. He pleads innocence, and instead accuses others of wanting to do it to him.

He refers to his homosexual fears many times during the course of the interviews. He is in a constant state of anxiety that people will look upon him as feminine: "I try to make myself appear to others what I really am not. If they could see into my mind, they would get a different impression than they have. I have always been bothered with a tendency toward effeminacy. I was called a sissy when I was smaller. I had a high screeching voice and a tendency to holler. I had feminine gestures. But I've outgrown all that. I'm just wondering what in my appearance now suggests a feminine person?" The answer is: nothing. It's all in his mind. A more masculine-looking person than R.R. can hardly be imagined.

The interviews are replete with incidents of projection. The following is typical: "Yesterday I was sitting and listening to music on one radio at work. Everybody else was at another radio listening to the ball game. A person came in and said, 'Get up. Let's listen to the game.' I said, 'I would rather listen to music.' The boss came in and said, 'I always thought something was wrong with you. Now, I know it.' He wouldn't have said it if he didn't have something in the back of his mind. To him my behavior is not usual. Maybe to him it isn't normal for a young man to prefer music to a baseball game. Evidently, people have formulated ideas and opinions that I have an unusual personality. Rather than being a strong young man interested in athletics and sports, I am more interested in light things. I must appear effeminate to them."

His suspiciousness destroys his capacity for group relationships. He is much too referential to be comfortable. In consequence, he avoids group activity as much as possible: "I feel that people when they are in groups are talking about me. Especially if a person I have just been talking to goes over to another and they laugh. I feel they are talking about me. In my present job I feel people are talking and laughing about me. They kid me. I avoid people for that very reason. I feel they are poking fun at me. I have felt this way for a long time so I avoid social contacts. Then, too, I have one big fault. I'm so anxious to brag and build myself up. I give people the impression I think I'm better than they, but that's not the way I feel inside. I have a great capacity for being sarcastic. It's not always appreciated. It makes everybody angry at me. So to solve the situation I just stay away from people."

It must be emphasized again that the sexual conflict is not primary. The main struggle lies in the self-esteem system. The homosexuality is the major reflection of a failure to achieve status. His discomfort in the group takes origin from his desire to compensate for this lack. He is consumed with competitive envy. He feels himself always hemmed in by his competitors. He harbors murderous hostility toward them and magically conceives that they are aware of it. This produces both a feeling of guilt and, in a projected form, an expectation of retaliatory attack. It is his own feeling of weakness, his feminine-identification, that couches the retaliation as a homosexual rape. This is joined with the more simple fear of just being killed. He escapes both disasters by avoiding group relationships. In sum, this avoidance protects him from retaliation for his own competitive aggression. He would behave differently if he felt strong enough to hold his enemies at bay. He indicates as much in a repetitive daydream: "I think many times of going off by myself. My whole plan in this hideaway method is to wait 'til I reach my goal, then casually meet someone I know and show them how well I have done. I have daydreams about it: I'm driving my wife in an open car and I pass my father. He asks me what I have been doing. I tell him I have finished college and now I am working in my profession. It was a hard fight but I got through. That's the direction I am moving—to keep myself concealed 'til I reach my goal; then, meet people." Here again the acme of his ambition is the infantile one of surpassing his father. The great hitch, of course, is his lack of discrimination. No one escapes identification with his father; hence, he must surpass everybody. This is an impossible task and one guaranteed to keep him in a perpetual stew.

So much for the familial roots of R.R.'s low self-esteem. Let us take up next the influence of social factors. The caste system in which the Negro is forced to live provides fertile soil for the intensification of R.R.'s struggle. It constantly confronts him with the reality fact that society looks upon him as an inferior product. This is the very piece of information that his internal psychic economy is least able to tolerate. The result is a tremendous elaboration of the significance of those status attributes considered most valuable by the whites. Most important here for the Negro is color. Second, come such things as wealth, social position, professional achievement, etc. These are R.R.'s true goals. He is not, for example, interested in his technological training for its own sake, nor in the gratification it alone can offer him. No, his major concern is with the impression successful accomplishment will make on his rivals. His goals have little intrinsic value in their own right. That is one reason he finds it so difficult to sustain his drives. As he puts it: "I always start with enthusiasm, but it isn't long before it peters out."

He spent many sessions discussing his need to make an impression: "I want to impress everybody, but mainly my cousins. They're the better half of the family. They have lots of money. They're always throwing things in our face like the new Cadillac they just bought. The only thing we have over them is that we're going to college. They always had better clothes. They grew up with a superior feeling toward us. All my cousins are almost white. My sister and I are darker. My wife is light like my cousins. Grandma accepted my wife. Grandma is very color-conscious. She speaks constantly of dark Negroes as 'black bastards.' She has a terrific prejudice against darker people. My father can pass. He has blue eyes and blond hair. He had high goals for his children. We could go only with certain crowds. There are only two crowds among Negroes—light and dark. He wanted us to go with the light. He always objected if he saw me with a dark Negro. All my girl friends were of one type, one color—light and fair."

He dwells on the color theme again and again: "My wife's hair is straight and she doesn't look colored. Where we go on the beach we go purposely to avoid the colored. We go to Jones Beach. It's not like Rockaway where there are blocks and blocks of Negroes. It's awful, but the conversation in any group I'm in seems always to drift to this color business. So many of my friends are fair and feel so superior and really are not. I was brought up in this clique. Shades to them are the most important thing. I've had some of my friends rejected because they weren't light enough. One of my wife's girl friends was over last night. She wants to get married but her family doesn't like the fellow. Her family are all very fair with straight hair and sharp features. The fellow doesn't conform to the family looks. He is of my complexion with soft features. The concern is with the quality of the hair and nothing else. He doesn't have nice hair—straight hair—but just colored (Negro) hair. It's just ordinary colored (Negro) hair. The quality of the hair is more important to them than the color of the skin. It's a strange thing, but the majority of the families in my community think the same way when matching up the kids. They don't look into their backgrounds. They are not interested in that. They only care about the looks. They must have some outstanding Caucasian feature. If not color, then hair; if not hair, then blue eyes—or something like that."

The interaction of familial and societal factors in reproducing R.R.'s central conflict can be demonstrated within the transference.

One day he wishfully dreamed that his wife gave birth to a baby girl with blond hair and blue eyes. He readily admitted such a preference when questioned by the interviewer. The next night he had the following dream:

> I was sitting in a classroom. It seems as though I was on trial for something. I looked out of the window and saw what at first looked like Arabs, but as they came closer, I saw they were Indians. They were rushing to attack. Against them came some soldiers in costumes of the Revolution. These soldiers were all dressed in white pants. A fat man was giving a lecture in the class. Then Mrs. Roosevelt came in. She pointed to the other room which was full of colored children, extremely dark and definitely Negro. She made remarks in their defense.

He relates the classroom to the interview situation. He felt on trial for his attitudes toward color: "I was concerned about our talk last time. I was jumping to my defense in my own mind. I don't want to be prejudiced against my own race. I would love the child even if it weren't blond. Mrs. Roosevelt has always defended the colored. I felt I was on trial for something in the dream and she came to my defense. The teacher was very angry and talking against me. That is probably you. He is big and fat—just the opposite of you. Maybe that's my own way of getting even. When you insinuated I had a leaning toward whites, I didn't like it very much. I get particularly irritated when I am called color-conscious. I know it's true, but I don't like to be that. I don't feel it's a healthy attitude. The Indians bring to light the conflict, the fight, between us. The white pants emphasize the color, the difference between you and me—Negro and white. It reminds me of a costume play, 'Catherine Was Great,' with Mae West—a raw comedy, a series of bed adventures. The soldiers wore the same costumes as in the dream. They all had white pants. In one scene, she lined them up and chose the one she wanted to go to bed with—I suppose from the size of what she saw in his pants."

This dream is a remarkable condensation of the essential dynamisms responsible for R.R.'s behavior. He reacts to the interviewer in a typical paranoid fashion. An innocuous remark becomes a violent attack upon him. He is persecuted by a white man simply because he is colored. The superior strength attributed to his white attacker is symbolized sexually in the possession of a large penis. Here, he re-enacts his fear of anal rape by the father. Thus, in one dream, he simultaneously expresses his conflict on three different levels: body-organ, familial, and societal. Added together, they represent the sum total of his personality.

This subject describes the status and color conflicts of the middle-class Negro with remarkable accuracy and completeness. He has two introjected images: the white man and the colored man. In this particular case, the father, because of his light skin, is able to represent both. Each of these images has strongly ambivalent feelings attached to it: hatred and love. R.R. tries to dispose of the hated aspects of both by projecting them into the outer world. This maneuver enables him to say: "It is not myself that I hate, but that other fellow—the dark Negro." However, he cannot love the introjected white object either. In the end, he is left with nothing within himself that he can love. The resultant self-hatred is all too frequently the common lot of many Negroes.

L.H.

L.H. is a 30-year-old, married, white-collar clerk for a government agency that employs many Negroes. He has handsome Caucasian features, white skin, and straight hair. There is no way whatsoever from his appearance that he can be labeled a Negro. At first meeting, he settles down to speak to the interviewer as though they have been friends for many years. He seems very much at ease and is extremely graceful socially. Very quickly, however, there becomes apparent an almost imperceptible, but all-pervading, note of depression. Questioned about this, he at first denies that he is depressed, but as the interviews progress, he finally admits it. Another incongruous note is his dress. It is not in keeping with his good looks and social grace. Instead, he wears an inconspicuous, dull-black, poorly tailored suit with a dark, colorless necktie. One cannot but conclude that he is hiding his light under a bushel.

Technically, L.H. is a patient in psychotherapy, but actually, he comes to the interviews more out of curiosity than for anything else. One of his friends prevailed upon him to volunteer his services in return for possible aid in the resolution of a personal problem. He defines this problem in the first interview. He does not seem to have any particular goals in life. He feels he is just "drifting aimlessly" without any direction. He feels he ought to have a better idea of what he wants and where he is going than he has at present. He has considerable doubt that therapy can help him in any way, but nevertheless, he is willing to try.

L.H. is an only child. He was born and raised in a large Northern city on the borderline between a Negro and a white neighborhood. The father was a light-skinned Negro who could pass as Mexican or South American. He had a grammar school education and owned a small business at which he was quite successful. The mother, too, was a Negro, but had white skin, straight hair, and looked "Irish." She had a high school education. She took care of L.H. full time until he entered school. Then she took a part-time job as a cashier in a restaurant. L.H. describes both parents in identical terms: "They were very similar to each other. They were both placid people. There were never any arguments in the house. There were no disturbances or uprisings. Mother and father enjoyed going out. They always did that. They ran around a lot and had a pleasant time. They had lots of friends and all of them belonged to the same social group."

The family occupied their own private house, which his mother kept "very nicely, neat, clean and without disorder." Their economic status was always quite comfortable. He feels he was a rejected child, but not in the usual sense. The parents were affectionate and understanding, but they were too busy leading their own lives and their ties to the child were loose. He could not help but feel that they really were not particularly interested in him. The situation was more one of live and let live. Discipline was practically non-existent. He was free to do anything reasonable that he wanted to do. His religious training was characteristic of his parents' attitude toward him. He was given his choice about church. He could either go or he could stay home. He went a few times, but in the end he chose to stay home. Sex was treated in the same way. There was no intimidation, his questions were answered, and he could engage in sexual activity or not, as he desired.

In grammar school he got along well with his teachers, but he did not join into group activities and had few friends. He is not certain why this happened, but as we shall see later, it had to do with his fear of non-acceptance by Negro children because of his white skin. After school he did a great deal of reading and played mostly by himself. The situation changed markedly at the age of fifteen when he entered high school. He fell in with a group of Negro boys and neglected his studies: "We had a great social life. We spent each week end together, plus every afternoon after school. We would hang around the drug store, play cards, go to parties and dances. I failed all my courses for two years." He had his first sexual experiences during this period and since the age of fifteen has had intercourse regularly. Ocasionally, when a girl was not available, he filled in with masturbation. He has never had any potency disturbance.

He finally managed to graduate from high school and set out to look for work. He was not very serious about it and concentrated more on carousing: "I had a gay time again. I was free and on the loose and at an age I considered myself a full-grown man. The social group was the same, but progressed. Several fellows married, had homes, cars, a round of parties. I began drinking. I thought it a smart thing to do on parties." At first, he drank for social purposes only; now the drinking is an end in itself: "It's become something I enjoy doing. Now I will drink before dinner, or at work, or if I have time on my hands. I drink beyond the point of getting a lift, but not to the point where I am stuporous."

He came to New York to escape his parents' objections to his behavior. He continued to indulge himself socially: "I had a social group in New York that amounted to the same thing I had before, except in my home town the groups met at homes. In New York the apartments are too small and bars are the meeting places." He became a clerk in a government agency and has retained his job to the present. Five years ago, he met and married his wife, a light brown Negro girl. His life has changed little since the marriage. He spends most of his free time wandering from bar to bar. His wife goes with him when she feels like it, but usually she is not interested, so he goes alone. Occasionally, he stays home with her and reads. He appears to know literally hundreds of people and his major occupation is socializing with them. In fact, for him this seems to be the primary function of life. L.H. can best be categorized as a specialist in making friends.

This socialization, of course, is only a means to an end. Just what is L.H. trying to accomplish? Why does he devote so much of his energies to it? Let us examine the very first hour of free association. Here, put on his own, he spontaneously elaborates his conflict:

"Well, the thing I want to get from therapy is the ability to stick to a job and see it through. Usually I tell people I want to write, but I fear I won't be any good, or it won't satisfy me or other people and I would be very unhappy. I frequently write—in my head—without putting it on paper. Nobody can see it then or laugh at the content." (You seem to be quite concerned with what others think of your efforts.) "I am. For instance, I'm not having difficulty with people on the job, but I have gone out of my way to know their names, to pick them up, to buy them drinks, because I see clearly they are suspicious of me. A woman in the office I am friendly with told me that nobody in the place disliked my personality, but all are envious of my complexion and looks. So the only way I can get them to accept me is to be nice to them. I never could let them see what I had written because most people are suspicious of writers and expect them to be different from the ordinary. This is something I've had all my life. Other Negroes find it difficult to warm up to me. Because of that I have gone all out to be on their level, to speak their language; when I was a truck driver, I talked a worse language than they did: if they drank bad whiskey, I drank worse. I always succeed in getting liked. I never have petty arguments with anybody. I always spend more time listening than anybody else. I agree with everything that is said." (Doesn't that constrict your individuality?) "I suppose that is the basis for my not having any aims, like being an engineer or a doctor. It is of greater concern to me to be accepted by the whole group rather than to set myself apart. Most of them don't have any such goals. Negroes are very suspicious of other Negroes who have and do things they can't have and can't do. Some people decide they don't care but I do." (Your goals are blocked by the fear of non-acceptance by Negroes?) "Yes. My wife says I try too much not to do anything to make even a slight acquaintance or a stranger uncomfortable. For instance, I don't push in the subway." (You avoid aggression?) "Yes. I avoid any type of aggression. My wife will see some one and call twenty yards. I could never do that because it focuses attention on me. I sort of want an N.A.A.C.P.[1] job. I would be in the limelight and a lot of attention would be focused on me, but in this case I don't feel that the attention would be hostile because I would be doing things for the good of the whole people. I don't mind that. I would be telling

[1] National Association for the Advancement of Colored People.

them something they want to hear." (Attention is all right as long as you are helping people. Otherwise, it connotes an aggressive act.) "That's right. I don't want attention focused on me. That's why as a young child I sat home—reading and daydreaming. It was a complete escape. But now I am not afraid to go out and meet people because I feel I have become practiced enough to make friends of everybody."

In this one session L.H. makes very clear his dilemma. Already, as a young child, he became aware that his light skin, through no fault of his own, incurred the hostility of other Negroes. His color thus became a piece of aggression against the very group with whom he sought identification. Full of guilt and fearing retaliation, his first impulse was to withdraw. He remained by himself. That is why he failed completely to integrate socially until he entered high school. It was here that he was taken up by a gang of Negro boys and for the first time felt accepted. The result we have already seen. His exhilaration knew no bounds and he sacrificed everything for the new-found pleasure of social acceptance. His rejection at the hands of his parents gave additional stimulus to his behavior. The group, by virtue of its approval, gave him the love he felt he had never received. As he grew older, the hostile nature of color became generalized to include any attribute which operated to his advantage. Any attempt to advance his status—professionally, socially, or intellectually—became an act violently hostile to the far less fortunate bulk of the Negro population. It could lead only to equally violent retaliation as well as to rejection by the group.

This dynamic construction effectively blocks off all forms of self-assertion. L.H. is so burdened with guilt that his whole behavior is calculated not to alienate, offend, antagonize. Only in this way can he insure his safety and permit himself to feel loved. To make the scheme airtight, he invokes a self-referential mechanism as a warning signal. He avoids the limelight because it is a symbol of prominence. It is exhibitionism conceived as a hostile act. Placed in such a position, he magically feels that others symbolically interpret his behavior as aggression: he is trying to get ahead, push himself, be better than they, etc. The immediate anxiety he experiences is a constant reminder of the retaliation that will come his way should he ever fail to inhibit his assertive impulses. Seen in this light, the excessive socialization, with its need to prove friendship, is primarily a defensive maneuver that stems from attributes and activities that he classifies as hostile.

This conflict is the central theme of the interviews and he is constantly preoccupied with it. He never stops examining it from every possible direction. He comes back again and again to his fear of non-acceptance by Negroes. The following is a typical example: "Negroes resent my light color. That's why I go to all the effort to show them I am one of their boys, I am with them, on their side. Otherwise they won't associate with me. 'Who the hell do you think you are just because you're light?' That's a common phrase and I don't want them to say that about me, and they don't, and that makes me happy. Being accosted and jeered at in the streets isn't pleasant. You can't just say, 'The hell with it!' That's why light-skinned people move out of the area, out of the jungle. It's like a Jew in a community in Germany."

He correctly places drinking within the framework of his basic problem: "I probably drink so I will be less inhibited. Alcohol releases inhibitions—the control of emotions. My inhibition is stronger than drink. The control is always there, but with alcohol it isn't as great. I can have a more enjoyable time when I'm not so concerned with what everyone is going to say, do, and think. I don't see how I could get along without the controls altogether. I'm afraid the society within which I function wouldn't find me acceptable. If I lost some of these controls I would end up being lonely. Negroes in general would find me a bitter pill to take because their color bars would be operating at full force, and if I wasn't doing anything to appease their bars, then they just wouldn't accept me. I don't know what way I could act without controls because I have never done it, but I feel they would find it distasteful. And since I get a lot of pure pleasure and enjoyment at this time in associating and being accepted by Negroes, if I was not accepted, I would be very unhappy. I am not very religious, but I have changed the Commandment around a little: Act unto others as they would have you act toward them. I do that and I am happy. If I were antagonistic, I couldn't do that. I feel it's an investment. So I give up some things I might want to do, but I get something else in compensation for it."

In spite of all his efforts, L.H. never succeeds in establishing a complete identity with his group. He perpetually feels an outsider, a bystander instead of an active participant: "I am usually a bystander. That is the way I function in this society. I sort of stand around and watch how human beings exist in Harlem. I am just an observer watching what is going on and what other people are doing. I never really feel I am a part of it. I never feel that I am really a participant. When I am participating I am drunk. Probably that is the main reason I drink—to let the barriers down so I can participate."

He considers many people his friends, but actually he is really intimate with no one, not even his wife. In this connection, the following is a very telltale remark: "I always wait until you finish writing before saying something new, because I am very concerned you get down everything important. Another thing, I would like to read what you have written some day, and also I have a number of friends I would like to have read what I say—friends I want to be intimate with, *like my wife*, John, and others. There are lots of people I want to be more intimate with and that requires that they know more about me. I could never tell them but if they could read what I am, then a greater intimacy between us could be reached." It is significant that he refers to his wife as a "friend" with whom he wants to be more "intimate." It indicates the difficulty this man has in getting emotionally close to an object, as well as the desperate longing to do so. And, in fact, his relationship with his wife seems little different from that with other "friends." For the most part, like the rest, she is just another person who is "around."

Few of his needs are satisfied. He neither secures the total acceptance he wants nor does he achieve any of his ambitious goals. Such a failure in self-realization cannot help but end in depression, hopelessness, and apathy: "Your remarks about my depression are well taken. I'm aware of it. It's there. What may possibly be the cause of the depression, I think, may be the fact that I am in a sort of aimless situation. Being aimless and having no goals ahead would make me at any time to be in a frame of mind: What the hell is the use?"

His dreams reflect his non-participation, his aimlessness, and his hopelessness. The following dream, his first, represents his initial response to the treatment situation:

This is typical of the kind of dreams I have. Nothing happens. Not very exciting. I was going somewhere with an unknown man. We go where we can catch a trolley car. The car is standing there empty. The operator didn't come. We got in. I drove. I collected fares from the passengers. When we got to where we were going—the end of the line—we got out. I went down the subway steps, and that was all. The dream ended.

He associates: "I got the impression the man was white. Most people I dream of are very shadowy and don't seem to contribute anything. They're just sort of along. It was just sort of an aimless wandering, just going casually, no anxiety about being late, not in a hurry. I had no sense of disappointment when the dream was over or that I had accomplished anything. That is usually what happens in my dreams. Most of them involve traveling—going from one place to another. The other man was just sort of around, standing at the side behind me. He wasn't doing anything." The dream is an accurate representation of his basic attitude toward life and his relationships to people. He places the therapist (the unknown white man) and the treatment situation within the same context. He foresees no aid from the therapist and his expectations from therapy are nil. The therapeutic relationship will be just like all the others—an empty and meaningless contact. It will be pleasant enough, but nothing will be accomplished, and when it is over, he will get into another vehicle (the subway) and continue his aimless wandering.

In practically all of his dreams he is a non-participant. The following two dreams are typical and are presented to reiterate the point:

Somebody was trying to do away with everybody named Anderson. I don't know anybody named Anderson. They just seemed to be chasing everybody named Anderson. *I was just sort of a bystander and watching.*

It was similar to a final scene in the movies, but I don't know what it was the end of. It was a fadeaway scene. *I wasn't in the dream at all. It seemed as though I was just outside of it as though watching a movie.*

He comments only: "I played my usual non-participant part."

L.H. does have one avenue of escape—he can pass: "Negroes live in a ghetto and if I want other things I can go out of the area and get it, like going to Carnegie Hall, and I don't have to worry about color because Negroes won't see me, except Negroes in the same boat as I am. So any place I want to go I can, so that's why I don't feel trapped so much." His concern that other Negroes will see him denies his conclusion. He is far too guilty to pass with impunity. He does it on occasion, but it must inevitably be accompanied by an intensification of his unconscious sense of guilt.

This subject strikingly illustrates the intrapsychic difficulties that attend the accomplishment of a much-sought-after Negro objective: to be light-skinned. The resultant guilt feeling places him in an unfortunate dilemma: if he sides with the Negroes, he is considered a fool; if he takes sides against them, he is considered a traitor. This attitude revolves not just around the color conflict, but is extended to include the successful achievement of any status goal denied to the majority of Negroes. The hostility so generated is a potent force that helps undermine the cohesiveness of the Negroes as a group.

B.B.

B.B. is a dark brown, 26-year-old, college-trained technician, a recent arrival from the South. He is exceptionally well-groomed and flashily dressed in bright-colored clothing. He is unmarried and lives alone in a rooming house. He has just been hired by a government agency—his first job in New York—but for reasons which at first he does not disclose, he has been under so much emotional tension that his work has not been up to standard. He comes to psychotherapy for the exploration and resolution of his anxiety.

B.B. was born and raised in the capital city of a deep Southern state. His father was a professional man, a graduate of a Negro college. He was somewhat pompous and overbearing, but never really severe or mean. His interest was mainly in his work, rather than in his home or family. The mother, too, was a graduate of a Negro college, but devoted all of her time to running the home and taking care of the children. B.B. describes her in a much more favorable light than the father. She was warm, congenial, and generally liked. There are two older sisters, both college graduates, and an older brother who left high school before graduation. He is a laborer and the rest of the family look upon him generally as a failure.

The economic status was always comfortable. The family owned a large house in the best Negro neighborhood. The parental relationship was a good one and things ran smoothly with a minimum of arguing and bickering. Both parents were affectionate toward the children, but the mother much more so than the father. She was the real "boss" of the household and it was she who made all the major decisions. Ethical and moral standards were extremely high.

These were made necessary by the father's high position in the community. Discipline, therefore, was strict and was administered by the mother, either with a switch or through denial of pleasure. Sex was never discussed in the family, but on the other hand, neither were the children intimidated. In fact, B.B. appears to have had almost unlimited sexual freedom. He had first intercourse at seven with a playmate and regularly and frequently thereafter with girls of his own social group. He has also masturbated occasionally since puberty, but this has been infrequent, since his needs are so readily met through intercourse.

He showed an early inhibition of aggression. He has rarely been capable of an overt display of hostility: "I never had any temper—until recently." He spontaneously volunteers that he has always had a terrible fear of "dead folk and of rats." The dynamic significance of this observation is of the greatest importance. It lies in the fact that the rat is a "biting" animal. Such an association—between dead people and rats—symbolically represents his fear of being bitten to death by his siblings in the struggle for the maternal breast. The persistence of these fears into adulthood indicates that his competitive efforts are still couched in infantile terms. He has emerged from the sibling rivalry situation with the concept of oral aggression intact. Evidently, for him, competition is simply a revival of breast-envy in which he risks the retaliation of being killed by his opponents. On this basis, we would expect B.B. to be quite incapable of strong assertive action.

He was a good student at school. He got along well with teachers and playmates alike. He always had "gangs of friends." After school he usually worked. He sold papers, shined shoes, and ran errands. He graduated from high school with honors. He went on to a Negro college where he continued his good record. He was also very active in social and extracurricular activities. He took two years of graduate training and then secured employment in his specialty. Soon he became dissatisfied and decided to come to New York in search of greater opportunity. He had excellent recommendations and had no trouble finding a suitable job. It was not long, however, before he found himself in the anxious state for which he comes to treatment.

B.B. gave no inkling in the initial session of the sources of his anxiety. Instead, he waited until the second interview. Then he revealed with great embarrassment that he was involved in a homosexual affair. He had been seduced by a young man with whom he had become friendly since his arrival in New York. One evening the two had gone to a party and gotten drunk. Subsequently, they retired to the friend's apartment where he proceeded to perform fellatio upon the subject. B.B. submitted, but did not reciprocate. Afterwards, in disgust, he berated his partner. The latter, of course, was quite hurt and expressed himself to that effect. Filled with remorse for his remarks, B.B. apologized. A few days later his friend seduced him again and now the act repeats itself at frequent intervals. B.B. is always the passive partner, his friend the aggressor. Try as he might B.B. appears unable to extricate himself from this relationship. This is his first homosexual contact and he insists he has no homosexual desires whatsoever. He expresses disgust with himself and is petrified that he will be publicly disgraced. Why then is he so completely unable to break the contact?

The interviewer focused on this problem and B.B. responded with the following explanation: "He says he can't live without me. He threatens me that if he can't have me, no one will. I'm chained by it. He drinks a lot and he gets violent. I'm afraid he'll actually kill me. Besides, he is in bad shape. It wouldn't be right to leave him. He quit his job. He is going down hill. I try to help him straighten out. I always do that for any of my friends. I have always been a considerate person. I do what people want me to to give them pleasure. But this really takes my heart out. Why is it I keep going with him? Is it because I'm soft—or homosexual—or what is my responsibility to him?"

B.B.'s behavior bears out our expectations. He is a victim of this seduction, not because homosexuality is his activity of choice, but because he is utterly incapable of asserting his protest. He simply can't say "no." His degradation in this situation, for reasons that will be explained later, satisfies his need for punishment. In this sense, he is unconsciously homosexual, but his main trouble is not with sex; it is with aggression. Subsequent events confirm this conclusion.

He came to the next interview with a massive bandage on his thumb. He was very disturbed: "I had a terrific week end, I'm telling you. I was in a terrible state when I left you. The discussion really upset me. I was so weak I could hardly make it home. I no sooner got there than in came J. (his homosexual friend). He was roaring drunk. He raved and cursed. He called me all kinds of ugly names. He said he was going to kill me. I was as nice as I could be. I tried to reason with him. I carried him to a cab and took him to his house. I undressed him and put him to bed. All the time I was very solicitous and trying to pacify his anger, but it didn't work. He went into hysterics. He was like a maniac. He hit me—and I didn't even hit him back. Then he went into the closet and got un upholstery needle eight inches long and tried to use it on me. So I took that away from him. Then he got a razor blade and cut a gash out of my thumb before I got it away. That's why I have this bandage. I had to throw him down and sit on his neck. Once or twice I got angry enough to hurt him until I got hold of myself and stopped. Finally, I got out. He was still raving. I had feelings of guilt, but I went. I thought maybe he needed help. I felt sorry for him and here I was going."

A man practically kills him, yet it is B.B. who feels guilty. He went on to elaborate this contradiction: "I don't like to think evil of anybody. You know, I never had but one fight in my whole life. I have never made any enemies. It kills me to think somebody doesn't like me. The rest of my brothers and sisters, if they are angry, they get angry. Not I. I hold it back. I always try to help people. My mother said I was the most helpful person she ever saw. People have always taken advantage of me. I think a person could do me the worse damage in the world, and if he said he was sorry, I would forgive him. What people do to me really hurts sometimes. When I was young and someone hurt my feelings I would go away and cry. Now I don't cry; I just groan."

The therapist counseled that B.B. break off immediately with his so-called friend. B.B. protested: "He will blackmail me. He threatened to tell my mother and all my friends. He threatened I would lose my job. He said he would get a gang to do me bodily harm and kill me. And I believe he can do it. He has very influential friends. He's friends with the Willie Smith gang. He would tell them and they would just ruin me, murder me almost. I'm a stranger here, and New York is a very treacherous place. I have no protection. He knows all the angles. So I have been terrified and have tried to reason this thing with him. I have been very fair and honest, as though talking to God. I said this and this was the reason I didn't think it was good for us to continue. I proposed we be very casual friends, because I felt this was the only acceptable thing. But he won't listen to me. What should I do?"

The therapist remained adamant. There was no choice but to break off with J. If J. talked, so he talked. B.B. would just have to take his chances. The tug-of-war with J. continued for several more days. There were repeated meetings, telephone conversations, threats, and recriminations. Finally, buttressed by the therapist's insistence that he stand firm, he seemingly terminated the relationship. He refused to see J. and hung up the receiver when he called. It is true he did this, but not without considerable misgiving. He devoted much time in subsequent sessions to the resultant feelings of guilt. He worried constantly that he had hurt J., and J. would never forgive him for it.

One day, for the first time, he began to talk about his brother. It turned out that he left the South not so much to seek greater opportunity, but to escape his brother's exploitation of him. To put it bluntly, his brother ran him out of town. Their relationship smacks very much of his current involvement with J., but less the homosexuality. The circumstances were the following: His brother, for reasons unknown but doubtless bad, was suddenly discharged from the Army. He turned up on B.B.'s doorstep and moved into his apartment. B.B. not only gave him free food and lodging, but also provided him with spending money. The brother then began openly to use the apartment as a rendezvous for his many amours. His indiscretions were so blatant that B.B.'s friends began to raise their eyebrows. B.B. was mortified and pleaded with him to stop. However, the situation only got worse, and, instead of further remonstration, B.B. gave up the apartment to his brother, settled half the furniture upon him, and moved out. But even this did not end it. People continued to plague him with remarks about his brother's behavior. Finally, unable to stand the humiliation any longer, he left and came to New York.

We have already touched upon the genetic origin of this astounding inhibition of aggression. We saw that it derives from his sibling relationships. The account of his difficulties at the hands of his brother is a case in point. B.B. came out of his childhood with the unshakable conviction that any degree of assertion in his own behalf, any gratification of his own needs, any furthering of his own ambitions were acts of the most violent aggression against his brother and his sisters. This conviction led not only to a fear of retaliation, conceived as death, but also generated an overwhelming sense of guilt, which he expiates through endless attempts at self-punishment. He has generalized this behavior toward his siblings to include each and every member of the human race. This entire dynamic construction is unconsciously integrated. B.B. knows what he does, but he is not in the least aware why he must do it.

Matters are not helped any by the fact that he has tremendous ambitions. These greatly magnify both his guilt and his fear of retaliation: "I daydream an awful lot. It's always about something successful. I've got a terrific drive to make something of myself. I dream about wealth, fine cars and fine homes, a top job in my profession. I've got standards for myself I want to live up to. I've never wanted the same things that everybody else had. Take suits, for instance. I wanted something different with a little taste in it; or if I'm having a party, I want it to be a little better, something set apart from other parties. Now, take my apartment in the South. It wasn't just ordinary. There was something a little better about it. That's what I want to be—different and better. It's part of my ambition—something attractive, unusual, something to get attention from whoever might see it."

In his attempts to further his ambitions, he is in competition, of course, with both whites and Negroes, but particularly with the latter. Competition with whites is bad enough, but this he can tolerate, because whites, in general, are fair game. He seeks only to approximate what they already have. He knows he must always fall short and can never go beyond them. It is a different story when he competes with Negroes. It is here that the main pressure of being a Negro falls. He is striving for goals that few Negroes ever reach. He considers these attempts to surpass members of his own race as an unparalleled piece of aggression, far more certain to incite hatred and envy than that against the whites. This fact, more than any other, is responsible for the fantastic proportions of his guilt. Similarly, he is obsessed with an expectation of their revenge. He fears that the punishment for his efforts will be death. So certain is he of ultimate doom that he has no hope of survival beyond early adulthood. He must accomplish what has to be done in the limited time due him, or else forever give up his goal: "I've never felt even as a child that I would live to be a very old man. I don't know why. I always felt if I hadn't done what I wanted to do while I was young, I wouldn't be able to do it. There's a point in my age I always felt if I hadn't done it, I never would, and the time is drawing near. I give myself only to thirty-five. There has definitely been a feeling there that I wouldn't have too long to work."

His fear of death makes him phobic of dead people. This is simply an all-too-clear reminder of the fate that awaits him: "I told you once I was very much afraid of rats and dead folk. It seems so stupid to everybody else. I don't know why, but I am just as afraid of a dead person as I can be. It is embarrassing. I often think suppose someone in my family should die. I wonder what people would say if I didn't go to the funeral. I would feel awful bad about my mother's death, but I couldn't go. I couldn't look at a dead body and feel comfortable." We have here the operation of a vicious circle: his great ambitions can lead only to an early death, but the sooner he dies, the greater his ambitions must be. This is merely another way of saying that he is sowing the seeds of his own destruction.

After breaking with J., he began to feel some oats. Bolstered by the therapist, he made attempts to be more assertive. He rebelled against a supervisor on his job, who he had felt for some time was unfairly critical of him. He began to hound several dozen people who owed him money. He talked back to waitresses and he pushed in the subway. Unfortunately, his improvement was short-lived. The first show of real strength against him and he collapsed. Once again, J. appeared on the scene. B.B. began to receive poison pen letters. Either he reinstate J. as his lover, or he faced certain doom. He became literally paralyzed with fear: "I don't know how to describe my feelings. I'm just shaking away with fear. I have a lump in my stomach. I am so preoccupied I can't concentrate on anything. I haven't been able to work. I couldn't decide today what to eat, what to put on, where to go, what to do. So I stayed in bed 'til I came here. The only thing I haven't stopped doing is eating." Simultaneously, there was a resurgence of guilt: "I keep wanting to call J. I haven't done it, but it's a very hard job not to. I've been feeling awfully guilty. Those letters sound as though he is insane. If he has lost his mind, I would feel responsible. I fear what somebody on his side might do to me. They might sneak up on me and beat me up, or maybe shoot me, or cut me. I'm really afraid to go out at all."

The therapist took the position that his fear of retaliation was far greater than realistically was warranted. It was exaggerated by the underlying neurotic conflict. Unhappily, the therapist was theoretically correct, but practically wrong. A blow did fall. It took place within the week. Early one morning some men broke into his apartment, tied him up, and ran off with all his clothes and money. He was too fearful to apply to the police. Neither could he fight back alone. The only other alternative was to leave town. This prospect deflated his self-esteem and he found it thoroughly distasteful, but he felt he was given no choice. He left New York and returned South, but not before reporting a final dream. He reproduced the struggle with his brother in the context of the current situation with J.:

I was at home. My brother and I had some misunderstanding. He was after me with a gun. He was trying his best to shoot me. Someone called him off. Later, everybody was giving him hell for what he had done. They called him all kinds of skunk and things like that. I got violently angry and couldn't stand it any longer so I took a heavy ahstray and started beating him in the worst way you ever heard. At this point I was going through the motions of the dream actively and it woke me up.

He explains: "Very obviously I wish I could express my hostility to someone and the occasion I choose is for some of the things my brother has done. The gun part comes from the experience I had the other day. To me my brother represents any enemy I might have because he is one of the people I know has taken advantage of me. He and J. appear to me in a very similar way. There has been a great deal of envy on the part of my brother. I felt toward him as I did toward J., that I had the better break, so I guarded against taking advantage of either of them. I gave them the benefit of every doubt, even if they were wrong. And I felt responsible for my brother, even though he was older. He and J. are the same age." This dream confirms our initial premise that B.B.'s major difficulty takes origin from the rivalry with his siblings, particularly with his brother.

This subject illustrates the same principle as the previous one. The accomplishment here is not whiteness, but status, in the form of education and the ability to get a good middle-class job. No one can save this man from himself. His guilt is too great. He requires degradation to even up the score between his guilt to the Negro and his success in accomplishing middle-class white objectives. He buys his peace, but at a high price.

W.M.

This subject is a married, 35-year-old, light brown, college-educated Negro, who is a patient in psychotherapy. He has a professional training and suffers from inhibitions in the consummation of his work. He erroneously attributed the onset of this anxiety to lack of preparation for his job and, therefore, concluded he was incompetent. So great was his anxiety that on many occasions he started out to work and had to turn back. He began to spend days at home in an anxious agitated state. He fell so far behind in his work that the only alternative seemed to be resignation before he was asked to leave. He talked the situation over with his employer, who recommended psychiatric help. Instead, he changed jobs and at first there was some improvement, because the new organization was much less important than the one he left. However, the improvement was short-lived and soon the anxiety reappeared even stronger than before. This time he applied for treatment.

He was born and raised in a border state. His mother was a domineering person, who had some higher education, but did not work. His father was a college-trained minister who was also the political boss of the Negro community in his town. He used his church primarily as a springboard to further his political ambitions. He set very high standards for W.M. and enforced his ideals by the weight of his prestige. This made him rather pontifical and arbitrary. When he was a child, W.M. thought most highly of him. There was one sibling who died when W.M. was three months old. For all practical purposes, therefore, W.M. was an only child.

The family had a house of their own and their economic condition was very comfortable. The parents got along smoothly and there was an atmosphere of great affection in the home. In childhood, W.M.'s preference was largely for his father. Thus, he remarks, "I discounted mother." Discipline was not severe and most of it was by appeal, not force, though occasionally there were beatings. W.H. attended his father's church regularly, but there was no fanatic emphasis on religion, since his father's main interests lay elsewhere. Sex was not generally discussed but the father was always easily accessible for information on sexual topics.

He remembers the home environment as a happy one, but in his social environment he ran into difficulty. His father's standing in the community made W.M. vulnerable with respect to the other children. He was constantly exposed to their taunts, because they resented his privileged position. He was upper class and most of his playmates were lower class. His parents stressed this social distinction and overemphasized every aspect of respectability, much to his discomfort. In this manner he became involved in many fights, in which he usually took the beating. This situation made him very miserable. To make matters worse, he excelled in his studies, which provoked still more resentment from the other students.

He attended a Northern college and graduated with honors. Here he met the girl he married. Their courtship was prolonged for several years until his professional standing had been secured. He was much in awe of his wife's family. He considered them on a higher cultural plane than his own. His wife is very light and can "pass." She is extremely snobbish. They settled in Harlem where he advanced in his field and finally got a very desirable and responsible job. It is in this latter situation that he collapsed with severe anxieties.

He thinks sex is tied up with his problem. He volunteers that he and his wife practice cunnilingus, a "perversity" concerning which he expresses much guilt. Recently, since the onset of his anxiety, he has engaged in this practice more than ever. Another source of guilt feelings are his fantasies. As his symptoms intensified, he has been plagued by incessant fantasies of sexual conquest, particularly with older women. He has never had the courage to carry any of these out, but the greater his anxiety, the more insistent the fantasies have become. Simultaneously, they have dwelled with increasing frequency on the practice of cunnilingus.

Another source of his inner conflicts was his competitiveness with his superiors. The chief executive of his organization was a man of considerable prominence. The latter took W.M. under his wing and taught him the executive end of the work. But to W.M. this was no source of satisfaction. He was disgruntled about getting too little pay, and about being his superior's stooge, especially since greater responsibility brought no increase in salary or status, and only increased the standing of his superior. Finally, he was offered a most desirable job in a rival organization. This offer he used first as a wedge to get his increase in pay and elevation of status. When both came through, he resigned to take the other position, an act which enraged his superior.

Having accepted this new and most desirable job, he discovered to his dismay that he couldn't work. He was consumed with contrition over his presumptuousness in throwing up his old job, and was in constant fear of retaliatory measures by his erstwhile superior. He felt strange in the new organization which seemed large and impersonal. Worse, he began to feel unequipped for the new tasks assigned to him. He felt guilty and incompetent and reproached himself for unethical conduct—breach of contract.

Now his panic became intolerable. He had left a good-paying job for one he could not fulfill. And so he resigned his new job and became dependent on his father. It must be noted that the new position represented one of the highest a Negro could reach. In this dilemma, he decided to take a job much lower than either of the two he had. In this less desirable status he was in a measure able to function. Meanwhile, he kept trying to keep an option open on the more desirable job in which he had failed.

The central conflict in this man is, therefore, concerned with the achievement of high status, but once he achieves it, he collapses. He gets some relief from taking a lower status, for castigating and belittling himself, but then his ambition gives him no peace. He thinks this trend has something to do with his father, who was a prominent and influential man, and through whose influence he achieved some of his success, but certainly not all. He tends to deny his success and even takes active steps to fail. Apparently success carries with it some unknown dangers of which W.M. is not aware, and his anxiety is to some extent relieved when he renounces the goal. As a child, being prominent caused him much embarrassment. He felt he got this prominence unfairly through his father's high position. He considered it a hostile act toward the other boys, who were of lower status. Now, any piece of ordinary self-assertion becomes magnified into a hostile act for which he fears retaliation. The high position he achieved but could not hold is a case in point. It was a position which would make him the target of hostility from those who did not get the job, as well as from his elders with whom he was competing.

He has a great deal of resentment at being so driven. He longs for the free and easy life of lower-class Negroes, a longshoreman, or a sailor: "I was reading this book, *Back to Harlem* by Claude McKay. It's a fiction story of a nearly illiterate Negro, his life and loves, and you get the sense of freedom of the longshoreman, the sailor. This man was a free spirit, not hemmed in by taboos and conventions. As a matter of fact, the life of the Harlem masses is converged in that fashion. Sex, gambling, and so on are the acceptable, really dominant motifs of this fictional description, but I think that what struck me most was that there was no pressure on the major characters to be somebody. I found myself contrasting that kind of character with my own experiences and sort of wishing I was in his shoes rather than the way it is; yet, if I were I couldn't have that kind of freedom I ascribed to. Not now, anyway. I don't think my past experiences would permit it. I've had fantasies of being a postman, a human machine—get in and do your work and nobody pays any attention to you. But it's too late for that now. I can't escape striving until I reach my goals. They represent success with a capital S—for a Negro."

Another clue to W.M.'s distress is that he is following in the footsteps of his father, who was a great success. His own position now, however, is much greater than was his father's. Early in treatment he expressed his discomfort at this situation. He felt he was surpassing his father. He did not understand, however, why this should give him so much anxiety. At this point he had a series of dreams which provided the answer:

A woman, who seems to be my mother, and yet is different. She was crippled. Her legs were stiff from the hips down. I was behind her, supporting her, trying to get her somewhere. We were both trying to escape from some danger. I woke up frightened.

He identifies the woman as his wife. She holds him in bondage with her incapacity, making it impossible for him to escape the dangers he faces. She compels him to be ambitious. He thinks of another couple in which the wife helps the husband and they collaborate together. That seemed a desirable combine. His own wife seeks to "consume me, really." She is possessive and wants all his attention. She is very jealous of his efforts at advancement. He then thinks of an older woman, the wife of one of his superiors. She was the most beautiful woman he ever knew. Many times he indulged in the fantasy of winning her from her husband. He always sought older women. His wife is a rare exception; she is younger than he. The dream expresses in a negative way the unsatisfied wish to have someone relieve him of his burdens—at least while he is incapacitated. He wants some older woman to take care of him. That is to say, he wants a maternal object with a breast to feed him (cunnilingus). He does not like the role reversed. He resents caring for a woman.

The next dream shows him cringing before his father, asking forgiveness and attempting to expiate his offenses by being subjected to menial tasks:

I was a child, singing in the choir. I can remember a great sense of unhappiness standing there. It seemed to me the choir was rehearsing and I didn't know whether I began to cry in the middle of a song or whether the rehearsal was at an end. We were on a stage and I began to cry and I wanted to explain to the choirmaster what the trouble was, and I began, 'Sir, I got lonely . . .' I meant to go on and tell him what the trouble was, but instead I said, 'As the days get warmer, may I come to your house and mow the lawn?' Then he came and put his arms around me and he seemed to be my father. I felt a kind of a sense of revulsion.

He remarks: "Apparently, it is something I am ashamed about, because it seems I had screwed up my courage to tell him, but when I started to tell him it came out something else I hadn't started to tell him at all." The meaning of the dream is quite clear. He expresses the sentiment: Papa, I have been a bad boy, but now I'll be a good boy. Whatever the sin he committed, he did it because he was "lonely." Following so soon on the heels of the previous dream, the "sin" can only refer to his infantile wish for the breast, couched in terms of sexual fantasies toward his mother. He cannot risk alienating his father, especially now, when he is so in need of paternal help. He wants very much to be loved by his father (and also by the therapist). He would like to assume a passive feminine role toward both of them in the hope that they would magically resolve his troubles. In the end, he rejects his wish for fear that it might be interpreted as homosexual. The approaching awareness of these underlying conflicts had its effect. He overslept and failed to appear for his next appointment.

These two dreams form a complementary set consisting of the infantile love for his mother and the incompatibility this creates with his hostile feelings toward his father. This, of course, is the constellation commonly known as the oedipus complex. The passive feminine, submissive role is typical of the infantile resolution of this conflict.

Another type of dream which bears on the same constellation is the next one in which he is obliged to marry, under some compulsion, the daughter of his erstwhile superior:

It seemed to be my employer's wedding, except the only incongruent part was that I was the groom. His daughter seemed to be somewhere in there. It seems she proposed to me rather than I to her. I wasn't particular about it, but some pressure was put on me to do it.

This dream demonstrates a way of establishing a bond with a father surrogate through the agency of a woman. He again rejects the passive feminine implications by stating he is doing this under compulsion. In part, this constellation is a defense against his wish to surpass his superior or his father. By getting ahead of both he cuts himself off from their support, which he very much needs, and puts himself in a rival position. Hence, he must cringe, fail, and accept a passive feminine role; and this in return is responsible for an anxiety about homosexuality. Against this unconscious tendency, he mobilizes all his masculinity and uses it for the adventitious purpose of reassuring himself by conquering in fantasy one woman after another. Simultaneously, he cannot help but undermine this reassurance by engaging in cunnilingus, a practice that is most highly tinged affectively. This is the child-mother (and child-father) game of which he is so ashamed. It is based on the equation: vagina = breast = penis. In this act, he symbolically seeks to reestablish, through oral incorporation, the infantile dependency of his childhood. Other variations on the same motif are dreams in which he allies himself against a father figure with the aid of another boy; or he has fantasies of sexual relations with the wives of his best friends, especially if the women are older. Both patterns satisfy his need for allies against his father, reassure him of his masculinity, and give him secret revenge.

The masculinity conflict plays into the status struggle quite conveniently and the two reinforce each other. The masculinity conflict by itself would be enough to give him the anxiety he has; add the status struggle to it and he is caught in endless turmoil. The stereotype which conceals the whole status drive is "respectability." In his wife's family, the entire respectability complex has as its cornerstone the fact that they come from "free Negro stock." Additional prestige derives from education and their light complexions. They thus lay claim to respectability without money, of which no one in the family has any. Segregation in any of its forms, undermines all the efforts in the acquisition of status and respectability. As a compensation for this, W.M. thinks that the entire status struggle is diminished by the fact that competition is less keen for the Negro; that, after all, he lives in a second-class world. This is decidedly not true; it is doubled. He, himself, draws the conclusion that the status struggle impoverishes emotional life: "I think it makes for conflicting loyalties in almost all aspects of living. I certainly am not a fighter for Negro rights." He feels he is "the marginal man," on the periphery of two worlds, uncomfortable and torn between the two: "I can't believe in these principles of equality and freedom. I and all Negro professionals have a hemmed-in feeling. That's why we drink too much. You just can't forget being a Negro."

This weakening of his ties to his fellows stems from his profound contempt for them all. He wants to belittle them, degrade them, and deprive them of status. Thus, in one dream, he represents a successful friend in the fields next to a bale of cotton. This merely connotes: "You're nothing but a slave anyhow." One of the significant commentaries of this man's inferiority feelings is his identification, by his own word, with feces.

The personality picture of this subject is complicated by an obvious neurotic superstructure. The manner of dealing with his problems and conflicts is characteristic of anxiety hysteria. That is, the conflict reaches an impasse which expresses itself in neurotic anxiety, so strong as to block off any action. The form of this neurotic picture differs in no way from the corresponding picture in the white man. The same is practically true for content. W.M. brings with him typical white middle-class morality. He shares in the white man's capacity for idealization of the father, a feature not often found in the lower-class Negro. This merely means that disciplines in childhood were strict and enforced not so much by coercion as by the ability of the father to provide or withdraw need-gratification. W.M.'s father had a great deal of prestige and stood out in the family as the ultimate source of authority. He is squarely in the center of all of W.M.'s conflicts. This is typical of the white middle class where the father is dispenser of all boons and thus is the most feared. W.M. came from a father-oriented family. His mother is distinctly in the background as a provider and a disciplinarian, but stands high as the prototype of erotic patterning. Hence, we find in him a typical oedipus complex. It would be an error, however, to account for his difficulties merely as an elaboration on this motif. In a case like this, where the basic constellations of childhood so completely dominate the adult life, it is of the highest importance to examine the actual life situations on which these infantile patterns are projected, and it is precisely here that we find a situation that is typically Negro. The caste system within which W.M. is forced to live acts only to consolidate his neurotic conflict. It puts an exaggerated premium on success and lends reality to his fear of retaliation.

The paternal ideal, which W.M. so completely embraced early in life, became disqualified for two reasons: first, its attainment means killing and displacing his father, which blocks all efforts at success; and second, he fears aggressive retaliation from all other Negroes because success and elevation of status mean to him a piece of violent aggression against them. The result is that the second component strongly reinforces the first. The only form of refuge which he can institute is to keep his status down, but this in turn sets new anxieties in motion.

The conflict about surpassing his own kind in the pursuit of high status began in his school days. He had to make an early choice: to be one with his fellows and have low status, or to have high status and be hated by them. No wonder he is inhibited about the achievement of all high-status goals, and wants to shake off the burden of success which is both onerous to carry out and which brings him envy and hatred from everyone. No wonder he envies the situation of the lower-class Negro, who, he thinks, escapes this terrible dilemma. In his effort to achieve some peace of mind, something must be sacrificed. The chain of psychological events breaks at its weakest point—the tie between Negro and Negro. Thus, it comes about that these ties between Negroes, already weak for reasons that will be discussed later, become still weaker because the struggle for status in the Negro creates more intra-Negro animosity than it alleviates. This particular situation prevails largely with upper middle-class Negro technicians. It does not obtain with such figures as Joe Louis, Lena Horne, or Jackie Robinson, all of whom can be accepted by most Negroes as common ideal figures. In this regard, the educated Negro technician is out on a limb.

II. FEMALE

A.T.

A.T. is a very attractive, light tan woman of thirty-seven who is employed as a bookkeeper in a government agency. She is married to an uneducated laborer. They have one child, a son aged fourteen. Her hair is straight and long and she wears it upswept into a bun on one side of her head. She is exceptionally well-groomed and dramatically gowned. The over-all effect is a rather exotic one. She is most anxious to impress, uses big words, and is quite verbose. There is a haughty air about her and she does not like to be interrupted. She then indicates her displeasure by waiting with obvious impatience until she can begin talking again.

A.T. is a patient who comes reluctantly to psychotherapy as the mother of a problem child. She has been informed that her son's behavior difficulties may be an emotional response to improper parental attitudes. She feels she, herself, has no problems, but she wants the child to have "every chance to get better" and so is "willing" to undergo an exploratory period of treatment to find out if the "fault" may be hers.

She was born and raised in Harlem. She knows nothing of her father. He disappeared before she was born and she has made no attempts to trace him. She was turned over by her mother to foster parents a few months after her birth. The mother then visited her once or twice a year. However, her identity was hidden and A.T. knew her only as a friend of the family. She disappeared when A.T. was twelve and was never heard from again. A year later, while rummaging through some drawers, A.T. accidentally came across her birth certificate and her adoption papers. She confronted her foster parents and they confirmed her adoption and disclosed the true identity of the visitor. She remembers her mother as a "light brown, refined, well-dressed, good-looking woman, not the type you would expect to abandon a child." The foster mother was a medium brown housewife, who had something less than a high school education. She was a soft, unaggressive person, warm and affectionate toward the adopted child. She was very indulgent and A.T. easily manipulated her. The foster father was a dark brown, regularly employed handy man with a grade school education. He was the exact opposite of his wife—loud, violent, tyrannical. There were no other children and A.T. states that the foster mother adopted her over the foster father's protest.

The family lived in a small but adequate apartment. The foster father was employed throughout the depression and their economic status, though occasionally pinched, generally remained secure. The home atmosphere was a turbulent one. The foster father was an habitual drinker who liked to talk, and the more he drank, the more he talked. Usually his wife and A.T. remained silent and like as not he would talk on by himself for hours. At times he got very violent and struck the foster mother. However, he rarely laid a hand on A.T. He set the standards and discipline was strict: "He wanted you to lead a prim and proper life. He smacked me once or twice but I never actually got a whipping. He just raved and insulted you. It was worse than a whipping. I couldn't go to a show. I couldn't be out after dark. He came home at five and everybody had to be home then. He had a low opinion of everybody. He never thought too much of what I would accomplish. He accepted no excuses and made no allowances. He never held out any hope that I would amount to anything. Even if you were sick he didn't want you staying away from school. That meant you didn't want any education. If you got a high mark he wouldn't give you any credit. That was only what was expected. He was very ambitious for me." The foster father frowned on religion and A.T. had little religious education. The sexual mores were puritanical, to such an extent that boys were not even allowed in the house and A.T. was under constant suspicion. Failure to be home at the demanded hour invariably brought down accusations and insinuations upon her.

At school her relations with her teachers were strained. She was sarcastic and insolent, but she had good marks so the teachers made allowances. She was a bright youngster and skipped two grades. She was extremely competitive in all respects, but particularly in matters of status and dress. She aped her foster father's opinions, thought highly of herself, and looked down on others. She would turn down party invitations if she thought her clothes were not as nice as other girls'. Preferably, they had to be better. She continued to do well scholastically and graduated from high school at the early age of sixteen. She began to go out with boys clandestinely. Her social aspirations were quite high and she protests her companions were beneath her: "My foster father wouldn't let me have company at home, so I went out into the street. It wasn't the type of company I wanted but it was all I could get. We met fellows on the corner and went to shows and neighborhood beer gardens. It was something I didn't like but there was no way of meeting the type of people I like." She met her husband in this gang, an older dark-skinned man of twenty-five. She was flattered by his attention and after a brief acquaintance, eager to escape her foster father, she accepted his offer of marriage. She took time out for her pregnancy, otherwise she has always worked.

The status conflict overshadows all of A.T.'s behavior and everything she says, does, or feels can be understood only against this backdrop. A.T. never forgets she is a Negro. She is engaged in a perpetual struggle to retrieve the resultant deflation of her self-esteem. Her ambitions, ideals, and goals—mediated genetically by her foster father—are completely those of white middle-class respectability. She rejects the Negro and everything identified with him; yet, since she is a Negro herself, there is no escape. Neither can she identify with the whites. She is well aware of this dilemma: "I know I don't want to be identified with Negroes, but I am identified regardless of how I feel." Her solution is to limit all social contacts and maintain distance in interpersonal relations. In this way she perpetuates the illusion that she is "different" from the members of her group and superior to them: she may not be a white, but at least she is not a Negro, either. The end result is social isolation.

Let us begin first with her marriage. From her point of view, the marital relationship is quite devoid of feeling and exists mainly for economic reasons. It is necessary to maintain a home for the child, and, if it were not for this, she would leave her husband tomorrow. She feels she married only for expedience, and there is no compatibility between them. In many respects she is right. He is an uneducated, uncultured Southern Negro, who cannot possibly share in her social and cultural interests. On the other hand, he seems genuinely in love with her, a steady provider, eager and anxious to effect a marital adjustment, but, of course, within his limited capacities to do so. Unfortunately, her own conflicts prevent her from even meeting him halfway; instead, she rejects him totally. To her, he personifies her own self-hatred: the despised Negro stereotype. This is best illustrated in the following incident: One day she arrived for her interview thirty minutes late. She explained with considerable embarrassment, "My husband is outside. He was just curious, so he came along today." Her lateness had resulted from their argument in which she had tried to dissuade him from coming. The therapist suggested that he speak to the husband at the end of the session about their son's problems. She reluctantly agreed, but it was quite clear she felt trapped and did not know how to get out of the request gracefully. The interview ended and she attempted to leave as though nothing had been said about her husband. The therapist stopped her and asked if she wouldn't bring him into the office. She appeared bitterly ashamed that the therapist would have to see him, but nevertheless consented. He was a small, dark brown man with typical Negroid features and wooly hair. He was horribly ill at ease with the therapist and quite inarticulate. His behavior can perhaps best be described in terms of the insecure Southern Negro suddenly confronted with the "superior" white man.

She never lets him forget the disparity between them but maintains an incessant pressure upon him. She criticizes his behavior mercilessly. He cannot help but grasp her shame of him and in self-defense he avoids social situations and companions of her choosing. She, in turn, refuses to accept his friends and her haughtiness has alienated all of them. The interviews abound in derogatory references to her husband's social intimates. She sees them all as crude, ill-mannered, uncultured, illiterate, shiftless, without ambition and aspiration, and perfectly content with their sordid lot. In sum, she evokes the classical anti-Negro stereotypes. She must reject her identification with them at all costs: "I don't want to be identified with them and their problems. You've heard that saying, 'There but for the grace of God go I.' If I associate with these people I will have the same troubles. I want a smoother life. I don't want anything to make my life more disgusting. There's just a thin difference between me and them. I'm in contact with them all the time." This statement brings her self-hatred into sharp focus. It underlines the conclusion that her rejection of the Negro is primarily a defensive technique designed to give at least illusory inflation to a thoroughly depressed self-esteem.

The relationship with the husband is further complicated by her refusal to accept the necessary femine role. This is essentially a derivative of her familial background where the potestas of power were held by her foster father. Obviously, she would prefer to emulate him than to accept the secondary position of her weak foster mother. In consequence, she attempts to reverse positions with her husband, and it is she who is the "man of the house," not he. A dream her husband described to her attests to the success of this reversal. He dreamed that she was getting dressed to go out and put on a man's suit. He ordered her to take it off, but she refused. He took the suit off of her and tore it up. He then forbade her ever to wear a man's suit or to go to work again. She is perfectly aware of the dream's meaning: "The man's suit is rather obvious. He thinks I'm dominant in the house. And whenever he gets resentful he wants me to quit my job. That way he would rob me of my independence. I didn't tell him what the dream meant, though." She frequently taunts him with her "superior" work and greater salary. She knows what she is doing, and at least in this one aspect of her marital relationship, she is satisfied. "He is lacking in some things, but he measures way up better than most men in others—like taking care of the boy, cooking, cleaning, and bringing home money."

A.T.'s interpersonal relations external to marriage fare no better. They, too, are warped by the status conflict. The social contacts readily available to her consist of co-workers in her office and other wives in her neighborhood. She cuts herself off from all of them. At first she gives only one reason, the same one as for her husband's friends: they are beneath her. Actually, this is only part of the story as she herself finally admits as the interviews progress. The truth is there are people who would be acceptable to her, but she cannot allow herself to get close to them for fear her actions will betray that she is not quite the grand lady she pretends to be. She dare not risk putting her illusion to test. Her social behavior, therefore, is based on a single premise: she must do nothing that will expose her to gossip. Thus, in her office, she maintains a cold detachment: "The people in the office gossip and talk a lot about personalities. I don't want to join in. They'll talk about you, then. So I try to skirt their gossip, but I do wonder what they think of me. It disturbs me. They say such cruel things about people. They express such violent dislikes. They try to undermine people by criticizing their work." She is aware that they label her a snob: "Lots of times they say things but fall silent if I'm there. I offer no comment and they think I disapprove. I wonder if they think I'm a prissy or a poor sport." However, she willingly accepts this label in preference to risking exposure through more intimate contact. She is equally unbending at office parties. She describes a rare attendance at one: "It was nice in a way. I didn't get into things. I enjoyed myself, but as a bystander, not as one of those participating. The next day all the fellows were critical of the director because of her conduct at the party. She was not staid enough. That is the penalty you have to pay for enjoying yourself. If people made remarks about me that way it would worry me. I really didn't feel part of it. I just felt I was looking on. The people didn't seem my type, the kind I could enjoy myself with. Maybe it boils down to the fact that I'm a snob. I just didn't wholeheartedly enjoy their company." She goes on to discuss a prominent public official recently sentenced to jail for graft. She concludes by identifying with him: "I think how would I feel if something like that happened to me. The price people pay for their good time is more than it is worth. The small things people jeopardize their reputations for don't seem to be worth it. It would disturb my peace of mind and I set that above everything." The identification with such a well-known figure demonstrates how grandiose are her fantasies, and conversely, how shrunken is her self-esteem. She must maintain her "peace of mind" at all cost.

The extent to which she restrains herself, and the reason for it, is revealed in the following dream:

I went somewhere in the South. I found myself in a country town. In one part of the town the neighborhood was mixed—white and colored. At the other end of the town was the center of Negro life—Broadway and Reno St. There were cafes, colorful dance halls, pool halls, music. I just walked and walked slowly down the street looking at everything, but I didn't go in anywhere.

Her associations further differentiate the two parts of the town: "One part was quiet. The respectable whites and Negroes lived at this end. It was daytime while I walked through there. The other end was the Negro section—gay, life-loving, colorful. There was music, lights. I enjoyed the sights. I would like to be part of something like that sometimes—just wander through the streets and look at things instead of hurrying through—but if I lived a life like that I would lose respect." She contrasts Negro with white recreational activities: "The scene was like in a Negro musical, like in 'St. Louis Woman.' White people enjoy themselves, too, but not in the way Negroes do. The whites are prim, proper, not as robust or as zestful. They don't seem to be enjoying themselves as much. When Negroes enjoy themselves, they really enjoy themselves. It seems to be a deeper thing with Negroes." We need hardly ask with which group A.T. casts her lot.

As the dream shows, her need to identify with the whites forces her to sacrifice pleasures that otherwise would be available to her. A.T. never has a "good time": "I've never been able to do anything I call fun without somebody taking me to task afterwards—either my father or my husband—sometimes just for talking to people. So I have cut myself off from everything in order to eliminate the wrangling and to have peace and harmony. I can't ever remember doing anything I wasn't criticized for or had a guilty conscience about. Some people drink and get gay; I just feel the same all the time or I just get sick. I don't isolate myself from people, but I don't mix, either. I don't attend meetings. I don't go to church. The only place I come in contact with people is in the work situation. For the past year it's been work and home only. Social life is rare. It doesn't bother me. I don't like boisterousness or crudeness in any form. I don't like an embarrassing situation. I'll run every time."

A.T.'s relations with people are further hampered by her need to be dominant in group situations where cooperation is called for. This need, too, stems from her struggle for status. She must be acknowledged the leader or she won't play. We see this attitude in her description of a brief flurry into community activity: "I don't belong to any civic organizations. I went to the P.T.A. once. I was disappointed and didn't go back. The neighborhood has deteriorated. The problem is one of character education for the children, but they don't go into that. Instead, they discussed a bazaar. I felt that wasn't what should be discussed."

The rigid application of her own perfectionist standards to her son has produced disastrous results. He bites his nails, sucks his thumb, wets the bed, stammers, has numerous tics, and is a failure at school where he is unable to pass any of his subjects. He is wild, unruly, and unmanageable, fights constantly with the other children, and is always under reprimand from his teachers for misconduct. These behavioral difficulties are all manifestations of revolt against his mother's dictates. She has gotten the exact opposite of the result she desired: "I want my son to stand on his own two feet. I don't want him to become a derelict. I don't want him to get into trouble and get locked up. I don't want anybody to question his home or background. I want him secure, poised, confident. I want him to have a happy life, but I anticipate he will do something wrong. He's heading in that direction. I'll feel badly."

She has drawn the boy into her own status orbit. She feels every criticism of him a criticism of herself and reacts by putting even greater pressure on him. This, of course, only causes him to behave worse than ever: "He never chooses friends I want him to associate with. Their mothers and fathers don't take good care of them. They're unkempt. I wouldn't associate with their parents. The boys I think are nice are too mild and not exciting enough for him. His friends are a gang. They roam all over. Maybe I'm unfair and should let him play with whom he wants. It disturbs me when people stop me on the street and tell me that he is doing something. It's my own dislike of criticism. I'm always hurt by people criticizing me. I'm always striving."

She is particularly furious with her boy's behavior because it fits in with the prejudicial anti-Negro stereotypes: "I'm familiar with all the stereotyped notions whites have of Negroes. His failure in school falls in with those stereotypes. He won't be able to get any kind of professional job if he can't get through school. I always tell him he has to behave wherever he goes, because Negro children are not expected to behave well." This latter remark reveals most clearly the true reason for the severe pressure she puts on the child. He can belie his race through exemplary conduct associated in her mind only with the whites. It is simply another attempt to deny her Negro identification.

Sex to A.T. is ridden with fear and disgust and if she had her way she would have nothing to do with it. She denies masturbation at any time, has had intercourse only with her husband, and has never had an orgasm. She has always thought of sex as "nasty and dirty." This attitude, instilled originally by her foster father, has been perpetuated and strengthened by her social strivings, which put a premium on chastity and purity. It is small wonder, then, that intercourse is simply a "bother." Her version of appropriate relations between the sexes is highly romanticized in keeping with her social orientation. She even has an occasional romantic, but strictly asexual, fantasy in which she and a cultured gentleman engage in something akin to a "meeting of the minds." In actuality, she does not dare to have even so diluted a relationship with a man as this. Her husband is much too jealous and she is too fearful of social exposure and criticism. As a result, although she is an extremely attractive woman and undoubtedly has many opportunities, she rejects all advances: "I don't like things like that and I avoid them. When girls have what they call a good time, like going out with somebody else, it's always off-color, something is not right. I would have too guilty a conscience."

As we have seen, A.T. is not loath to be aggressive—but after her own fashion. Here again her channels of expression are determined by her conceptions of social propriety. She is overtly aggressive in her home with her husband and child where she cannot be observed, but she changes her tactics in public. There she does not fight back directly, but demolishes her opponents with a snobbish technique of social withdrawal that brands them as her inferiors. In other words, she subjects them to her own personal coventry: "I don't like to argue at work. I don't like to argue in public. I think it's crude. I don't settle an argument by arguing. I ignore you. You just don't exist. I don't hate you. I won't allow myself to do that. I just ignore you. If anybody does anything to me, I ignore them from then on. I have another habit, too. I have the habit of not listening. I do it with lots of people. If I don't like what you're saying, I seem to listen intently, but I'm really not listening at all."

This subject describes an adaptation made up wholly of denial and self-deception. She uses every situation in life to beat herself with and makes every experience a source of fresh misery. Her biography defines the cancerous proportions to which the psychic constellation of identifying with the white man can grow. In the Negro this can never be a source of ego-enhancement; it is always a source of self-degradation. The projection of self-hatred on to other Negroes of lower status does not solve the problem. However, it is one of the few half-pleasures she has in life. Thus, she cannot give up her husband for he serves her too well as a reliable whipping boy. She has also cast her child into this role; but he is avenging himself on her through his neurotic behavior. All possible pleasures of living are sacrificed to the fictitious image she has created of herself as she would like to be. A.T. lives as though she is waiting for a train whose journey has been canceled; but she is still there, waiting for it, just the same.

N.N.

N.N. is a paid subject. She is an attractive 33-year-old divorcée with light brown skin and straight black hair. At the present time she is unemployed. She lives in an apartment in a better section of Harlem with her four children, her father and mother, and both her grandmothers. These are the permanent residents, but from time to time various relatives temporarily in distress will come and live with them. The apartment only has six rooms, so even without the relatives it is overcrowded. All the adult members of the household pool their resources in order to pay for its upkeep. In this way they are able to maintain quarters that would otherwise be beyond their social station. The father is a stevedore and the mother works occasionally as a beauty operator. Most of the other tenants are substantial middle-class Negroes. A neighbor known to the interviewer expresses the general sentiment: "That family is very much out of their element."

N.N. was born and raised in Harlem. The family consisted of the parents and six children. She is next to the oldest. She has two brothers, one older and one younger, and three younger sisters. Their housing was quite adequate. The parents, the two brothers, the two older and the two younger sisters were paired in separate rooms. A fifth room was rented out to transient roomers, usually a man. Their economic status was always comfortable, even during the depression years. The father's role was mainly that of breadwinner. He worked, gave the money to the mother, and then went his separate way. He was not often home and had little to do with the children. However, he was not mean, and in the contacts he did have with them, he was pleasant and warm, even though he was never particularly interested. It was the mother who managed the house and ran the family. N.N. describes her as "a lovely person, kind and good to everybody." The parents got along well and there was little tension in the house. Discipline was "not too strict" and the children were given a "lot of leeway." Punishment was rare, and when it did occur, took the form of a mild spanking. Ethical standards were taken as a matter of course and not especially emphasized: "We had no cause to be deceptive and steal. We had everything we wanted." Socialization was encouraged. The family always maintained an open house and friends of the children could come up whenever they wanted. The girls were allowed "company" and were dating by the time they reached their early teens. Sex was generally taboo and morality was stressed. The girls, particularly, were expected to be virtuous. The family attended church regularly every Sunday, but religion otherwise was not very important. The siblings apparently got along with no more than the normal amount of friction. In sum, the early environment as presented by the subject was mainly one of live and let live in which easy-going comfort and casualness predominated.

Her developmental history is in no way remarkable. She grew up, to all respects, a healthy and normal child. She played easily with other children and was an average student. She was a very popular girl and always had more offers for dates than she could accept. She belonged to two social clubs and there were many dances and parties. At fifteen she met a young man of twenty-one: "I thought then that he was the last word. Now he's still the last word, but words have changed. He was nice-looking, browner than I. He worked as a carpenter. He'd been around quite a bit. He knew a lot more than I did. He had a car. At first he was not acceptable to Mama, but finally she said O.K." She was married before she was seventeen. She dropped out of school and the couple moved into a room in her parent's home.

She and her husband got along poorly from the beginning. They quarreled constantly about everything. After some six months of marriage, N.N. packed his things, placed them outside the door, and locked him out. He left, only to return in a week, and they were reconciled. They got along "better." She had her first, second, and third children. He took a job in a neighboring state and came home only on week ends. She became pregnant again and he rebelled: "When he discovered I was pregnant for the fourth time he stopped writing and sending me money. He said I had too many children and he didn't want to be bothered. We broke up and that was the end of him." A few years later she secured a divorce.

Saddled with four babies, N.N. did not shirk her responsibilities, but immediately looked for a job. The depression made this difficult, and for a time she was supported by relief agencies. Finally, she was hired as a hat-check girl in a night club. She acquired a succession of lovers who, for services rendered, contributed to her support. The war came and she took a job in a defense plant. She began to go steady with Gurney, an uneducated, semi-skilled laborer, a recent arrival from the South. After the war she obtained work as an operator in the garment industry. She also accepted Gurney's proposition that she be his permanent mistress and in this manner she rounded out her income. Without his support she could hardly manage. A few weeks ago she lost her job but she is in no hurry to return to work. This makes Gurney more important to her than ever. It is at this point in her life that the interviews begin.

Throughout the study she maintained a façade of flippancy and gaiety. Only rarely did this break down and reveal the underlying insecurities. She began the first session with a description of her lover, Gurney: "My boy friend's mad at me. He stays mad. He's just evil. I think I should bring him to you. He's the one you should see. I met him a year ago. He's a nut. A fellow I knew said he had a fellow who wanted to meet me. He had a good job and made plenty of money. So I went. He was loud. Every three words were disgusting. He swore and talked nasty. He didn't care about dressing. He was very dark brown. He said 'mens' and he said 'peoples.' He came here from Mississippi. When Mama first saw him—I don't have to tell you! 'Mens, peoples, childrens' got on my nerves! I told him it was 'man, person, child.' I reformed him. I told him, 'No bad words.' I don't sound as though I like him, do I? You're probably wondering why I took up with him. Well, I'll tell you. I needed the money. He asked me what my expenses were a month and I told him. He pays half my rent and twenty dollars a week. Oh, he's a nut! He's suspicious of other men. We quarrel a lot. But he has a great big heart. He's nice to the kids. Everybody likes him. He used to have women every night. Now it's just me. I spend most of my evenings with him. In general, it's pretty nice when he's not evil, but I couldn't ordinarily put up with it if it weren't for the money."

That night N.N. had two dreams:

I was on a boat. There were a lot of people on it. We got stranded on an island. All the people on the island were sick. They were tied to a rack. They were crazy from the sickness—men and women both. They were so dirty! They laid there in all their mess. It was a disgusting scene. I had two pictures with me and a whole lot of little animals, little whatnots you put on a mantle. I stood up the pictures on something. I thought we'd be there for a while. Men were chasing women on the beach. They were out for a wild time. A man chased me. He was dirty. We got back on the boat and shoved off. We left the whatnots and pictures. I was terribly frightened.

A fellow was holding another fellow and pouring lye on him. It was a big house, a mansion. The fellow pouring the lye ran all over the house. People were chasing him. They were trying to catch him. I saw him under a table, but he was not a man then; he was a dog, a police dog. The people shot him. I was awfully scared.

She reports these nightmares in the next session and then associates as follows: "Oh, the people were terrible, awful! One young woman was lying there on her stomach. She was very young and very dirty. It was an awful mess." (Pictures? Whatnots?) "The pictures were one of me and one of my sister. I've always had whatnots around." (Men chasing women?) "I went to the show that night. The people downstairs said, "Mmm! How nice you look!' I said a joke, 'Me is clean and my dog is clean, too.' Jughead is my dog. I call Gurney 'Jughead,' too. I went to Gurney's place. He was asleep. He thought I looked good, too. He told me one of his rare compliments. He didn't want to go to the show so I went alone. On the way to the show more people wolfed at me. Everybody was saying 'hello.' When I got back to Gurney I asked him if I looked different. I thought I was getting old, but I sure scored last night." (Why are you so afraid in the dream?) "The people were sick and dirty and I didn't want them to touch me. I have always been lucky. No one has ever molested me in the street." (Where was this movie you went to?) "Seventh Avenue and 125th Street. People down there look dirty and act dirty. It depresses me. The streets are dirty."

At this point she became visibly tense and was obviously reluctant to associate further to the dreams. She blocked repeatedly and several times claimed she could think of nothing else. The interviewer, however, continued to press her, with the result that by the end of the interview she was quite upset. (Are you sensitive about the dirt?) "I sort of think people ought to clean and freshen themselves up. I thought that on my way to the show. I glanced in a private house. There was a big room with drapes. It was so dirty! The house looked so depressing! People were hanging out on the sidewalk and the street. You don't see that up my way. It's always halfway decent up there. Down there it gives me the willies. I know I shouldn't be snobbish. Still, I think people can raise themselves." (You seem to fear being dragged down.) "We used to live down there. It didn't seem as horrid then. Mama can't understand how we ever lived there. But where we live now is such a bunch of phonies. They're scared to speak to you. I told Mama I would rather live where we used to." (What about the other dream?) "It's a rare thing for a man to do it. Usually it's a woman who pours lye—when she has a broken heart or is a discarded victim. It's silly—a man turning into a dog. Then somebody shot him. I jumped out of the window. They were chasing this fool, so I jumped." (Who is the fool?) "The fellow upstairs came and told me what I needed was another dog. He gave me Jughead and Jughead still can't stand him. I guess I'm not living right—any time people chase me in a dream. I went back to Gurney after the show." (How do you feel about him?) "I said I loved him. I must have been drunk when I said it." Here, the interviewer suddenly asked, "Do you think Gurney is in the dream?" This question really shook the subject. She appeared acutely uncomfortable and gradually became embarrassed, ashamed and depressed. "I don't know. When he's not nice, he's bothering me. He fusses, screams, and quarrels. It used to worry me, but it doesn't affect me now—but I wouldn't say he would turn into a dog . . . (pause) . . . Gurney is one of the common people—and I live where the big shots do." (Where does Gurney live?) "Lennox Avenue. Maybe he has some kind of power over me. I do find my way down there every night. When I first went down there his friends thought I was a snob. He stopped buying them whiskey and giving them money. They called me 'Hincty' . . . (pause) . . . I hold back my anger with Gurney. I had to learn that." In conclusion, as she left, she remarked weakly, "Please, no more dreams."

These two dreams express the degradation, the resentment, and the hatred she feels in the relationship with Gurney. She has sold herself sexually for economic gain, but the toll in terms of her self-esteem has been disastrous. The island in the first dream represents the house in which she lives. Symbolically, it is an island of respectability surrounded by the great morass which is the rest of Harlem. The whatnots and the pictures are tokens of the status she wishes to maintain. They lend sanctity and stability to the home. As she puts it: "A home is not a home without them." Her association with Gurney undermines this beautiful vision. It generates too much guilt and she can only feel soiled and degraded. He drags her down to his level and in the end she is no better than he. The idealized image of a fashionable home is paradoxically destroyed by the very act of prostitution that makes it possible. The action in the second dream also takes place in her building. This time she depicts it as a mansion. The tranquility is disturbed by Gurney, whom she sees as subhuman—a dog who is out of his element. She resents the fact she must sell herself to him and hates him violently for it. The identification forced upon her is unpalatable, and much of her fury undoubtedly consists of projected self-hatred let loose upon her lover's head.

Her self-esteem is further undermined by the color conflict. She equates blackness with the white man's anti-Negro stereotypes: "It's when you see someone very black, uncouth, dressed like a bum in a bus. It's times like that I wish I weren't a Negro. It's when you see them acting a fool in the subway, bus, or street. I just want to commit manslaughter at times like that." Her lover's black skin is hardly compatible with such an attitude. Yet, she swallows her revulsion in the service of economic need: "In going around with fellows I automatically pick out the dark ones. Now my friend, B., she's a Washingtonian. She can't understand how I can stomach them. I can go with anybody as long as their behavior is all right. I don't care what they look like as long as they don't look like an ape. Light-skinned men are the most conceited asses I ever saw. You can't even walk down the street with them. If you want to sit down, he takes the chair; if you want to look in the mirror, he is there first; and he won't work, and he expects you to give him something. And the dark fellow, when he has something light, he won't let go of it."

So she prostitutes herself in favor of the black man, but only at the cost of heightened self-hatred.

This discussion of color prompted the following dream:

I was at the ball game. I was laying up there in a bed at the stadium. Jackie Robinson hit a ball—a black ball—and I caught it. The ball came right to my bed and I just reached over and picked it up. Then Jackie began doing back flips. He caught his head on a wire. He tried to get loose and it turned out he was wearing a wig and the wig came off. Everybody laughed. It was so funny.

In attempting to associate to the dream, she became flustered, very embarrassed, and blocked repeatedly. Finally, it was brought out that she wishes she had a "wonderful" man like Jackie in her bed. She insists not Jackie, himself, but "just someone wonderful like him." Jackie, of course, would be the ideal lover for her. He is devoid of the usual stereotypes, yet black enough to appreciate her light skin. His exploits as a race hero cancel out the stigma of his dark color. He would satisfy all her needs without subjecting her to further degradation.

The second half of the dream expresses her fear that Jackie may not succeed and make a fool of himself before the white populace. Jackie here stands as a symbol for all Negroes: "It's exactly what I said the other day about being a Negro. They can act pretty awful sometimes and naturally when they start acting a fool everybody thinks it's a joke. I'm sure Pee Wee Reese (a white Brooklyn Dodger ballplayer) or none of those people would act up like that. You hardly find them making fools of themselves. Some of our people make fools of themselves all the time. It's just the opposite with Jackie, because he doesn't. He doesn't fight or argue with umpires. He knows how to conduct himself. I'm sure I wouldn't laugh if he did. It would just make me disgusted. It would upset me. It would make me feel bad." This dream is graphic evidence of the tremendous emotional investment that all Negroes put into such race heroes as Jackie Robinson and Joe Louis. It explains the wild exhilaration that stems from their successes and the funereal despair that accompanies their failures.

Her sex life is a contradiction. Strangely enough, in spite of her "moral" laxity, she has little to show for it in the way of sexual pleasure. In fact, she suffers from the usual sexual inhibitions found in the middle-class woman. She has never masturbated and in intercourse experiences orgasm only rarely. However, in the interests of her desirability as a courtesan, she puts on a good act: "I don't let the men know it though. I make them think they're hell on wheels. I act—wooooo! As though they are doing something. But they really ain't doing nothing. I never get no kicks out of it." During the interviews, whenever relating the details of her sexual behavior, she invariably becomes embarrassed, tense, and fidgety.

As the interviews progressed, N.N. became more and more dissatisfied with her relationship with Gurney. She began to talk of giving him up and going back to work. Finally, they had one of their more violent quarrels. She appeared for an early morning interview looking disheveled as though she had just gotten out of bed: "I had a wild hell-firin' night! Can you kill a person and not think anything of it? I want to kill somebody but I don't have the guts for it. It's that Gurney! I never seen anybody so evil, so malicious, so stupid! In all my life I've never had anybody say things to me like he did." She went on to explain that he called her last night at 2 A.M. She happened to be on the telephone talking to a girl friend. He became suspicious because the line was busy for so long and came up to her apartment. "He accused me of calling men. He accused me of turning tricks in my house. He said I was this. He said I was that. We were up all night quarreling. It really upset me. God, it don't make sense! Why does a person put up with all that nonsense from somebody so far below them? Oh, I know why! Why don't I be a smart girl? I better leave that man alone or I'm going to get hurt."

That very day she began to look for a job. She came to the next interview in a despondent mood. She had been turned down by a large firm presumably because she was a Negro: "The ad said no experience needed, we train you, good salary—blah, blah, blah! I filled out the application. Then they told me I wouldn't qualify. I said, 'Why?' She said, 'We don't give you any reasons.' So that's that. They do hire Negroes every once in a while though. I would have wanted something like that. I don't want to sew, I don't want to operate, I don't want to stand up all day and be a waitress. It's too hard. There are so few choices for me. I guess I'll be forced to go to the garment industry and sign up for a job. I've made up my mind to stop fooling around with Gurney. I can't stand it any longer. I feel like I'm wallowing in the gutter. The next time you see me, I'll have a job." Suddenly, for the first time, she lost her flippant façade and burst into tears. She wept bitterly. "I just feel so at a loss these days. I feel so alone. I just feel there is too much on me. I have to go and work. I saw Gurney last night. Not to speak to. He was sleeping. I just walked in and walked out. I started giving him his key and then I changed my mind. I'm afraid of the future. I feel insecure. I feel I'm up against the whole world. I always took care of myself and the kids—always. Years ago I could stand up all day and work at anything, but not now. I'm too old. I've got the jitters."

She failed to keep her next two appointments. Attempts to reach her went unanswered. Two weeks passed before she reappeared. Gurney had beaten her up. She had a black eye, but her good spirits had returned: "This time we really had a fight! I hit first and he hit back. My face was all swollen. I couldn't go home with my face looking like that. Boy, was my face a mess! He softened up after that. Oh, what a sweet, lovable person! So that's where I was the whole week. I stayed at Gurney's. I couldn't go anywhere. I stayed in bed and was treated like a queen. Gurney had to take care of the kids. He went up to the apartment and saw that they got food and everything. Oh, from the time Gurney hit me he's been the sweetest person in the world! Another black eye and I'll be God's gift to earth! He's been sending me papers every day, sodas—oh, he's really been wonderful! But I still intend to go to work."

The study ended here and she was not seen again for two years. A follow-up interview revealed that she had been good to her word. She was working and, for the greater part, had loosened her ties with Gurney: "Well, I've been providing for myself. Since I saw you we had two more fights. Yes, honey, not just one, but two! He blacked both eyes both times. Four black eyes! Isn't that wonderful! Well! When that happened I decided now it was time to leave Gurney and go to work, so I got a job in a factory and I been there ever since. I see him occasionally, but it's not like it was. Oh, if I go there he'll give me some money, but otherwise—uh, uh! I have to work for anything he gives me. He's so mad that I'd have to sleep with him day and night now instead of just night in order to get enough food to feed the family. I have another boy friend now. Isn't that interesting? He thinks the sun rises and sets with me, but he can't do anything for me. He can't give me money like Gurney. He can't pay my food bills. He wants to marry me, but I keep backing out. He can't give me a home. He can't take care of me. He talks to me as though I'm his equal. We'll work together. We'll build a home together. He doesn't seem to realize I'm an old woman. I want a home already there. I want someone to take care of me."

This subject illustrates, perhaps more effectively than any other, the psychological cost of maintaining middle-class ideals with lower-class means. N.N. has champagne tastes, but with a beer pocketbook. The image of herself that she can accept, if not admire, is modeled on middle-class respectability. However, in order to maintain this façade, as we have seen, she must sell her soul to the devil. The resultant shame is almost unbearable, but she nevertheless thinks it is worth the price. There is nothing about this behavior which is characteristic of the Negro. It is essentially a *class* struggle. Plenty of white women pay the same price for the same commodity. The motive force for this drive to respectability in N.N., however, has the Negro denial of race as a constituent.

E.W.

E.W. is a paid subject. She is a 27-year-old, medium brown, unmarried schoolteacher. She was born and raised in Harlem in the very apartment which she still occupies. Her father is light enough to pass for white. He is a high school graduate and a government clerk of many years service. He prides himself as an intellectual and at one time had aspirations for a professional career, either as a doctor or a lawyer. The frustration of these ambitions have left him an embittered man and "hepped" on the subject of discrimination. He launches into tirades at the slightest provocation. Emotionally, he is extremely volatile: vile-tempered, high-strung, overly energetic. E.W. thinks of him as thoroughly disagreeable. She complains he is aggressive and argumentative and has a faculty for making people miserable. The mother is medium brown in color, the daughter of a white man and a Negro woman. She is a college-trained schoolteacher just like the subject. E.W. is quite ambivalent about her. On the one hand, she remarks, "She is very sweet and very kind. On the whole I am very thankful for the kind of mother I have, considering the kind of father I have. It's a relief to have someone I can talk to, someone understanding." On the other hand, throughout the interviews, she repeatedly expresses great resentment at the frequent and unjust punishment meted out by the mother. There are two siblings, an older sister and a younger brother. The sister is a college graduate and works as a private secretary to a "race leader." The brother is a student in college. Both parents, particularly the mother, openly favored him. This, of course, was further cause for resentment in E.W. His skin is a very dark brown and hence a source of considerable disappointment for the mother, who is quite color-conscious. In this connection, E.W., is often the butt of the mother's ire: "My mother has always resented that my sister and I were lighter than my brother. She has always wished he were the lighter. Whenever she gets mad at us she calls us 'black.' "

The family's economic circumstances have always been adequate. The father has never lacked for a job. The mother stayed home with the children until they were old enough to go to school. She then returned to teaching. The parental relationship was not too good. The father's temperament led to frequent quarreling concerning any and all subjects. The mother, however, was not entirely innocent of provocation. She never let the father forget that he had failed in his pre-marital promise to become a professional man. In status terms, this was perhaps even more of a disappointment to her than it was to him. Another point of conflict was sex. It was an open secret in the household, shared also by the children, that the mother hated anything connected with sexual relations and rarely allowed the father access to her. The children were indoctrinated in the mother's attitudes. E.W. grew up to look upon sex as something dirty, painful, and indecent. Both parents showed the children considerable attention and interest. Affection was also present, but in a much lesser amount. Discipline was fairly strict and enforced by the mother. The children were expected to lead a "decent, moral life" and they acted accordingly—or else. The parents were very religious and E.W. and her siblings participated regularly in all church activities.

E.W.'s early development contains several items worthy of note. They all indicate a frustration of infantile dependency needs and a terror of violence. She was a very insecure child. She bit her nails severely between ages five and eight. She still bites them sporadically, but now only mildly. She was enuretic until nine. She had many childhood fears. She was afraid to sleep alone and was afraid of the dark. Accounts of accidents, fights, and death threw her into a panic.

She would vomit after a horror movie such as Frankenstein or Dracula. Once she saw a picture of a Negro being lynched and she had to sleep with her mother for six months. She was always a feeding problem. She was very finicky about food and had many stomach upsets. She fought repeatedly with her mother over eating. The mother insisted she eat, and E.W. swallowed the food, only to regurgitate it later.

She was sent to a private school that accepted Negroes. This occurred because the mother considered the public schools in their neighborhood inferior. She was one of a handful of Negro girls. They were made to feel their difference most keenly. The white girls had very little to do with them. E.W. was an excellent student and well-behaved. In fact, she was always a teacher's pet. This incurred the envy of the other students and served only to isolate her even further from the group. She was never very happy in grammar school. Things improved in high school. There were many more Negro girls and she greatly enlarged her circle of friends. She was fearful of boys and did not date at all. Neither did she go to many parties, and for the same reason. She graduated from high school first in her class.

She attended a large Middle Western university. Here, relatively speaking, she blossomed out socially. She joined many clubs and participated in many extracurricular activities. She began to go out with boys and had several offers of marriage. She even became engaged once, only to break it off. Her relationships with men were never very good. In her own words, she was always a "fault-finder," and inevitably the men found her "disagreeable." Simultaneously, she "lost interest" in them. Following graduation from college, she returned to New York and secured a job as a teacher. Her school has both white and Negro students, but the former greatly outnumber the latter. There are two other Negro teachers in the school. At the present time, then, she moves professionally in predominantly white circles. Her social life, however, is almost exclusively Negro.

E.W. has several emotional conflicts. These have to do with self-esteem, the handling of aggression, sex, and interpersonal relations, especially with men. Let us start with the self-esteem. It is not very high. Here, her familial relationships did not hold her in good stead. The parents' behavior created doubts concerning her self-worth and lovability. Neither parent gave her sufficient emotional support and both frankly favored her brother. This already is enough to create a serious disturbance in a child's self-esteem, irrespective of color. Add the Negro problem and the child is really in trouble. The mother, herself, equated worthlessness with the color black. In addition, the family was constantly reminded of the father's failures, and these in the end, were attributed to the stigma of race. No matter that he was the unhappy victim of discrimination. The common-sense conclusion is still the same: it is better to be white. The family atmosphere, therefore, was not conducive either to idealization of the parents or to the self-love that goes with it.

The self-esteem problem became even more acute as soon as E.W. entered an all-white school. Her inferior position as a Negro was confirmed daily. We can hardly expect an individual to think well of herself under such circumstances. Now, as an adult, E.W., in her work, associates daily with whites. Again, numerically, she is very much in the minority and can never forget that she is colored. This state of affairs has two major effects. First, it maintains the self-esteem at a very low ebb. She is plagued by constant feelings of worthlessness. This occurs in spite of her good performance, for everybody recognizes that she is a most competent teacher. During the interviews she repeatedly comments on her own low opinion of herself. She always expresses it in the same way: "I do good work but I still feel inadequate, and in my relations with people I feel insecure and ill-at-ease. It's hard for me to join in and I have a tendency to respect other people's opinions more than my own." The second effect is an around-the-clock preoccupation with anti-Negro discrimination. The interviews are replete with discriminatory incidents. Practically every interview contains such references. Many sessions are devoted entirely to them. It is not that E.W. is self-referential in an unreal sense; unfortunately, the episodes she reports are all too real.

Discrimination was always present in school: "Negroes had quite a time in college because of the teachers. I heard of many instances where teachers put 'N' next to the student's name so they could mark them accordingly. About the time I was going to school I remember the students were up in arms because they claimed the teachers were prejudiced against Jews and Negroes. 'A' students would end with 'C's' and 'D's' for no apparent reason. Three times I got 'A's' in all the exams but the final grade was 'C.' When I went for an explanation, none was forthcoming. We'd get into little groups and we'd try to organize and see what could be done. Every Negro I knew had this happen to him at least once. One time six of us went to a teacher. We went in a body, but she just refused to answer us. Then I was on several committees, but nothing ever came of them."

The whites, even inadvertently, never let her forget she is "different": "I am very sensitive when whites make any remark I can take as an insult to Negroes. For instance, when I was a freshman in a sociology class, a remark was made that Negroes were supposed to have flat noses and kinky hair. I was the only Negro in the class so of course everybody in the class turned around and looked at me. I don't think he should even have made the remark. Everyone knows what Negroes look like. Then there are jokes about color and about Negroes as domestics, and so forth. I know white people insist Negroes are always supposed to fit a facial pattern, so just for fun I looked at my friends to see if they followed the stereotype, and none of them did."

During vacation from college she made two brief excursions into the job market. The results typify what every Negro is up against: "One Christmas vacation I applied for a job at a department store. I went on the recommendation of a white friend of mine who was working as a salesgirl. I didn't know whether they were hiring Negroes or not, but I went. Just as I thought, they said they would hire me as a wrapper, but not as a salesgirl. Well, they gave me the usual story. They had no openings for salesgirls, but just the next day they hired five of my white friends. But a colored girl and I took the wrapping jobs anyway. I stayed about six weeks and I think I wrapped about three packages. They used me as a relief cashier, but paid me the lesser salary of a wrapper. They were doing this with many Negroes. I asked about this several times, but they always gave me the runaround. One day I short-changed a customer one penny. She was fairly dripping in sables and diamonds. She called the floor manager and created a row. She said she objected to having a Negro serve her and she didn't know what was happening to the department stores. He took her aside and I don't know what happened, but my guess is he apologized for hiring the help. The usual story was that help was hard to get and that's why they had Negroes. Well, I had given her back her penny and he advised me there would probably be more incidents like that and I should try to overlook it. But after that I left. The next summer I got a job as a baby sitter. They were very nice people, but finally the tenants forced me out. It was a luxury apartment and they objected to my going up and down the elevator. The little boy had a lot of problems and his mother wanted someone trained in psychology. I liked her immediately. She was telling me how to treat the little boy. She told me to be sure to give him a lot of affection, to kiss him a lot. I thought that was very odd. I didn't know they'd want Negroes kissing their children. So I got along very well with the boy, but it wasn't very long before people started complaining and I was known to everybody in this big apartment house as 'the Negro girl who comes in and out of the elevator as though she owns the place.' Finally, the landlord made a rumpus and threatened to make my employer move. She insisted I was not a domestic and would not use the servants' elevator, but finally it got so unpleasant, I had to leave. And she paid me very well. After that I stopped trying to have such jobs. Never again!"

So now she is a teacher, but the pressure upon her still remains: "I'll tell you what happened to me at school this morning. This is very usual, but I'll tell you anyway. I went into the front office and passed the receptionist's desk. I've been knowing her now for a year and a half, so I would assume she would know me. But she called me Mrs. M. There are three colored teachers there and one of them is Mrs. M. I'm getting tired of that nonsense every day, so I refused to answer. So then she called me Mrs. K. That's another colored teacher, so I still didn't answer. Then she said, 'Well, the only one you could be then is Miss W.' And there was a time when she'd say, 'Which one are you?' Well, recently, I've been asking, 'Which one what?' I think it's stupid that she can't recognize individual differences. It's because we're Negroes and she assumes all Negroes are alike—big mouths, flat noses, and all that. Actually, there are only three of us, and we are the ones who ought to have trouble distinguishing the whites there. And that's the general attitude of all the teachers as regards the Negro children. They're all alike, regardless of how light they are. They are all reported as 'dark and ugly.' I even came across a phrase: 'This child's mother is dull and lazy—like most Southern Negroes.' "

None of these incidents is exactly calculated to bolster her self-esteem. To the contrary, literally a hundred times a day she is reminded that she is considered an inferior human being. The normal reaction to such intimidation is hostility, and E.W. has plenty of this. She is full of resentment, but she is hardly in a position to express it. For the most part, it must be held back. Retaliation from the whites is too costly and too certain to be risked. This means that she must rely on techniques of control to siphon off the aggression. These are both conscious and unconscious, i.e., suppression and repression. In E.W., the end-products of such control are overt anxiety (tension), headaches, nausea and vomiting, and high blood pressure.

One day she arrived for her interview thirty minutes late. Before entering the office, she went to the bathroom and vomited. She then related the following incident, which illustrates the difficulties she has in handling aggression: "I'm very sorry to be late. Everything happened. Now I have a splitting headache. I was just furious. I was trying to get down here and the bus was going too slow so I got out and tried to hail a cab but every one I hailed said they were going on in. So the first one said he was going in, and he immediately took a white passenger, practically in front of me. Another one said his clock was down and he took a white passenger. So the third one said he was going in, too, but I was so mad I decided to report him. I said, 'That's fine. What's your number?' He told me a sad story how he had to go and get his cab fixed and I believed him and didn't take his number, but then he took a white passenger, too. I hate to investigate something, even though I feel badly about it. So immediately I was saying to myself, 'Discrimination! Discrimination!' By that time I felt a little beaten and didn't bother any more. I walked eight blocks and took a bus again. I practically got on the same bus I had gotten off. And all the way down here I was getting a headache. I tried to tell myself it was so stupid and trivial and it certainly wasn't worth getting a headache, but I still got the headache. I don't know why I couldn't get up the gumption and the nerve to say something when it happens. I can only talk about it afterwards. I'm still steaming! I should turn people like that in, but actually, if you turned in every case of discrimination, you'd be busy all day." One can well imagine what such an encounter does to her blood pressure.

E.W.'s difficulties with aggression do not stem only from societal forces. They also have a familial origin. She was frequently punished by both parents. Her father, especially, thoroughly frightened her: "I was thinking about my father and myself. You know, I've always felt I had a rather unhappy childhood. I was never very contented and I have a feeling my father had a great deal to do with that. I had my bad relationship with him and then I had the worries and fears and scariness connected with growing up. By the time I was seven I realized every time he got angry he was going to slap me or hit me. It was usually for something trivial. Once he slapped me on the head, so I pretended he struck me so hard I fell to the floor, just to see what my mother would do. She told him he was never to touch the children again. After that, he would often clench his fist to keep from hitting me because he didn't know how my mother would react. Well, you know, I guess it must have been before I was ten, I remember writing a note to my mother. I explained to her I hated my father and I wanted to jump out of the window. I don't remember what happened. All I remember is the letter and I was upset." Suddenly, E.W. became nauseated. She jumped up and dashed to the bathroom. She returned in tears. "I don't want to talk about it any more, I guess. I haven't cried about this for a long time. I remember I used to cry a lot over it as a child. When I wrote that letter, my mother read it and just said, 'Stop being so stupid.' If she'd only said something to make me feel better."

Few children can stand up to such treatment. The usual outcome is a protective inhibition of aggression. The above description goes a long way toward explaining E.W.'s many childhood fears. It also explains the difficulty she has with interpersonal relationships. She distrusts others just as she did her parents. This limits her ability to establish close emotional relations, and, indeed, she admits to only casual friendships. A white child, given the same treatment, would end up with the same problem. For the Negro child, confronted in addition with a hostile social environment, it is proportionately that much worse. This is not to say E.W. lacks the capacity for warmth. This she has in abundance, but she can express it only when she feels safe. Her work with children is one such situation. A great deal of her bottled-up affection comes out here. Her principal attests to her great popularity as a teacher.

E.W. does have many "acquaintances," and she socializes with them a great deal, but they are mostly women. We heard earlier that she has trouble with men. This is as we would expect, since her father was much the more threatening of her parents. Now, as an adult, she gets her revenge. She mistreats the men just as her father mistreated her: "Whenever I meet somebody, they think I'm very nice, and I act nice until they get to know me. Then, the more they like me, the nastier I act. That's not with girls. It's with fellows. I get along with girls all right. It's beginning to worry me recently. It starts off with little things. I get stubborn and won't talk and I deliberately do things to hurt the other person. Then if something annoys me, I don't discuss it and drop it. I keep on talking about it and getting angrier and angrier until I seem to be consumed by it. As it is now, I could never make a happy marriage. There would be an argument every minute. I just don't know when to stop. I am kind of worried about this. I always said I would never want to marry anyone like my father, but now I act just like he did." Her behavior gives her satisfaction, but as she herself recognizes, the cost is high. No man puts up with it for long.

There is another reason for her poor relations with men, which is probably even more important. E.W. is markedly inhibited sexually. At twenty-seven she is still a virgin. She has been kissed a few times, but that is all. She denies ever having masturbated. Parental attitudes were instrumental in her inhibition. Her mother's rejection of the sexual role made a great impression upon her. Several times she was beaten because she asked for sexual information. The mother said that even kissing was a sin. Part of the inhibition, then, lies in the persistence of her infantile fear of maternal punishment. The rest stems from her father (and brother), but of this E.W. is entirely unaware. She is unconsciously enmeshed in a classical oedipus complex and falls victim to the usual inhibitions derived from it. This is demonstrated in thinly disguised and repetitive incestual dreams of sexual assault. Thus, she also conceives of sex in terms of violence. This is a necessary outcome of her father's violent behavior toward her.

E.W.'s neurotic conflicts are run-of-the-mill. They are qualitatively the same as in any white girl exposed to a similar family configuration. Yet, there is a difference. The difference lies in the intensification of these conflicts by the extra pressure of the caste system to which only the Negro is subject. This is the special significance of E.W.'s case history. It demonstrates that the professional Negro who is in constant and daily contact with whites, is in a peculiarly vulnerable position. His problems, particularly those having to do with self-esteem and aggression, will be magnified manyfold.

E.S.

E.S. is a very attractive 24-year-old, married woman, presently employed as a sales girl in a small business run by a white man. She has a pretty face with Caucasian features, a light golden skin that can easily pass for white, and jet black straight hair. Her figure is quite shapely and she shows it off to good advantage in simple but attractive clothing. She could well be a chorus girl or a model. She is warm, friendly, and cheerful and relates herself easily to the interviewer.

E.S. is a patient in psychotherapy. She comes to treatment in order to resolve a marital conflict. She has been married for five years to a light brown semi-skilled electrical worker, who is cold, rigid, argumentative, and domineering. They have one child, a boy aged four. The marriage has steadily deteriorated. They fight and argue constantly. He is interested mainly in saving money, does not care to socialize, and gives her very little affection. She has begun to lose her usual happy disposition. She has become nervous, irritable, and tearful. In addition, she finds herself daydreaming about other men. She feels she should take her son and leave him, but she is not sure this would be the right thing to do. She hopes through therapy to air the problem and come to a final conclusion.

She was born and raised in Harlem. Her father was a mailman, an easy-going and kindly man. The mother was a grammar school graduate, who for a time worked as a domestic and as a dressmaker, but after the children were born, devoted herself exclusively to them. There are five siblings—two boys and three girls. E.S. is the youngest. Next come two sisters, then the two brothers, and finally the oldest sister, who is fifteen years older than the subject. The family group was close-knit and the children got along fairly well with no more friction than is usually expected in such a large family.

The economic situation was always a little tight. The father did not earn enough for such a large family and there were occasional quarrels about money. Aside from this difficulty, the parents appeared very much in love with each other and presented to the children an example of marital harmony. Household affairs were mostly in the hands of the mother. It was mainly she who ran the home and raised the children. Both parents were demonstrative and affectionate, but here again, the mother more than the father: "Daddy loved us, but he wasn't as expressive as mother. He mostly sat and smoked his pipe and read his Bible. He never played with us. Mother used to play with us all the time. She used to put on boxing gloves and box with us. She would ride bicycles with us. She helped us with our homework. She was very, very nice. Everyone liked her." Discipline, too, was maintained by the mother, but was not very strict. Standards were high and the children usually did what was expected without coercion. The father was quite devout and stressed a religious up-bringing, but the mother had much less interest in it than he and greatly attenuated his pressure upon the children. As a result, none of the children today, beyond occasional attendance at church, is particularly concerned with religion. Sex was not a topic for discussion. The father died when E.S. was nine, and the mother when she was thirteen. The oldest sister, who was married, took the mother's place, and the siblings stayed together as a family unit, until, one by one, they left to get married.

E.S., as the baby of the family, was the parent's favorite and received a great deal of attention not only from them, but also from her siblings. In school, too, she was very popular and liked by everybody. She was not, however, a good student and in high school she failed several courses. She was far too interested in other things: "I used to daydream quite a bit and not pay any attention to the teachers. I daydreamed about romance. I used to like to read those love story magazines. I would think about anything, except what the teachers were talking about. I just couldn't wait for three o'clock to come to go see my friends or go to the movies or just to go out. I used to like to go skating and walking and bicycle riding."

She began dating early, but it was "strictly proper" in accordance with her mother's restrictions: "Oh, I always went out with boys. The first time was about thirteen when I was in junior high school. They liked me, but I guess I was particular about a boy's behavior and when they found I was so nice, I guess that chased them away. There were lots of parties and dances. My brothers and sisters all went so I went along with them. I was always like 'the little sister,' you know, and my brothers sort of watched over me." She was very attractive to boys and in spite of being a "nice girl" she always had more dates than she could accept. She quit high school in her last year and went to work in a defense plant.

She was an excellent worker and, relatively speaking, made good money. Her popularity with men continued; if anything, because of her beauty, it became enhanced. She had literally dozens of marriage proposals before she accepted her present husband. His personality difficulties undermine his work relationships and he has lost one job after another. As a result, it has been necessary for her to continue working. She took time off only for her pregnancy. Things got slow in her plant after the war and she was laid off. She then took a job as a sales girl in a small store and this is where she now works.

Her immediate problem is clearly outlined in her first two dreams:

My husband was on a stage. He was playing a piano. He had on these tails and a white front and black suit. He looked very nice. He looked so happy. He had this smiling, pleased expression. Even in my dream I felt he hadn't looked so happy in so long. I began to dance to the music. Then he got up and began to dance, but we were dancing separately. I felt that was wrong. I thought we ought to be dancing together.

She interprets the dream as follows: "I feel my husband and I are not getting along. I can't make him out. I can't understand him. The things I like, he doesn't. He doesn't enjoy talking to me, but he will sit and talk with his friends for hours and enjoy it; yet, we can't seem to laugh together. I make him look happy in the dream because that's the way I want him to look. He's always so sour." Thus, the dream focuses on the incompatibility she feels with her husband. It states very simply that they are ill-mated. The next dream shows her response to this frustration. She is tempted with unacceptable impulses toward other men.

I was in an office building. Someone was chasing me and I was trying to get out. I was trapped. Green dragons were being sent to close in on me. I got downstairs and was running to the fence to get out. The doors were closing. I didn't think I had time to get through. So I ran fast and took a big jump over the fence. Then I was running down the street. I was still being pursued when the dream ended.

She immediately identifies the locale as her place of business. Her boss has been making advances toward her. She has felt attracted, but has refused. Nevertheless, she recognizes that she has played the dangerous game of teasing him, and this has been provocative. The day of the dream he was counting out some money to go to the bank. He had several thousand dollars, all in greenbacks. Suddenly, he peeled off a hundred dollar bill and offered it to her if she would sleep with him just once. It is this offer that prompted the dream. The money is symbolized by the green dragons that threaten her. The dream, therefore, comes under the heading of "Get thee behind me, Satan!" It represents the conflict between her conscience, on the one hand, and her desire for the money and sexual gratification, on the other. She is hard put to resist the temptation. In the dream she falls back on projection: it is not she who seeks the devil; rather, it is the devil who seeks her. This construction is verified for us in her very next dream:

> I drove to a house. A lot of men were there with their wives. One man took a liking to me and started making advances. He actually started to rape me. I was struggling like mad. I was calling out to my husband and people around me for help, but nobody paid any attention or came to my rescue. Finally, he left. It seems he actually had intercourse with me. I was very embarrassed about it. Two other men came over and started talking to me. I told them this was terrible since I had never slept with anyone but my husband. One of the men looked at me. His wife was there. Suddenly, I picked up a box of pepper and threw it in his face. Everybody laughed. A woman said, 'Don't do that again. That's what started all the trouble in the first place.' It seems she meant that by throwing pepper in his face I made him have a desire for me. I said, 'Oh, my goodness!'

She explains in her associations that she, herself, is not entirely innocent: "My boss always used to tell me jokingly, 'I'm going to rape you one of these days. You just prepare for it.' I would say, 'Oh, my goodness!' The man who raped me in the dream was my boss. I was in a playful mood when I first came there. After work, instead of leaving right away, I would stay and comb my hair. He would sit there and watch me and say how beautiful I was. I realized I was teasing him but I still did it. My husband never compliments me. It was something I was getting I wasn't getting any more. I enjoyed it. I've never been with another man and my boss says I'm too pretty to be so good. It just slipped into my mind once that this man was bothering me so much, I might weaken."

This dream proves an old axiom: The woman who protests the loudest about rape is usually the one who most desires it. In brief, the dream states: Help! Help! Get me out of this before I give in and let him rape me. Nevertheless, in actuality, she manages to hold out against the temptation. This fact demonstrates the efficacy of her conscience in sexual matters.

E.S.'s capacity for affectivity is excellent. Unfortunately, her husband is utterly unable to reciprocate. Over and over again, throughout the interviews, she dreams that the marriage is in ruins. The following dream is typical; it expresses the sentiment of all:

There was a cliff overlooking a big canyon. On top of the cliff were ruins of some houses. It seems as though there was a house right on the edge and it was covered over with white stuff like snow. And it was all inside the house, too. Those people had cleared out the inside but couldn't clean one room just on the edge of the cliff because they feared it would fall off. I looked into this room. It wasn't fit to live in—no furniture and dilapidated and all this snow in it. Then there was another room and somebody told me not to go in there because the floor was weak and I would tumble through.

She explains: "The dream is me looking at my house. I felt that was the way I felt about my marriage—that it was ruined. It was full of snow—like a hard rock—frost. It means my husband is cold to me. Like yesterday, we went to the beach with some friends and he acted as though I wasn't even there. He just talked to the fellows and didn't pay any attention to me. It was just lacking so. It doesn't seem to me that's the way a man should act toward his wife. I feel the house is teetering. The marriage is actually going."

Sexually, she is quite normal. She masturbated throughout adolescence. Prior to marriage, she engaged in necking and mild petting but no more. She has had intercourse only with her husband. On a purely physical basis, she finds him a satisfactory partner. She achieves orgasm regularly without difficulty. She relates her capacity to respond sexually to her familial background: "As far as I know my whole family is normal sexually. Daddy and mother were very affectionate. If you went into their bedroom and saw them in bed he would have her in his arms with her head on his shoulder. So I guess growing up in an atmosphere like that had a lot to do with our being normal." She is quite right. It did.

There is nothing very much the matter with her self-esteem. In fact, it appears to be exceptionally high: One day she described how she felt about herself: "I like for everybody to like me. I like to hold myself in the highest esteem. My brothers, they think I'm very nice, and I'd like to stay nice. Maybe I'm very proud. Ever since I can remember, people have told me I was very nice. People have always trusted me, liked me, maybe admired me. There's one woman who comes to the store, she thinks I'm so pretty! Why, she brought a friend just to look at me! I just love things like that. Oh, my ego just swells! My husband gets so mad at me. He says I get too many compliments. I always tell him if I don't think well of myself, nobody else will! I don't like to have bad thoughts about myself or to have anybody else have bad thoughts about me. I guess sometimes when I'm here I do hold back thoughts about myself that aren't so nice." As she got up to go at the conclusion of the interview she began to laugh hilariously: "You know what thought I had just then? I had the thought: 'There's nothing not so nice about me!' " She turned and skipped out of the room.

She appears to escape many of the problems that confront Negroes: "I go wherever I want and everybody that meets me likes me, whether they are colored or white. There are a lot of people who don't like being colored, but I don't know why they worry. Those that like you, all right; if they don't, that's all right, too. But maybe I just don't come in contact with the problems other Negroes do. My husband, he lets it bother him. He just hates to have anybody take advantage of him, but I just laugh it off. Sometimes you just have to put up with having some advantage taken of you. In the summer I'm a little dark but in the winter I'm fair. People look at my husband and me when we're together in the subway. He gets uncomfortable. He says I look Irish when I laugh. I pass sometimes, not purposely now, but I used to do it on purpose."

The attenuation of her status conflict is easily explained. To begin with, her self-esteem was given a solid foundation in her formative years. Her parents and siblings gave her plenty of attention and affection. This made identification and idealization easy. This foundation was not later undermined by inordinate aspirations, either social, material, or vocational. These have remained on a very modest level. Actually, she asks for no more than a "nice husband, a nice family, and a nice home," all on a lower middle-class basis.

Her light skin and attractive appearance further enhance her feelings of worth.

Toward the end of the interviews, her boss became so insistent in his overtures that she felt compelled to quit her job. She decided to relax for a few weeks before going back to work. Her husband thereupon issued an ultimatum: either she find a job immediately or he, too, would stay at home; he would not be the sole support of the family. She stood pat, and he promptly resigned. A tug of war began in which each refused to be the first to return to work. The subject felt there was little chance the marriage would survive, but she wanted to give it one last chance. On this note, the interviews ended.

She was seen next six months later: "Well, it took me a very long time. I had to make up my mind. I bent over backwards, but it didn't work. I just waited and waited and he wouldn't get a job. I went back to work before he did. I worked in the factory, as before. After that he still didn't get a job. I was working and all the money was going so I told him I wouldn't feed him any more. I started hating him. I decided to separate and I kept after him to move. I couldn't move because I had the baby. We began to quarrel and he slapped me. Then he struck me and we really began to fight. My mother had taught me if a man attacked me I should put my finger at the angle between his teeth and lips. That's supposed to be very painful. Instead, I put my finger in his mouth and he bit on it and wouldn't let it go. He bit it right down to the bone. I grabbed his testicles and we fell down and he got a hammer-lock on my head. I blacked out and he let me go. Then he packed his clothes and left. Work got slow and I was laid off for a while, but I managed to get another job. My husband wants to come back, but I guess I've gotten a little more independent and I don't want to go through that again. Right now I feel fine. I don't have any problems. And my conscience is clear. You know, I wanted to try everything before I gave it up. I never wanted him to say I didn't try. I wanted to squeeze the last drop of trying out of me, and I did. I tried and tried and tried, and finally I saw it was no use. I know now we can never be happy again."

This subject can be categorized as essentially "normal." She is caught at the moment in a crisis situation which stimulates neurotic tendencies that otherwise would lie dormant. The underlying adaptation, however, is basically sound. She has plenty of resources and is capable of mobilizing them and putting them to effective use in time of danger. Her affectivity is of a high order. She can establish warm and meaningful interpersonal relationships with facility. She has adequate patterns of aggression and does not shrink from self-assertion. Her sexual behavior is normal. Her conscience has normal tonicity, her self-esteem is reasonably high, and she does not lack the capacity for idealization. The possession of such an integrated personality is not happenstance. It is directly derived from the stability of her family unit during her formative years. Here again we have a clear-cut indication of the point at which social engineering must be applied.

C.E.

C.E. is a former schoolteacher, thirty-five years of age, who now devotes herself exclusively to social and domestic duties. She is married to a Negro technician fifteen years her senior and they have two sons, ten and eight. She is exotically beautiful, with sharply molded features, light golden skin, and naturally straight black hair. Her figure is shapely and her clothing expensive, fashionable, and in the very best of taste. She does not, however, carry her striking beauty with an easy grace. She is much too preoccupied with the impression her appearance and behavior are making. In consequence, she is self-conscious, tense, and unsure of herself. She comes to psychotherapy because she is having marital difficulties. Her relationship with her husband is marked by endless quarreling and bickering. She is resentful and irritable and frequently has explosive outbursts of temper.

She was born and raised in a large Southern city. The father was a highly successful Negro physician. He was a hail-fellow-well-met and liked by everybody. The mother, a graduate of a Negro teachers' college, did not work, but occupied herself entirely with the household. C.E. describes her in glowing terms: "She is vivacious, attractive, decidedly independent, very friendly, and always put the family before everything." There are four older siblings: two brothers, both college graduates—one a physician, the other a lawyer—and two sisters, also college graduates—one employed by a Negro uplift organization, the other a housewife like C.E. The subject is the "baby" in the family. She and the two parents have the same skin color. The brothers and sisters are all slightly darker. The five siblings got along quite well, but C.E. feels she was, without question, the favorite child, particularly of her mother. Not the least of the reasons for this was the fact that she had a lighter skin and straighter hair, attributes of great importance to the parents.

The father was wealthy and the family's economic status was very comfortable. They belonged to the Negro "society" of their community. They owned a large home, two automobiles, and maintained a staff of servants. The mother and father appeared to be very much in love and their relationship was smooth and amicable. Both showered the children with attention and affection, the mother, since she was home all the time, more so than the father. For this reason, maternal influence was the dominant force in the children's lives. Standards of behavior were fairly strict, but rigid only on issues of social status. The parents were extremely "race-conscious." They wanted to be very proud of their children. They insisted the children always be aware of their high social status in everything they did, i.e., manners, dress, selection of playmates, etc. The family led a very extensive social life. The parents entertained members of their own social set frequently and lavishly, and the children were inducted early into the social graces befitting their station. Otherwise, they had the run of the house and freedom to play. Punishment was usually verbal, rarely by spanking. Religion was stressed, but not so much for religious, as for social purposes. Church attendance every Sunday was a great social event, an opportunity for all to display their finery and compare themselves, one with the other. C.E. enjoyed going because neighbors would later tell her mother how pretty she looked, how well she played the piano, how beautifully she sang. Sex was not hidden and the mother gave the children information whenever they asked, but in keeping with their social position, the moral code was strict and the girls were expected to be virtuous. In sum, C.E. remembers life in the home in which she grew up as a very happy one.

The idyllic setting which she describes, however, is belied to a great extent by the history of her early development. She was a nervous and active child, who had many temper tantrums, wet the bed to seven, and bit her nails to sixteen. These are unmistakable signs of unbearable parental pressure and the breakdown of her ability to cope with it. They point to a constant state of anxiety, frustration, and underlying rebellion.

In school she was well-behaved, received good grades, and worked hard to impress her teachers. She succeeded so well she became a perennial teacher's pet. This served to antagonize her playmates and marred her social integration with them. They were all jealous of her, but nevertheless, because of her family's prestige and her good looks, she was quite popular, especially with boys. She associated in a small, exclusive group—the "upper crust." They were all light-skinned and their parents would not allow them to mingle with children of dark color. They engaged in a very active social life and hardly a night passed without a party or a dance. All of the girls in the group were very attractive and competition for the boys was very intense. Invariably, C.E. was the winner. She graduated from high school first in her class. Her parents and teachers wanted her to be a teacher—the most elevated occupation for a Negro woman. This was to be combined with marriage to a doctor, lawyer, professor, government official, or race leader, which automatically would guarantee the perpetuation of her high status.

She took the next step for achievement of these goals and entered an exclusive, Northern, interracial women's college. Following graduation she came to New York and completed her training as a teacher. She taught for only a few months in a progressive school and then left to marry her husband. He was a Negro technician, handsome and light-skinned, but at that time without social position. Also, he was fifteen years older. Sensing parental disapproval, she rebelled and married him secretly. Later when the news leaked out, she was severely criticized by her parents and in the society columns of the home town Negro press. It was claimed she had erred on a number of counts: there had been no social glitter to the marriage; a person in her position was expected to have a "proper" marriage; the husband's social position was obscure; she had failed to inform her parents; it was not the kind of behavior expected from a goddess who had gone out to carry the torch.

The husband has achieved both professional and financial success. This enables C.E. to lead a life of leisure. However, she considers her social life essentially a failure. This she attributes to her husband's lack of interest in dances and big social events. Further, he works hard all day, and when he gets home, he claims he is very tired and frequently refuses to go out. On week ends, when he does have free time, he doesn't care for the things she likes to do but is mainly interested in sports. She cares little for these, so he goes to various athletic events alone, or with his male companions leaving her once more to herself. He also seems to have an inordinate attachment to his mother and insists they spend a good deal of time with her. Their children make further inroads on the amount of attention her husband can give her. As a result, most of what C.E. does, she must do alone. This is a sore point, a never-ending source of bitterness between them.

C.E.'s background hardly prepares her for the treatment she receives at the hands of her husband. As a girl she was a favorite child not only with her parents, but also in the entire community. Her security, as well as her self-esteem, now depend upon this kind of recognition. She has developed an exorbitant need for affection, attention, and services. Now, as an adult, she relies on the same system of security she used as a child. She must always be first—on top with everyone. If she is not, she becomes anxious, enraged, and depressed. In her attempts to achieve these ends she has extended the original sibling rivalry, first with the siblings, then with her playmates, to anything and everything. Thus, she makes of her husband a parental substitute and then engages in rivalry for his favor with her own children, her mother-in-law, his work, his friends and athletic events. Granted, her demands are disproportionate, but it is also true that her husband fails to fulfill them even to the minimum degree that would be considered normal. He admits as much in an interview with the therapist, although, in self-defense, he is careful to point out that she is well-nigh insatiable. Such is the core of their conflict. As she puts it: "The man I went with before my husband waited on me hand and foot, but not my husband!" Her reactions to this frustration are aptly described by the husband: "She is insatiably demanding of attention, a constant nag, and chronically irritable."

She has been equally unsuccessful in her struggles to receive recognition on a social level. Here, again, the infantile patterns are recapitulated. She must be the center of attraction in every social group. Social acceptance implies to her the original maternal acceptance. Unfortunately, C.E. is doomed to failure from the beginning, and with this failure, comes a thorough deflation of her self-esteem. The trouble lies in her values. These revolve around the class-status-prestige constellation. The attributes she considers valuable are those of white middle- and upper-class respectability: race, color, appearance, class, wealth, achievement. There is hardly a moment in her life that she is not concerned with one or more of these items. She stews in a constant state of competitive envy and hatred of everybody who possesses them in greater amount. Her struggle is hopeless for the simple reason she is a Negro. No matter how hard she strives, she must always fall short of being white. Yet, C.E. never stops trying.

She rejects totally her identification with Negroes. She cannot be white, so she compromises by associating only with light-skinned Negroes. The color black to her is anathema. In fact, her reaction is practically on a physiological level. She remarks with great distaste: "Ugh, black is dirty, bad, no-good, evil!" She then describes the actual nausea that seizes her when, at a social gathering, a dark man asks her to dance. She is revolted by such close physical contact. She describes her reactions to the bulk of the Negro population in the most prejudicial stereotypes: "I was waiting for a bus at 120th Street and 7th Avenue today. The people are all so loud and unclean. Two men tried to pick me up. They made a lot of loud wisecracks. It made me mad and disgusted. Why do people have to be like this? All those people (the whites) come by in cars and see them. You can imagine what they are saying. Then the bus came. It was full of Negroes going to the ball game. They had their whiskey bottles and their lunches. There was a lot of swearing and pushing. They don't bathe and they smell bad. I try to be calm about it but I get awfully discontented. I say to myself, 'Why must I be a Negro?' Sometimes I feel it is all useless. I might as well give up. The people on 7th Avenue and on Lennox Avenue will never learn." This is a favorite topic with her. Throughout the interviews she delivers many similar harangues. Always the Negroes are ill-clad, dirty, loud, boisterous, coarse, ill-mannered, odoriferous, drunk, stupid, etc.

Both of C.E.'s children are dark brown in color. Their births were a terrific shock to her. The first time, C.E. was sure she had been given the wrong baby. She shared a room with another mother darker than she. Perhaps there had been a mixup and the baby really belonged to her roommate. She was very disturbed and demanded an investigation. This was done and the child proved to be her's. She had no choice but to accept it. The baby was quite black and C.E. was horror-stricken. She was beside herself with shame. To make matters worse, when the baby's hair began to grow, it came out crinkly. C.E. protests: "That was the final straw! How could I ever be proud of hair like that?" To her, the child represented a piece of everything that she hated in herself. Whoever saw the child, in reality saw her. Small wonder that she rejected the child completely, and then projected upon him the full force of her own self-hatred. For a time, she could not bring herself to appear in public with the baby. Gradually, she began to go out, but kept the carriage covered so that the baby was hidden. She gave the baby daily baths in water containing hydrogen peroxide in an effort to lighten his skin, but this proved to no avail. Finally, in desperation, she tried Clorox, but this, too, failed to bleach the child. After two months she stopped trying, and as best she could became resigned. Two years later, it happened again. She gave birth to another dark-skinned, wooly-haired boy. After this she gave up and against the pleas of her husband, who wanted a girl, refused to have any more children.

She cannot, of course, come out directly and accuse the children of having dark skins. Instead, she displaces her fury to minor items for which she never stops berating them. She is engaged in a ceaseless effort to remake them in terms of the perfectionist white image she desires for herself. However, nothing the poor children do ever satisfies her. In them, she sees constantly all of the dreaded anti-Negro stereotypes. Thus, for example, she comes to the interview one day, enraged because the boys and their playmates are going through a "giggling period." She complains bitterly: "I'm supersensitive about things like that. I don't want them to do anything wrong. I want them to be perfect. They step on other people's toes, and probably mine, too. It's like in the subway when I see Negro school children. I want to tell them to sit down and behave. I compare Negroes with whites. The Negroes are noisier. They're on the spot and should watch their behavior. It affects me especially when they are in the midst of it. If I see a group making noise I think, 'Thank God, they are not in it!' The oldest one is a comedian, too! It annoys me. Why in hell should he be a comedian and keep people laughing? That's what the white people think about the Negroes. They think they're all clowns, that their purpose is to make other people laugh. His father is the same way. I told him to sit and read. I had to toe the line when I was a child. We did what mother wanted. I have to make compensations because they are dark. It's a handicap for them. If everything else were balanced it would be okay, but this way, I don't want them to do anything that would call attention to them. I want them to be perfect gentlemen. They giggled for two hours. They made faces. Ugh! The other kids go to operas and read." In a similar vein, she unleashes a steady stream of criticism against the children: they don't read well, they can't eat properly, they are too loud, they are ill-bred, etc. Indirectly, in her efforts to mold the children, she makes them aware of their dark color. Thus, even though the children, themselves, are dark, she will not allow them to play with other dark children. They must play only with the light ones. We can well imagine the demoralizing effect this must have on the boys' self-esteem.

It is not enough that she rejects the sons for reasons of color. As we have seen, she is also in rivalry with them for her husband's attention and affection. This intensifies even more her antagonism toward the children. She remarks one day, "It annoys me when my husband wrestles with them on the bed when he comes in." First she rationalizes, "The noise annoys me. People hear them in the hall. I don't want the place to be noisy." Then, finally, she comes out with the true reason: "I get annoyed at the attention they're getting. I feel they come between us."

As we would expect, even though she places her husband in a maternal role, at the same time she also makes of him a sibling and cannot help but be in rivalry with him, too. She must invariably show him up as her inferior. Thus, for instance, every time he is involved in an argument during a social evening, she always takes the side of his antagonists, regardless of whether she agrees with them or not. She has noticed that he habitually asks for a cigarette before telling a story or a joke. She never fails to comment later that this is evidence of his insecurity. He, of course, denies it, and she then proceeds to belabor the point. She vies with him for attention in every social group. She complains angrily: "His loud voice always gets the floor and it keeps me from contributing. I have lots of good comments to make, but I never get to make them." She adds contritely: "It's the same old thing. I always have to be queen. I have to be perfect. It comes from my childhood. I have grown up with this feeling and I still do it. I got angry with myself for feeling that way, but I still feel it." Sometimes her competition with her husband borders on the ridiculous: "Once I got a rash of the groin. It drove me crazy. I thought I didn't want to have anything to do with my husband like that. I thought it would matter to him. I went to a specialist on Park Avenue. He told me to get resigned to it. I was almost ready to commit suicide. I was afraid any time we had intercourse he would know. It finally went away. I think I know why I was so sensitive about it. I have always been a person everybody thought was perfect—pretty, nice figure—any detraction worries me. I can't have anything to mar me. I must be unblemished. After all, *he* (the husband) is unblemished! It makes me angry! Why should he be perfect? Why should his body be without blemishes and not mine? I've gotten some satisfaction because he is losing his hair. Mine is getting thicker. It all comes from my mother, my home. I was brought up to feel I was a perfect person—perfect in looks, personality, intelligence. Society was proud of me. I'll show you the clippings. I felt the rash was a punishment being put on me—to take a feather out of my cap. I can't be everything mother wanted me to be. All of us had things that didn't please her. I had acne. My oldest sister's hair was bad, both my brothers liked to fish. They got so sunburned, they were too dark. She didn't like that. Last summer, when my sons returned from camp, they were just black. I didn't like it, but for once I let them out to play. There have been summers when I wouldn't. That's why I won't go swimming. I'm in competition with my husband's color. I don't want him to get more fair than I."

One day she was asked to come to an early morning interview. She came on time, but remarked, "It broke my heart to leave early today. I hadn't cleaned the place up enough. I must have everything straight. If anything should happen to me, if I got killed or something and people went to my apartment, at least they would find things in order. I feel it's expected of me. I was brought up in that pattern. I can't afford to let down. My in-laws can't come if there's a speck of dust." The interviewer wondered how she ever had any fun. "I don't! That's what bothers me. I want to do otherwise but I just can't. If I do these things, I don't have any fun. If I don't do them, it worries me so much, I don't have any fun that way, either. My husband isn't bothered by these things, though. He goes around with his coat wrinkled, his shoes not shined. Oh, it irritates me! But it doesn't bother him. I'm going on my vacation in July. I don't look forward to my trip. I won't have any fun. I won't go in the water. I don't want to get sunburned—I'll get darker. I don't swim well, either. When I went to the beach as a girl, the main object was to impress the fellows. I was always among the first five. I guess that has carried over, too. I want to be admired. My husband can go around in an old moth-eaten pair of trunks. It doesn't seem to bother him. And he doesn't care if he gets darker. He has the most fun, but I've worked too hard to get my color. I got lighter as I grew older. I don't want to lose it now. I found out the lighter you are the better off you are. I'd rather not go into white restaurants—I fear I might get kicked in the pants. I'm timid about going into good stores to buy clothes. They might turn their nose up at me. I can't even go into a grocery store unless I'm completely dressed and made up. It's ridiculous! Whoever heard of making up to go to the corner grocery? But I can't do it otherwise."

She is not very interested in sex. It is important to her only as a vicarious device that gratifies her needs for affection and attention: "Sex is not too big a problem. The other (attention and affection) is much more important. I don't seem to have any need for intercourse at all. I feel I can get along with it, or I can get along without it. It's enough for me to lie next to my husband and have his arm around me. For the other, I don't want to be bothered." She is hazy about orgasm. She is "not quite sure" whether she has had any or not. It is a safe bet that a woman who has such doubts on the score has not.

This subject got off to a bad start, not because she suffered too many frustrations and deprivations, but because her childish omnipotence was overstimulated. She has lived the rest of her life in the expectation that every life situation should continue to reflect her grandiose image of herself as it did in childhood. There was, however, one serious obstacle to this continued grandiosity, and that is that she was Negro. This put her in the unfortunate position of "almost" having everything. This element of "not quite" spoiled her life and made her take on defenses and compensations of children who are very deprived. The actual picture that emerges is therefore the negative of the original exaggerated self-love. It is now self-hatred, with the proviso: I could love myself if—. Against this she is constantly trying to protect herself by seeking repeated reassurance from somewhere in the outside world that the self-hatred is not justified because other people do love her. Another way in which she tries to dilute the effect of this self-hatred is to project it on to others: I am not the one who is hateful, but you—because you are blacker, louder, more ill-mannered, etc. This projection, however, ricochets back upon her in the form of guilt. This guilt surely does not exist on a conscious level. It is most likely a feed-back from the hatred she has to other Negroes on whose shoulders she wishes to stand in order to elevate herself. It is, in other words, a retaliatory fear that is always felt by those who hate the ones they seek to degrade, but whose love they still want. She cannot legitimately expect the love of those whom she despises. This is also the formula for her relation to herself, for it is in the absence of self-love that we find the secret of her maladaptation. This is the motive that sets off all her frantic efforts at compensation and restriction, all of which miscarry. She is left a thoroughly miserable and unhappy creature, frustrated at every turn. The prime mover in her destruction is the fact that she is a Negro. This makes all her compensatory maneuvers futile. The total personality collapses under the weight of a monstrous superstructure—the struggle for status.

CHAPTER SEVEN

The Adolescent

I. MALE

H.V.

H.V. is a paid subject. He is a medium brown, 15-year-old high school student. He was born and raised in Harlem. The father is a Southern-born porter with a grammar school education. His main role is that of the breadwinner; otherwise, he enters little into the daily life of the household. The mother, also Southern-born, does not work, but devotes full-time to her duties as a wife and mother. She is a high school graduate. H.V. says about her: "My father is the head of the house, but my mother really runs it. She's not stern, but she seems to hold us all in check." There are three brothers, two older and one younger. The four boys appear to get along with no more than ordinary difficulty.

The family occupies an apartment in the central section of Harlem. The father has always had steady work and their economic status has been relatively comfortable. The home atmosphere is peaceful and quiet, broken only by occasional arguments between the brothers. The parents get along smoothly and very seldom argue. A good deal of interest and affection is shown the children, more by the mother than the father. Standards are high and stress the simple virtues of courtesy, avoidance of bad language, honesty, and cleanliness. Discipline is not too tight and is maintained by the mother, usually without the aid of corporal punishment: "When we was small we could get whipped with a strap by my mother mostly, but now she sort of tells us. We more or less know by now what to do ourselves. She don't have to tell us." Little attention is paid to religion and the boys do not attend church. Sex is rarely mentioned in the household.

H.V.'s world consists primarily of school and activities "on the block." It is a world of relative violence. The boys in the neighborhood are divided into two opposing factions: good and evil. H.V., his brothers, and their friends, are always on the side of law and order. They are the "good guys" as opposed to the lawless gangs and hoodlums who are the "bad guys." The former are under constant threat of attack from the latter and must maintain ceaseless vigilance in order to defend themselves. As much as possible they try to avoid trouble, but if confronted with it they are not hesitant in fighting back. Sometimes, to choke off an expected assault, they will even take the offensive. Thus, the necessity of maintaining a common front unifies the in-group. Their solidarity is further enhanced through their organization into a club, the functions of which are social, recreational, and athletic. Nevertheless, in all these areas, each is markedly concerned with his own status and engages in individual competition with the other. This competition can be quite intense, especially in matters of athletic prowess, which occupy the greater part of their free time. School is relegated to a minor role and, for the most part, is simply another backdrop for the external conflict in the streets and the internal rivalry within the group.

In the light of such daily activities it is not hard to understand H.V.'s major preoccupation. It is with self-assertion in all its forms, positive and negative. The interviews follow a constant pattern with monotonous regularity. Each consists of a series of vignettes that deal with the following topics, singly or in various combinations, involving either H.V. or one of the boys in the neighborhood: dominance—submission, success—failure, violence, fighting, competition, discrimination, prejudice, being cheated, being taken advantage of, being deprecated, etc. He is not, however, easily intimidated. His handling of aggression is quite uninhibited and he rises readily to a challenge. These occur almost daily: "Yesterday, in school, we had a fire drill and a guy kept pushing me and telling me I had to get in line. I said he didn't have to push me, so he said, 'You think you're bad?' So I said, 'Yeh.' So then he told me to meet him outside at 3:00 o'clock. So I said, 'All right.' So at 3:00 o'clock there he was—with all his gang. He said did I want to fight him? I said, 'No, not with all your gang,' because I seen him fight before and when he started losing, all his gang jumped on the other boy and beat him up. So when I wouldn't fight him, all his boys jumped on me and started to beat me up, so I had to run home that afternoon. The next day I saw him in school and all his gang weren't there, so I caught him and I beat him up."

He explains the source of the animosity between his group and the gang up the block: "There's a guy around our block, they call him 'Tip.' This guy, Tip, he doesn't like us guys. I told you about these two groups around our block. Well, he's with the other group. So every time he sees us, he goes out of his way to make trouble, like we had our movies and instead of coming in and watching the picture, he'd sit around and make a lot of noise and cause a big disturbance. The other day we were playing ball and he comes in and stands right in the middle of the court talking to his sister across the street, and different other things like that. So the other day one of the fellows asked him why he didn't like us, what he had against us, so he told him that he didn't like us because he'd been to jail and every time he goes around the block, people point at him and say 'Look at that boy. He's been to jail. He's a hoodlum,' and different stuff like that. Whereas, in our group that hangs out together nobody's been to jail and we keeps to ourselves mostly. He seems to resent the fact that nobody in our group has been to jail, so he's just against us. And another reason, I asked him the same thing one time and he told me the first day he got out of jail, some of the other fellows saw us going down the block and they pointed to us and said, 'See those guys? They think they're the upper crust. They think they're better than us.' That's what they call us. They call us the upper crust."

Throughout the interviews, H.V. related many stories of gang activities, all in a violent vein. The following is a typical example: "There is this guy Nate who lives around our block. He used to be a nice guy, one of the regular fellows. We used to have a lot of fun. Then about a year later he got in this club around our block and they had these gang wars and things like that. So after a while he started to change. He used to do real simple things like he'd go to the park and catch pigeons and then he'd take them home and take a hunting knife and cut off their heads. He became a regular bully around the block. After a while guys began to call him 'Butcher' because he used to kill these pigeons. After a while he became the leader of this club. Last summer, one night him and the rest of the gang were in this candy store right across the street from my house. A bunch of guys came down from a rival club and so they saw these guys in the candy store. They had guns and they started shooting at these guys in the candy store. So right away these guys came out of the store and started running down the block. Butcher grabbed a cardboard box out of the store and he rushed at these guys. I guess he thought he was going to scare them. They blew his brains out—killed him. Then some of his gang were taking up collections for his funeral. One of the guys taking up the collection, he made off with their money. That's about all for that."

H.V. attributes to maternal influence his refusal to participate in gang activities: "So far as I'm concerned, for me that's definitely out. I know this guy, Wilson, and he belongs to a gang, and one day they were going to fight another gang, and I asked him why he was going to fight, and he said, 'I don't know. They just told me we was going to fight.' I can't see that at all—this fighting and shooting. My mother kept a pretty close watch on us and she wouldn't let us hang out with those guys."

His dreams are mostly reflections of his waking thoughts. Every dream he reported during the study was concerned with some aspect of self-assertion. Two examples will suffice:

Me, my cousin, and one of my friends went to a show and my cousin took off his shoes in the show and he put his feet on my friend's lap. My friend got mad and pushed them off.

The dream was prompted by an encounter with his older cousin, who the day before had pre-emptorily ordered H.V. to take his suit to the presser. H.V. was doing his homework and was reluctant to go, but nevertheless, out of respect for his cousin's age and authority, he went. He comments, "It seems to me he always expects everybody to drop whatever they're doing and look after him." Thus, the dream means: My cousin steps all over others.

A minor irritation with his brother produced the next dream:

My biggest brother and me, we was walking down the street. He said something to me. I don't know what it was, but I remember I slapped him in the face. Then I said, 'Get wise to yourself.'

One day the interviewer pointed out to H.V. that the only topics he discussed were those concerned with rivalry, fighting, violence, etc. This comment produced the following response: "I guess it's just the sort of thing that goes on all the time. I'm a Negro. For me, life is a fight. I know that trying to get a decent job and pretty good pay, that will be pretty hard for me to do. I see all these guys around my block having a tough time getting a job. And when they do get one it's not a very good job, and I know it will be just the same when I get out of high school. Right now, at this present stage, around my block, the only way that you can get respect from these other fellows is just show them you are tougher than they are—and usually you have to fight to do that. I guess that's it."

H.V.'s aspirations are quite clear as to the ends, but the means are rather nebulous. This is the universal problem of Negro youth: (Ambitions?) "Well . . . uh . . . I don't know. I've given it a lot of thought, but everything that's mentioned doesn't appeal to me at all. The only thing that really appeals to me is athletics, but not as a career." (What do you want to go into?) "I don't know. Everything that's been mentioned to me doesn't appeal to me. Everybody in the family, sometime or another, keeps asking me what I want to be. I don't know. The only thing I really want to do is open a business, but I'm undecided about that, too. I don't know what kind of business I would open up or where I would get the money to open it. I definitely don't want to be a doctor or a lawyer or anything like that. It takes too many years to study and usually you have to have a considerable amount of money to set yourself up in practice. I'd like to get some kind of unusual business—not just a grocery store or butcher shop or bakery—practically every street has that—but something unusual you could make money at." (Life goals? What do you want?) "Me? I want money. If I got it, what I want to do is get a home, a car, and put some money away in the bank, and have a steady income coming in from the business." (Anything else?) "Well . . . If I can't have a business I feel I should have a job making at least . . . (laughs) . . . $150 a week." (What kind of a job do you propose would pay you that much?) (Laughs) . . . "That's the whole thing. I don't know."

His sexual experiences are still to come. Other than some infrequent necking and even less frequent petting he has had none. Moreover, at the present time, he professes he "really isn't interested." He denies masturbation and vaguely expresses the idea that it is the wrong thing to do. His behavior would appear to differ from that of most Harlem boys of the same age on his socioeconomic level. This is further evidence of the relatively greater stability of his familial background. One of the penalties of middle-class respectability is delayed sexual maturation and a varying degree of sexual inhibition.

H.V. is about as "normal" an individual as it is possible to be. He has effected a successful adaptation to his social situation. This adaptation, in its overemphasis on self-assertion, is markedly different from that usually found in the white. However, his preoccupation with assertion is not neurotic. It is entirely a projection of the social realities which confront him, and as such is the healthiest possible response, especially in a boy of fifteen, who for the first time is learning to stand on his own. In fact, it is precisely this hypertrophy of his aggressive drives which lends stability to the total adaptation. It is his major device for maintaining confidence and self-esteem. In addition, it is subject to voluntary control and is appropriately activated, which further attests to its normalcy. Otherwise, as we have already seen in too many cases, the individual is overwhelmed by the hostile world in which he is forced to live.

Effective patterns of aggression and a relatively high self-esteem are not his only strong points. H.V. also possesses resourcefulness, good affectivity, the capacity for warm and meaningful interpersonal relationships, strong conscience mechanisms, and the power to idealize. In these respects, he is in decided contrast to the majority of the lower-class subjects in the series. These positive traits are directly traceable to the stability of the family unit which nurtured him. This fact neatly demonstrates the point at which social engineering must be applied.

S.A.

S.A. is a paid subject. He is a 15-year-old boy of dark brown complexion. He lives in a small apartment in Harlem with his mother and younger brother. Technically, he can be classified as a high school student, but this is mostly in name only as he has been in the same grade, 10-A, for two years because of truancy and failure to study.

S.A. was born and raised in Harlem. The father is a high school graduate, currently employed as a mechanic. His skin color is very light and when he wishes he is able to pass for white. The mother is literate, but has not had very much formal schooling. She has worked off and on as an operator on dresses. Her skin color is dark brown. The parents separated when S.A. was two years old and the mother never remarried. He has had little contact with his father and consequently does not know very much about him. The mother he describes as a pleasant person, who is friendly with everybody and rarely gets angry. He has one sibling, a brother aged fourteen, who like the father is so light-skinned that he can pass for white. S.A. is particularly proud that there is white blood in his background. He emphasizes that both his grandfathers are Irish—"pure white."

The family's economic status has always been marginal and at times they have been on relief. Still, S.A. does not feel he suffered too much. As he puts it, at least he never went hungry and he always had a roof over his head. The mother has tried hard to provide for the children's basic needs. In addition, she has always been warm and affectionate toward them. Discipline has never been strict and only rarely physical. Church attendance is required, but religion has not been unduly stressed. The mother has been unable to discuss sex, but she has encouraged the boys to seek information in books and from friends. They learned quickly and at a very early age.

S.A.'s first years in school passed without incident. In fact, he got exceptionally good grades and graduated from elementary school as an honor student. His behavior changed for the worse in junior high school. He began to play hookey and did very little studying. Nevertheless, he managed to scrape through and at the age of 13 entered the first grade of high school. Here, he stopped studying completely and stepped up his truancy. In consequence, he has failed all his subjects, and in two years has yet to be promoted. He, himself, is not clear as to the reasons for his behavior: "I just don't like it. It seems to bore me. It seems silly just going there and sitting. And most of the time it is so hot and they don't do anything about it and the teachers just talk, talk, and you never learn anything." Thus, he put in only an occasional appearance at the school. The rest of the time he loafs or "fools around" in one way or another. He goes to the movies or the pool halls, plays in the park, runs around with girls—or older women, stands on street corners and gossips, and so on. Of late, he has begun to think of giving up all pretense of going to school; instead, he will look for a job. This is the point in his life at which the interviews begin.

At the present time, then, S.A. is like a ship without a rudder. He is drifting aimlessly and is engaged in no constructive activity whatsoever. That is not to say he has no ambitions. He has, and he indicates what they are in his opening remarks during the first session of free association following the history: "One thing I've always wanted is a car. Why—I don't know. My mother wanted to get me a bike a few months ago, but I said, 'Don't bother,' because I don't seem to want one. I just don't like them now. Before, when I was in junior high school, I wanted one, but now I don't seem to care for it. I don't know why. I would like to get behind a car, though, and go riding. Another thing I want is a job, a nice job, doing something—anything to get out of the streets, even working nights so I could have a little change and get out of the streets. Now I just come home and sit down in the candy store at the corner and play the juke box and listen to the records. If I had a job I wouldn't do that because I don't like it, sitting in the candy store, but there isn't anything else for me to do now." The difference between wanting a bicycle and wanting a car is the difference between being a boy and being a man. Having a job likewise falls into an adult category. This is S.A.'s basic conflict. He aspires to full masculine prerogatives, but he lacks the means for their implementation.

S.A. would like to "get ahead and be somebody." He returns to this theme again and again during the interviews, but always with a sense of defeat: "There's a couple of Jewish boys at school. They're about the only boys I hang around with. I like them a lot. The rest of the boys ain't got nothing on their mind. They don't want to get ahead. They're always running around, always want to hook something. But these boys I go with, they want to attain a golden life. They want to be something, be somebody, attain a big name. I figure if I stay around with them I would feel the same way they do, but right now I can't seem to care much."

Every time he mentions the future it is with the same air of hopelessness: "At first I thought I'd be a doctor, but now I'm thinking of a trade. I gave up on being a doctor. Most likely it was because of my uncle. He started a whole lot of crap: 'Oh, you ain't going to be a doctor.' He started nagging and nagging and I got sick and tired of it. Then I thought if I could get a diploma I could get on the police force, but I been in high school so long and ain't done nothing, I don't think I could get on the police force. My family just keeps on nagging me and, you know, I can't stand that. They keep saying I'll never amount to nothing, that all I'll be is a bum, and all that. Well, when somebody keeps on telling me something like that over and over again, I get mad and do just the opposite. When they keep telling me I got to go to school or I won't amount to nothing, I just get mad and I won't go. I want to get a job. I'm fed up with school. These schools around here just make me sick. Why it is I don't know. You go to school and the teachers nag you. Then you come home and your parents nag you. Right now I wouldn't mind getting back in school if I knew I had a chance to get promoted, but I know I'll never get promoted. I didn't take my mid-terms. But even if I did take them I don't believe I could pass."

He blames much of his failure on discrimination against Negroes: "I'd like to get out of high school and go to a trade school, but they say I have to pass one term at high school before I can do that. Me and another colored boy—when I was in junior high—took a test to get in the School of Science. We was the only colored boys. There was four other boys who were white. Well, two of the white boys passed and they told the rest of us we failed. My junior high school teacher told me there were only two colored boys and one colored girl in the school and she thought we had passed but they discriminated up there and don't want colored students. That's why I went to my high school and there I started messing up. I saw all these boys going down town to the show and all that so I started, too. Then they flunked me and it got more and more boring so pretty soon I gave up. The first term I was there I worked pretty good. I admit I was absent several days, but I don't understand why I flunked. After they flunked me, I thought, 'What the hell?' And after that I started being absent more and more. I believe I'd passed if I'd gone through from the beginning, but after I worked and failed, I couldn't understand it, so I just quit working, especially after I saw boys who didn't do nothing and they passed."

One can't help but wonder how many Negroes in our society react in this way: "What the hell?" It is quite true that when S.A. evokes discrimination as the reason for his failure he is, at least to some extent, rationalizing. On the other hand, neither can this explanation be minimized. Immobilization of the kind he displays can result only from one or both of two factors: lack of innate resources or reality obstacles. There is no gainsaying the fact that the Negro's aspirations are realistically far more blocked than the white's. The inhibiting effects of these obstacles cannot be lightly dismissed. This means that among the Negroes, irrespective of resources, casualties such as S.A. will be proportionately much more numerous.

His inability to achieve his goals is symbolized in the following dream:

I was just walking and walking. Seems I was just walking on this long street. I could see a light down on the corner and I kept walking toward it, but I never seemed to reach it. Seems like I was on a treadmill. I felt kind of scared because I was walking toward this light and I couldn't reach it. Then sometimes I would think somebody was behind me and I'd turn around and nobody was there. It was like an alley with high brick walls on either side, and I just kept walking and walking.

His associations run to his frustrated ambitions: "All I want to do is get me a nice job and get to be somebody, but right now I'm not getting nowhere—I'm not doing nothing. I want to be somebody. You know, someone achieves something great and wants to be known and I want to do the same thing. You know, like I was a scientist or something—find out different things. Say I'm working in this big factory and I find a way for them to produce at a cheaper rate. They'd say, 'We have a smart worker here,' and they'd look up to me. I want people to look up to me. It's not the money. When I was small my family used to say how nice it would be if we had a doctor or a lawyer in the family. So I said I would be a doctor, but by the time I got to junior high school I saw that there were a lot of doctors in New York and by the time I got through there would be too many, so I gave that up. Then I used to think of how I would get into a profession and, you know, people would say how smart I am and I'd get to be known. Then, my parents told me if I achieved something great I'd be a big help to my race, but I ain't never paid much attention to that."

It is not enough that he considers himself a failure, but his self-esteem is further deflated by his race and his color. He repeatedly denies to the interviewer that these constitute a problem for him. He insists, "That stuff has never bothered me." His productions and his behavior during the interviews, however, belie him. The superiority he attributes to whites is clearly seen in the following exchange: (Who are your heroes?) "Einstein, Darwin . . . let me see . . . Shakespeare— He got known for his great plays . . . Louis Pasteur . . . Alfred Roentgen . . . Those are the people. They each did something and made themselves well known. Then there's one Negro. He became Emperor of Haiti." (Emperor Christophe?) "I don't know his name. He was a Negro and he made himself world-known and it improved his race. I figure if it wasn't for some of those Negroes who did what they did, the Negro race wouldn't have what they have now." (What Negroes?) "Like Booker T. Washington and George Washington Carver. They came up when the Negro race was considered no good. They proved the Negro was just as good as any race even though his skin was a different color." (What Negroes today would you want to be like?) "Oh . . . I forget their names . . . (pause) . . . let me see now . . . (pause) . . . I know several but I can't think of their names." He pauses again and becomes embarrassed. (Who are the big Negro names today?) "I know of a lot of them, but I can't think of their names . . . (pause) . . . Let's see . . . (pause) . . . Joe de Mag— . . . No, I mean Jackie Robinson, Joe Louis, Satchel Paige . . . This is in sports." (How do you account for your trouble in thinking of Negro names? You didn't have any trouble thinking of white names.) "I don't know. They just seemed to skip my mind. There's one Negro who's a cult leader—George Baker." (Who's he?) "Father Divine, but I call him George Baker. If I had my way I'd put him where he belongs—in hell! Going around calling himself God! And many a simple fool believes him. He's broken everything the Bible teaches. I'd like to beat his brains out, this George Baker!" The blocking on the Negro names and the subsequent derogation of a Negro figure are telltale signs that S.A.'s loyalties are with the whites.

The unconscious rejection of Negro-identification becomes even clearer through his attitudes toward color. He castigates his brother for deriding the whites: "My brother hangs around with these colored boys who have light skins. They go around the white kids and call them names and yell at their mothers, 'You white so and so's!' They curse them out and all that. If I find my brother doing that, I kill him. That's why the kids don't like me around there because they say I'm colored and they see no reason I should take up with the whites. You know, these light Negroes think they're better than the rest of us who are dark—I mean brown-skinned—because they get better opportunities and all that. Well, if they think they are better than the rest of us Negroes because they're light, then why do they go yell at the whites who they think they're like? It would be all right if they yelled at other Negroes, but it don't make no sense to me he yells at whites. He has white blood in him, himself, so it just don't make no sense, his yelling and making fun of white people. If my father had heard him do that he would break his neck He would kill him in a minute! And he has white blood in him! He's Irish!" The last two remarks, of course, are the crux of the whole matter. In his unconscious mind, S.A. would prefer to believe that he were really white.

S.A.'s reaction to his sense of failure is to take refuge in apathy, rebellion against authority, pleasure pursuits, and crime. Some of this behavior has already been described. Perhaps his most important pleasurable activity is sex. For a 15-year-old boy—in our culture—he gets around quite a bit. He has been having regular and frequent intercourse since the age of nine. Hardly a week passes that he doesn't have intercourse several times and usually with more than one girl. Masturbation is rare, for the simple reason that intercourse is too readily attainable. He has never had any potency trouble. He prefers older girls who are past the age of consent. He explains that it is difficult to register in a hotel as "Mr. and Mrs." with a schoolgirl and besides he can always place responsibility on an older girl: "That's why I lay these girls older than me. If anything goes wrong, I can get out of it. You know, if she gets a baby, I can get out of it . . . (laughs) . . . I'm younger than her . . . (laughs) . . . I'm too young. I don't know what I'm doing. If she forces it on me, what the hell can I do?" From his stories, his services are apparently in great demand by many of the women in his neighborhood. He is not, however, without discrimination. Out of deference to his mother, he tries not to have intercourse with "nice" girls—although he slips more than just occasionally—and neither will he go to bed with a girl in his house during the time that his mother is at home, but only when the mother is out: "Some boys will take girls to their homes and lay 'em there whether their mother is working or not. Not me. I could never do that if my mother was home. It would be funny. It would lose respect for the house, and you'd have to worry your mother might come." S.A. spent many sessions regaling the interviewer with animated tales of his many carousings.

S.A. used to belong to a gang, but it disbanded after one of the boys was killed in a fight. He has not yet joined another. Instead, he has been thinking more and more of "solitary" crime. For some time he has toyed with the idea of "running numbers," i.e., acting as a courier for the numbers racket: "I'm getting very nervous just loafing around the house. I can't stand to be still. I could have had a night job—running numbers—made a lot of money, too, but I got scared. Then my mother said if I got caught and put in jail she wouldn't come and see me." One day he announced to the interviewer he had accepted a commission to deliver some narcotics. The interviewer remonstrated with him but to no avail. He insisted he was too smart to get caught, and besides it was far too easy a way to make money. He went ahead with the delivery as per schedule.

We must not be fooled by the perpetual activity of this boy's life, with its opportunities for free sexuality and lots of adventure. Rather, we must note the utter emptiness. The single recorded dream is one of complete lostness, a complete lack of direction and goal. He is bewildered and disoriented. It is in the light of this inner desolation that we must evaluate his activities. He does lip-service to his mother; and one cannot say that it is devoid of feeling. But his tie to his mother can by no means overcome his sense of isolation, nor can it influence him from entering on his many delinquent activities. He is too numb, too bored; he cannot take too seriously the formal efforts into which society forces him—like going to school—none of which has any real bearing on his prospects in life. How seriously can a boy, who has his pick of women up to twice his age, take a "D" mark in deportment, or be much troubled about a truant officer's opinion of him?

The insight this boy has about his position in the world is quite remarkable. He acts as though he had made a complete appraisal of his chances in life, written them off as not for him, and then abandoned himself to a pure hedonism and opportunism. The sham world in which he lives, in the candy store gangs with their rivalries and battles, is his vicarious way of beating the real world to which he has no access. His difficulty in recalling the names of Negro heroes reveals just how little he thinks of his own chances as a Negro. The ready accessability of white heroes indicates the incorporation of the white man as ideal. In other words, the discrepancy that exists between his ideal and his real self comprises a wide gap which is filled alternately by depression (boredom, apathy, emptiness) and abandon.

II. FEMALE

B.Y.

This subject is a 16-year-old, high school girl who was referred for psychotherapy because of somnambulism. She has Caucasian features, light olive skin, and fairly straight brown hair. She could easily pass for Spanish or Italian, as well as Negro. She lives with her mother, father, and older brother in an interracial housing project. She and her brother share a bedroom but sleep in separate beds. Since the age of seven she has suffered from somnambulism, which during the past five years has occurred with increasing severity and frequency. Currently, she walks in her sleep on the average of once or twice a week. During these episodes she appears terribly frightened, screams loudly, and runs crazily around the apartment as though she is trying to escape some danger. Sometimes, she becomes violent and strikes out blindly. The mother comments that she behaves as though a gorilla were after her. This is in marked contrast to her behavior during the day. Ordinarily, she is a calm, quiet, soft-spoken girl.

B.Y. was born and raised in the Bronx. Her mother is a light brown, Northern-born housewife, who occasionally works part-time as a domestic or as a factory worker. She has had something less than a full high school education. She has always given the children a great deal of interest, attention, and affection, but simultaneously has insisted on obedience to her standards and demands. The father was a medium brown, Southern-born grammar school graduate, who was employed as a laborer. He died when B.Y. was seven and she does not remember too much about him. She does recall, however, that he was a kindly person who was always nice to her. The mother remarried when B.Y. was twelve. The step-father is a medium brown, Southern-born, grammar school graduate who works for the Department of Sanitation. He seems to have taken over the parental role without any difficulty and the subject feels he is everything her own father would have been had he lived.

The family has always lived in an interracial environment. Their economic status has been fairly comfortable except during the interval between the father's death and the mother's remarriage, at which time they were on relief. The home atmosphere has always been placid and relatively free from friction. The parents rarely fought or argued and B.Y. feels they were very much in love. The same is equally true of the relationship between the mother and the step-father. The mother is the disciplinarian and as stated, she is quite strict. She punishes the children either by denying them pleasures or by hitting them. B.Y. is quite fearful of her wrath and hence is usually well-behaved. Thus, for example, she explains why she is so good at school: "I never get in bad with the teachers. I'm afraid they'll give me bad marks and send home for my mother and all that. I don't like to make my mother mad. I'll only suffer for it. I have everything to gain by behaving, and everything to lose if I don't. Doris (a friend) smacks her mother back. Oh, that's one thing my brother and I would never do—and if we run, we get it double." The family religion is Baptist but neither of the parents or step-father has put much emphasis on it. The mother's attitude toward sex has been a mixed one. On the one hand, she has always answered B.Y.'s questions and given her information about intercourse, menstruation, and birth; on the other hand, she has indoctrinated B.Y. with Victorian morality, and what is worse, thoroughly frightened her by repeated warnings of possible attack and rape. An interview with the mother reveals that these began when the subject was six. At that time, the mother did not trust the superintendent of the building in which they were living and daily cautioned her daughter against going into the basement alone for fear she would be molested. Her advice was couched in such dire terms that for a brief period B.Y. became phobic and on occasion, if she were out of the house alone, she would suddenly become fearful and run to her mother in a panic. Shortly after, she began to walk in her sleep. As the child grew older, the mother expanded the area of danger to include the entire neighborhood, and to this day never fails to remind B.Y. that she must be careful when walking alone, especially after dark, or she may be raped.

It is this fear that is responsible for the somnambulism. B.Y. is engaged in a constant struggle with sexual impulses that she dare not even recognize, much less allow herself to gratify. During the day, while awake, she does a thorough job of repressing all sexual feeling. She consistently denies to the interviewer that she has any. If evidence from her own productions is presented to the contrary, it makes no impression upon her. Instead, she maintains the characteristic *belle indifference* of the hysterical patient. She is not so successful at night. During sleep, the repressive forces are weakened and the forbidden impulses are released. Unfortunately, conditioned by her mother, she conceives of sex only as violence. That is why instead of stimulating pleasure the wish for sexual gratification arouses images of a violent attack upon her. This is the symbolic meaning of her somnambulistic behavior. The unacceptable sexual wishes are represented in their negative as a fear of rape and she hysterically acts out her panic in the attempt to escape.

This psychodynamic reconstruction was validated several times during the course of therapy. The parents were instructed to report the subject's behavior and remarks while sleepwalking. B.Y. would then associate to the material so furnished exactly as she would to a dream. One example will demonstrate how this procedure bore fruit: "Father said I was up last night calling 'Henny!', and 'Let me go, Henry, let me go!' " (Who is Henny or Henry?) "Alice used to tell me about a girl named Henny. And the boy who is leader of that gang in our neighborhood—the Scorpions—is called Henry." (Henny?) "Alice told me she was put in a home a year ago. She had a baby." (Henry?) "Oh, I never bother with him. I avoid him as much as possible. He's no good. He's been in and out of jail five times. He was in jail for rape. He just got out a few months ago. If he speaks to me I walk on. I never saw this girl Henny, but Alice told me how she used to go out with all the boys. Sometimes she would go with a whole gang of fellows and have relations with them. My mother always tells me to be careful when I come home in the evening. The Scorpions hang out around the block. And there are a couple of other gangs. They all go around shooting and stealing and raping girls. A few boys have tried to get fresh with me but I don't let them."

B.Y.'s sleeping arrangements do not help the situation any. Her brother's presence in the room at night stimulates her sexually and serves to enhance both the wish and the fear. She denies any sex play between them but she has on occasion feigned sleep so that she could observe him as he undressed and walked about in the nude. A dream illustrates her fear of sexual attack by her brother. The underlying wish for a sexual overture is implicit:

I dreamt the cops came to my house and took my brother to jail and were holding him on a rape charge.

She associates: "I thought it was a terrible thing to do. Lots of times I hear my mother talking to my brother. She reads in the paper of things like that. She tells my brother often never to do such a thing. Maybe I dreamt it because I read so much of that in the paper. I come home at night and I think of those things sometimes. My mother is always telling me when I come home alone at night to be extra careful and look behind me. One day this last week I was reading in the paper how they caught this fellow that raped that 80-year-old woman."

B.Y.'s neurotic conflict is sharply localized within the framework of her personality and during the daytime she adapts very well around it. It does not appear seriously to interfere with her daily activities. For the most part, her interviews sound like those of any other adolescent girl. She chatters endlessly about such things as school, play, parties, dates, friends, etc. She seems to be well-integrated socially. She has many friends and of both sexes. As is usual for a girl her age, her closest companions are girls, but she dates frequently, and on occasion even does some mild necking. She is forever engaging in group social activities—parties, dances, athletic events, hikes, picnics, etc. These—together with television, jazz, and comic books—are her main recreational interests. She appears to have no intellectual pursuits, whatsoever. She plays an active role in her group relationships and is quite capable of establishing strong emotional ties.

Her self-esteem seems fairly adequate. There are several reasons for this: First, she comes from a stable family background and has not lacked for parental love and protection. This has facilitated parental identification as well as the capacity for idealization. Second, her aspirations are really minimal and hence do not overload her capacity for achievement. She has no desire to go to college. After she finishes high school she wants to get "some factory job" in the garment industry and "around twenty" she wants to "get hitched." Beyond this—job and marriage—she insists she wants nothing at all. Third, so far, anti-Negro discrimination has not caused her much trouble. She has always lived in an interracial neighborhood and has attended interracial schools. In both places active measures have been taken to combat prejudice. The socioeconomic make-up of the neighborhood population is homogeneous—all are lower to lower-middle class. The same is true for her classmates. She attends a textile high school where all the students are in preparation for a trade and most have aspirations similar to hers. All of these factors combine to minimize the status conflict and help maintain the stability of her self-esteem. Fourth, her light skin color enables her to pass for white, if she so desires. This, in itself, is a status attribute, and in addition protects her from many of the manifestations of overt discrimination.

B.Y. nicely demonstrates the advantages of a family life and a social climate that, at least, begin to approximate that of the majority white culture. She has a neurosis, it is true, but she has successfully compartmentalized it so that it has not markedly hindered her adaptation in other than sexual areas. She is resourceful, reasonably assertive, has strong conscience mechanisms, an adequate self-esteem system, good affectivity—except where limited by neurotic defenses (*belle indifference*), and the capacity for close interpersonal relationships.

There is a strong temptation here not to see the forest because of the trees; that is, with such a prominent neurosis that occupies her entire façade, it is a little difficult to see that the neurosis, itself, is an indicator of strong attachment to the parents. The neurosis is the result of the successful internalization of parental discipline, a vigorous struggle of the sexual drive against internalized parental injunctions. However, the essential part of the picture is not in the neurosis, but in the underlying personality traits of which the neurosis is only one expression. This picture is a healthy one, the product of good parental care and a normal development of all the relevant personality functions, with but the single exception. Had her relations with her parents been poor, she would have had no base on which to rest her efforts to comply with parental demands. The latter, however, are of a restrictive character and lie mainly in one direction—not to be raped. These demands do not encourage this child into more expressive activity, like accomplishment. She is, in this regard, content just to get along and get what pleasures she can within the framework of parental approval.

R.H.

R.H. is a medium brown, 18-year-old, high school student. She is the only child of a broken home. She was born and raised in a large city of a border state. Her mother and father were divorced when she was a baby. All of her life she has been a pawn in court battles between them. They are both high school educated, white-collar workers, people of better than average means, but neither has particularly wanted to assume responsibility for her. Finally, the mother was forced to take over, but primarily by default. The father simply refused to have anything to do with it. R.H. has seen him only rarely to this day. She and her mother moved in with the maternal grandmother. The family unit consisted of only the three of them. They occupied a well-kept private home in the best Negro neighborhood.

The mother was an embittered, hard-working, ambitious woman, who never gave the child either attention or affection. In fact, she never forgave her existence. She considered it only a burden. R.H.'s description of her is concise and to the point: "Mother is a very cold person. It is like meeting an open door on a very cold day—cold, very cold." She was always aware that she was an unwanted child. She was told many times that her birth was an accident: "She didn't want me. It was just something that happened." The grandmother was somewhat more mellow than the mother, and from her R.H. did get a measure of affection. The mother, however, ran the house, and the grandmother, of necessity, fell into line. Discipline was very strict and enforced by whippings. The child was repeatedly derogated. The mother never stopped reminding her that she was "stupid." In truth, R.H. did have difficulty in developing the usual childhood skills, but this was the fault of her mother, who would not allow her to play with other children: "When you are younger, things are impressed on you. Everything somebody told me—like 'You're stupid'—I never forgot. I always carried it around with me. Then I could never keep up with the other kids. Mother wouldn't allow me to play with them—like riding a bicycle and skipping rope. She always said, 'You can't do that. You'll be hurt.'

So I began to feel I couldn't do it—things like that—that the average kid does so easily." The family attended church regularly. Sex was completely taboo and never discussed.

She stayed with her mother until she was fourteen. Then, on the pretext that proper schooling could not be obtained in the South, she was shipped to a white family in a small Northern city. Here, she did housework in return for her board and room. This enabled her to attend the local high school. There were few other Negroes and she felt herself completely isolated. She stuck it out for two years, but was so unhappy she finally threw it up and returned home. This time she was sent to New York to stay with friends of her mother, a Negro family in one of the better sections of Harlem. She has been with them for the past two years. The head of this family is an elderly, very religious woman, who is decidedly set in her ways. R.H. has developed a wishful attachment for her, so much so that she refers to her variously as "aunt" and "mother." This attempt at affection, however, is not really reciprocated by the older woman. She admitted as much to the therapist. She makes a pretense at warmth, but only because she considers the child "her Christian duty." In actuality, as far as she is concerned, it is a nuisance having the child and she would just as soon be rid of her as not. Three grown children of the foster parent make up the rest of the household. R.H. attends a private interracial school in which the students are predominantly white. She and another girl are the only Negroes. This, of course, has not helped her socialization any.

R.H. is a patient in psychotherapy. She comes to treatment at her own insistence. She has read recently of psychiatry and feels that her many problems can be resolved only in this way. She outlines her conflicts very clearly. Let us listen to her own description of what is wrong: "I have many problems. I'm nervous—like when I got up I knew I had to see you and I got awfully nervous. I told my 'aunt'—'mother'—about it. She is my aunt, mother and father, everything to me. I'm a great one for remembering things from the past and if anything drastic happens today I think of these things. For instance, I remember once when I was nine my mother was going out. This happened all the time. I wanted her to stay. She wouldn't and I cried. She spanked me and I cried. I've never forgotten that. Things like that. One day I was trying to see exactly how she felt toward me. I asked her, 'Would you approve of my going out with boys?' I was about seventeen. She was very abrupt, and said, 'No.' I know she would never have agreed to what I asked. I've never been able to go to her and discuss anything. These people I am staying with are just strangers, but I can go up to her and say, 'Hi, "mother"!' I can tease her and go and talk to her. She is more a real mother than my mother. Another problem is money. My mother has money. She is employed by the government and she owns a rooming house—but she won't give me things. She was always delinquent paying where I was concerned. Right now I have a few piano students and that is a very small way of caring for my needs. It gives me a small amount of money and perhaps a garment or two. But it's not enough. 'Aunt' makes up the rest, but it is really my mother's responsibility. My father and I are out. He has given me up and I receive no help from him at all. I have no feeling toward him. It's just as though he were a stranger. Then I'm having trouble with school. I would like some day to become a person of importance and the way things look now I'll never reach that goal. I want to be a teacher but I'm having an awful time with my subjects. I can't concentrate. I don't believe I'm lazy or indifferent, but I act that way. Another thing—my 'aunt' says this is important, but I don't see why it is—she says I don't seek companionship with fellows and it is not normal. Also, people think I am stuck up and a snob. I don't feel that is true. If people get to know me they will see I like them. Perhaps I've grown up alone so long I give that impression of being retiring and modest—an old person. Now the one thing I am trying to do is grow up and be somebody, so if I'm not a credit to my mother, I will be to people here. I've never been able to settle down. I've never been able to feel a part of the world. I just feel I am existing. I never feel that people accept me. They say, 'You're a snob.' I'm not. I like people and I am fond of animals, but I just feel something is missing somewhere—something I have failed to get and should have gotten. I'm never happy. Somehow, I feel upset all the time. Others have troubles, but they seem to get over them and enjoy themselves all the time. I never do. Even 'aunt' says I am very stubborn and unbearable and she can't talk to me. I do feel there is someone bigger than man himself, a Supreme Being, who will do something for you. This is something I have accomplished since I have been in New York. Someone is helping, someone I never realized. But sometimes I lapse into a state of ungratefulness and try to reject this person. I reject God himself. I get so full of my own troubles, I feel no one is helping me. That's why I have come here. I would like to get my mind freed. Right now I am very depressed. I feel I am not really living at all. If I talk to some person I will be able to see just what is going on in my mind. Right now I feel I am standing still. Life is going on around me and I am not a part of it. I feel very inferior. I don't want to be superior, but I would like to feel I can be as good and accomplish as much as anyone else . . . I think those are my major troubles. I have enough to last me a lifetime." She is right. She has.

Her account demonstrates many of the pernicious effects of rejection upon the growing child. Basic here are the unsatisfied cravings for attention and affection. Unfortunately, these are paradoxically coupled with an inability to relate emotionally to the very people who could be in a position to satisfy her. It is not only that distrust and resentment stand in her way, but she simply never learned how. Her induction into affectivity was too poor. This comprises her central conflict and throughout the interviews she returns to it again and again. Thus, she is in constant fear of abandonment and rejection: "I take things very seriously as far as living with the family. Sometimes I'm overanxious. You see, for a long time I never had anyone show me kindness and affection without feeling that if I said something, that person would hold it against me. I hope they don't get the idea I'm taking away the mother. Although these people are older, I wouldn't want them to think I'm just walking in and I'm taking over—especially O., because she is the daughter and the only one. Another thing, all of a sudden I will begin to feel very lonely at times. I know sometimes they will have to go away and I won't be included. Maybe it's a feeling of possessiveness. I feel if they go away I ought to go along. I'm always trying to figure out why I act that way because I realize when I look at it truthfully they don't belong to me. They have only befriended me. Yet, I have taken over. I imagine it's because I have never had anybody to love me before. I have a great many fears. Because I was alone so long I feel someday it will happen again, and when it does, I feel something drastic will happen. I don't know what—it's just a feeling."

She refers to this feeling many times. Essentially, it is an infantile fear of disaster—the fear of facing the world and its dangers alone:

"I love 'aunt' a great deal and I can talk to her and not feel it is going to be held against me, but in spite of all that, I have a feeling something just isn't complete. I don't know what it is—I'm never quite relaxed. I'm always tense, and here lately, even if somebody speaks to me, I know they're not going to harm me, yet I jump. I wish I could really feel I am happy. I think I am, but there is still a question in my mind: always, what's going to happen next? In one of the pictures in the ink-blot test I saw a figure standing on a high cliff. That's the way I feel. He was ready to fall any minute. I'm always afraid that nothing good will come, that I'll be forgotten, and all my hopes and dreams will be lost. I'm afraid that I will be left all alone. I feel trapped. I don't know where to start. I don't know how to go out into the world. Everybody else seems so much more competent. I guess I'm just a baby."

Her frustrated dependency needs are reflected in her dreams. The following are typical examples:

I was 10 years old, or young enough to wear short clothes. I was among all of these people. I was the only child around and everybody was ignoring me. I wandered all around and saw some funerals and finally I came to my grandmother. She was sitting on tiers like at a parade. I went to her, but there were a couple of steps before I could reach her. She put out her hand to me and we embraced. Then I had to leave.

She remarks: "Well, it's my mind at work continuing into the night from the way it is in the day. I ought to forget it, but at night I dream of things the way I would like them to be instead of the way they are. As you know, whenever I am in trouble, I dream of my grandmother because what little happiness I've had in life, I found it there."

She has frequent dreams of food. These are symbolic of her search for the good mother (breast). In the following, a transference dream, she assigns the maternal role to the interviewer (the clerk):

I was wandering around—just wandering—where I was going I don't know. I decided to eat, and I ate so much, and I continued to ask the clerk for more. I just continued to eat. But before he gave me any more food I woke up.

She never stops mulling over her inability to make friends. This is an endless preoccupation during the interviews. People invariably think her stuck-up or take her for a snob. In actuality, she is neither.

She is leading from weakness, not strength. She carries with her a deeply rooted conviction of unlovability. She has been conditioned to expect rejection, and hence is suspicious of any overture in her direction. This causes her to be either standoffish and shy, or belligerent and defiant. These are protective devices by means of which she wards off hurt. Unfortunately, however well they defend her, they are hardly conducive to a successful social integration. Rather, they can only enhance her isolation. Thus, although she has been in New York for two years, she has no friends other than the members of her foster family. She has several rationalizations for this failure, but the true reason is her own emotional deficiency.

One day the therapist suggested she try to be more active socially. That night she had a dream in protest:

I found myself going to two parties. One was given by 'aunt's' mother and another person was giving one—I don't know who. This other person told us to go to another party, not her's. So I went to it, and somehow I left, and went to 'aunt's' party. She said, 'Why didn't you stay? Why did you come back?' I said I wanted to say hello to her and talk to her. Leaving her party I saw a woman about my age. I spoke to her and we had quite a conversation. I thought we were leaving together, but somehow I found myself on a strange street with cobblestones. I crossed it. I didn't know where I was going. I walked. All of a sudden I got pushed into a crowd and couldn't get my bearings. I found myself on an escalator going down. People were in front and in back of me. When the escalator got to its landing it was in a hotel and all the people were busy with themselves and didn't pay any attention to me. I went to a newsstand and bought a fashion magazine on the cover of which it said, 'Music.' The people still didn't turn around. They paid no attention. So I took another escalator up and went into the street.

Again, as always, she is the unwanted wanderer. She is isolated and rejected, no matter what the group. Only with her foster family does she feel any acceptance, but even here, her "aunt" is not exactly delighted with her presence. In the end, she, too, rejects her. There is only one recourse: she must substitute people with an interest in music and fashion. Thus, she informs the therapist that his suggestion of the day before is not well taken. How can she possibly go out with people when nobody wants to have anything to do with her?

Her sex life is nil. It is restricted not only by her social inhibitions, which prevent even non-sexual relations with boys, but she is further restrained by a Victorian code of morals derived from her mother and grandmother. She has never been kissed, much less masturbated or had intercourse. In fact, she has never even been out on a date. Her sexual inhibitions are cloaked in moralistic rationalizations: sex is "disgusting and dirty" and "men are out for only one thing."

We have already seen that she suffers from great feelings of worthlessness. She has keen insight into both the familial and societal origins of her low self-esteem: "I wish my people would think twice before they start raising a family. I mean the Negroes as a whole. I wish they wouldn't. It would save them a lot of headaches. Yesterday, as I walked through Harlem, I looked at the people and the buildings and I realized if you weren't optimistic you would do one of two things: either kill yourself or drink yourself to death. Now I understand why they do that sort of thing. I saw three little boys—Negro triplets. They were cute—but they were doomed. They will fall right into the pattern of Harlem and hang around street corners and discredit themselves. What struck me so hard was that nobody paid any attention to them, so I did something. I read a magazine to them and told them some stories. That's all they wanted—somebody to pay some attention to them. It made me very happy to do that for them. If people would only stop being so busy and pay some attention to the younger generation, they wouldn't have so many delinquents, as they call them. You know, I believe a lot of this business about Negroes being inferior could be conquered if the mothers would spend more time with their children." She elaborates this theme several times: "I notice this book on your shelf—*The First Five Years of Life*. I don't think many people realize just how important these first few years are. Recently, I met a person who has two children. She allowed them to be sent down South. This was a very bad thing. It retarded them and made them very stupid. The mother, because she worked, couldn't be with them. They were not taught properly and they are the victims of circumstance, of a broken home. The father thinks nothing of them and has no responsibility. In so many ways it reminds me of myself. It's something I would like to work with—I understand it so well. The mother just doesn't realize how important it is to spend time with her children. They are hers and she should take care of them. If we don't take care of ours nobody else will. My mother used to compare me with white kids. Finally, I stopped her. I told her she must not compare me with kids who had more opportunities than I had. She told me such things as, 'You're stupid, you can't do things,' and so on. That's one reason she drove me away from her. Every child won't take it. Children have feelings and they feel more than you think. This is something people should realize. So often they compare their children with white kids, but before they do it they ought to sit with their children and help them to grow up. Then they can make a comparison. By belittling children, especially colored children, you make them feel inferior. I feel that way right now. This feeling and this fear were instilled in me by my mother, believe it or not. It always makes me feel I can't do things. Negroes have a hard enough time without their parents making it worse. It's not easy when you grow up only to discover you are not worth while."

This biography is the story of a valiant effort at adaptation against the greatest possible odds. R.H. describes, more eloquently than any other subject in this volume, the causes, the course, and the consequences of parental rejection. This, in itself, would be enough to give her plenty of trouble. The added awareness of being a Negro finished whatever chance she had for an effective social adaptation. It cannot be emphasized enough that the problem here is not the lack of initial endowment. R.H. was born with the capacity for relatedness, like any other normal child, but it never got any encouragement to grow. The consequence is a picture of inner desolation that is appalling.

CHAPTER EIGHT

The Neurotic Elaboration[1]

I.B.

THIS subject is a small, alert, 21-year-old art student, who is unmarried and lives in Harlem with her parents and two older brothers. She is dark brown in color and has characteristic Negroid features. She does not wear her hair in an imitation of Caucasian hairdoes, but rather has it dressed wild and full. She has an excellent figure, which she accents with inexpensive but smart clothing. There is an air of vitality and intensity about her. She speaks without difficulty and is quite uninhibited, crying and raging with facility.

She comes to psychotherapy for the resolution of three major problems. The first of these, and the one she presents as the most important, is a sexual difficulty. I.B. has had several affairs, but she has been completely frigid in all. Not one has been in the least pleasurable to her. In addition to this problem, she has difficulties in group relationships. She is highly competitive with her classmates, particularly the boys. She is argumentative and gets into constant trouble with her instructors, whom she seems to force into fights with her. Her friends accuse her of being overemotional and protest that it is not possible to have a reasonable or logical argument with her. She is insatiably demanding of attention, insists on the limelight, and if denied recognition reacts with venomous hostility. The third problem is in work. I.B. has considerable talent, but she is hard pressed to put it to use. She has an art scholarship, but she

[1] This subject shows in great profusion the neurotic responses common to the American Negro. Her case history can almost be categorized a composite of all those that have gone before. We are presenting it under a special heading to highlight the neurotic elaboration of the Negro's defenses against the pressures of caste.

has produced so little, the school is threatening to throw her out.

She was born in the Bronx and lived there in a mixed but predominately white neighborhood until the age of eight. Both parents were of Southern origin and had migrated to the North shortly after their marriage. The father was a mild, passive man who had something less than a grammar school education and was employed as an unskilled laborer. He had little to do with the children. The mother was the central and dominant figure in the household. Everything revolved around her. She was a high school graduate who rebelled violently at her low status. I.B. recalls her as cold, undemonstrative, and demanding. She was a rigid and driving woman, who gave the children a great deal of attention, but showed them no affection whatsoever. The emphasis was always on the need to be an example to the white world. The children were kept spotlessly clean and great attention was paid to physical appearance. I.B. has always felt that these attentions were not due to any love on the mother's part, but rather to the mother's own need for approval. She did not want to be condemned because her children were messy or dirty. To make matters worse for I.B. both parents openly discriminated in favor of the two boys. I.B. learned at an early age that to be a woman was to be inferior. Religion was not particularly stressed. Sex was never discussed in the home, but there was no undue intimidation.

The family occupied an apartment not too different from those in which their white neighbors lived. Their economic status was poor, but at the beginning, I.B. did not suffer from any privation. Her early childhood was spent mostly in the company of white children. She appeared to be accepted by them and mixed freely with them, even though, as far back as she can remember, she was always acutely aware that she was black and they were white. She looks back upon these years as relatively happy ones. The Depression cost her father his job and the family began to suffer severe economic want. It became necessary for them to move to cheaper quarters in Harlem. I.B. was eight at the time and she still recollects the move with horror: "The difficulties of that year were awful to me. There were fights, and I resented being Negro in a Negro neighborhood. It was such a contrast from having lived in a good building in the Bronx and having gone to a good school. I will never forget how horrible that first night in Harlem was. I couldn't go to the bathroom and I thought I never would. It was filthy and it took weeks to clean out the filth. I can't recall a single pleasant experience in Harlem. It was nothing but disappointments and degradations. I hated it and I rejected it completely. I'll tell you what Harlem represents to me. It represents 'these are your people'." Throughout the interviews, she returns to this theme many times. Over and over again she recalls isolated, painful incidents—much humiliation, the meaninglessness of holidays, the unrelieved poverty and the drabness, her rejection by teachers, and most of all, the physical repugnance of being with other Negroes. Nevertheless, she has lived in Harlem ever since.

I.B.'s central conflict is her unceasing struggle for status. This struggle permeates her every action and her every thought. It has two sources of origin, familial and societal, each of which reinforces the other. The trouble began in infancy with the maternal rejection implicit in the mother's lack of warmth and affection. This produced in I.B. a concept of self that is extremely difficult to alter—an almost unshakable conviction of unlovability. To this first sense of worthlessness was added the family preference for the brothers, accenting inferiority as a woman. On top of this, the mother taught her to reject being a Negro and to aim for white aspirations. Such instruction was tantamount to teaching self-contempt. I.B. learned her lesson well and incorporated the white ideal. But the incorporation of a hated ideal is a guarantee for perpetual self-hatred. As she grew older, and saw for herself what society thought of her, the initial feelings of worthlessness were both confirmed and consolidated. The deflation of her self-esteem is now on a completely permanent basis and there is not a minute of the day that she is free from such awareness.

Her opening dream focuses on this underlying conflict:

I was in a hospital. Someone forcibly reached into my vagina and brought out a white baby. I denied that it was mine.

Her associations all dealt with her shame over a sexual affair with a white man. This dream contains her impossible expectations from therapy. The dream is a rebirth fantasy in which she sheds her blackness and is reborn white. Whiteness is the cure for all her troubles. This metamorphosis will magically take place through an erotic association with the therapist, an association of which she would be ashamed and hence must deny. Such a delusional goal can only have a poor therapeutic prognosis. It forecasts a stand in favor of magic as opposed to realistic alteration.

Her convictions that she is worthless, inferior, and unlovable—and that these states because of her blackness are unalterable—give rise to a wild resentment, characterized by explosive tantrums and hysterical outbursts. Hostility is her main defense and she is primarily an aggressive personality. However, her uncontrolled use of aggression alienates all her friends and only serves to entrench still more her basic convictions. Any manifestation of aggression is followed by guilt, depression, and a retreat from contact with people. She emerges with an even lower self-esteem and an even greater need to prove herself. She becomes more coercive and more demanding. In the end, failing to get what she so much desires, she turns the rage on herself and engages in self-destructive activity. This takes the form of provoking the very rejection she seeks to avoid. Such behavior is calculated to assuage her need for self-punishment. This is the pain-dependent mechanism commonly referred to as masochism.

The following dream reveals her anxiety about her own aggression. It was stimulated by a quarrel with her parents:

It took place in an apartment with two people. It was a couple. I think they were my parents. I was deathly afraid of a cat with human characteristics. It climbed on the man's body. It was spitting and changed to a baby suddenly. They put the cat in another room. The cat was displeased at being locked up.

She identifies both images as herself: "The cat could have been myself. I am changeable even in the middle of a sentence. The cat was changeable. It became a baby." She explains that she jeopardizes all her relationships by creating an atmosphere of hostility; then she becomes frightened and turns back. Thus, the dream indicates that she thinks of herself as a cat with catlike aggression. No one can love such a creature. She attempts to escape this aggressiveness by becoming a helpless baby. This sequence not only is a genetic prototype of her original relationship with her parents, but is also reproduced in her daily life today. She will spit out at a friend, and then, through guilty fear, suddenly act to elicit sympathy and tenderness. Unfortunately, with I.B., it is always the cat that wins out.

Her patterns of hostility are directly related to the work problem. I.B. suffers from a "success phobia." She interprets her competitive strivings for status as a hostile act against those whom she surpasses, both Negroes and whites. The resultant guilt and fear of retaliation force a willful failure: "I'm supposed to be a superior dancer. I could have had the dancing scholarship, but during the tryouts I couldn't handle myself well and I was suddenly self-conscious because I was being watched. I didn't want to be good and so I fell down. This failure, at the point of success, is a pattern with me. I used to do this in tests at school. I want to give but I can't. I'm afraid I will do well."

Her hostility destroys all her relationships with people. Her perception is fixed and she "knows" in advance that she will only be rejected. This creates endless distrust and suspicion. She is elusive and wary. Overtures of friendship are misinterpreted as tricks to ensnare her. They mean only that the inevitable rejection will be that much more painful. In consequence, she generally rewards kindness with hostility. She is vicious to friends and enemies alike, unpredictable and volatile.

Her relationships are undermined by still another factor. It is true that she purposely holds back for fear of being hurt, but this is not the whole story. She does not intrinsically have very much warmth to give. Her capacity for tender affectivity has been greatly diminished. Her mother's coldness and disapproval did not permit its development. In addition, the constant presence of the emergency emotions, rage and fear, do not leave much room for anything else. However, the capacity for the warmer emotions is not entirely absent; rather, it is markedly constricted. Its presence, and also her fear of its expression, can be demonstrated within the transference. For many months she kept fleeing from treatment and constantly tested the therapist. She was chronically late, frequently failed to appear altogether, explosively hostile, expressed resentment at having to expose herself to a white man, repeatedly derogated the therapy, and so on. Finally, one day, after a year in treatment, she became aware of some tender feeling: "Underlying my flight to and from you and my feeling for you is a strong desire to love you as a friend. I would like to embrace you even though one doesn't do that to a doctor. I have to work hard to suppress that and I am ashamed or guilty in having that feeling. I feel good and bad about it. I am inching along. I am embarrassed sometimes by the feeling that I want to call you up. After all, attachments lead to dependency and my previous experience with dependency has been disappointment and rejection. Mostly my mother was guilty of this." In the very next hour, frightened at this exposure, she retracted her remarks: "I feel I shouldn't have let you know that I want to love you and accept you as part of my life. I must be independent. Somehow, if a person knows you are dependent on him, he will do something to you. Love is nice but it is like being enclosed in something. It can destroy you. It isn't good to depend on someone for affection and love because that person can always withdraw. Being independent is like saying, 'I don't need love and affection'."

This, of course, is a rationalization. I.B. really means that "the grapes hang high." Actually, she is furious when love is not forthcoming. For example, a few days before her birthday she speculated that no one would remember her. How could she expect to be loved or remembered? Maybe she has no right to affection. She concludes it's not important anyway and she is really indifferent. Then her birthday came and her family completely forgot about it. They made no mention of it whatsoever. She raged that she had been a fool to let herself feel. She should have hidden her feelings; then she wouldn't have been disappointed: "I am determined not to feel humiliated by my need for love. I was humiliated by not being able to feel affection and I equate that with wanting revenge when I am angry at my mother. I have promised myself I will punish my mother for the injuries she did me in childhood. I am always resentful that I could never punish her because I needed her food and shelter. I have the same mistrust of you. I need you and this implies loss of control and further hurt."

But her guilt is too great. The need to punish her mother invariably ricochets back on herself. In the end, she alone feels to blame. This self-condemnation is illustrated in a transference dream:

I was in a cafeteria. I picked out lots to eat but I had no money to pay for it. I called for my friends to pay, but they didn't hear me. Then I was at a party. I took a man away from another girl and had intercourse with him in front of this girl. The man I took was white.

The girl in the dream is one who in reality is going with a white man. I.B. recounts some of the uncomplimentary things that are said about this girl. Her own feeling is that a Negro girl who goes with a white man is degrading herself. This dream focuses on her conviction of unlovability. It is her own "badness" that stands in her way. She reaches out for love (food), but it is denied her because she has nothing worthwhile within herself to give in return. She appeals to her friends, but they, too, are deaf to her pleas. Finally, she buys affection by giving herself sexually to the white man (the therapist). The price she must pay is further degradation.

This triad—the conviction of unlovability, the diminution of affectivity, and the uncontrolled hostility—is hardly limited to Negroes. All three occur in whites as well, although it is apparent from the case studies they are much more frequent in Negroes. However, the erosive effects on interpersonal relations need not be quite so disastrous in the whites. To these obstacles the Negro adds self-hatred on a caste basis. This additional feature in I.B. ruins whatever chance she may have had for altering her relationships for the better. First of all, it tends to fix the triad, and renders the separate items immovable; second, the hatred is projected upon other Negroes, and she must hate them as she hates herself; and lastly, she hates the whites not only for what they have done to her, but also because she envies their status, a position to which she aspires, yet is prevented from reaching.

She gives voice to these attitudes many times during therapy: "I don't fully accept the sincerity of a white person. I think so little of myself that no one could possibly accept me. If I believed in myself as a Negro I wouldn't be so skeptical. I was told by a Negro leader that there are out and out bigots and people who make honest mistakes. He criticized me as damning all whites. I felt unloved and inadequate as a child and as a Negro child. I incorporated the concept of inferiority in relation to my home. I was treated this way because I was a Negro. I am ashamed of Negroes and I have shared the attitudes I have damned the whites for."

Early in therapy, S., a Negro girl friend, married a white boy. I.B. refused to go to the wedding and fought with the bride. She came to her interview very late and in a rage: "I am late because I am trying to get back at every one. I was violent with S. I cut her down as though she were white. I can't face my anti-white feelings. I haven't been honest with you. I doubt treatment. You give a white person your confidence and then you mustn't. They leave you. My relationships with whites means I must work out not being white. I identify with them even when I hate them. Anger gives me confidence. S. suffered and I felt happy." These remarks go beyond just clarification of her attitudes toward whites. Actually, in castigating S. so mercilessly, she is by proxy punishing herself. Her first dream accomplished in fantasy what S. has just succeeded in carrying out in reality. I.B., too, wants to marry a white man. Her guilt for this desire explains her ferocity toward S. As we shall see, she finally follows in her girl friend's footsteps.

All people are her enemies, white and black, but she divides them further into male and female. She has little rapport with other women because she rejects her own femininity, and all women with it, as inferior products. On the other hand, she fares no better with men, but for a different reason. She considers them superior by virtue of their masculinity. This she resents and engages in constant competition with them. I.B. is a "castrating" woman. She is overtly aggressive toward all men and her relations with them inevitably degenerate into open struggles for dominance: "Emotions are feminine. When I can't be domineering, I'm weak. If I'm accused of being feminine in an argument, I'm petrified and feel defeated. Anything feminine makes everything wrong. Men are better off. You are not listened to if you are not a man. I am still trying to be on top intellectually with C. (a current boy friend) to compensate for my inferior position as a woman. You have to give in to a man to get any kind of relationship. What's so terrible in being a woman is being subordinate to a man. If you top a guy who is tops, you are as good as a guy. If I don't reach the top I devaluate myself."

The competition with men spoils her sexual adaptation. She uses sex as an arena of the struggle for superiority. To her, intercourse is a violent, bloody, and damaging act in which the woman is both used and abused. She is promiscuous with Negro and white men alike and often chooses partners who are of diminished potency, ranging from homosexuality to complete impotence. She is thus enabled to indulge the fantasy that it is really she who is the male. On the few occasions that a man pleased her sexually, she immediately devalued him and sought a new relationship. She could not bear the display of masculine power, and with it the proof of her femininity. If there is no satisfaction in a relationship, the responsibility for failure is placed on the man. Her fears of intercourse are qualified by her desire to destroy the man's penis, or to remove it and appropriate it for her own use. These hostile wishes bring an inevitable fear of retaliation in their wake. The result is a violence-concept of sex. Unlike most women, I.B. makes no attempt to disguise either her intentions or her fears. They are fully conscious: "Intercourse is too dangerous. Sex play is safer and more enjoyable. I used to be afraid my breasts would be torn off and if my vagina was aroused I feared something drastic would happen. When I touch a penis, I do it viciously. I would like to tear it off. I am disgusted with myself when I think of sex as soon as I meet a man. I always turn a relationship with a man into revenge and retaliation. I get upset if I'm aroused. I'm afraid the penis will stick me and I will be shattered to pieces." These fears explain her frigidity. The inhibiting influence of anxiety is far too great for a successful performance.

As therapy progressed, I.B. took concrete steps to achieve her illusory goals. She began to act out her magical involvement with the therapist by displacing it to the real world. One day, out of the clear, she suddenly announced she was in love with a white man and intended to marry him. Not only was he white, but also he was partially impotent. Thus, through marriage, she would fulfill her two major fantasies. She would become white and, simultaneously, she would be the "man" of the partnership. She stated openly that she was angry for having revealed her intentions to the therapist. She was sure he would oppose the relationship because her husband-to-be was white. The therapist analyzed with her the true reasons for her behavior and counseled caution. She was adamant and went ahead with plans for the marriage despite opposition from both families.

The period that followed was a stormy one. She railed constantly at the therapist and accused him of anti-Negro feelings. A good deal of her rage came down on her lover's head. She systematically provoked him and they had one fight after another: "I have many fantasies that I am not a Negro. I don't want to be a Negro woman. That's why I fight so much with R. (her fiance). I must test him. I seek ways to prove that he doesn't love me. My jealousy and need to be on top is from the effort to divorce myself from Negroes and prove I'm not inferior. To stop competing and fighting would mean I would have to go back to this feeling of inferiority. I fight R. because I want to be loved for something I can't be. He accepts me as a Negro woman. I reject this." Nevertheless, in spite of such clear insight, she continued to insist the therapist was wrong. Her only motive for marriage was "love." Her dreams, however, belied her.

She had a series, all in the same vein. One typical example will suffice:

> I and R. were already married and we were to visit his parents. The family was indifferent. The parents were away on a trip when we arrived. There was a feast for R.'s sister. It was the sister's wedding. At the table we were worried about the return of R.'s parents. R.'s sister made a speech about happiness. No one listened to her. I started to run and suddenly I was in a red light district. It was full of prostitutes. I was stopped by two men. They said R. was white and rich because he was with a Negro woman. The men attacked us and we fled. I felt guilty that R. was marrying me. He should change his mind.

She related the dream with great chagrin. The meaning was too obvious. She immediately identified the sister as a stand-in for herself. She really doesn't love R. as a wife, but feels more like a sister to him. She knows his family will never accept her. The racial difference can never be reconciled; he will always be white and she will always be black. The looks people give them on the street when they are together make her feel like a prostitute. No wonder her speech about happiness fails. There is no use talking about happiness in the face of such obstacles. The marriage cannot possibly be a success. The best thing to do is to get out of it now.

Her dreams and all discussions with the therapist notwithstanding, she married the man of her choice, but for a brief time continued in treatment. As her own dreams had predicted, the marriage was not a successful one. The sexual problem did not ease up and she continued her attempts to belittle and reduce her husband. However, he turned out to be not as weak as she would have liked. He protested violently and they fought like cats and dogs. Her lot was made worse by guilt over the marriage which stimulated a fear of being ostracised by her own people. She was generally quite depressed. As the meaning of her act became clear, her rage at the therapist mounted. She had a series of dreams the details of which she could not remember, but all of them were concerned with the destruction of the therapist by the atomic bomb or through plotting with other people. In all of these dreams, she wanted to warn the therapist not to trust her, but she was paralyzed and could not. At this point, unable to face her own destructiveness, she bolted treatment and was never heard from again.

This case, more than any other recorded in this volume, points up the problem of whether neurotics are people. To this we must reiterate that a neurosis is a special method of dealing with a problem, rather than a definition of the problem itself. The problems of adaptation that confront this girl are no different from those of any other subject; but she deals with them in a unique manner that spreads with equal intensity over every facet of her adaptation.

A more unhappy, anxious and aggression-ridden human being is hard to conceive. At the same time, we cannot overlook the enormous drive behind her conflicts, and the high proportion of her energy that is wasted in compensatory and corrective moves which leave her no better off in the end. This girl is crippled in every aspect of her social life. She cannot cooperate with other human beings and enjoy her relations with them, she is maladjusted sexually, and she lacks the capacity to become a useful citizen through work.

There is little doubt that the basic integrations which she now uses as her adaptive tools were molded by her mother. Typically, her home was female-oriented. Yet, she cannot follow the maternal ideal because this was disqualified by the mother herself, through the overt discrimination in favor of the brothers. The craving for her mother's love is at the basis of her neurotic conflicts. This is amply demonstrated by her eager endorsement of all the conditions, in terms of her childhood experience, that would have brought her this emotional reward. The wish to be a boy and the wish to be white or the acceptance of the attenuated version of the same thing —to acquire status—all are efforts to establish conditions for being loved by her mother. The maternal ideal of acquiring status means to her: to be white = not to be dirty, with the obvious identification of herself and all Negroes with feces. This excites the most violent compensatory activities to wash herself clean (= white). With her this is tantamount to a dirt phobia. To be a boy is likewise in line with the maternal ideal. Her frigidity is therefore not a product of terrorization in connection with sexual disciplines, but an end product of the hatred and envy of men on the status level, which she rationalizes as a fear of being destroyed by them in the sexual act. The reverse is true. She hated her brothers, impounded her hostility, and now meets it in the projected form of a fear of being injured by them.

In the center of her whole adaptive apparatus there is this main constellation of *self-hatred*. Generated in her childhood for one set of reasons, this constellation received ample reinforcement from the impact with caste and class, so that now, in addition to the necessity of becoming a boy, she must also become white as the condition for being loved. Hence, she is engaged on the hopeless quest of becoming both male and white. The rest of the psychological picture is the outcome of this pursuit. The psychological parallelogram of forces can be depicted in the following diagram:

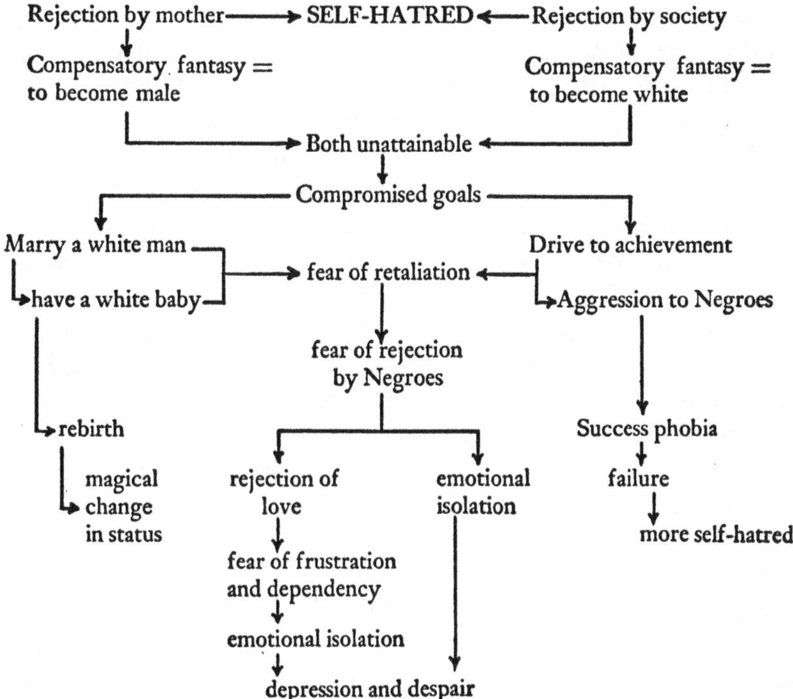

The nuclear constellation in this girl's psychological economy calls for some comments on the meaning of self-hatred as a motivating force in adaptation in contrast with self-love. Several authors [2] have written extensively on this subject.

[2] Deutsch, Helene, "Uber Zufriedenheit, Gluck, und Ekstase," *Int. Z. f. Psa.*, 1947. Fromm, Erich, *Escape from Freedom*, Farrar and Rinehart, 1942, and *Man for Himself*, Rinehart and Co., 1947.

Approval of oneself, as Fromm has aptly pointed out, is a much neglected topic, commonly confused with narcissism on the one hand and selfishness or greed on the other. Self-approval is an indicator, on a self-referential basis, of one's social orientation. In other words, indifference to one's social orientation means practically a break in all meaningful relatedness to the group in which one lives. Disturbances in self-esteem and self-love or self-approval can stem from a variety of causes.

Children have no automatic or autonomous devices for social orientation. They think well or poorly of themselves depending on parental approval or disapproval. In general, one can say that a healthy state of self-esteem–love–approval is compounded of the following constituents: (a) being loved by parents and internalizing their disciplines, which makes for a healthy conscience; (b) taking on their ideals, or at least ideals not incompatible with theirs; (c) effective performance, be it in learning or skills; (d) a healthy affectivity potential which leads to the expectation of emotional reciprocity with others; (e) being identified with individuals and ideals that are harmonious with the group in which one lives.

This is an ideal picture. In the practice of growing up and living, the child learns to make compromises with antisocial (or what is so considered) impulses without serious impairment of self-esteem or self-love. Thus, many children learn to tolerate conscience conflicts proceeding from breach of parentally taught sex mores without much damage to self-esteem. Many fail in this respect, and in them, sexual guilt can poison an otherwise healthy self-esteem. A high aspiration level with poor performance can do the same.

Self-approval is, therefore, a record of harmony between what one is and what one wants to be, an acceptable compromise between ideal and actuality. Contentment is the feeling which accompanies this compromise. Its presence means there are no serious demands being made by an unsatisfied conscience and neither is there too much protest from too high an aspiration level. To be contented with oneself is very like the experience of an enamored man with his enamorata. He sees her faults but they do not diminish his love. He diminishes their importance in order to preserve his dominant feeling of affection.[3]

[3] It must be observed parenthetically that frustrated parents have a way of transferring their self-hatred to their children, whom they expect to be geniuses, to

There is a type of self-love (very common in Western society) which may be called compensated self-love. This is basically a self-hatred in which the hated attributes have been projected upon some accepted stereotype of hatred (like Jew, Negro or any other minority) which leaves the subject in the position of what looks like a restored self-love. This kind of self-restorative maneuver is not only costly to the groups who are favorite targets for the projected hatred, but moreover it does not restore self-love. It merely sets up a trumped-up claim for self-love, but does not achieve the real thing.

It is easy to see from this inventory that the Negro has no possible basis for a healthy self-esteem and every incentive for self-hatred. The basic fact is that in the Negro aspiration level, good conscience and even good performance are irrelevant in face of the glaring fact that the Negro gets a poor reflection of himself in the behavior of whites, no matter what he does or what his merits are. The chief disturbing factor in the Negro is that he must identify himself with the Negro, but this initiates the compensatory identification with the white, who is also hated. The enormous amount of aggression that is mobilized in the Negro in itself prevents any healthy self-esteem from getting a foothold. Here, retaliatory fears and conscience mechanisms interfere.

This case is a remarkable demonstration of the endless vicious circles and blind alleys that are set in motion by the frantic efforts to remove the causes for self-hatred, which in this subject is a ceaseless irritant. Every adaptive maneuver she starts ends in more failure, more isolation, and leaves her self-hatred intact. She differs from most other subjects in the extreme and regressive means she uses—like marrying a white man in order to be reborn white. All these efforts only add more sources from which she feeds her ceaseless need for degradation and misery.

---

look like Athene or Apollo, failing which the disappointed parent heaps on the child an ill-concealed disappointment that the child correctly interprets as hatred. Negroes have no monopoly on this constellation. We have seen several instances of such self-hatred in whites passed on to several generations. These people all had the idea that no matter what their achievements, they were still no good. They identified themselves with feces, and passed their self-hatred on to their children by this route. Self-hatred in varying degrees is a constant feature in all minority groups.

PART THREE

Negro Adaptation: A Psychodynamic Analysis

CHAPTER NINE

Psychodynamic Inventory of the Negro Personality

A PSYCHODYNAMIC summary of the findings on twenty-five cases is a very different story from a statistical study of incidence. The psychodynamic composite picture records incidence also, but incidence of patterns of intrapsychic accommodation. Whereas the study of employment vicissitudes in the same number would be totally without significance if it were treated as a sample of what transpired in fourteen million people, the corresponding study in patterns of intrapsychic accommodation has a much higher range of validity. It is doubtful whether we could get much more out of the study of fifty or one hundred cases. The real handicap of studying a small number intensively is not that our findings are unlikely to be representative, but that their representability takes too little account of characterological and vocational differences. This is the trouble with any pilot study. We cannot tell from our studies what comprises the personal adaptation of the successful Negro businessman, the successful actress, the successful baseball player, the successful racketeer, and the like. On the other hand, how important is it for us, in trying to establish a composite picture of Negro adaptation, to include these types of character, who are statistically unimportant, because they are the exceptions and not the rule?

We do not believe that this issue of representability is the most important issue that concerns us. There are other much more troublesome features which will emerge in the course of this summary. There is the question whether caste or class is the dominant

Negro source of conflict, and whether the conflicts about caste are so prominent that they submerge differences that would otherwise arise from class distinctions, as is likely to be the case with whites. In this study, we cannot avoid the conclusion that the dominant conflicts of the Negro are created by the caste situation, and that those of class are secondary. This is due to the fact that the adaptation of the Negro is qualified primarily by the color of his skin—an arbitrary but effective line of demarcation.

At best, the question of representability of our findings is secondary to another more important issue. Namely, in what form shall we describe the various kinds of adaptational variations? This opens the whole question of characterology and the study of personality functioning and modes of adaptation generally. To this we can only say that psychodynamics is not the only way that it can be done. It has the limitation of studying adaptation from the point of view of effectiveness and ineffectiveness. It is not tied to any absolutes or archetypes. It has the advantage of having been the subject of experimental verification for over sixty years by many people, and of being internally consistent. We have heard objections of an academic kind that what is described here is not "personality" at all but something else; but we have never heard of any substitutes for describing the vicissitudes of adaptation that do not include the successful or unsuccessful modes of handling life situations. Let those who object supply us with a better frame of reference.

It is a consistent feature of human personality that it tends to become organized about the main problems of adaptation, and this main problem tends to polarize all other aspects of adaptation toward itself. This central problem of Negro adaptation is oriented toward the discrimination he suffers and the consequences of this discrimination for the self-referential aspects of his social orientation. In simple words, it means that his self-esteem suffers (which is self-referential) because he is constantly receiving an unpleasant image of himself from the behavior of others to him. This is the subjective impact of social discrimination, and it sounds as though its effects ought to be localized and limited in influence. This is not the case. It seems to be an ever-present and unrelieved irritant. Its influence is not alone due to the fact that it is painful in its intensity, but also because the individual, in order to maintain internal balance and to protect himself from being overwhelmed by it, must initiate restitutive maneuvers in order to keep functioning—all quite automatic and unconscious. In addition to maintaining an internal balance, the individual must continue to maintain a social façade and some kind of adaptation to the offending stimuli so that he can preserve some social effectiveness. All of this requires a constant preoccupation, notwithstanding the fact that these adaptational processes all take place on a low order of awareness. The following is a diagram of a typical parallelogram of forces:

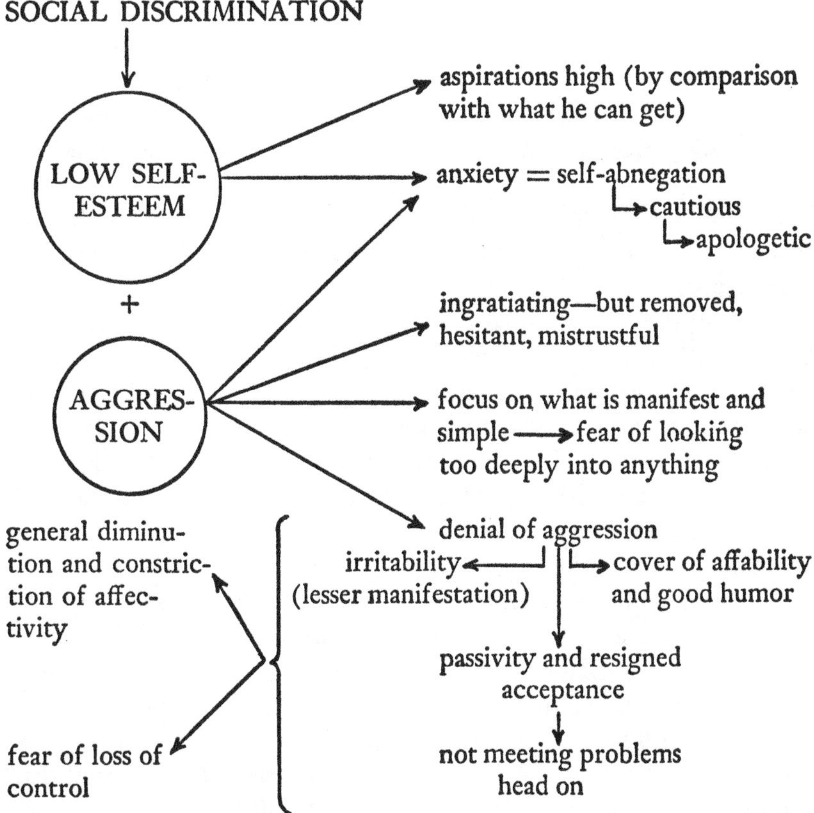

In the center of this adaptational scheme stand the low self-esteem (the self-referential part) and the aggression (the reactive part). The rest are maneuvers with these main constellations, to prevent their manifestation, to deny them and the sources from which they come, to make things look different from what they are, to replace aggressive activity which would be socially disastrous with more acceptable ingratiation and passivity. Keeping this system going means, however, being constantly ill at ease, mistrustful, and lacking in confidence. The entire system prevents the affectivity of the individual that might otherwise be available from asserting itself.

This is the adaptational range that is prescribed by the caste situation. This is, however, only a skeletal outline. Many types of elaboration are possible, particularly along projective or compensatory lines. For example, the low self-esteem can be projected as follows:

Low self-esteem = self-contempt → idealization of the white →
frantic efforts to be white = unattainable ↗ hostility to whites
↘ introjected white ideal →
self-hatred → projected on to other Negroes = hatred of Negroes.

The low self-esteem can also mobilize compensations in several forms: (1) apathy, (2) hedonism, (3) living for the moment, (4) criminality.

The disposition of aggression is similarly susceptible to elaboration. The conspicuous feature of rage lies in the fact that it is an emotion that primes the organism for motor expression. Hate is an attenuated form of rage, and is the emotion toward those who inspire fear and rage. The difficult problem for those who are constantly subject to frustration is how to contain this emotion and prevent its motor expression. The chief motive for the latter is to avoid setting in motion retaliatory aggression.

The most immediate effect of rage is, therefore, to set up a fear of its consequences. Fear and rage become almost interchangeable. When the manifestations of rage are continually suppressed, ultimately the individual may cease to be aware of the emotion. In some subjects the *only* manifestation of rage may be fear.

The techniques for disposing of rage are varied. The simplest disposition is to suppress it and replace it with another emotional attitude—submission or compliance. The greater the rage, the more abject the submission. Thus, scraping and bowing, compliance and ingratiation may actually be indicators of suppressed rage and sustained hatred. Rage can be kept under control but replaced with an attenuated but sustained feeling—resentment. It may be kept under control, but ineffectively, and show itself in irritability. It may be kept under sustained control for long periods, and then become explosive. Rage may show itself in subtle forms of ingratiation for purposes of exploitation. It may finally be denied altogether (by an automatic process) and replaced by an entirely different kind of expression, like laughter, gaiety, or flippancy.

Rage may ricochet back on its author, as it does in some types of pain-dependent behavior (masochism). This is only likely to happen when rage is directed toward an object that is loved; the rage is then accompanied by strong guilt feelings. In this case the only manifestation of rage may be depression.

The tensions caused by suppressed or repressed aggression often express themselves through psychosomatic channels. Headaches of the migrainous variety are often the expression of rage which is completely repressed. These are usually not accompanied by amorphous anxiety—though the latter may be the sole vehicle for this aggression. Hypertension is another psychosomatic expression of the same, but predominantly suppressive, process.

In the case histories, we found all these varieties of the expression and control of rage. All kinds of combinations are possible. The two commonest end products of sustained attempts to contain and control aggression were low self-esteem and depression. These are merely the results of the continuous failure of a form of self-assertion.

The adaptational scheme we have charted above takes in the impact of discrimination but does not account for the integrative systems due to other conditions operative in the process of growth. This division is purely arbitrary for actually both series run concomitantly. There is no time in the life of the Negro that he is not actively in contact with the caste situation. The other personality traits derive, however, from the disturbances in his family life. This source gives rise to the following constellations: the affectivity range, the capacity for idealization and ideal formation, the traits derived from reactions to discipline, and conscience mechanisms. In these categories there is some difference as we proceed from the lower- to the upper-class Negro. Let us take up the lower-class Negro first.

Affectivity range means the range of emotional potential. In appraising the role of emotion in personal and social adaptation, we have both quantitative and qualitative features to take into account. The total adaptation of the individual will depend on how much and what kind of emotion he has in a given situation. Emotion in man's adaptation tends to operate on a mass action principle. That is, the predominance of one emotion tends to stifle all others.

Emotion has the function of orientation toward objects in the outer world that can be the source of frustration or gratifications. The individual responds to a frustrating object with the emergency emotions of fear and rage, and their derivatives of hate, suspicion, distrust, apprehensive anticipation, and the like. These functions are self-preservative in intent and gear the organism for defensive action. The feeling toward objects which are the source of gratifications is the wish to be near, to perpetuate the influence of, to love, to desire, to have anticipations of continued gratifications, to trust, to have confidence, to cooperate with.

We must stress the point from this inventory that the emotions most conducive to social cohesion are those that pertain to the categories of love, trust, and confidence. All creatures are natively endowed with the capacity for fear and rage. The positively toned feelings of love, trust, and confidence, however, must largely be cultivated by experience. Hence, when we refer to the affectivity potential of an individual, we do not mean the emergency functions of fear and rage. We mean rather the capacity for cooperative and affectionate relatedness to others.

None of these emotions functions in isolation; they have a continuous adaptive interplay during the entire process of growth and living. What counts in the individual are the types of emotional response that become habitual and automatic. These fixed patterns of emotion are not only adaptive, in the sense that they are reaction types to actual situations; they also play a dominant role in shaping anticipations and to a degree, therefore, influence how events will shape up. For example, a person trained to be suspicious will shape the actual events of his life in such a way that his suspicions appear warranted.

The emotions play a decisive role in determining the sociability (peaceful cooperation with others) of the individual through the development of conscience mechanisms and the formation of ideals. The desire on the part of the child to be loved and protected is the dominant incentive for the child to be obedient to his protectors. He needs this because he is helpless himself. The child thus becomes socialized in order to continue the boons of love and protection. He learns to anticipate the requirements for these returns by internalizing them and making them automatic. He also learns the methods of escaping blame and of devising techniques for reinstatement. Thus, the fear of punishment and the withdrawal of love exert a powerful restraining influence against antisocial behavior. The reward for conformity is a sense of pride in the social recognition of "good" behavior, while the fear of detection and punishment leads to guilty fear and either an anticipation of punishment or self-punishment.

However, in order for these positive emotional feelings and the functions of conscience to be instituted, certain behavior by the parents toward the child is required. Thus, we cannot expect the child to develop affection and dependence on the parent who is not constant in his care, who does not love in return for obedience, whose punishments are either disproportionate, or have no relation to the offense. In this instance, conformity is of no adaptive value at all. A child who is constantly abused by the parent cannot be expected to have pleasant anticipations or to idealize the parent or wish to be like him. A child exposed to this kind of behavior from the parent will not love, trust, or cooperate. It can take flight from the hostile environment and try to seek another more friendly one. Or it can stay and hate the parent, and suppress all the hostile feeling.

On the institutional side, the family structure of the lower-class Negro is the same as the white. However, in the actual process of living, the vicissitudes of the lower-class family are greater and its stability much less. This is where the broken family through early death of parents, abandonment or divorce, takes a heavy toll on the opportunities for developing strong affective ties to the parents. First, the needs for dependency are frustrated. This makes the mother a frustrating object, rather than one the child can depend on. This does not mean that it is the intention of the mothers to neglect or mistreat their children. Quite the contrary, the intention is the usual one, and many lower-class Negro mothers have strong maternal feelings, are exceedingly protective, and try to be good providers. This is not, however, what one hears from the subjects. They tell chiefly the story of frustration and of arbitrary discipline by mothers. Not infrequently there is also the constant story of beating and cursing as disciplinary reinforcements. The rivalry situation between siblings in the lower classes is greatly enhanced by the general scarcity in which they live. This situation, of course, is greatly magnified when the child is given to some other relative for custody, as a consequence of a broken home. These children fare worse than any of the others. They are the ones who, because of mistreatment, decide at the age of 10 or 12 to run away and shift for themselves. In these children, some of whom we studied, the premature independence hardly works to the advantage of the personality in the long run. They become shrewd and adjustable, but at the cost of complete mistrust in everyone.

The result of the continuous frustrations in childhood is to create a personality devoid of confidence in human relations, of an eternal vigilance and distrust of others. This is a purely defensive maneuver which purports to protect the individual against the repeatedly traumatic effects of disappointment and frustration. He must operate on the assumption that the world is hostile. The self-referential aspect of this is contained in the formula "I am not a lovable creature." This, together with the same idea drawn from the caste situation, leads to a reinforcement of the basic destruction of self-esteem.

Thus, many of the efforts of the lower-class Negro at emotional relatedness are canceled out by the inner mistrust in others, the conviction that no one can love him for his own sake, that he is not lovable. Under these conditions, not much real social relatedness is possible. It is, however, very significant that the lower-class Negro is an inveterate "joiner" in one kind of social voluntary organization or another, of clubs and cliques with high-sounding names and with much ritualism in initiation rites. In these organizations, which have a very short life span, there is continuous discord, jockeying for position and prestige, and insistence that each member must have his own way. In other words, through these clubs and associations, the Negro tries to compensate for his lack of relatedness. But for the greater part, he fails. The intrapsychic mistrust and need for dominance destroy the effectiveness of these compensatory efforts. This is a noteworthy feature of Negro life, because the social organizations are supposed to facilitate cooperative endeavor and to give the members the satisfaction of belonging to something, to diminish their isolation. This end is not accomplished because most of the energy of these "associations" is taken up with overcoming mutual distrust and very little energy goes into the mutual supportive aspects of the organization.

Closely related to the question of the affectivity potential is the capacity for idealization. This trait is a general human characteristic, and is rooted in the biological make-up of man. It is the most powerful vehicle for the transmission of culture. During his helpless state man must place his trust in the parent who is his support. If this support and affection aid the individual in his adjustment, the natural tendency is to magnify the powers of the parent to magical proportions. This projection of magical attributes on the parent is the most powerful implement the parent has in enforcing discipline, because the threat of withdrawal of this support creates anxiety in the child. It follows, therefore, that the idealized parent is the satisfying parent whose authority is less enforced than it is delegated, and the acquiescence to discipline is a method the child has for perpetuating those boons he has already enjoyed in the past and hence expects to enjoy in the future.

The formation of ideals to pursue is a corollary of the idealization of the parent. It is easy to identify oneself with the idealized parent if the expectations from him have been realized. If these expectations are frustrated, then there may develop a reactive ideal or the opposite to the one experienced. This is generally a rare phenomenon, where a mistreated child becomes an ideal parent by living the opposite of what he has experienced. It does indeed happen. But it is far from the rule. The commonest outcome of this situation is that despite the hatred to the parent, the child takes on and identifies himself with the hated and frustrating attributes and becomes the replica of the frustrating parent. Here one must draw the line between an activating ideal and the unconscious identification. The activating ideal may be "I will be a provident parent"; the unconscious identification, however, may be with the frustrating parent. In some instances, the mistreated child when it becomes the parent is actuated by the idea: "Why should I give you what I never had myself?" These are the cases in which the frustrated dependency cravings interfere with the protective parental role.

The question of Negro-ideal formation is hardly limited to the parental role. The "ideal" answers the question: "Whom do I want to be like?" This is where the Negro encounters a great deal of difficulty. The parent is a member of a despised and discriminated-against group. Hence, this ideal is already spoiled because it carries with it a guarantee of external and reflected hatred. No one can embrace such an ideal. Furthermore, until very recently the Negro has had no real culture heroes (like Joe Louis and Jackie Robinson) with whom he could identify. It is therefore quite natural that the Negro ideal should be *white*. However, accepting the white ideal is a recipe for perpetual self-hatred, frustration, and for tying one's life to unattainable goals. It is a formula for living life on the delusional basis of "as if." The acceptance of the white ideal has acted on the Negro as a slow but cumulative and fatal psychological poison. Its disastrous effects were due to the fact that the more completely he accepted the white ideal, the greater his intrapsychic discomfort had to become. For he could never become *white*. He had, therefore, to settle for the delusion of whiteness through an affectation of white attributes or those that most closely resembled them. This also means the destruction of such native traits as are susceptible of change (kinky hair, etc.). In its most regressive form, this ideal becomes the frantic wish to be reborn white. (See biography of I.B., page 284.) Pride in oneself could not, therefore, be vested in attributes one had, but in attributes one aspired to have, that is to say, on borrowed ideals. This maneuver, calculated as a restitutive one, ends by being destructive of self-esteem.

The reactions to discipline and the dynamics of conscience mechanisms are closely interrelated, and these in turn are related to the general affectivity potential and ideal formation.

In general, there are several factors operating on the parental side of the induction of disciplines which differ from the situation among whites. The Negro parent has no authority in the social world in which he lives. It is, therefore, a strong temptation for the Negro parent to tend to be authoritative in the only place where he can exercise it, namely in his own home. Hence, we get repeated stories of children being subjected to disciplines that are both arbitrary, instantaneous, and inconsistent, depending often on whim, and at the same time without the ability to offer the child the appropriate rewards for obedience and conformity. Children recognize these rewards chiefly in terms of need satisfactions. These the parent, more often than not, cannot implement. They often fail on the sheer subsistence level. Such a parent cannot have much delegated authority or inspire much dependence. Hence, the authority of the parent is destroyed. A second factor occurs especially in those cases where the mother works. She has no time to be the careful and provident mother. After a day's work, during which time the child often shifts for itself, she is inclined to be tired and irritable which accounts for much of her impatience and insistence on immediate and unqualified obedience.

As between mother and father, many factors conspire to make the mother the chief object of such dependency as is possible under the circumstances. The male as provider and protector definitely suffers disparagement. The mother's objective—since she has so little time—is to make the child as little nuisance as possible. This makes her both an object to be feared and at the same time the only one that can be relied upon.

In passing, we must mention here the place of street life for the Negro child and adolescent. In many ways this street life is no different from corresponding street life in lower-class whites. The crowded home is not a happy place for the growing child, especially when parents are so often away. Since the family does not implement its disciplines with appropriate rewards, the children tend to get their ideals and pattern their amusements on the opportunities of the street, with its values, its heroism, its ideals, and its factionalism. They differ from corresponding white groups in the quantity of the savagery of their mutual aggression, in which the boys get seriously hurt and in some instances killed. Part of this street life pattern is the result of sheer boredom and the irrelevancy of education. Hence, they cannot be attentive at school or get the feeling that they are engaged in a meaningful and ego-enhancing activity. Many of these high school boys have been to bed with women the age of their female teachers and the disciplines and obligations of school life make no sense to them. In consequence, school is treated as a meaningless routine. The street, on the other hand, offers adventure, struggle for dominance, mock and real hostilities. It is, in other words, a better training for life—according to their sights—than education. Delinquency among adolescents runs high for very good reasons.

In this general setting we can evaluate the effects of the socializing disciplines.

We have seen but little evidence of rigid anal training in childhood. There is no serious contest of will between parent and child over this aspect of socialization. It is largely neglected, and in those who came from the South, there was little emphasis on order, neatness, or systematization. Hence, in this group we would not expect much adventitious use of the anal zone for elaborate constellations about expulsion and retention. If there are any compulsive traits in the Negroes of this group, they do not derive from this source.

A more important aspect of socializing discipline is in the sexual domain. Here the picture is very confused. In the lower classes, the sex morality taught is of the Victorian variety. However, there is but little effort made to implement it. There is, on the whole, much less anxiety introduced into sexual disciplines than is the case with the white middle classes. The result is actually more sexual freedom among lower-class Negro children than among whites. And it is by no means unusual for boys and girls to be inducted into sexual activity quite early (7 to 13). It is therefore highly unlikely that potency troubles in both males and females of this group derive from anxieties introduced into the picture by parental threats. In those cases observed these difficulties usually arose from another source. They came from the confusion in the sociosexual roles of male and female. The male derives these difficulties from his inability to assume the effective masculine role according to white ideals, as against the dominant position of the female, first in the dominant mother and later in the dominant wife. The economic independence of the female plays havoc with the conventional male-female roles, and this in turn, influences the potency of the males. In the case of the female, her sociosexual role is reversed. She is dominant, and rebels against the passive and dependent role. Thus, the sexuality of the Negro in the lower classes is confused by the sexual significance of the social role.

Contrary to expectations, the sexual drive of the adult Negro is relatively in abeyance. We saw no evidence of the sex-craved and abandoned Negro. This playing down of sex is the result of the socioeconomic hardship and the confusion in the sexual roles.

What kind of conscience mechanisms can be integrated under these conditions? This situation is, if anything, more complex than in the white. Basically, the tonicity of the conscience mechanisms depend on the ability of the parent to act as provider of satisfactions.

Hence, in the lower-class Negro, we cannot expect strong internalized conscience. If we add to this the disastrous effects of the caste system, then the lower-class Negro, in his hatred for the white, is robbed of any incentive for developing a strong conscience. However, the effects of the caste system are such that they inspire a great deal of fear. Therefore, antisocial tendencies would be held in rigid check by fear of detection. In fact, we can say that conscience in the lower-class Negro is held in tow by his general vigilance over his hatred and aggression, and that the fear of detection of his aggression and antisocial tendencies are both governed by the same control mechanisms. The great danger for the lower-class Negro is that these control devices may occasionally and impulsively be overwhelmed—a factor that is of enormous concern to every lower-class Negro.

This group of constellations sets up in the Negro a strong need for compensatory activities, to help establish some semblance of internal harmony. These compensatory activities have the function of (a) bolstering self-esteem, (b) narcotizing the individual against traumatic impact, (c) disparaging the other fellow, (d) getting magical aid for status improvement.

Among the activities for bolstering self-esteem are flashy and flamboyant dressing, especially in the male, and the denial of Negro attributes, such as doing away with kinky hair.

Narcotizing the individual against traumatic influences is effected largely through alcohol and drugs. In these activities, the males predominate. Alcoholic psychoses in Negroes occur with twice the frequency that they do in whites.[1] Narcotics have a wide use among Negroes, but their high cost makes alcohol much more available.

Disparaging the other fellow is widespread among urban Negroes. It is of a vindictive and vituperative kind and derives largely from the status strivings. The street corner and candy store are favorite places for malicious gossip.

In the domain of magical aid to self-esteem, gambling takes a high place. This takes the form of card playing but more often of participation in the numbers racket. Here everyone has a chance at

[1] *See* Malzberg, Benjamin, "Mental Disease Among American Negroes: A Statistical Analysis," in Klineberg, Otto (ed.), *Characteristics of the American Negro*, Harper, 1944.

beating fate, of being the favored one, if only for a day. The lure of this tantalizing game must be very high, judging from the vast fortune spent annually by the bulk of the Negro population.

In addition to these, there are occasional outlets, chiefly by males, which stem from their inability to plan or have any confidence in a future. Since the general tendency is to live from day to day, explosive spending when they have money is not infrequent. An occasional illusion of plenty and luxury can thus be created, even if to do so means to mortgage one's energy for months ahead to pay for the luxury.

This psychological picture is to some extent changed in the middle and upper classes. Here the family organization corresponds more closely to the middle-class white group. The emphasis shifts from subsistence problems to status problems. There is also a shift from female to male dominance in the family. The chief conflict area is that concerned with status. In general, the benefits derived from better parental care, better induction of affectivity, better ideal formation and more tonic conscience mechanisms are to a large extent canceled out by the enormous increase in status conflict caused by the caste situation.

In appraising the adaptation of the middle- and upper-class Negro, we encountered a good deal of difficulty in differentiating the real from the apparent. For example, the affectivity potential is much better in this group than in the lower class. But against this we must discount the fact that the representations of better affectivity rest largely on a formal basis. Their marriages are more stable; they induct affectivity more appropriately, etc. But these features are due largely to the fact that the upper- and middle-class Negroes strive hardest to live and feel like the whites. They are more conventional, have more rigid sex mores, set more store by "respectability" than do lower-class Negroes. They know what the "right" feelings are for a given situation and they try very hard to have them. But whether they do or not depends on the quantity of the conflicts they have on the issues of skin color and status strivings, all of which tend to detract from the freedom of feeling.

In the specific integrative areas this group approximates the white. Parental care is good in the same sense and with the same incompatibilities as with whites. The affectivity potential is apparently higher than in lower-class Negroes and they have more capacity for relatedness. They have a high capacity for idealization, but what is idealized is white and not Negro. Here again the ideal formation in the Negro has two layers. The natural figure to idealize is the provident parent; but he is a disparaged figure. Introjecting this object means to hate it to the accompaniment of perpetual guilt. The substitution of a white object as the source of the ideal does not solve the problem. It, too, is hated and likewise must give rise to guilt. The Negro cannot win in either case. As one upper-class Negro observed: "The only thing black that I like is myself." Their ideal formation is of a high order, but founders on the rock of unattainable ideals. The fact that these ideals are relatively more capable of achievement than in the lower classes renders the conflict sharper. Thus, they tend to drive themselves harder, make greater demands on themselves for accomplishment, and are obligated to refuse the compensatory activities open to lower-class Negroes. This greatly augments the internal self-hatred and makes it more difficult to accept the Negro status. I could love myself "if" is all the more tantalizing because they can almost make the grade, but for skin color. They are therefore more vulnerable to depressed self-esteem than the lower class.

The need to conform to white standards of middle-class respectability gives the upper classes a harder time with their control of aggression. And this in turn has a constricting effect on all their affectivity.

In view of the good parental care, one would expect that their tendencies to passivity would be accentuated. But this is countered by the strong pressure against any form of passivity or subordination especially to other Negroes—since they cannot avoid subordination to the white. This constellation would be very valuable to follow through in Negro homosexuals. As we saw in the biographies, the conflict about passivity in the males was enormous.

The points where the intrapsychic conflicts are sharpened for the middle- and upper-class Negro, then, are in the disposition and compensations for lowered self-esteem, the disposition of aggression, and in the uncompromising acceptance of white ideals.

The self-hatred of this group takes the usual form of projection on both white and on Negroes lower than themselves. However, they have more guilt about their Negro hatred than is the case with lower classes. To the whites, the formula is hatred + control = disguise; to the Negro the formula is hatred + guilt = anxiety of retaliation. Thus, every middle- and upper-class Negro has increased competitiveness with whites, but his psychological task is merely one of control and concealment. The hatred to the Negro has a way of ricocheting back on its source. Every Negro who is higher than lower class has a sense of guilt to other Negroes because he considers success a betrayal of his group and a piece of aggression against them. Hence, he has frequently what might be called a "success phobia," and occasionally cannot enjoy the fruits of his achievements.

In his acceptance of white ideals, the Negro often overshoots the mark. He overdoes the sex mores so that the incidence of frigidity in the women is very high. In his acceptance of the white man's cleanliness obsession, the Negro ends by identifying himself with feces, and becomes extraordinarily clean and meticulous. However, the obstructions to the accomplishments of white ideals lead to increase in aggression, anxiety, depression of self-esteem, and self-hatred. This compels him to push harder against the social barriers, to drive himself harder, and ends with more frustration and more self-hatred. This vicious circle never ends.

Thus, as we stated above, it is difficult to appraise the advantages and disadvantages of the upper classes as regards their intrapsychic effects. The shift from female to male orientation at least saves this group from the confusion of social and sexual roles. It is one of male dominance and clear definition of sexual role. However, they overdo the rigidity of sexual restrictions, and this affects the female more than the male. The marriages are more stable, but the importance of conventionality is very high; hence the impression remains that as an average the marriages are not more happy. Affectivity is better; but its betterment is largely on the formal side.

The chief outcome of the psychological picture is that the upper classes of Negro society have so much controlling to do of their psychic life, that they must be extremely cramped and constricted and unspontaneous. There is too little self-contentment for true abandonment, and too much self-hatred and mutual mistrust for effective social relatedness. They must constantly choose the lesser evil between spontaneity and getting hurt by retaliation. Hence, they prefer not to see things as they are, or to enter too deeply into anything to the accompaniment of apathy and resignation.

Is there such a thing as a basic personality for the Negro? This work proves decidedly that there is. Though he lives in American culture, the Negro lives under special conditions which give this personality a distinctive configuration. Taking as our base line the white middle class, the conditions of life for the Negro are so distinctive that there is an actual alteration of the pressures to which he must adapt. Hence, he develops a distinctive personality. This basic Negro personality is, however, a caricature of the corresponding white personality, because the Negro must adapt to the same culture, must accept the same social goals, but without the ability to achieve them. This limitation in social opportunities accounts for the difference in personality configuration.

CHAPTER TEN
The Rorschach Experiment

By William Goldfarb, ph.d., m.d.

The Rorschach Test is probably our best psychological test for the delineation of character structure. This is so because it permits the analysis of personality at different levels; for example, conscious and unconscious. In addition, the various aspects of personality are viewed in interaction. The test has definite limitations, too, as a clinical and, especially, as a research tool. We shall touch on some of these limitations later.

Rorschach Test responses of twenty-four of the twenty-five subjects discussed in this volume were made available to me. Obviously, in employing the test originally it was not thought that the test could justifiably replace or give the detail and richness of understanding that a prolonged psychodynamic analysis is able to offer. Rather, it was presumed that, in itself, it is a valuable and valid instrument for the assay of personality, capable of enriching insights derived from other sources. More specifically it was the plan to test out major hypotheses derived from comprehensive psychodynamic analysis by seeing how closely these hypotheses were borne out by Rorschach Test findings.

The following experimental procedure was employed. The tests were administered by a trained examiner. Then, the individual test records were interpreted by the present writer. This procedure separated the administration and the interpretation of the test, a fact which undoubtedly increased the difficulties of interpretation. Nevertheless, it was not completely without justification, inasmuch as direct observation of and personal interaction with an individual while administering the test, doubtlessly permit one to reach a degree of understanding regarding that person. From a research point of view, it was desirable to check the findings of psychodynamic analyses by a method quite different in its approach.

The Rorschach interpretations were to be made "blind." This meant that the Rorschach analyst was to know nothing regarding the life histories of the subjects. The only data made available to him included the sex and age of each subject. In addition, the fact of Negro derivation was known. It goes without saying that the findings and hypotheses of Dr. Kardiner and Dr. Ovesey were not discussed with the Rorschach analyst till the latter's findings were a matter of written record.

The scoring employed was that of Klopfer.[1] Inferences were drawn in the usual manner from an analysis of manner of approach, important determinants, and content. It should be stated that our primary approach was that of interpretation of individual Rorschach Test records. Such interpretation has a conspicuous intuitive-integrative element. We were more interested in the perception of meaningful, dynamic, individual patterns than in the statistical manipulation of discrete Rorschach variables. To control the individual interpretations, use was made of an extensive clinical experience with subjects of widely varied circumstance and background, and the approximate standards and norms upon which Rorschach workers agree. (See, for example, Klopfer,[2] Rapaport,[3] Rorschach [4] and especially the very fine summary of group findings by Davidson and Klopfer.[5]) Following individual interpretation, we sought for those individual patterns or character trends which were present in most or all of the subjects.

Presently, we shall offer a description of those character trends which we found in all or nearly all of the twenty-four subjects in the course of individual Rorschach Test interpretation. Composite or group Rorschach data will also be presented to clarify and high-

[1] Klopfer, B., *The Rorschach Technique,* World Book Co., New York, 1942.

[2] *Ibid.*

[3] Rapaport, D., *Diagnostic Psychological Testing,* Vol. II. Yearbook Publishers, Inc., Chicago, 1946.

[4] Rorschach, H., *Psychodiagnostics*. Huber, Berne, Switzerland, 1942.

[5] Davidson, H. H., and Klopfer, B., Rorschach Statistics: Part I. *Mentally Retarded, Normal and Superior Adults*. Rorschach Research Exchange, 1937–1938, 2, 164–169.

light our inferences regarding universal character trends in the group. A review of the literature does not reveal completely suitable norms or contrast groups against whom one might compare our present group of subjects. It is a fact that most mature workers have had experience with many more subjects of wider range of background than that found in any single normative investigation. Shall we, for example, compare our group with that of Rapaport's Kansas Highway patrolmen? [6] The latter group contains no women, and differs culturally and economically from our group. It should also be noted that Rapaport's patrolmen offer far fewer responses than do our Negro subjects. For example, the group of well-adjusted patrolmen gives a mean total response number of about 17, while our subjects average about 39 responses. This difference in the total number of responses is an obvious stumbling block in any comparison of both groups with regard to specific Rorschach variables. Similar limitations are characteristic of other groups described in the literature. In the main, therefore, I shall stress those Rorschach findings in the group data which clinical experience in individual interpretation as well as prior reported group investigations would permit one to interpret as significant.

Group Data

Composite Rorschach data are presented in Tables I and II. These data shall be discussed in terms of approach, determinants, and content.

Approach

The response total (R) is 39.2 (Table I). Most adult groups offer an average of 20–40 responses. Rapaport's normal control group averages only 18 responses. It is clear that the total number of responses of our present group tends to be high and at the upper range of normal. Total number of responses is of little significance in itself and attains meaning only in terms of the general constellation of personality tendencies. In our group, we have correlated the high response with a number of tendencies, namely: (1) the good intelligence of the group (i.e., average or better); (2) their high aspirations; (3) their apparent compliance and adjustability; their

[6] Rapaport, *op. cit.*

wish to give the overt impression of conforming to external requirements. This is not to say that these subjects are characterized by a truly liberated and creative output. Indeed, qualitatively, there is not the organization and elaboration of response, the varied content, and the rich combination of determinant that would go with effective creative productivity. Nor does the overt appearance of conformity and compliance mean genuine social rapport, as will be seen.

The individual's approach to problems and situations in his actual living are reflected in his approach to Rorschach's ink blots. The average adult offers one whole response (W) to every two detail responses (D). The normative approach according to Klopfer is 20% to 30% wholes (W), 45% to 55% usual details (D), 5% to 15% small but frequently chosen details (d), and less than 10% of unusual details (Dd) plus space details (S). It is apparent (Table I) that the average W per cent and D per cent are within normal ranges. However, mean (Dd + S) per cent tends to be high. Table II demonstrates that 50% of the subjects show an exaggerated attention to unusual detail (Dd + S). In addition a majority of the subjects (79%) show either above average D per cent or above average (Dd + S), or both. This is in accord with the inference, to be mentioned again, that these subjects avoid complicated adjustments. In spite of elevated aspirations, they seek out the simple and uncomplicated. True drive is not present. Rather there is a tendency to limit one's efforts to the apparent, to give the impression of complying, or perhaps to bustle with superficial and vacuous activities.

Determinants

As one would expect from the high response total, the average frequency of all the major determinants is above average. Thus, for example, the means of kinesthetically determined response (M) and also of color-determined response (Sum C) are above average. Average M is 4.8 and average Sum C is 3.9. The mean per cent of responses which are purely form-determined (F%) is 52.7 and within normal ranges. To outward appearances, therefore, these subjects are spontaneous, not overly constricted, free in their use of their imagination and in their affective expression. This is not the fact, however. We are merely confirmed in our belief that single Rorschach variables can have no meaning, except as interpreted in the light of personality constellations and configurations. In addition they need to be enriched by qualitative analysis of the Rorschach variables.

As many as 71% of the subjects have a Sum C score above 2. This is interpreted as potent, assertive, affective strivings. However, responses in which color is the dominating determinant and form is of secondary importance (CF) or where color is the only determinant (C) exceed the number of responses with clear, definite form and integrated use of color (FC). Mean FC is 1.6 while the sum of Mean CF plus Mean C is 2.9 (Table I). More significantly, 79% of the subjects demonstrate a (CF + C) higher than FC (Table II). One-third of the subjects show at least one pure C response—an unusual finding indeed. On the other hand, in the face of the Sum C, only 29% of the subjects show 2 or more FC responses. The inference is made that the bulk of their emotional strivings are organized along the lines of aggression. Their inner existences are turbulent with the urge to hit out, hurt and destroy.

Yet a qualitative analysis of the records leads one to the inference that they cannot accept frankly and are unable to tolerate these pushing destructive impulses. This manifests itself in a variety of ways which represent anxiety when aggression is provoked. One sees manifest expression of conflict (shock), denial and rejection reaction, aloofness, attempts to intellectualize and depersonalize, or the substitution of a thin, insincere, pollyanna-like response for the disturbing aggressive impulse. Part of this adaptive response is to resort to withdrawal and active wish-fulfilling fantasy, such as is represented in the high average M. An evaluation of the quality or direction of movement in the M responses is of even greater interest. Are the M responses extensor and moving away from the center of the figure? Or are they flexor and moving to the center of the figure? Extensor emphasis is observed in individuals who are assertive, striving, and energetic in their own behalf. In their dream and fantasy existence, they have taken on the pattern of throwing off and struggling against that which blocks them or is dangerous to them. In contrast flexor emphasis in M implies passivity, submission, resignation, and ofttimes apathy. Sixty-three per cent of the subjects demonstrate more flexor M than extensor M, while only 29% of the subjects show more extensor M than flexor M. There is thus a greater trend to flexor M than to extensor M. This trend becomes even clearer if one analyzes those responses included in the extensor M tabulation. The latter M include all references to dancing figures.

It is a fact of some significance that 54% of the group offer one or more "dancer" responses; and that such responses total 24% of all the extensor responses. In the light of their aggressive urges and their equally conspicuous adaptive pattern of compliance, dancing would seem to reflect an inability to express emotional impulses frankly and an attempt to find socially disguised and acceptable outlets. This observation is further favored by the fact that 38% of the group offer extensor M involving restricted extensor motion such as pointing, reaching, or simply extending without objective. Such responses make up 22% of all extensor M. We may conclude that the basic pattern of social adaptation is one of submissive docility and obsequiousness. As already stated, however, their resentments and aggressive inclinations are by no means completely submerged. Indeed, they continuously assert themselves, disorganize and cause our subjects to be at odds with themselves.

In view of their special interest, illustrations of flexor M are reproduced:

1. Card II: ". . . the figure taken as a whole looks like two figures bending perhaps, holding their hands together in prayer. It seems that the two knees come together where the red is. Perhaps the red could be fire or some symbol of tribal tribute—in adoration, holding something up to God . . ."
2. Card IX: "This looks like an old lady scrubbing the floor or something. Bowed down."
3. Card VII: "This is two men with big rocks or something on their heads . . . Rocks are so heavy they bend his back."
4. Card II: ". . . woman down on her hands and knees."
5. Card III: "These look like two slave servants. Look as if they are bending down to pick up something. Look like Negroes to me. I associate that right away with a servant." (This is the only reference to a Negro in all the records.)

Light-determined responses are common in the group. Three or more such responses are found in 71% of the subjects. A dysphoric trend is tentatively suggested. In reviewing the individual records, I found as a particularly salient feature the extent of achromatic color responses (C′). The mean C′ of the group is 1.9 and C′ is found in 58% of the group. Klopfer suggests that such responses are found among those individuals who have had extensive traumatic experience. We have interpreted the trend to C′ in accord with Oberholzer's hypothesis that black and white, as a significant determinant, is evidence of apathy and resignation. Other evidence for such a tendency has already been described.

Content

Average percentage of animal responses (A) is 37.3%. In addition the great majority of the group (88%) has an A per cent less than 50%. This would indicate normal intellectual adaptivity.

The average number of popular responses (P) is 5. Seventy-one per cent of the group has a P score of 4 or more. This, too, is consistent with the inference that the group is an outwardly adaptive one.

Anatomy responses (At) occur frequently. Mean At per cent is 10.2; and one or more anatomy responses are found in 88% of the records. It is my belief that an At per cent of 10.2 is high in a group with trend to high R total. (This point is stressed in view of Rapaport's finding [7] that his well-adjusted controls also gave an average of 10% At responses. We have already commented on the fact of small average R in Rapaport's control group.) I have interpreted the trend to At response to be evidence of a sense of intellectual inadequacy with the need to impress, as well as an undermining anxiety which our subjects try to cover and deny by a process of intellectualization.

Finally, our attention has been drawn to two meaningful facts: namely, (1) the sizable number of subjects (38%) who offer blood responses and (2) the even higher percentage of subjects (88%) who offer one or more images in which human physical mutilation is fantasied. Both types of response would indicate pressing, straining hostility and aggression. In the face of what has already been said about the group's dominantly compliant mode of adjustment, however, is it inferred that their aggressive drives are not permitted to find expression. Instead, they act to disturb and disorganize by bubbling, incessantly and complainingly, below the surface.

Color shock and shading shock

Color shock refers to a startle reaction demonstrated on presentation of the colored cards with evidence of delay, conflict and abrupt paucity of response. Shading shock refers to similar disturbance on presentation of the black and white, shaded cards.

[7] *Ibid.*

Color shock is seen in 88% of the group. A pattern of conflict is the interpretation. In association with the color tendencies already described, the interpretation has been made that the group has hostile impulses, which it tolerates poorly and to which it reacts with subjective sense of conflict and doubt.

Shading shock is seen in 100% of the test records. The inference drawn is that these subjects are characterized by intense, pervasive anxiety and overriding fear of external threat.

Individual Test Interpretations

The total constellation of findings gives direction and meaning to the single Rorschach factor. In individual test interpretation, conclusions are reached on the basis of multiple, mutually confirmatory Rorschach findings, all seen in patterned relationship to each other. Thus, for example, intelligence is inferred from the response total, content and range of content, perceptual accuracy, organization level, number and quality of W, number and quality of M, and succession. Similarly, intellectual efficiency is interpreted from consistency in such factors as form accuracy or organization level. Again, aggression may be interpreted from the handling of color and content. Or anxiety may be interpreted from reaction to light-determined stimuli, shading shock, and content. Understanding, therefore, the configurational basis of interpretation of an individual's Rorschach Test responses, the dominant trends noted in the 24 subjects will be presented. These trends are summarized in Table III.

An exact estimate of global intelligence is not being offered. However, a summary of ratings of intellectual status on the basis of Rorschach Test results indicates that all the subjects are assayed as average or better. However, 92% of the group give evidence of reduced efficiency and incomplete utilization of potential capacity.

Profound anxiety is hypothesized in all the records. Life is viewed as dangerous, hostile and assaultive. They feel small and inferior; and they have a persistent fear of mutilation and destruction.

Another universal trait in this group is a sweeping, pushing, impelling hostility or aggressive inclination. Equally conspicuous in all the subjects is their inability to give free rein to their assertive aggressive drives and destructive impulses. These impulses are a source of conflict and disability; and they are not accepted complacently. The subjects are tense and strained; and they sit uncertainly on the lid of a turbulent and explosively simmering cauldron of hostility. They expend great energy in containing and controlling aggression. Yet, always, it remains a problem to them.

Their defenses against their intolerable urge to hurt includes denial or rejection of the impulse and the assumption of a cool, reserved exterior. Of importance is the defensive adaptation of ingratiating compliance observed in all of the subjects. They tend to be passive, submissive, and resigned to their dangers and insecurities. Although they typically present the external features of social conformability, it is interpreted that they are all characteristically distrustful and suspicious. They tend to be isolated and in poor rapport with other humans.

In the individual test interpretations, a compelling, keen desire for status is interpreted in 54% of the group. This wish manifests itself in such qualities as intellectual pretentiousness, cultural and aesthetic striving, wordiness, and the investment of great value in outward show and decoration. Verbal expression, too, is often highly valued though words may be used stiffly and awkwardly. While aspirations are elevated, potentialities are not well fulfilled. Indeed the majority are prone to turn from difficult accomplishment and to be more comfortable with the simple and uncomplicated activity and life experience.

Finally, in 46% of the cases (7 of 13 males, 4 of 11 females), sexual maladjustment is conspicuous. This expresses itself in sexual conflict and uncertainty with regard to sexual integrity. In this group with manifest sexual problems, the men appear particularly confused with regard to their sexual role and they are perplexed and doubtful of their masculinity.

The 24 subjects described in this chapter show definite differences in personality among themselves. However, the remarkable uniformity and the universality of certain important and dominating character trends within the group are startling findings, indeed. Similar conclusions were not noted in a previous Rorschach study of 100 white and 100 Negro subjects by Sicha.[8] However, this investigation was highly limited in its objective and was merely a study of the Rorschach "Erlebness-Typus" or M to C ratio. The

[8] Sicha, M. H., "A Study of Rorschach Erlebness-Typus of Comparable White and Negro Subjects" (thesis), Columbia University, 1939.

major finding was that the Negroes were more extrotensive than the whites, though both groups were more extrotensive than introversive. Other than this, no findings are presented. Interpretation is avoided, so that Sicha's conclusions are of no help in the present study.

We have hypothesized major personality trends in a group of 24 Negro subjects, on the basis of their responses to the Rorschach Test. Responsibility for the selection of the subjects, for the interpretation of the broader implication and significance of our results, for comparing the results of the Rorschach Test and those of psychodynamic analyses, and for integrating the findings of both techniques is that of the authors of this volume.

In concluding, it is believed that the Rorschach Test is profitably employed to test conclusions regarding individual traits, derived from other sources. In so doing, however, certain qualifications are in order:

1. The test cannot hope to offer a picture of all aspects of personality. This principle holds particularly where the interpretation is "blind." The Rorschach Test may be said to simulate the X-ray film in physical diagnosis. The X-ray film cannot by itself reproduce the warm, full-bodied, alive human being.

2. Overt behavior is predicted with difficulty. The test points to potentialities for reaction. Actual behavior, however, is also based on total life circumstance, about which the Rorschach Test is quite unenlightening.

3. The most conspicuous tendencies tend to dominate the test. Where pathology is prominent, subtle signs of health are often obliterated.

4. The test gives a cross-sectional picture of the individual at a given moment. He is not seen in the process of change and development. The dynamic genesis of character traits is not observed. This would preclude a complete grasp of an individual's personality.

5. Finally, the significance of trends inferred from the Rorschach Test still needs evaluation. To what extent are the observed tendencies unalterable reactions or reactions to specific experience or even mood? How shall the inferred trends be weighted? Are suspicion and distrust representative of paranoid or projective trends where assault and danger are a reality? Is it ever possible to interpret the Rorschach Test accurately without knowing what has been the life experience of the subject under investigation?

TABLE I

RORSCHACH DATA (A): FREQUENCY OF RORSCHACH VARIABLES

	Kardiner-Ovesey *Mean*	*Kardiner-Ovesey* *Standard Deviation*	*Gardner*[9] *Mean*	*Guirdham*[10] *Mean*	*Rapaport*[11] *Mean*
R	39.21	21.21	22	33	17
W	8.21	3.22	7	9	7
D	24.08	13.05	13	21	9
d	0.54	1.08 }	{ 1–2	{ 2.5	{ 1
Dd	5.92	7.47 }			
S	0.54	1.31	0–1	2	1
W%	26.67	19.08			
D%	59.04	14.94			
d%	1.29	2.24			
(Dd + S)%	12.67	12.28			
M	4.79	3.91	1	1.6	1
FM	3.17	3.14			
F	20.75	13.64			
C′	1.92	2.39			0.6
FC	1.63	2.37	0.4	1.6	1.0
CF	2.42	2.08	0.5	0.9	0.7
C	0.50	0.95	0.6	0.2	0.0
Sum C	3.92	2.81	1.5	2.0	
H	5.04	4.41			
Hd	4.58	5.13			
A	10.08	5.57			
Ad	4.38	4.32			
At	2.54	2.50			
F%	52.66	15.16			
H%	23.63	15.15			
At%	10.17	14.65			
A%	37.25	12.65			
P	5.00	2.33			
P%	14.63	5.03			

[9] Gardner, G. E., "Rorschach Test Replies and Results in 100 Normal Adults of Average IQ," *American Journal of Orthopsychiatry*, 6:32–60 (1936).

[10] Guirdham, A., "On the Value of the Rorschach Test," *Journal of Mental Science*, 81:848–869 (1935).

[11] Rapaport, *op. cit.* (well-adjusted patrolmen).

TABLE II

RORSCHACH DATA (B)

	Number of subjects	*Per cent of total*
Approach		
W above average	8	33
D above average	14	58
Dd + S above average	12	50
D or Dd + S above average	19	79
Determinants		
M > 2	20	83
Sum C > 2	17	71
CF + C > FC	19	79
Pure C	8	33
FC, 2 or more	7	29
Total light-determined response, 3 or more	17	71
Vista responses, 1 or more	9	38
Flat gray responses, 3 or more	12	50
C′, 1 or more	14	58
More flexor M than extensor M	15	63
More extensor M than flexor M	7	29
1 or more dancing extensor M	13	54
1 or more reaching or pointing extensor M	9	38
Content		
A%, 50% or less	21	88
P, 4 or more	17	71
At, 1 or more	21	88
Blood response, 1 or more	9	38
Mutilation fantasy, 1 or more	21	88
Shading shock	24	100
Color shock	21	88

TABLE III

RORSCHACH TEST INTERPRETATIONS

	Number of subjects	*Per cent of total*
Intelligence		
Average	14	58
Good average or better	10	42
Intellectual efficiency		
Average	2	8
Reduced	22	92
Deep anxiety	24	100
Aggression	24	100
Conflict with regard to aggressive urges	23	96
Suspiciousness, emotional isolation, deficient rapport with other humans	24	100
Apathy, passivity, compliance	24	100
Sexual conflicts and doubts	11	46
Above average desire for status	13	54

CHAPTER ELEVEN
Synthesis of Experimental Data

THE VALUE of the Rorschach Test in establishing basic personality was first demonstrated by Emil Oberholzer in connection with the research on Alorese culture.[1] We have made use of this test in the study of the Negro partly to confirm the psychodynamic findings, partly to get fresh insights. Considering that these Rorschachs were all done "blind" by Dr. Goldfarb, except for the knowledge that the subjects were Negroes, the correspondence between the two procedures is quite remarkable. The findings from the Rorschach report that are of aid in helping us reconstruct the psychodynamic picture are the following: the discrepancy between the potential and effective intelligence; the imagery used to describe fear of the environment through mutilation fantasies; the predilection for flexor responses; the use of dancing to express blocked affect, particularly aggression, through diversion into disguised, but socially acceptable channels; the absence of the "adaptational improvement," particularly in terms of affectivity range, that we found in the psychodynamic picture of the middle and upper classes. This is the most startling feature of the report. Dr. Goldfarb denies any evidence in the Rorschach protocols of essential psychological differences along class lines. This discrepancy between clinical and Rorschach findings needs to be explained.

The discrepancy between potential and effective intelligence is the result of the divided attention, the destruction of spontaneity, the vigilance consumed in anticipation of hostile stimuli and the

[1] Du Bois, Cora, *The People of Alor*, University of Minnesota Press, 1944.
Kardiner, A., and Associates, *The Psychological Frontiers of Society*, Columbia University Press, 1945.

necessity to curb aggressive response. These maneuvers, though they are automatized, detract from the utility value of the intelligence because reality is greeted with anxious expectation and spontaneous response must be controlled. The diminution of intellectual capacity by emotional preoccupation has long been known to psychiatry in the form of hysterical "stupidity." This kind of "stupidity" is usually limited to a specific subject matter. Thus, a clinical example is that of a patient who was hopelessly stupid in learning a new technique invented by some of his younger competitors in a technical field. The hysterical preoccupation proved to be an unconscious conflict between dependent and aggressive attitudes. This patient surrendered to his passive cravings by enormously exaggerating the achievements and technical virtuosity of his younger competitors and correspondingly belittled his own considerable achievements. His "stupidity" was an inhibition created by the false identification of his assertive efforts with equivalents of murdering his rivals. There are other variations of this neurotic mechanism.

It is not this mechanism, however, that is characteristic of the Negro's failure to use his intelligence fully. In his case, the explanation is largely in his conscious appraisal of external reality and the necessity to exercise stringent control over his responses. We have here, in other words, a loss of efficiency due to preoccupation with factors that have prior claim to attention. This discrepancy between potential and effective intelligence also has a bearing on the ability to translate aspirations into achievement. The social barriers are enormous; hence, there is a great temptation to be satisfied with symbolic equivalents that have only a slight resemblance to the real thing, e.g., flamboyance instead of status. The amount of push in back of the aspiration is tremendous, but the accepted satisfaction is only a fraction of that desired. This may have the effect of diminishing the intensity of the frustration involved, but simultaneously it may create the impression of a lowered intelligence.

The high frequency of mutilation responses in these Rorschachs raises the question of their psychodynamic significance. This type of response is found commonly in two syndromes, the traumatic neuroses of war and schizophrenia. In the former the response represents an inadequacy of the ego organization due to massive inhibition of personality functions. The consequence is a real discrepancy between the stimuli coming from the outer world and the available resources for organized mastery. The subject therefore feels himself mangled by the environment. The same problem exists in schizophrenia, though the character of the inner disorganization is quite different. Here, the affective base of the relations between people and things is seriously disturbed, and here, likewise, the subject is robbed of one of the essential elements of control over the environment. Delusions are an effort to reinstate such control, but at the price of a further serious distortion of reality. The large number of mutilation responses in these Negro Rorschachs indicates that it does not matter where the control is lost, be it through neurotic impounding (war neurosis), affectivity disturbance (schizophrenia), or sheer inability to control the environment because of externally imposed barriers; the mutilation response comes through in all three. It is therefore a general indicator of a discrepancy between available resources and the challenges in the outer world. The Rorschach does not tell us whether the origin of this discrepancy is inhibitory, affective, or social, but it registers the correct impression that the subject feels he is being disintegrated by the onslaughts of forces he cannot ward off. In the case of the Negro this disintegrative process is facilitated by the fact that even such a response as disorganized rage on a hedonic level (pain-pleasure basis) must also be checked. Hence, the aggression must be denied, impersonalized, treated with aloofness, intellectualized, watered down, replaced by pollyanna-like attitudes, or made into wish-fulfillments. All of these modifications in the aggressive response distort reality, and, when they are carried out repeatedly and habitually, they permanently disturb the effective integration of the self to the environment.

The predilection in the Rorschach for flexor responses is another indication of how the relations between the self and the environment have been settled in the interests of staving off anxiety. The disintegrating effects of the display of aggression are resolved by taking the submissive attitude in advance and resigning oneself to it.

However, the next factor we note, the predilection for dancing as a movement (M) response, indicates an attempt at a more active disposition of the problem of aggression. We must conclude from these Rorschach configurations that dancing, for which the Negro has such remarkable talent, is not a positive and abandoned joyful expression, but a socially permissible vehicle through which his aggression can be expressed. We are reminded, in this connection, of a play (*Burlesque*) which was a great Broadway success in the twenties. Here, the husband of a neglected wife, who threatens to leave him for another man, shows his enraged jealousy by performing an abandoned and hysterical dance. No one in the audience is ignorant of the fact that the dancing is a rage equivalent, and the dramatic effect is thereby enormously enhanced. Moreover, it wins his wife back to him.

This motivational backdrop is missing in the white man's appreciation of the Negro's dancing. It appears to us as a form of hedonistic abandonment and our enjoyment of it is due to our ignorance of its motivational source. It is by virtue of this that the Negro has become the vicarious vehicle through which we express a hedonistic abandonment. The same is true of his rhythmic and rhapsodic jazz inventions and his specialization in "blues" songs. Negro hedonistic abandonment in song and dance exists on a denial basis, for it cannot have any basis in his actual feeling of well-being, triumph, or euphoria. It is a strange paradox that a by-product of Negro suffering and denial should have become a vehicle for the expression of a euphoric abandonment which is identified the world over as an American cultural product.

Dancing also has other meanings in addition to the siphoning off of aggression. It undoubtedly serves as a permissible vehicle for otherwise constricted affectivity no matter what the source. Nevertheless, in the case of the Negro, the predominant emotion which finds expression through dancing is rage. The same can be said for the Negro's acknowledged proficiency in competitive sports. Here, again, his performance is greatly enhanced by the energizing action of aggression that under other circumstances must remain suppressed.

The most important discrepancy between the psychodynamic and Rorschach findings lies in the failure of the Rorschach to confirm the improvement in affectivity range that was noted in the psychodynamic picture of the middle and upper classes. What can this discrepancy mean? Does it mean that the Rorschach is not delicate enough to catch such a gross factor as improvement in affectivity range? Is one or the other wrong, or is there a third factor at play, a consideration of which would enable us to reconcile the discrepancy? We are not disposed to throw the Rorschach report out because of this. On the contrary, we prefer to reconcile the one approach with the other. In so doing we open a very troublesome technical issue concerning the diagnosis of social behavior.

We do not know how fully to explain this discrepancy. Any reflections we set down must therefore remain tentative. This discrepancy needs much more investigation before anything conclusive can be demonstrated. Meanwhile, the following are a few guesses.

In our psychodynamic summary we pointed out that the distribution of anxiety in the upper and lower classes was a bit different. The sum total of frustration is about the same, except for the fact that the anxiety proceeds from different sources. In the lower classes it is largely a subsistence anxiety, in the upper largely a status anxiety. This distribution would not, however, account for the discrepancy reported for affectivity improvement in the upper classes. Another factor is at work. The improvement noted is primarily in form, not in emotional content. That is, the middle and upper classes, driven by the mimetic urge to emulate the white middle-class standards, do so on a formal basis. They are well aware of what is expected of them, and actually do behave as if the affectivity were better. What happens, then, to the better emotional integration that supposedly arose from the more adequate child care, the happier relations between the sexes, and the lessening of rivalry between the siblings? This is in all likelihood greatly spoiled by the depredations created by the caste system and the self-contempt it induces. In other words, the makings of a more effective integration are there and behavioristically are definitely present. But the inner organization of this better affectivity is spoiled by the interference of self-hatred and aggression. In the lower classes this control of behavior to conform to middle-class white standards is less insistent, and aggression is played out more directly. In the upper classes a great deal more control and attention are concentrated on "face" and appearance in the interests of conformity with the accepted white ideal.

This glaring fact emphasizes the importance of our original classification of behavior from the point of view of integrative, learned, or mimetic systems. The better affectivity of the middle and upper classes, as it showed up in the psychodynamic analyses, is to a large extent of mimetic rather than of integrative origin. That is why it fails to register on the Rorschach Test, which is designed to pick up integrative responses. The better integrative setting for the middle and upper classes is vitiated and destroyed by the caste system with its many ramifications and devastating effects. This is the same problem that was posed by the difference between potential and effective intelligence. In the case of affectivity, what is left is the formal response in the interests of mimesis.

A second tentative explanation of the discrepancy is possible on the basis of a *mass action* influence of predominant emotion. A predominant emotion of momentary anxiety or rage at the time the Rorschach is taken can polarize the responses that might be different were they elicited under more favorable conditions. Such momentary shifting in responses can be observed in answers given to the Rorschach by the same person at frequent intervals when the subject was under different emotional moods. We doubt, however, that momentary emotion could restrict Rorschach responses to such a high degree. The mass action principle works on a long term chronic basis in the adaptation of the Negro.

The mass action and the mimetic principles are actually not incompatible. The simplest form in which mimesis operates socially is contained in the formula of "keeping up with the Joneses." In the case of the Negro, however, this formula is not purely imitative; it is a part of the Negro ego-ideal and serves in part to create the attributes of "whiteness." This principle is very active in all forms of acculturation.

Restrictions on space prevent us from publishing fully the results of the Thematic Apperception Test (T.A.T.). For the greater part they show much the same thing as the Rorschach experiment. However, some points come out with greater clarity because the T.A.T. is semi-structured (while the Rorschach is completely unstructured) along the lines of social interaction. The T.A.T. asks the subject to interpret a social situation which contains a planned ambiguity. The responses demonstrate the influence of the integrative systems in operation. A trait that shows up with particular clarity in our T.A.T. series is the mechanism of denial. It is well illustrated in a response to a card which depicts night, gloom, and fog, as "a spring scene with flowers." Whatever the motivation of this denial, such distortion of a mood into its opposite cannot be an isolated experience. If the subject can do this simply on the provocation of a picture stimulus, he must be actively engaged in doing the same thing a thousand times a day. Another point that comes out with considerable clarity in the T.A.T. is the equation: aggression + control = emotional flatness. That is to say, the sheer mass of effort used in controlling aggression can choke off other forms of affect which are potentially there.

The T.A.T. also adds a bit of body to the conclusions of the Rorschach concerning sexual difficulties. Here, this difficulty shows itself in different ways in the male and the female. The female tends to regard the male as irresponsible and as an exploiter. There is a great deal of protest against his failure as a provider and protector. (This is why Father Divine makes such an appeal to the Negro female.) Hence, men are seen as dangerous. The males, on the other hand, tend to confuse the sexual and social roles and see explicitly female figures as masculine and authoritative. Therefore, their attitudes to women are mistrust, hostility, and a resentful dependency. Females also represent conscience and ideals to several of the males. Judging from the T.A.T. responses the "sexual" difficulties between male and female are largely the result of confused social roles.[2]

On the whole, we must be satisfied that the conclusions derived from the three different experimental approaches—the psychodynamic analysis, the Rorschach Test, and the T.A.T.—are essentially the same. The major features of the Negro personality emerge from each with remarkable consistency. These include the fear of relatedness, suspicion, mistrust, the enormous problem of control of aggression, the denial mechanism, the tendency to dissipate the tension of a provocative situation by reducing it to something simpler, or to something entirely different. All these maneuvers are in the interest of not meeting reality head on.

In conclusion, we must reiterate that the psychodynamic, the Rorschach, and the T.A.T. points of view specialize on defects in adaptation. That is what they are for. They do not, therefore, give a picture of the total adaptation, but mainly of the motivational sources for miscarriages of adaptation. Perhaps more than in any other group that has come to our attention, with the possible exception of the Alorese, was it as clearly demonstrated that the defects in adaptation are not of mysterious or racial origin, but owe their existence

[2] The protocols on which these remarks on the T.A.T. were prepared were drawn up by Ethel D. Kardiner.

entirely to the arduous emotional conditions under which the Negro in America is obliged to live. The defects in his adaptation are truly the mark of oppression.

Nor must we overlook what is perhaps the most important lesson of this study. The defects of adaptation that we have described, together with their social sources, make a dismal picture of human misery, one for which it is hard to find a parallel. However, in spite of its defects when compared to white standards, we must not forget that in the face of such hardships it is a heroic achievement to be able to adjust and to survive. The authors have often been amazed at the remarkable ingenuity and stamina that most of these subjects showed, and each of the authors has privately thought that under similar conditions of living, neither could have done as well.

CHAPTER TWELVE

The Expressions of Negro Personality

HERETOFORE, in previous research,[1] we relied on an adaptational scheme to furnish us with a program of study. This scheme was based on the principle that certain experiences mold the personality, and that, in turn, the personality then creates certain varieties of expression, either in the form of institutions, or in the form of a specific type of fantasy. These were arbitrarily called projective systems and could be identified in religion, folklore, and other forms of communal expression. These systems are, for the greater part, unconscious in origin. They could be used as a demonstration that certain specific factors were operating in the personality in a given culture, or they could be used to indicate where certain pressures were falling. These projective systems had a high adaptational value and played the same role for the culture that fantasy life does for the individual. For example, among the Alorese, we found a distinctive motif in the folklore, the theme of vengeance on parents. In view of the fact that the Alorese child is neglected by its parents, this motif in the folklore makes motivational sense. It serves as a common vehicle of discharge of a suppressed feeling tone which cannot be discharged in real life. Or, in the case of the Marquesas, the folklore was filled with a hostile representation of the female that is unique in all folklore. This representation was not fortuitous; it had a distinct relation to the experience of the child, and had a high

[1] Kardiner, *op. cit.*

expressive value—that of contempt and fear of the female—to the community as a whole.

The attempt to apply this same technique to the Negro must be made with certain cautions in mind. In the first place, have we any right to expect anything distinctive about the Negro expression since his culture is American? The answer, if based on our studies of "primitive" cultures, would be *no*. Since the personality is American, we can expect nothing new that is not found elsewhere in American culture. However, this position does not do justice to the facts that we established in the biographical studies, nor does it do justice to the distinctive history of the Negro in America. As we have already indicated, the slave personality had distinctive features, and we have a right to expect that the fantasy productions of this period of Negro history should likewise be expressive of certain trends—surely not all—in this personality. We ought to be able to find some communal expression of this period, in the spirituals and in the fragments of folklore contained in the Br'er Rabbit and Uncle Remus stories.

Spirituals and folk tales

We can pause for a moment to make a few observations about these forms of expression. The Spirituals are undoubtedly survivals of the slave years, and represent an accommodative trend toward slavery. They do not ring with protest or hatred. They all contain a resignation to the slave status and a wish for liberation by a higher power. They contain identifications with the Hebrews, who were slaves in Egypt, but were liberated by the Lord; there is identification with the suffering Jesus, who "never said a mumblin' word"; with "li'l David," who slew Goliath; with a lamb and with a motherless child. The self-representation is that of fatigue, of sufferings that no one knows about, of sinking down, of anticipating deliverance, of waiting for a chariot "comin' for to carry me home." These folk songs are devoid of rage and of guilt. They undoubtedly had a high value in creating emotional release, as well as a community feeling for the oppressed people.

The Br'er Rabbit and Uncle Remus tales are the only remnants of anything that can be called a folklore. True they were gathered and edited by a white man (J. C. Harris), who placed these stories in the mouth of Uncle Remus, a white stereotype of the compliant and accommodative Negro. The general pattern of these stories is very like those found in many parts of aboriginal America and Africa. The chief protagonist is an exceedingly clever animal—a rabbit or coyote—who outwits all those who try to best him. He has a thousand lives, and is never beaten no matter how many hair-breadth escapes he has. He is resourceful and clever without limit. Br'er Rabbit and Coyote are still with us in the form of Mickey Mouse and Donald Duck.

The adaptation of these stories to the conditions of slavery is all too obvious. It is always the clever rabbit who outwits the strong and wily fox. This was a vehicle for expressing hatred to the white, the wish to torture, outwit, ridicule and destroy him. This hatred is clearly envisaged, but kept under suppressive control. These tales permitted consummation in fantasy of aggressive attitudes, and one could gloat freely over the torture and demise of the fox, since the overt expression of such attitudes to the white man was blocked. These tales must have had a good deal of release value.

These Spirituals and folk tales do not belong to the contemporary scene, and hence, cannot be used in any way to supplement our study of the present-day Negro personality. Where, then, can we look for such expression? Can we look to the vast protest literature that has grown up for a hundred and fifty years? This would have some value; but in it, we would only expect to find and appeal to the white man's sense of justice and fair play. It contains a repeated appeal through the demonstration of the damage and suffering wrought by continued injustice and discrimination. This literature represents the conscious and articulate protest which needs no psychological explanation. It contains no hidden trends. On the other hand, we do find, particularly in the contemporary novel written by Negroes, some faithful representations of factors that do need explanation and are truly distinctive. Why, for example, do most novels by Negroes about Negroes have predominantly females as their chief characters? Why, in so many of them, is the fate of the male decided, not by his paternal ideal, but by his female relatives? Why are there so few really masterful male figures? Why is female father-attachment so rare in these novels? Why is there a paucity of dialogue between two people? Why is uncommunicated self-expression so common, and why the common device of describing a scene in terms of what each person is feeling, yet ending without either making contact with the other? [1a]

These are all features that deserve special study. But this volume is hardly the place for it. Perhaps some of these will be explained to some extent by what we do undertake to explain. Shall we look for these hidden trends in statistics about crime or the incidence of nervous and mental disease? We do not expect to find anything distinctive in either case.

Crime

In the case of crime, the statistics concerning incidence are notoriously unreliable and the features that are established speak for themselves. Arrest rates among Negroes are higher for petty offenses: assault, burglary, petty larceny, disorderly conduct, drunkenness, vagrancy, and juvenile delinquency. They are not conspicuous in fraud, embezzlement, and forgery. They have no conspicuous place in big-time rackets, a fact that can be ascribed to discrimination against the Negro there too, though they are used as flunkeys, dope runners, and the like. The Negro predominates in impulsive and not in long-range, planned crime. This is probably why homicide figures for the Negro run higher than in whites proportionate to population. Impulsive crime has an immediate discharge function.

The problem in connection with crime in the Negro is not to account for the fact that the rates are so high, but rather to account for the fact that they are not much higher, considering that the provocations, in the form of continuous frustration, are so much stronger and more frequent than in the white. To this we can only say that the Negro is trained by experience from earliest childhood in the suppression of aggression. He has plenty of aggressive affect, but fails on the executive side. Watchfulness over this aggression is a constant preoccupation with every Negro. He does not discharge it because he is afraid to do so. There is less resistance to discharge from Negro to Negro and most of the violence we have observed is of the beating up variety, taking place largely between husbands and wives, parents and children.

[1a] These features of the Negro novel were called to our attention by Thelma B. Goldberg, graduate student at Columbia University, in her unpublished paper, *A Content Analysis of Negro Fiction.*

Nervous and mental disease

The same difficulties face us in the evaluation of nervous and mental disease in the Negro as we encountered in the evaluation of crime. But here the situation is a bit more complex, because most authors writing on the subject have not standardized the basic Negro personality. Hence, their observations record certain oddities which seem to be idiosyncratic to the Negro and so are ascribed to racial origin. About this we can only say that mental diseases have form and content. The form of schizophrenia, as a type of mental aberration, is pandemic in every culture ever observed; the content will vary according to the basic personality, which is ontogenetically integrated. Thus, schizophrenia in Western society is largely inclined to paranoid configurations. This is not necessarily so in all cultures.

There is only one blatant fact that stands out in the statistical studies of insanity in Negroes as compared to whites, and that is the great increase in organic psychoses in the Negro due to alcoholism and general paresis (cerebro-spinal syphilis).[2] The latter is due to ignorance and the former to the increased necessity on the part of the Negro for narcotizing himself to his traumatic world. No such decisive differences appear in relation to manic-depressive and schizophrenic disorders. This is a startling fact, because we would tend, a priori, to assume that the incidence would be much higher, owing to the greater general hardship that accompanies adaptation for the Negro in America. These factors apparently do not increase the predisposition to the "functional" psychoses.

The so-called idiosyncratic factors found in these latter types of disorder must be standardized against the known conditions to which the Negro must adjust. For example, in our Rorschach records, mutilation fantasies with considerable fear of the external environment are extremely common. Such anxieties mean one thing in the white and another in the Negro. In the white, they mean paranoid tendencies; but not in the Negro. For the latter, to see hostility in the environment is a normal perception. Hence, we must guard against calling the Negro paranoid when he actually lives in an environment that persecutes him. In the same way, we must reserve

[2] *See* Benjamin Malzberg, "Mental Disease among American Negroes: A Statistical Analysis," in Otto Klineberg (ed.), *Characteristics of the American Negro*, Harper, 1944.

judgment on the significance of such observations, for example, as those of Lewis and Hubbard [3] concerning the Negro's "comparative lack of self-consciousness" and his reported tendency to "draw a fainter line of demarcation between will and destiny, illusion and knowledge, and dreams and facts, and make less distinction between hallucinations and objective existences." These all await standardization of the norm for the Negro personality in the light of the social realities that confront him.

For true expressions of the Negro personality (and by this we mean, to repeat, the impact of the distinctive features of Negro adaptation on a personality that is otherwise like the white) we must look elsewhere. We do not aim to be exhaustive in this inventory; we merely aim to deal with the most prominent features, to give us a framework for further research. If our studies of the personality are correct, we ought to be able to explain some prominent features of Negro social life: the psychological antecedents of the broken home in the lower classes, the distinctive and atypical character of male-female relations, the social cohesion of the Negro, and the fate of the religion adopted from the whites by the Negro.

The broken home

In discussing the broken home as one of the expressions of Negro personality, we seem to commit the error of using it both as a cause and as an effect. This is not an error. It is the kind of cycle that is easily demonstrable in any culture. Beginning in Alor with maternal neglect, we can trace the effects of this in the individual so that when the child becomes a mother she then repeats the same thing; she neglects and rejects her children. This is not an imitative process by any means; it is the end result of an integrative process.

The broken home in the lower-class family is very commonly attributed to the precarious economic conditions under which these families live. This statement is not untrue; it is merely incomplete. No single factor operates in such direct line to so complex an end product as the broken home. This is the culmination of a large number of factors, each of which adds to the momentum of the rest.

Let us begin arbitrarily somewhere in the cycle, with the father

[3] Lewis, Nolan D. C., and Hubbard, Louis D., "Manic-Depressive Reactions in Negroes," Vol. XI of Research Publications of the Association for Research in Nervous and Mental Disease, *Manic-Depressive Psychosis*, Baltimore, 1931.

who abandons his wife and offspring. On the face of it, this is very easy to explain by merely saying that the father has no sense of responsibility, and since this is a very reprehensible trait, the Negro male bears the brunt of the accusation. Moreover, since this is generally considered a character trait of the Negro—presumably of racial origin—that seems to settle the matter. Our researches in personality do not bear out this trite conclusion.

More often than not, the father who abandons his children was himself the product of a broken home. Which means that he never had the patient care of a father to whom he, as a child, could look for protection and take as an ideal. On the contrary, he was generally in the custody of some foster parent who treated him cruelly; he commonly had violent sibling rivalry with step-siblings and usually got the worst of it. His mother, if she cared for him, had to work and was generally irritable and demanded immediate obedience. He never received tender and affectionate care. The end result of these factors is that he grew up to think little of himself, to expect nothing but frustrations from his mother and siblings; he trusted no one and his capacity for cooperative affectivity was severely damaged in the whole process. In addition to all this, he did not grow up with a very exalted ideal of masculinity, which he heard repeatedly disparaged by his female relatives who, to be sure, were the mainstays of his life.

Here, another factor enters to make a contribution to the damage. His mother image is not an affectionate and loving one; it is harsh and demanding; the woman is one toward whom he seems foredoomed to take a submissive attitude, contrary to the commonly accepted ideal. This spoils his sexual attitude. He may or may not emerge with some gross sexual disturbance, like impotence. But he surely comes out of it with a disturbed, unconfident, untrusting attitude. If he marries, he knows the woman has much better economic chances than he has. Then, his position in the home is already jeopardized by his preparation for submissiveness to her—in our male-oriented society.

With this as a preparation, he enters marriage, usually impulsively. Neither he nor his spouse have any great tolerance for mutual incompatibilities. Now come the vicissitudes of employment. If he finds work, it is hardly ever permanent, nor does it last for long periods. Or he must go to another city in search of work. He tries, and in many instances tries very hard, to live up to his obligations. But he cannot do so and he fails continuously. It is at this point that the dissatisfied wife takes a hand at berating and browbeating—and often invites him to leave—or he leaves at the end of a long saga of frustrated efforts.

The antagonism in the broken home is mostly due to the incapacity of both mates for continuous relatedness. There is generally fear and suspicion on both sides. Several of the males we studied continued for long periods to have tender feelings for their children; but few retain much for the wife. Not infrequently, the deserter gets a job in another city, gets caught up in serious debts, and begs and borrows—in addition to working hard—to pay them back. These harassed men often go on sprees, for a bit of self-indulgence, or spend out of proportion for their clothes, to bolster their fallen morale. The deserter is not generally a vindictive or self-righteous figure. He is generally a very defeated person, who now tries to drown his sorrows in drink or in a not very abandoned hedonism with women, to whom he can discharge his obligations with money —which means more indebtedness, etc., etc. . . .

Let us consider the instance of the male who does not desert the family, but stays on and lets his wife take up the slack. She works to supply the main support of the family while his sporadic earnings help occasionally. He is now definitely subordinate to his wife. Some of the histories indicate that under these conditions the man is submissive and unassertive, or he is overassertive and domineering over his children.

The abandoned wife usually tries marriage a second time. Meanwhile, she leads a harassed existence between work and caring for her young. Generally, she tries to do this herself. Her mother, if alive, is frequently helpful. Failing this, a sister or a brother takes the child, where he is not wanted and he is exposed to bitter rivalries with other children. The second marriage is commonly undertaken in the hope of relieving her economic distress. Often she succeeds the second time. Should this fail, she is then completely disillusioned and hopes for little from marriage. Her lot, from this point on, is hopeless and incessant toil. Most of the time she is not able to give her children either satisfactions or love. There are, of course, many exceptions.

The effects of this general situation on the children is catastrophic

—in comparison with what happens in the middle-class white or Negro home. These factors, mentioned below, do not concern the fate of a single individual. What happens is a major concern of the entire community, because the total fabric of social relatedness is undermined—at least for the kind of society we live in. The following constellations are affected:

The affectivity potential is lowered.
The paternal ideal is disparaged.
The maternal ideal is injured.
The sexual or male-female relationship is spoiled.
The conscience mechanisms suffer.
The self-esteem systems suffer.
The capacity for idealization is destroyed, partially or wholly.
The potentiality for parenthood is spoiled.

The deserting or improvident father serves as a poor ideal for his children. Many of the females in this group remember the father without any fondness, chiefly as a punishing figure. These women grow up to fear and distrust men. Their sexual attitude to men suffers and the number of gross sexual disorders in this group is astonishingly high. We see none of the expected sexual hedonism. The greatest damage to the group as a whole is done by the injury in the boy's mental life to his paternal ideal. He never hears his father's role lauded, only condemned. The common imprecations are indolence, good-for-nothingness, and moral lassitude.

The male child, whose parental ideals have thus been injured, takes to the streets. Here, he has his own world, his group morality, loyalties, and animosities. It is action and adventure. Here is a chance for elevating self-esteem, of performing exploits that give pride, and of letting off steam on the hostile world or on those delegated to represent it. Here, there is also the chance to be a "man" with the girls. There is a great deal more that the boy gets from the streets that he cannot get at home; he gets praise, admiration, pride in achievement, cooperation and competition, hero-worship, confidence. It does not matter to him, nor does he know, that he has bought these satisfactions at the cost of engaging in activities that are antisocial. The maternal ideal, however, in most of these adolescents, has a permanent restraining influence for the better. The mother is, for the greater part, feared and respected, but not especially loved. Thus far, the only decisive influences toward ideal-formation have come from an ambivalent mother-image and from the street gangs. This is not a firm basis for lasting self-confidence. On top of all this, now add the never escapable effects of caste. What equipment do either boy or girl have for effective parenthood? And so the vicious circle is endlessly repeated.

Male-female relations

It is not commonly recognized that the poor relations between male and female in the lower classes is a serious disrupting influence. This tension between the sexes is not a calculated or a "cultural" trait; it is an accidental by-product. The importance of peaceful and cooperative attitudes between the sexes, together with mutual acceptance of the established social role for each, is a factor that has endless repercussions in either the smooth or the disorganized functioning of a society. This tension cannot be kept private or quiet; ultimately, it always takes on an expressive and public form.

The origin of this tension lies in a single factor in Negro lower-class life, a factor that is blatant in all employment statistics. These show clearly that the male has fewer and less enduring chances for permanent employment. In the actual practice of living, this is a factor of astonishing regularity in the life of any lower-class male.

This disparity of economic chances today has a long history among the Negro people. In the slave years, the female had a higher use-value to the group, because of her sexual value to the white male. She was the only member of the group who was capable of entering into some emotional reciprocity with her white masters, as mistress, as mother of lighter-skinned Negroes, and as mammy to the white children. The Negro male slave only had utility value; the female had this, and a sexual and emotional value as well. This gave her a head start in relative prestige, while that of the Negro male fell. She always did and still does remain the most permanent and dependable member of Negro society—insofar as the children are concerned.

For entirely different reasons, the free Negro female has retained her prestige, but now because of her better chances for employment. This heightened prestige and dependability does not remain an isolated phenomenon. Its influence spreads into the ideal-formation of the children and in the sexual attitudes of male and female to each other. What is the result? The female now has some of the social value attributes of the male, and the male those of the female. The lower-class Negro female cannot be "feminine," nor the male "masculine." Their roles are reversed. Since these values are just the opposite from what they are in white society, and since the values of white society are inescapable, the male fears and hates the female; the female mistrusts and has contempt for the male because he cannot validate his nominal masculinity in practice.

This becomes a tension point in the social and sexual relations between the two, which is a powerful factor in disrupting lower-class marriage. As a submissive and dependent object, the male cannot have any pride; and whether she has pride or not, the female carries the bigger load of responsibility. This means that the male must seek compensations for his defeat in other ways: clothing, spending, gambling, drugs, extramarital sexual conquests, and other self-validating pursuits. To the female, it means the devaluation of the sexual role and a dedication to ceaseless toil and unrewarding responsibilities.

It is therefore, no surprise that in the lower classes there should be such a high proportion of sexual disorders in both sexes.

Religion [4]

Religion is one of the most important expressions of personality; in fact, it is the most universal. Since this discussion is essentially about the devices man uses to adapt successfully, we shall keep the discussion on this level. In other words, we shall not discuss religion theologically, but psychologically.

It has been amply demonstrated that all religions have certain features in common: they all assume the existence of a superior being, whose interest in human affairs is paramount, and that he regulates, in ways best known to the deity, the affairs of man. The relations of man to the superior power vary a great deal from culture to culture. Freud pointed out in *The Future of an Illusion,* that the probable origin of this universal idea lay in an experience common to all human beings; namely, that they are born helpless and are assisted in their adaptation by a pair of benevolent giants (the

[4] In this discussion on Negro religion we have been aided by researches on the subject by Aaron J. Weiss, graduate student at Columbia University. Other references are Embree, E. R., *Color and Christianity in Religion in the Post War World,* Harvard, 1945; Hoshor, John, *God in a Rolls Royce,* Hillman Curl, 1936; Cantril, Hadley, *The Psychology of Social Movements,* Wiley and Sons, 1941.

parents) who do their every bidding. In many religions, the origin of this deity is still preserved in its pristine form, viz., ancestor worship. This simply means that the parent after death continues to exert his magical powers in behalf of his own offspring. The Romans, at their peak, still preserved the household gods (*gentes*) as their personal or private gods. Kardiner [5] has further shown that the procedures and rituals for invoking this solicitude of the deity have their origin in the methods the parents use to enforce their disciplines, and these are contingent on the methods of upbringing—the induction of affectivity, the punishment-reward systems, and especially on whether the relations between parent and child are reciprocally pleasant. For contrasts in the aspect of religion, those of Tanala and Alor are most striking.

All these considerations are to a large measure irrelevant in the discussion of Negro religion in America. The aboriginal religion could not and did not survive the smashing of Negro culture through slavery. We have no record of the disintegration of the aboriginal cults under this impact. We do, however, know that the question of permitting the Negro to take on the religion of his masters was heavily debated before it was allowed to take place. There were certain complications: Christians could not be enslaved, and several Negroes had been able to obtain their freedom by proving that they had been baptized; hence, it was considered that a slave could not be a Christian, because of the evil effects of education on him, i.e., it could result in his freedom. However, about 1700, the slave was granted the right to be Christian owing to the efforts of missionary societies and some of the more liberal slaveowners. Simultaneously, doctrine was altered to conform with economic necessity; Christianity and slavery were deemed compatible.

The history of the career of the Negro as a Christian does not concern us here. It is the story of caste in the churches. The point is merely that the Negro absorbed Christianity as he did all other aspects of American culture. Our real task is to find what the Negro did with his adopted religion. If there are any basic problems of adaptation, then these will show themselves in the form and emphasis they give the adopted religion. Here, no specific trend is visible in the gross. The Negroes adopted all Christian denomina-

[5] Kardiner, *op. cit.*

tions, mostly Baptist and Methodist, and added a few of their own. These latter take the form of "sanctified" sects, cults, and store front churches, and their appeal is largely to lower-class Negroes.

Most students of the role of religion among Negroes tend to stress the segregational aspects of it. This is hardly the place to look if our interest is in content. Other students look upon the store front movement [6] as the machination of impostors who exploit Negroes with religious hocum. This may be so; but this does not gainsay the basic fact that there is a need by many lower-class Negroes which they try to satisfy through these "churches." We can grant that the segregated church offers better feeling of expressing common ideals or wishes; but the content of a religion or cult expresses much more than a wish for equality with whites. Caste in religion, as has been pointed out repeatedly, is part of the white man's dilemma.

Our interest is in the content of the adopted Christianity of the Negro. We do not find any evidence that the Negro has in any way altered Christianity to his specific needs. If we find any such evidence it will not be in the churches of the upper and middle classes. We cannot expect to find it anywhere but in the cults of the lower classes. The reasons for this are apparent from our discussion of the Negro personality, the pertinent aspects of which we can briefly recapitulate.

We have indicated that because his own culture was destroyed, the Negro was forced to accept the white man as his ideal. This did not happen to the Ghetto Jew, because the latter's culture was not broken up. To him, the extrinsic culture remained foreign; the Jew in the Ghetto never took the ideals of the out-group as long as he was persecuted. This only happened when persecution stopped and he enjoyed some social mobility. Then he became acculturated but was never forced to abandon his religion. The incompatibility between the two religions was not too great. The case of the Negro is quite different. The slaveholder was not only his persecutor; he was also his benefactor and protector. This is the strange fate of a persecuted people who become acclimated to the passive and dominated role; they tend to identify themselves with their persecutor. The self-hatred of the Negro is the best testimony we can offer in

[6] *See* Reid, Ira de A., "Let Us Prey," *Opportunity*, Vol. IV, September, 1926, pp. 274–78.

evidence; he hates himself as the white man hates him (or as he thinks the white man hates him). This self-hatred can only cease when his social mobility increases.

Meanwhile, there is enough in the Old and New Testaments to give the Negro the opportunity to identify himself with the downtrodden Hebrews who were slaves in Egypt, and with the suffering Christ, and to make some aspects of Christianity compatible with his inner needs—the promise of being loved equally with the white man after death, and the like. The chief reason why the white man's religion is acceptable is the identification with white ideals. In the Negro upper classes, the complete acceptance of Christianity is compatible with their social strivings. This is not the case with the Negro lower classes. The standard versions of Christianity probably do not take care of the terrific tensions generated by their suffering. Here, we can expect some explosive religious striving, which the upper classes ridicule. We cannot possibly expect any modifications or adaptations of orthodoxy from upper- and middle-class levels, because they are so completely identified with the whites and so imitative of white ideals, that the endorsement of orthodoxy further enhances the illusion of equality—segregation notwithstanding. Moreover, fantasies about status-striving leave little room for fantasy-play on a religious level.

In spite of the inability of some of these lower-class cults to find an original ideology, the mere fact that they all get a following is sufficient evidence that they fill a need. The chief requirement a Negro preacher must meet is to have a "call," to be an effective and dramatic orator, to be able to describe parables vividly, to be able to give the impression of being inspired and carried away. This is an essential part of the success of any preacher. The reason for this is probably that the audiences have only a vague and amorphous idea of what they are after. However, they are receptive to having certain emotions expressed and vicariously discharged. The ranting preacher, who seems to be going through these emotions, can in this way induce the same feelings in his listeners, at least momentarily. The preacher's performance thus becomes a good "show" with lively participation from the audience. The chief features of these performances were uninhibited expressiveness, excitement, and rhythm, to the accompaniment of hallelujahs, rhythmic clapping and stamping. Occasionally, there is also crying, running, flaying of arms, jumping up and down the aisles. Whether this is a copy of white revivalist evangelism or a vestigial hang-over of African ritual is neither here nor there.

In view of the paucity of content and ideology represented in these lower-class religious cults, what can their function be? They offer "escape" from hardships of life, some social cohesion, opportunity for emotion, and possibly act as a vehicle for dissemination of political and social ideas. They have a high entertainment and release value, and nothing happens there that depresses the Negro's self-esteem; quite the contrary.

There is, however, one Negro cult which has acquired not only a large following, but an ideology as well. And that is the cult of Father Divine. Few of the Negro cults have had a persistent career, and although much "release" is afforded by them, they have nothing, apart from the energy of the preacher, to keep them alive. There are too many pressing actual problems of living for which occasional release is not the answer. The life of these individual cults has generally been brief. Much more progress has been made in Negro education, press, secular uplift organizations, all of which have competed successfully with these cults for popular support. No escapism or entertainment or release can withstand the constant barrage of stimuli that come from both Negro and white sources, which stimulate the drive for a higher standard of living. But, most important of all, none of these cults has any enduring effect in improving the Negro's most vulnerable psychological handicap, his depressed self-esteem. From this point of view, the Father Divine movement is of considerable importance. This movement was built on the ruins of the one propelled by Marcus Garvey. The latter began as a reaction against the intensified nationalism and race hatred following World War I. This protest movement was dressed up in an Utopian ideology, the chief emotional constituent of which was a stimulation of *Negro race pride*. It was a Pan-African dream, which introduced a brand of Black Chauvinism. Everything "black" was not inferior, it was superior. This movement collapsed; but the Negro race pride which it generated lived on, though in another form.

For our purposes, it hardly matters who Father Divine is, where he came from, and what accidental factors, aided by a good press, brought him into prominence. The simple fact is that he devised a formula for Heaven on Earth. Only one of these factors deserves mention in our hasty survey. Father Divine, who had been a roving preacher with a very original twist in the form of serving a "banquet" with the religious meeting, had set up his heaven in Sayville, Long Island. This was discovered by a reporter, who wrote Father Divine up as a "worker of miracles" and "a good provider." This began the big rush. Sayville was mobbed by Negro visitors as a consequence of which Sayville real-estate owners and operators went into a panic, tried to buy Father Divine out, and failing this, trumped up a charge of "public nuisance" against him. He was convicted. But four days later, the judge who convicted him died of a heart attack and Father Divine in his cell was heard to say that "he hated to do it"; that is, he hated to kill the judge by his supernatural powers. This was excellent newspaper copy, and this coincidence touched off a big rush into the world of magic on which Father Divine now had a monopoly.

The success of this movement can hardly be judged merely by the accidents that made it prominent. Its success rests on the fact that it made good its promise of devising a formula for Heaven on Earth. In other words, it is a practical cult. It is not an idle theology which like other cults left its adherents in the terrible quandary of trying to reconcile a hostile world with an ideology of submissiveness and guilt. The Divine movement left none of this quandary to his followers. He solved it for them. But how?

In the first place, his followers are left in no doubt as to who Father Divine is; he is no plenipotentiary, he has no mission, he is God. His kingdom is run on the principle of a big business which has chain-store extensions. That is, it is an organization of which he is the autocratic president; moreover, it is an organization which has a sound financial basis, with plenty of methods for collecting or making revenue. The chief slogans of the movement are: no race; no sex; no money; no responsibility; no hate; no rage; no war. He is married to a white woman and has a white secretary, which destroys the myth of color and race. The "angels" surrender their sexual rights and their money (i.e., their earnings). In return for this sacrifice, all their earthly needs are provided, and for this, each "angel" has no responsibility. He is housed, fed, and entertained. Dancing and singing enjoy high favor. Drinking and smoking are taboo. There is no color nor caste in heaven, a condition often breached, because there are favorite "angels," and white "angels" enjoy preferred privileges. Moreover, the movement has a political program, which is not very different from the secular brand of progressivism. And it has a press, and instructs citizens on how to vote. The movement is careful to avoid leftist causes.

The effects of this movement could best be appraised by the personality studies of a few "angels." We have had no opportunity for such studies. But we have had lengthy interviews with two, about whom no generalizations can be made. Both of these, females, were schizoid personalities, and both had had long histories of severe maladaptation. In both of these instances, the help they received from being "angels" was enormous. Almost completely incapacitated before they became "angels," they have since been able to keep their pathological symptoms under control, to function effectively, to enjoy a feeling of pride and even prestige, and have a deep devotion to their leader. This is a great therapeutic gain. Neither thought that the restrictions under which they lived were too difficult. The fact is that both had severe sexual maladjustments and the injunction against sex was a relief and not a burden. Neither of them felt exploited and both carried around an air of eery beatitude which was not obtrusive. They were both fearless and felt very protected. Neither spoke of being "saved," but their attitude to the interviewers was one of "you don't know how well off you could be if you'd join us." But neither proselytized. Both were dependable and honest.

We are in no position to say how general the effects recorded about these two instances are. They cannot be universal, judging from the simple fact that there is a good deal of shifting membership in the organization. No doubt, a normally constituted individual would find the restrictions imposed rather irksome, especially those pertaining to sexual abstinence among married "angels." The success of this movement can only be judged from the relief it affords to those pressure points we have located in the Negro personality. It can only attract the most naive, because the rational aspects of the movement cannot be very acceptable to the educated Negro, who would probably cast his lot with those who are seeking the same ends by secular means.

Firstly, it does not aim at equality with whites in the remote future; it practices it now. Moreover, being a Negro movement, the Negro has the initiative, and it is he who tolerates the whites. This puts the shoe on the other foot. To those who are "angels," it matters little that the movement itself is small and the number of whites in it is insignificant. "Heaven" is their world, and in it they do enjoy equality with whites, with the added prestige that God is a Negro. This is a complete reversal and denial of the actual position of the Negro in America. This gain is, therefore, an illusory one.

On the other hand, the freedom from responsibility for oneself is not illusory. Since the organization is run on the basis of an insurance company, it can guarantee this freedom from responsibility as long as the intake is higher than the expense of running the organization. An economic depression could easily collapse the financial structure, notwithstanding the great savings in cost by buying supplies in huge quantities and by diminishing overhead through the employment of unsalaried "angels," who work for maintenance and lodging, in addition to the other boons which are free. For those who turn their earnings into the organization, the emotional gain is still very high. It is an organization that cushions the blow and anxiety of unemployment—the great bane of the lower-class worker. There is no evidence that it encourages indolence. But it does give economic security.

Under these conditions life in "heaven" must do a great deal to diminish self-hatred and mutual envy. Since class distinctions are wiped out, the struggle for status is nominally non-existent. At least it is not played out on the standard of living stage, which is set by the organization. There is no special climbing on the status level and no struggle for existence on the subsistence level. The feeling tone of mutual dependence must be enhanced and the feeling of mutual hatred diminished.

Another gain is to be found on the emotional level. Here, there is no emphasis on inborn sin and none on suffering divinely imposed as a means of reinstatement into God's good graces. There is high emphasis on communal pleasures of singing and dancing. These are both expansive, ego-enhancing and socially useful. There is very little, if any, of breast beating, penance, and atonement. In this sense, it has no resemblance to Christianity in any denomination. It, furthermore, is in a position to satisfy one of the deepest cravings of lower-class Negroes, many of whom bear the emotional scars of broken homes—namely, the frustrated dependency longings. Here is someone who really cares for them, and materializes it in tangible form. This is not preaching one thing and practicing another. The religion and living are united. The "angel" does not need to labor at enhancing his self-esteem; it is done for him.

The effect of this movement on family cohesion is questionable. We have already learned that in the lower classes cohesion is very low. It cannot destroy anything that is not there. For the abandoned wife, "heaven" is a great boon. Her children are cared for in a responsible way, while she works.

The success of this movement does not, therefore, depend on momentary excitement or a good show; its success depends on the fact that it relieves anxiety, elevates depressed self-esteem, and fosters a better feeling of the Negroes to each other. How strong and cohesive the group would be in an actual test would be hard to predict; but on its face merits, we would give it greater staying power than any other non-business Negro organization.

Can we look upon this whole organization as an illusory one? It is no less and no more illusory than any other cult devised by man. Its real weakness does not lie in its illusory character, but in that it takes its "angels" out of the society in which they live and places them in a fantasy world. The advantages enjoyed by the "angels" under present conditions could be easily destroyed if it grew to sufficient size. The whole organization operates on a principle of mass *denial*, and the harsh impact of the outer world on the "angels" must be counteracted by constant denial in the fictitious world. A good many "angels" complain of the difficulty of dividing themselves between the two contradictory sets of values. Moreover, the democracy and equality so much preached is, in practice, often breached. White "angels" are automatically treated with deference. There is continuous jockeying for favored prestige places and titles. The prestige fights within the organization are considerable, notwithstanding its theocratic structure. The renunciation of medical aid has led to catastrophic results, so that the original injunction against physicians had to be amended to read: no physicians shall be called before three days of illness. The sexual restrictions have caused many delinquencies and defections. The movement is predominantly a refuge for lower-class Negro women. In view of what we know of the lower-class marriages, the common abandonment by husbands who are constantly defeated in their efforts to maintain a family, this defection from marriage to "heaven" by the women does not surprise us. No doubt the Divine movement has often been accused, especially by irate husbands who lose their bed mates, of breaking up marriages. We do not think this is likely. The Divine movement could not break up an otherwise successful marriage; it recruits few from middle and upper classes where marriages are more stable. Furthermore, the Divine movement furnishes the lower-class female with an idealized male figure who really acts as a provider and protector. Few lower-class women observed by us have actually experienced this in real life from either father or husband.

This is not an inventory or appraisal of the movement; it is merely a discussion of the needs in the lower-class Negro which prompted the cult into existence and which the organization attempts to satisfy. In this sense, it is the only truly Negro indigenous religion. We regard this movement less a religion than a folk-cult, in which Father Divine is hardly more than a catalytic agent. If this is so, then this movement represents a considerable degree of self-assertion on the part of the lower-class Negro. It is a part of Negro protest, with all its illusory and contradictory trends; but it is a protest in fantasy only, and as such it dramatizes this protest, and gives it articulate form—by denying reality, and forcing new values in a make-believe world.

A word might be said about the "no hate," "no rage," "no war" slogans. These are all probably determined by several factors: the practical reason is to prevent the movement from becoming militant, and assuming a revolutionary character. But the more important reason is that it places an injunction against the exercise of the most deeply suppressed tendencies of the Negro—namely, aggression and hostility, by removing the necessity for them. The origin of this hostility and aggression lies in the frustrations of living, on the subsistence and status levels, this injunction is easy for "angels" to follow because the incentive for these emotions has, to a large extent, been removed.

Despite the many advantages that accrue to the individual members of the Father Divine movement, it further amputates the individual from the real world in which he lives and removes him from any effective social protest or action. Its relevancy to the problems of the Negro people is dubious; it adds nothing to the social cohesion of the Negro. It only encourages flight from reality and a "turn the other cheek" attitude to his oppressors. It is to discrimination what a cough medicine is to pneumonia; it tries to alleviate a symptom, but leaves the underlying disease untouched. In sum, the Father Divine movement is in direct opposition to the final goal of the Negro in America—the complete and equal integration into American society, of which he is part and parcel.

Negro personality and social cohesion

Social cohesion is commonly understood to be the ability of the individuals who compose a group to cooperate to the end of improving their common lot. There can be no difference of opinion concerning this definition. There can only be differences of opinion concerning the factors that bring it about or fail to do so. That the Negro lacks the capacity for social cohesion has been noted by many observers. One of the most recent of these studies, by Arnold M. Rose,[7] makes a very comprehensive survey of the entire problem and we must concur with many of his conclusions.

We must, however, draw certain distinctions between various types of social cohesion. There are acute emergency situations which call for social cohesion, as, for example, a natural catastrophe or a fire. These are not the kinds of situation which test the capacity of a group for concerted action. Once the emergency situation is over, the participants go back to their previous psychological positions and remain there.

Sustained social cohesion was in order for the issue of resistance to slavery. This was a concrete issue in which every Negro had a vital stake—his own personal freedom. What are the facts? There were only three slave rebellions of any consequence, involving small numbers of slaves. These were discovered by the betrayal of house slaves, who were always better off than the field slaves. This does not mean that there were not among the slaves powerful and resourceful leaders. Nor does it mean that slavery was accepted with docility. On the contrary, *individual* protests were many. But we are talking here of organized rebellion on a *group* basis. These rebellions were infrequent and failed for various reasons, the chief being that the fabric out of which social cohesion is made was eroded by slavery. Social cohesion depends on a capacity for relatedness, the locus of which does not lie in the group as a whole *but in each individual.* It is a common error to regard "liberty" purely from the

[7] Rose, Arnold M., *The Negro's Morale,* University of Minnesota Press, 1949.

political angle. "Liberty" from the psychological angle looks a bit different. The ability to exercise those rights which go with "liberty" requires, in addition to the capacity for cooperative relatedness, a certain working conception of oneself. The latter is probably the most fundamental. This conception of oneself in relation to the group can, for the sake of convenience, be called the *social ego*. This entity is self-referential, but not in relation to one's personal capacities alone, but to one's confidence, trust, and ability to participate in a common cause, i.e., to identify one's interests with the interests of others. In other words, we mean *social* self-reference as distinguished from *personal* (*individual*) self-reference. The latter is the result of the success or failure of activity to which the individual attaches importance. A successful or effective performance leads to a feeling of gratification, at times even to euphoria. It produces self-confidence. This personal self-reference is not, however, the same as the social self-reference. One can have enormous self-confidence and be isolated from the group. This self-confidence is not, therefore, available for common use. It sticks to the individual.

What, in the light of these considerations, was the social ego during slavery? Working as a slave had no self-referential value. This conclusion has been recognized as long as slavery has been known, and shows itself in the simple fact that slaves are not the most efficient workers. Why should they be, since the work has no relation to them, but to someone else, with whose interests the slave is not identified? To put it differently, no slave can take pride in his work, except perhaps in that it may serve another form of self-interest through *ingratiation*. The latter is, however, a bid for discrimination in favor of oneself, but to the disadvantage of everyone else. It is a bid for privilege, and in the case of the slave, this privilege was the opportunity to identify oneself with the *master*—no matter in what small degree. We are saying, therefore, that slavery was not conducive to a positive or confident social ego, nor to a personal self-confidence. It led only to corruption, to lessening the ties of Negroes to each other by introducing the corrupting motive of ingratiation.

There were a host of other factors which operated to destroy the social ego of the Negro, especially the breaking of his culture and the inability to form permanent familial ties. In fact, one can say that the destruction of the capacity for relatedness was one of the natural consequences of slavery. Not the least of these corrupting influences was the acceptance of the white man as an ideal, the inevitability of regarding him in part as a *protector*, notwithstanding the hatred borne him. In addition, there was the growing pride of being lighter-skinned—which bears out our contention that the Negro succumbed to the fatal influence of identifying himself with the white. Those who clung together because of their blacker color or more lowly function could not have pride either—because they had the despised attributes and the functions that were held in common contempt. This was a social ego whose chief ingredient was mutual contempt. These were the chief psychological factors which led to the mass inertia of the Negro. There were, of course, other potent factors. The Negro was permitted no education; there were realistic fears of overt rebellion against whites, and even fear of participating with those whites who espoused liberation of the slave.

Apart from all external barriers, i.e. the plantation police and spy system, there was no capacity in the individual Negro for concerted thinking, much less concerted action. Passivity and ingratiation are the natural antipodes of self-confidence and autonomy. The liberation of the Negro could never have come about through his own initiative. His participation with those who sought his liberation—for whatever political ends—could only have been half-hearted, for the very same reasons. Those slaves who had freed themselves psychologically from the influences described could, therefore, have only one objective—personal flight.

How was the situation after "Emancipation"? It must be remembered that no human being can alter his habits of adaptation overnight—even if it means transition to liberty. It takes time to acquire the capacity to implement it, in addition to the opportunity. There *was* such a brief opportunity, lasting exactly eleven years, 1865–1876. Then, as the result of a *political deal*, the Republican party withdrew its protection from the Negro and white supremacy was restored. This ended the opportunity and, psychologically, eleven years was not enough of a head start. Furthermore, Negro leadership changed its tone from the militant type of Frederick Douglass, to the accommodative type of Booker T. Washington. The authors do not hold any brief for this leadership theory of social change. Leadership is never any stronger than the people it is leading. We do not hold that the leadership policy was without influence entirely, but we do hold that the greatest drawback to Negro progress lay in the social factors we have stressed throughout this work, and the influence of these factors on the personality. Needless to say, when a group leader advocates the acceptance of subservience, it cannot do group morale much good, as was the case with Booker T. Washington. Another disintegrating factor was W. H. Thomas, who made a further split between light and dark Negroes, North and South. Both these men emphasized respectively the same factors that operated during slavery: passivity and the corrupting influence of identification with the whites by ingratiation and imitation. The kind of social cohesion that counts for a society in the long run is not the kind that is organized for emergency purposes, but for a constant, though slow constructive interplay. This kind of cohesion has its root, not in effective leadership, which at best is only a catalytic agent, but in the structure of the personality. Social cohesion cannot be taught by parable, nor can it be educated into people. It must be integrated into the personality.

Let us first glance at the efforts of enlightened Negro leadership. This has taken place largely as a reaction among the "talented tenth" of the Negroes against the policies of Washington and Thomas. W. E. B. Du Bois has galvanized this movement with the aid of the N.A.A.C.P. The white participation was prompted largely by the assumption that as long as the Negro is discriminated against, the white man suffers in a measure through his discriminatory activities, and in spite of his gains from so doing. The chief aim is to secure equal application of the law to Negroes and to make these laws conform everywhere to the Constitution and the Bill of Rights. This organization has had considerable success, though its job is far from completed. The legal method has won some victories; but new ways are always found to circumvent a legal decision. Another organization is The National Urban League and its aim is to secure good jobs, equal pay, and equal chances for advancement for Negroes. This is largely a Northern organization. No one can criticize the constructive efforts and the achievement of these agencies.

However, we still have some questions to answer about Negro social cohesion that were not touched by any of these organizations. Why, for example, was there no significant migration of Negroes from the South to the North and West between 1865 and 1915 (leaving out the one into Kansas after the Civil War)? The chances for advancement were undoubtedly better in the North, but it was not until 1915 that Negroes began to migrate in response to economic opportunities (World War I). The reason why Negroes stayed in the South was that basically there was not much change in personality organization—notwithstanding nominal political freedom; there was no galvanizing Negro ideal and there was no success in group action. This kept the social ego more or less within the confines that it had been. No opportunity was given for such development in the South. Whatever did take place, did so in the North, and among the educated classes. That is why migration was so long delayed, pending the development of a powerful stimulus *external* to the personality. The *internal* organization of the personality of the average freed slave was not yet capable of exploiting the minor opportunities in the North that were available prior to World War I.

The constituents of the *social ego* need separate treatment because often they do not operate simultaneously.

The constituent that is most easily observed goes under the heading of "race pride," which merely means the espousal of a Negro instead of a white ideal. The traditional background for the Negro ideal had been undermined by slavery when the culture was destroyed. It had, therefore, to be built up afresh, from the history of the Negro in America, or by pure fiat. The latter was the method used by Marcus Garvey, who simply proclaimed the Negro superior. The Garvey movement was supported largely by the lower-class urban groups. It had an ideology and a program. Its ideology was race purity for the Negro, and the program was Back-to-Africa. Crude as were his methods, and unsound his rational background, Marcus Garvey saw one important truth: that the Negro was doomed as long as he took his ideals from the white man. He saw that this sealed his internal feeling of inferiority and his self-contempt. He was wrong only in the means he used to free the Negro from it. Race pride cannot be induced by fiat—it must be integrated.

Negro ideal figures were not long in appearing. The enormous influence of the Negro on our popular music and song had a strong influence ideal-wise. More effectual than this was the universal admiration given such Negroes as Joe Louis, Jackie Robinson, and the famous dancer, Bill Robinson.

The Negroes have also had some success in group action in influencing political appointments, in political action where the

Negro vote is something to reckon with, and in slow but persistent action in labor unions.

We can place a high emphasis on alteration of the Negro ideal and on success in group action. But the most important source of the lack of social cohesion is to be found in the structure of the personality. According to the inventory we made from the direct study of the Negro personality, these constellations that have a bearing on group cohesion are:

Low self-esteem
Self-hatred—in direct and projected forms
Aggression patterns:

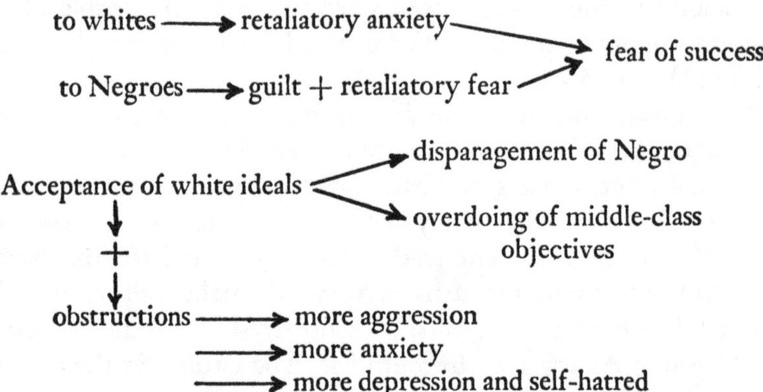

It would be very convenient if we could arrange these various factors into a simple causal sequence; but this is relatively impossible. They are a group of constantly interacting factors, which feed into each other. What makes this whole system a vicious circle is that it *begins* and *ends* with discrimination, based on economic vested interest and its social superstructure. The entire system is defensive and restitutive in intent; but it fails because no high self-esteem is tenable without implementation in some socially recognizable form.

The depressed self-esteem is basically a reflection of being a member of a despised group, but one which is also deprived of the opportunities for self-realization in those forms current in our society. No private virtue can compensate anyone to the extent of being able to counteract the impediments of self-realization. The Negro, being a member of our society, cannot invent new objectives for personal endeavor. The only objective we can think of that would not run afoul the white man's discrimination would be *yogism.* This type of adaptation happens not to be in vogue anywhere in Western society; hence, it has no value as an ideal. Being a member of a despised group, would, by itself, be damaging to self-esteem, as it is with Jews, or any minority group. The greatest damage, however, is done by the impediments to opportunity.

Depressed self-esteem almost always remains a *private* matter. But self-hatred is a stronger feeling and generally requires some form of projection to attempt to stay its damaging effects. The simplest form it takes in the Negro is to hate other Negroes, and to attempt some personal restitution by laying claim to one or another attribute of the whites. Thus, the lighter-skinned Negro can claim some "whiteness" and so use this as a basis for hating the darker-skinned ones.

Identification with the white oppressor has been the bane of Negro cohesion from the very beginning of slavery, when it took the form of pride in being a house slave, rather than a field slave. This sop of an illusory identification with the master did incalculable harm to Negro cohesion, because it formed one base for class distinction between Negroes. On the other hand, Negroes who can *pass* apparently have a bitter time of it, not only from the pressures of the fellow Negroes who know about it, but more particularly, from their own sense of guilt. That is to say, *passing* is regarded by the passer as a piece of violence and betrayal of his fellow Negroes. Hence, he fears detection—but most of all his own conscience.

Identification with the white ideal has innumerable repercussions in Negro society and destroys group cohesion by stirring up mutual animosity. A dark, successful man can always get, and is most likely to look for, a light-skinned mate. This does not do the darker girls' chances any good, nor does it improve their feeling toward the successful light-skinned girls.

The same fear that is associated with passing attends any other kind of *success.* It is also regarded as a blow against other Negroes. This fear of success is a powerful deterrent in many cases of successful Negroes we have observed.

We cannot tell how widespread fear of success is among Negroes. This, on the face of it, looks like a paradox, that individuals who strive to achieve success under the greatest possible odds, should have a sense of guilt about it. Yet, we have observed this particularly in upper- and middle-class Negroes. It is not universal to be sure.

Many upper-class Negroes take advantage of the handicaps and miseries of the lower classes in many ways—and it is a known fact that many wealthy Negroes do not contribute money to the relief of impoverished Negroes. Rose [8] believes that Negroes have a deeply ingrained sense of impoverishment. However, they do not spare money on conspicuous ostentation. We would attribute this rather to the contempt the successful Negro has for the poorer ones—that is, it comes from their projected self-hatred, rather than a sense of impoverishment.

Projection is not the only defense against self-hatred. The latter also propels the individual into more frantic efforts at validation, which means more aggression and more anxiety, which success only relieves to a slight degree. Naturally, failure augments self-hatred, which ultimately ends in an exhausted resignation.

The systems we have described above are not universal in Negroes. In fact, they predominate in the middle and upper classes—where there are some opportunities for self-realization. In the lower classes, the emphasis is much more on sheer subsistence, which attenuates the status conflict, although it does not completely obliterate it.

The causes of the lack of social cohesion in the lower classes originate in other sources. They depend essentially on the lower affectivity potential that results from the broken home, the absence of dependable parental figures, the vanishing father, the working mother who has no time to care for her children, the loveless discipline to which the children are exposed, the inability to idealize parental figures who frustrate more than they satisfy dependency cravings, the distorted relations between the sexes, the female-dominance in a male-oriented society, the disparagement of the masculine ideal, the universal mistrust and essential isolation of the lower-class Negro—all this in spite of the fact that the Negro is an interminable joiner. All of these factors have their origin in the lower economic opportunities of the Negro. In all the personality studies of lower-class Negroes, this vicious circle begins in the inability of the father to be a dependable provider. If the couple starting on a marriage come from broken homes, each already has a preconception of what to expect from his or her mate, based on parental example. They explode at the first frustration. Women who have better earning power leave or permit themselves to be deserted by

[8] Rose, *op. cit.*, pp. 70–71.

their husbands. The children are placed with foster parents who treat them badly, etc. In other words, in the lower classes, the psychological opportunity for creating strong affective ties within the family is lacking. In consequence, when they are thrust into prematurely independent positions to shift for themselves, they already have a distrust of all human relations, and do not join into them readily. They have too much suspicion and a long unconscious backlog of suppressed hatred. It is on top of all this that the frustrations imposed by discrimination are piled up. It is no wonder that the capacity for affectivity of the lower-class Negro in this group tends to be permanently shattered. We found a seemingly better affectivity potential in the middle and upper classes, where the conditions of living more closely resembled the whites, and hence, better and more persistent types of relatedness. We can refer to a single observation in lower-class families which bears this out: in this group, hostility between siblings is most violent, and in the majority of the cases no relatedness to siblings was maintained after adulthood. This was not the case in the middle classes; they maintained relatedness in spite of strong sibling rivalries.

The causes of lack of cohesion lie, therefore, in the kind of personality that is bred in lower-class families—and this in turn is traceable to the inability of these families to maintain the material and emotional conditions that conduce to strong, affectionate intrafamilial relationships to start with, and later to others outside the family.

Rose [9] points to another significant fact, that ethnic differences between Negroes account for some of the blocks to "group identification." He says that West Indian Negroes do not have the slavery tradition and are not accustomed to living under caste conditions. Hence, he is violent in his protest against it, and Negro protest leaders are largely of West Indian origin. There is much rivalry and antagonism between native American and West Indian Negroes. Some of our subjects were West Indian and from this source we know that they consider themselves very elite in comparison with native Negroes.

The ideological differences between Negroes are no greater than in any other group, and we cannot consider this anything but an end product of all the other factors we have described; hence, it is not a basic cause of the Negro lack of social cohesion.

[9] Rose, *op. cit.*, pp. 76–78.

CHAPTER THIRTEEN

The Psychology of Oppression

THE PURPOSE of this book was to describe the relation of the individual to social processes within a fixed context. We did this by using the adaptation of the individual as a medium for getting information to help us interpret a vast array of sociological data. This technique needs some justification to start with, and a disinterested appraisal of its merits. Since it is an extremely arduous technique, it is important to decide whether the effort is sufficiently rewarding to warrant its use.

Until the twentieth century very little attempt was made to study societal function through the medium of the functioning individual. In order to do so we required some knowledge of the fixed inborn characteristics of man, his methods of adaptation with their defects and failures, and his educability to the demands of culture. All these were a part of the equipment necessary for such an undertaking. Without this knowledge we could only use a quantitative evaluation of fixed phenomena through the statistical study of incidence such as employment, income, delinquency, abandonment, and the like. We could then attempt to explain these phenomena on a rational basis of cause and effect. On a theoretical plane, efforts were made to draw conclusions from the descriptive interrelationship of institutions to each other. It is remarkable how much accurate and valuable work was done by these means alone. The study of the individual can, therefore, be used to supplement our knowledge from these other sources. It is not too much to expect, if this technique is at all accurate, that the indications for social engineering may be defined with more precision than by methods previously in use.

However, our knowledge about how the human unit functions cannot be introduced precipitously, because many serious errors can be made, and many a false lead promulgated. One of the commonest of these is to make hasty analogies between processes taking place in the individual and those taking place in society. This procedure is based on the fallacious assumption that society, like the human unit, is also an organism. This is an erroneous assumption. Society is not an organism, much less a human organism. It is a human *organization*, the constituents of which are human organisms. Hence, one can with full justification claim that the adaptational equipment of the human unit plays a most significant role in the adaptation of societies.

In an organism, the various organs automatically regulate their functions with respect to each other through the medium of a central coordinating apparatus. This consists of the central and autonomic nervous systems and their related humoral mechanisms. The individual organs do not ask each other's consent to do what they need to do. They interact on a low order of chemotactic stimulus-response that has as its purpose the maintenance of the organism as a whole in a state of *homeostasis*,[1] an internal balance and preparedness for the vicissitudes of adaptation. There is differentiation of function to be sure; but the various parts do not have wills, minds, or emotions of their own to look after. In other words, the various parts have no independent adaptation, and no independent existence apart from the organism as a whole. This is never true of a human organization. The human unit always has an independent existence and adaptation apart from the society. The individual's integrity as a functioning unit may be severely crippled by the destruction of the organization of which he is a part; but he, the individual, need not necessarily be destroyed.

The hopeful assumption that society was a self-regulating organism was held by the social thinkers of the eighteenth and nineteenth centuries. It was this assumption that led to the policy of *laissez faire* and to the thesis that enlightened self-interest works itself out somehow to the good of the community as a whole. The documentary evidence in this book shows clearly that this is not true. There is no

[1] The concept of homeostasis was originated and elaborated by Walter B. Cannon. See *The Wisdom of the Body*, Norton, 1939.

automatic regulation. The latter takes place only through the agency of mutual consent or coercion.

The suffering of a large number of people cannot take place within a society without impairing the effectiveness of the whole. If society were self-regulating, there would not be such a long time lag between a noxious stimulus and a restorative response. Since social homeostasis is not automatic, it must wait upon common recognition of the disturbing influence. Such common recognition can long be withheld by denial, education, propaganda, and the like. In the long run, societies, too, have regulating devices. But few social ills are diagnosed during their incubation period; they generally wait until the subject is moribund. Those who doubt this can profit by a study of Roman history from 100 B.C. to 325 A.D. Why are homeostatic disturbances in a society so difficult to recognize? The reasons are readily discernible. All societies have blind spots. Few societies are willing to admit that long accepted measures or regulations have become damaging. Such institutions may start favorably, but in the course of application and enlargement undermine the common good, though they may continue to be beneficial to a special group, who therefore defends the harmful practice rather than surrender the privileges and boons that go with it.[2]

This discussion does not labor a pedantic or semantic point. Quite the contrary, it defines for us the most difficult of all social problems. How does the human unit lend himself to being coordinated into an organization, and at the same time preserve the autonomy of his individual adaptational equipment? He always surrenders a good portion of it in the process of socialization. But this is not quite as bad as it sounds. The human unit is not born with too many inherited reaction types; for the greater part, he learns them or has them integrated into him. Culture is more directive than it is coercive and the process is generally not too traumatic.

At this very point we touch on a serious matter. Does the individual unit initially consent to become a part of a social organization?

[2] This phenomenon is discussed by Norbert Wiener in his book, *The Human Use of Human Beings*, Houghton Mifflin, 1950, under the captions of Progress and Entropy—the latter being the measure of disorder. Wiener says: "It is one of the paradoxes of the human race and possibly its last paradox that the people who control the fortunes of our community should at the same time be wildly radical in matters that concern our own change of our environment, and rigidly conservative in the social matters that determine our adaptation to it." (Page 56)

Indeed he does not. He makes no prenatal choice; nor does he ask his parents to care for him. He is born helpless and if abandoned by his parents could not long continue to exist, nor could the social organization into which he is born survive if abandonment were a common practice. Consent or willful coordination into a social organization can only take place after the individual has already become an effective participant. Many types of organization depend for their existence on this mutual consent. However, these types are generally found within the total culture into which the individual is born. He does not give his consent to the latter; he is inducted and has no choice. Nevertheless, even in this involuntary socialization through which the individual unit becomes coordinated, his individual adaptive equipment is always at work. He does not take this process passively, nor is he put in place like the part of a complex machine. His adjustment to the coordinating process is always a compromise between the forces acting upon him and his own adaptive apparatus. This is why the personal adaptative equipment of the individual has two distinctive configurations: one that he shares with the norms in the community or culture in which he is coordinated (Basic Personality), and the other a record of his compromise with the social forces acting upon him (character). In other words, it is in the domain of personal character that the individual shows his *margin of autonomy*.

What we have described here is the double adaptational cycle of the individual in a society. He shares in the larger and slower motion of the big societal cycle while he moves within the smaller circle of his personal adaptation, much like the motions of the earth on its own axis and within the gravitational orbit of the sun. Naturally, the individual is far more aware of his own personal cycle and to a much lesser and variable degree of the larger cycle. We are therefore saying that societies as a whole have an adaptation too, in which the human units are participants as well. However, in order to get the human unit to function effectively in the larger social ambit which has many vicissitudes, the needs of the individual in his personal cycle must, within a certain margin, be met. This is the feature that defines for us the problem of what might be called *social homeostasis*, or intrasocial balance.

Were it not for the fact that man has an individual adaptational cycle, and that he reacts adaptively to the motions of the larger social cycle, we would have no intrasocial problems. This happens to be the case with certain species of ants, who are differentiated anatomically for specific functions, and hence social homeostasis is maintained by a differentiation of *non-conflicting needs*. Such a society need have no concern for the individual adaptational cycle. It is regulated automatically. All the ant society must look after is the societal cycle. This arrangement has a high survival value. But human beings are not ants. With the exception of differences in the statuses of sex and age, they are all alike, and have similar personal needs. This is a condition that presages conflict and defines the task of intrasocial homeostasis. Add to this the fact that each individual (by nature or nurture?) places a high priority of claim for his personal cycle of adaptation, then we can only say that it is nothing short of a miracle that man can maintain any social life at all. We are all witnesses to this miracle, but let us not forget that we have only a record of those societies that have survived. Many must have disappeared because the intrasocial homeostasis failed, or because the environment withdrew its hospitality. In those that have survived, the problem of homeostasis must have been solved to the extent that the society could go on, notwithstanding many tensions and accommodations. The most important factor in the survival of societies is the capacity of the original pattern of social organization to survive many alterations in the societal adaptational cycle and to continue to be expedient. This cannot be predicted. It is largely a matter of chance which influences the balance of progressive and entropic forces (Wiener). If the changes in the societal adaptation are too rapid, the social organization always tends to lag behind. This is the great advantage that "primitive" societies have; the discrepancies between progress and entropy are not great enough to become explosive because the societal adaptational cycle doesn't change rapidly. This is essentially the "disease" of Western society today. The societal cycle has undergone violent and radical change, the social organization some, but not rapidly enough to keep pace. This was probably the "disease" of Roman society; in fact, the inability to change its social organization was bolstered by the most violent artifices to keep it from changing, with the inevitable result that the cohesiveness of the society deteriorated and the society perished.

In appraising the way in which a society functions, we therefore have three aspects to watch: the personal adaptational cycle, the societal adaptational cycle, and the interaction between the two.

The personal adaptational cycle gets its directives from the cultural institutional pattern and presumably from the adaptive needs of the society as a whole. This is not strictly speaking always true. Many incompatibilities can exist between social needs and institutional arrangements. Hang-overs from the past that are no longer really useful have a way of persisting because man is not always aware of the function of all the institutions under which he lives. But no matter what their source or function, the personal cycle revolves around them. There are, however, several sources of variation: (1) the constitutional endowment of the individual which makes for aberrants; (2) the specific character of the parents of the individual; (3) his personal fate. In the latter, we find the status into which the individual is born, i.e. his class, if he lives in a society where function differentiation carries class implications. It is obvious from this study that though the culture demands conformity to certain institutions, the adaptive struggles of the class to which the individual belongs cannot always follow the norm. Family structure in the lower-class Negro is aberrant, though nominally it is the same as in the white. Thus, one can say that the basic personality of the lower-class Negro is different from the white middle-class norm, and that this norm is approximated more closely in the middle- and upper-class Negroes.

We are not in this work concerned with the adaptational cycle of societies. Little is known about this subject. We do know that the adaptation of societies seems hardly ever to be directed, but more often keeps on modifying itself on an emergent basis. In connection with societal adaptation, the problem of intrasocial homeostasis is of the highest importance because this is the point at which the personal and the social adaptation meet.

A long time ago a very convenient term was in vogue which was very adequate for describing a group of phenomena we must discuss. This term was called the *instinct of self-preservation.* Many psychologies have tried to deal with this concept in a methodical way, but for the greater part have failed. The reasons for this failure are several. First, the qualification of *instinct* tied the activities we attribute to it to a specific somatic origin. This origin cannot be located unless we elect to place it in the muscular system. This is obviously absurd; for the muscular system is only an executive. The sense organs deserve a place in its action, and so does the autonomic nervous system and the emotions of fear and rage. In short, if it is an instinct, the entire organism is its source and executive. Second, the term connotes an unlearned and goal-directed activity. Only the goal can be defined, but many learned as well as unlearned reactions contribute to the goal of self-preservation. In other words, it is not an *instinct* at all, but the result of highly coordinated activities. But we may be permitted to make a metaphoric use of the term whether we call it self-preservation, mastery, or any other synonym. The function of this complex of activity is to render the subject safe and secure against offending influences in the environment which may cause pain of one kind or another. Stimuli which threaten the individual can be perceived a long way off, and sense perceptors and intelligence have enabled man to perceive dangers in the remote future. Similarly, man is able to devise means for circumventing these dangers far in advance; in other words, he can anticipate and institute prophylactic measures. Insofar as these activities subserve the end of continuing existence and circumventing dangers, they can be said to have a security function.

To this category belong the following tendencies:

(1) Responses to threatening stimuli with fear and rage.
(2) The drive to mastery through combativeness leading to coercive aggression and the prevention of retaliation, either by annihilation of the threatening object or by the prevention of aggressive attitudes through domination over the object.
(3) The reactions of flight or submission.
(4) The ancillary tendencies to acquisitiveness and the adjunct emotions of envy and greed—all of which probably stem from the eating drive which aims at security by incorporation. There are a great many psychological derivatives and elaborations of these primary tendencies.

In the early phases of human evolution (as in all animal life), these tendencies had a high survival value. They were the instrumentalities of defense and security in a hostile environment—natural, animal, and human. No one can give any complete answer to the reasons for man's social life; but there is little doubt that it increased man's chances for effective survival. It diminished the anxieties that confront man and lessened the necessity for constant rage, fear, and dominance. This, however, has not always been the case. Some of man's anxieties have not diminished with social life, though one cannot say they have increased. The occasions for rage, the necessity for both poles of dominance and submission, and the need for acquisitiveness, envy, and greed have not disappeared.

These tendencies have always had a disturbing effect on all of man's efforts to devise social formulas for intrasocial homeostasis. However, even though no formula has ever been devised to quiet these feelings, it would be a serious error to regard them as instincts in the sense that they demand satisfaction as does, for example, the sexual "instinct." These tendencies can be stimulated greatly, or materially assuaged, by the particular rules that govern social relationships in any given society. Let us contrast several societies from previous research.

The Comanche [3] had a social organization in which the chief executives were the warriors, i.e., the young men. There were no vested interests outside of courage, daring, and skill. There was no property that couldn't be carried on the back of a horse. Prestige was not tenable unless constantly validated by exploits. The security was vested in the cooperation of the young men for the common good. Food was plentiful, requiring only skill in hunting. The hunt was divided among the hunters. There was not much insecurity in this society. There was no opportunity for greed or envy except in relation to women. The old men had no prestige. It was a day-to-day existence, but without anxiety. The individual's position in the society was assured. Leadership got only prestige that could not be transformed into any permanent claim. This culture did not, therefore, stimulate any great intrasocial strife.

In Tanala,[4] the problem of social homeostasis was solved by compromise. There was high gradation of status, but not in a closed system. There was some mobility: one could become a warrior or medicine man. Those who did not—the younger sons—had a nominally subordinate position; but since land was communally held, the produce was distributed by the family head according to need. There were vested interests defined by rank, but these could not be reified in better dress, better food, better housing, or other privileges. No one suffered want in any important area and everyone was

[3] R. Linton in Kardiner, A., and Associates, *The Psychological Frontiers of Society*, Columbia University Press, 1945.

[4] R. Linton in Kardiner, A., *The Individual and His Society*, Columbia University Press, 1939.

protected by the common endeavor. Social homeostasis was easy to preserve by this system, despite differences of rank.

The Kwakiutl [5] have a remarkable system of social homeostasis. Their economy is divided into (a) subsistence economy and (b) prestige economy. Though subsistence is guaranteed everyone by communal endeavor, the society is notwithstanding anxiety-ridden and filled with the most bitter mutual rivalry. There is a high degree of status gradation. This culture shows conclusively that a guarantee of subsistence does not render a society free of anxiety. The anxiety can be centered about prestige and self-esteem. This does not necessarily mean that subsistence anxiety and prestige and power anxiety are of the same cast. The former is more fundamental and has different social consequences from that occasioned by prestige. In Kwakiutl the prestige anxiety is expressed in the perverse form of the institutionalized *potlatch*, a type of public challenge in which both contenders consume by fire or other forms of destruction, property that could otherwise be useful. The winner is the one who has goods left to burn while the rival has exhausted all of his. The social homeostasis in this culture is maintained at a high cost in intrapsychic tension, as is well attested by their violent folklore.

Still another type of social homeostasis is illustrated by the culture of Alor.[6] This disorder of internal social cohesion has a direct bearing on the Negro. In Alor the social homeostasis is ruined by the accidental injury to the affectivity potential of the individual by a capricious division of labor between males and females. The latter work in the fields all day while the men gamble or dun for debts. The result is that the child is neglected and the capacity for human relatedness is seriously impaired. Hence, the Alorese are suspicious of each other, their marriages are unstable, they are all emotionally isolated, sexual and emotional relations between the sexes are chaotic, and they are incapable of forming common ties for cooperative endeavors.

From these four illustrations we can conclude that social homeostasis depends on at least two identifiable factors—if one can make any generalizations about this complex subject: (1) It can be disturbed by impairing the affectivity potential of the individual dur-

[5] Cora Du Bois in Kardiner, A., *op. cit.*, on data drawn from Franz Boas.

[6] Cora Du Bois in Kardiner, A., and Associates, *The Psychological Frontiers of Society*, Columbia University Press, 1945. *See also* Du Bois, Cora, *The People of Alor*, Minnesota, 1944.

ing the process of growth. This destroys the capacity for effective cooperation and affection by substituting suspicion, distrust, and isolation in place of affection, trust, and ease of identification. (2) However, even where affectivity is not impaired, homeostasis can still be disturbed by institutional arrangements which block off cooperation by division of interests, thus setting one group in antagonism to another, and so stimulating self-preservation anxiety. Some societies that suffer from disturbances in social homeostasis have only one factor or the other, and some have both.

In general, the culturally determined rules of social relationship decide how much self-preservation anxiety and conflict prevail within the society. The anxiety and conflict need not be limited to subsistence; they can be transferred to the issue of status and prestige. Thus, we can say that these anxieties and conflicts are best controlled by arranging the traffic rules of social relationship in such a way that they are not stimulated excessively. A word in passing may be said about "sublimating" these tendencies. This does not make any psychological sense at all. One cannot drain this anxiety or work it off in baseball or football. These sports are only small exercises of the same tendencies and the love of these competitive sports prevails in those societies where the competitiveness is otherwise very keen. Sport is not a substitute or "sublimation"; it is an accessory activity.

These tendencies can and do exist in complex societies which are supposed to obviate the necessity for them. Self-preservation anxiety cannot be obliterated from any society. As long as man's existence depends on how effectively he uses his environment to satisfy his needs, there will be anxiety contingent on the ability of the natural environment to satisfy these needs. The environment can and does cease to be hospitable, if not abruptly, then piecemeal. But this anxiety man has—at least in the civilized world—overcome most effectively. The anxiety of self-preservation with all its refinements and accessories comes from the pattern of intrasocial balance. This is the source of the so-called perversions of the instinct of self-preservation. These perversions take the form of privilege, power, and dominance. Their true nature is frequently hidden under the anonymous devices of economic practice—money, credit, and the like, so that no one is held personally responsible for anything. They are perversions in the sense that they do not subserve survival because they disturb cooperative endeavors, on which the success of social life depends. They can become pleasurable ends over and above their use for survival, e.g., hoarding money but dying of starvation, or killing for sport. In their perverted form, these tendencies are difficult to tame, and are accompanied by powerful emotions. They are capable of diverse and subtle rationalizations. We have civilized only the means, but not the end itself.

Western culture stimulates these perverted tendencies to a very high degree. It is difficult to appraise a culture in which one lives and get a detached opinion about the prevailing system of values. We must contrast it with other styles of social organization and compare its results in human impact with the denizens of our culture. For us, success by competitive effort is the highest expression of individuality. This is the common objective, but it is implemented in different ways according to class position. In the lower classes, this objective is the acquisition of the means of subsistence through work. In the middle classes, who have the greatest mobility, the goal is subsistence plus status or prestige, either through capital investment or through membership in a business hierarchy. In this group, the conflicts about self-preservation on the status level are keenest and the anxieties greatest. This is the norm; competitiveness and anxiety are routine. In the higher echelons, the struggle is for prestige and power. Labor is subject to the vicissitudes of the labor market, it being a commodity. The middle and upper classes are subject to the anxieties that accompany capital risk.

In other words, no class is immune from anxiety; but the anxiety is about different things and these vary in their psychological impact. One can suffer at being reduced to one's last yacht or last meal. But the last meal has a very different effect, on oneself and on family cohesion, if it persists. Every Western country knows that prolonged unemployment on a large scale is demoralizing and all seek desperately to prevent it. But, nevertheless, the basic anxiety for the greatest mass of the population continues to be an anxiety about subsistence, the reduction in capacity to work with advancing years, and the like. This is in accordance with the rules of our social organization. The ethics of this social arrangement are in the formula that when the "market" is good one doesn't need ethics and when it is bad ethics are irrelevant.

Since these were the basic rules (formed from the sixteenth century on), the dominance of the entrepreneur was largely a part of a social expedient, and when by accident or plan, slavery was introduced into America, the system worked itself effectively into the then current ethos of economic practice, especially in the South, without too much interference from conscience. The degradation of the Negro's status served to narcotize the white man's social conscience against the ethical issues involved in slavery. Degradation of status is very contagious and in three generations a group of people deprived of culture and social participation can become deculturized. At all events, the fact that even Southerners had to justify their attitude to slavery means that there always was some conscience reaction to it. This was toned down by common practice, the psychological rewards of dominance, and the material gains of economic expediency.

Slavery is thus the extreme manifestation of the ego perversion of dominance—the subjection of another human being to a pure utilitarian use. Once you degrade someone in that way, the sense of guilt makes it imperative to degrade the object further to justify the entire procedure. If you do not use the human being whose attributes you despise, you can escape the ambit of his influence by pure avoidance; if you use him, you cannot avoid the consequences. The only defense now is to *hate* the object. However, when the enslaved person is compliant and servile, this hatred can remain hidden and its place taken by condescension. Should the enslaved become refractory, then the hatred can emerge clearly; but when it does, the reasons seem very different from what they were when the slave was compliant. Now the reason for the hatred becomes the loss of dominance over an object that has already been degraded in status. This represents a claim by the Negro for a reciprocal emotional relation with the white and *hence a fall in status for the white*. In a revised form, this struggle has continued in the South to this day, and the slogan "white supremacy" betrays the fictitious struggle that the white man is engaged upon to salvage his relative fall in status, and to restore it by the device of "keeping the Negro in his place." [7]

[7] The scope of this book has precluded the possibility of entering on any lengthy research on those mental and emotional processes in man which make him prone to prejudice and discrimination. Much has been written on this subject, which on the whole has been characterized by a good deal of wanton psychologizing. The prime requisite for prejudice is to have the stereotype at hand. No one needs to be very original to be either anti-Semitic or anti-Negro. They have both been

This is something approximating the psychological processes that dominated the South during the agitation about slavery and after the Civil War. The white man had a bitter struggle within himself about this issue and has never quite solved it completely. Naturally, it was more difficult in the South when the abolition of slavery caused serious economic hardship in addition to the relative fall in status, not only in relation to the Negro, but also to the Northern White. The greater prejudice in the South against the Negro is the cultural hang-over of this psychological battle together with its economic overtones. This psychological struggle of the white man about the Negro, which Myrdal calls "The American Dilemma," demonstrates quite conclusively that slavery did *not* wholly remove the Negro from reciprocal emotional relationship with the white. This went on despite the powerful social barriers that were erected to prevent this seepage.

The self-preservation anxiety of all classes in our society is extremely keen because no class has any security against the fluctuations of the "market." To all this must be added the insinuating effects of new inventions and labor-saving devices which relieve one type of strain while they cause another. The labor-saving device always hits labor hardest until new adjustments can be made. All Western societies have instituted some type of cushion against this blow. "Social security" is one of these mitigating institutions.

We have no way of gauging the amount of anxiety generated by the risks and uncertainties that face each class—upper, lower, and middle. But we do have some way of checking on the effects of subsistence anxiety, not in terms of quantity, but in terms of quality.

In order to explain this quality, we must refer again to the place of the family in our social structure. There is a vast number of

---

available for a long time. How much use one makes of these stereotypes, publicly or privately, depends on the need for counteracting one's own depressed self-esteem or frustration. The work of Bruno Bettelheim and Morris Janowitz (*Dynamics of Prejudice*, Harper, 1950) shows that prejudice is most easily mobilized in those subjects whose status had fallen or was in process of falling. Those who felt protected by society did not have the need for violent anti-Semitic or anti-Negro sentiments. Also, those who had strong religious or political convictions were most tolerant, i.e., did not use prejudice as an internal balancing mechanism. The attempt to educate an individual out of a stereotyped prejudice while public approval for its exercise exists is quixotic. The only way to remove prejudice as a means of establishing internal comfort is to remove it from the group of permissible or even laudatory attitudes. (*See also* Bettelheim and Janowitz, "Prejudice," *Scientific American*, Oct. 1950.)

observations on record which point to certain general conclusions. Those societies seem to have the greatest viability in which the family is strong and unbreakable. Every society is alarmed at anything that disrupts family organization. And for a good reason. The family is the locus of personality formation, and hence the most reliable avenue for the transmission of culture. It is within the family that the characterological types best suited for the culture are formed. In Western society, the family is burdened with more obligations, personality-wise, than in other cultures, because the family is an economic unit, as well as a social one. It is the place where non-utilitarian relations exist. Here one can be loved and protected for one's own sake in return for meeting certain disciplinary conditions. It is a highly cooperative group, on a basis of affection, notwithstanding many tensions, like sibling rivalry, that take place within its confines. Outside the family, relations are governed altogether on a utilitarian exchange basis—labor for pay, for example. In this utilitarian exchange, the hire of the individual is governed by supply and demand. If there is no demand, there is no income. The "dole" or "social security" takes up the slack at this point on a bare subsistence level. But all this is comparatively recent. Before this there was "charity"—which was extremely uncertain in its function as a source of subsistence.

We wish particularly to stress the effect that lack of subsistence has upon the family. The position of the father in our patriarchally oriented society suffers. He is the great provider and source of all bounties within the family. When he fails in his provident function, his psychological position falls. This means his magical powers no longer exist and his wife and children are exposed to anxieties of survival. He cannot be idealized. If the mother can work and does so, the father takes his place as one of the siblings. One cannot retain paternal authority if one ceases to be the source of basic life satisfactions during the normally dependent period of the child.

If the mother now has to work, she cannot be the mother she ought to be. By her mere absence from the home for the greater part of the day, she imposes restrictions and frustrations on the child. She takes the psychological position of the father, in which case she automatically elevates the female role as provider and derogates the established role of the male. Her idealization is, however, mixed with a great deal of ambivalence; she inspires fear as well. If she works, surrogate parents must be found. These generally do not function as true parents and the psychological picture of the real parent suffers. The result of all this is that the affectivity potential of the child is undermined. The child has no one to trust and idealize. He is obliged to take his ideals from the street, where he forms new types of values; but these are likely to be asocial if not antisocial.

This is a brief sketch of the erosive effects of economic insecurity on the family. Such erosion destroys the family as the site of the most effective character-building for the benefit of the community as a whole.

If we apply these considerations to the lower-class Negro, we can see that this group is heir to the greatest amount of self-preservation anxiety in our culture. Whatever other effects discrimination has, the principle of "last hired, first fired" leaves the lower-class Negro the most unprotected member of the community. It attacks and erodes the family as a place of refuge against the hostile world, and destroys the opportunity for molding those traits in personality most harmonious with our social goals.

These considerations all bear on the psychology of oppression. Let us examine the individual who is subject to oppression in order to determine (1) the effects on his personal adaptation, and (2) the effects on the group as a whole.

We saw that during slavery the slave was used as a commodity, and the master who "owned" him treated him as an object of utility and as a vested interest. The slave ceased to be his own vested interest. He was deprived of the capacity for reciprocal action with his master or his peers. This was not altogether true of the female slave who had sexual value. The only records we have of the adaptation of the Negro slave are the slave revolts, the spirituals, and the rudimentary folklore. Here we find four types of adaptation:

(1) Overt aggression and flight.
(2) Passivity or submissiveness and the plea for rescue.
(3) The vicarious aggression in the folk tales.
(4) Suicide—which was rare, and occurred mostly in the early days of being captured.

Since the culture was smashed and communication was so difficult, few opportunities existed for the evolution of either mass protest or mass accommodative devices.

However, there was a large white protest against slavery of which *Uncle Tom's Cabin* by Harriet Beecher Stowe was a famous illustration. Here, the attempt was made to restore the Negro to reciprocal emotional relations with the white. The whites were urged to recognize the humanity of the Negro and hence, the injustice of using him so blatantly as a means to an end. This white protest literature was evidently the result of a very complex situation, but it had one major feature—it articulated the fact that the white man shared in the degradation he heaped on the Negro (Simon Legree). This character was not engaged in any self-preservative activity; he carried out brutality that served no useful end. It was this use of the Negro as a scapegoat and vicarious avenue of aggressions that reflected his master's or overseer's perverted need for self-aggrandizement through a perversion of mastery, i.e., brutality for its own sake. This was the moral harm that the white man was doing to himself. Moreover, as Stowe dramatically pointed out through the character of Simon Legree, brutality gave rise to violent retaliatory anxiety which could only be quieted by more brutality. All of which shows that while the slave was deprived of the outward avenues for reciprocal emotional relations with the white, the slave did nevertheless continue to make his human influence felt. The entire South was held in the spell of a violent retaliatory fear because of the brutality it meted out to the Negro. This fear was naturally aggravated after liberation and gave rise to such defensive organizations as the Ku Klux Klan. Stowe showed that the emotional price of human degradation was *anxiety*. History has proved that the white man's fears were paranoid projections of his own brutality.

On the other hand, the economy of the South had geared itself to slavery as an essential prop, without which the economy would collapse. The South was defending what had by this convention become a right and a vested interest. The Civil War was therefore an economic war as well, and as such it decided the economic future of America.

The Negro we studied is the one who lives in the postwar ethos, and what we see in him are the marks not of slavery, but of oppression which takes the attenuated name of discrimination. Dollard [8] has adequately shown what the white man gains from this social policy. We need not repeat what he has so well stated. We do, how-

[8] Dollard, John, *Caste and Class in a Southern Town*, Harper, 1939.

ever, want to recapitulate what this continued policy does to the Negro and to show the damage it does to the white man. Myrdal[9] has compiled an encyclopedia of the many and varied forms in which this policy is carried out.

After liberation, as we have already pointed out, the Negro was confronted with what may be called a liberation panic. This meant a transition into a new style of adaptation. First, it augmented his sense of responsibility for himself without much ability to do anything about it. He was given a nominal freedom, but without the opportunities for full participation. Such protective features as were attached to the slave status were removed. He now had to compete under very unfavorable conditions with low-priced foreign white labor. He had no culture, and he was quite green in his semi-acculturated state in the new one. He did not know his way about and had no intrapsychic defenses—no pride, no group solidarity, no tradition. This was enough to cause panic. The marks of his previous status were still upon him—socially, psychologically, and emotionally. And from these he has never since freed himself.

The Negro group now finds itself being divided into upper, lower, and middle classes. The little mobility the Negro did have made this grouping possible. Within these three groups there are all the gradations of status that exist among whites, and a few original ones of their own: Northern-Southern, urban-rural, lighter and darker—to each of which varying degrees of prestige attach. The struggle that all Negroes have about caste are violently augmented in connection with class. The snobbishness of the upper to the lower classes is the same as among whites—perhaps more so. The result is that all these groups and their subdivisions despise, hate, or envy each other. All hate themselves or find it necessary to project this hatred on to the Negro below him. From this source comes a loss of group solidarity so necessary for any concerted action or attitude, except of course for emergency situations.

The heaviest adaptational load is carried by the lower-class Negroes, who constitute the great majority of the Negro population. Here, not only the personal adaptation of each individual suffers, but an endless number of vicious circles are started that can never end anywhere because they are self-perpetuating. Those who are in the

[9] Myrdal, Gunnar, *op. cit.*

upper and middle classes are not subject to all of the disastrous effects on personality that strike the lower classes, but their lives are embittered by the constant preoccupation with status and self-esteem.

The chief of these vicious circles that plague the lower-class Negro are the broken home and the disturbed relation between the sexes. The capacity for positively toned affectivity is destroyed, and there is isolation, suspicion, and mistrust everywhere. This sets in motion the necessity for compensatory gratifications. Among these, gambling takes a high place, for in the chance to "win," one hopes to find a magical release, to be the favored one, to be "lucky." This penchant is amply exploited by both white and Negro racketeers, at a great cost to the Negro community. Other compensations are to be found in flamboyant dressing, drinking, drugs, crime (particularly among adolescents). The onus of the constant vigilance the Negro must exercise over his hostility to whites and other Negroes sets other accommodative mechanisms in motion, the need for flippancy, artificial gaiety, or servility. The imitation of whiteness or white attributes (e.g., loss of kinky hair) costs the Negro population a vast fortune annually.

These people have no fantasy escape. Many of them cannot imagine anything much further than a middle-class home. Religion does not answer their needs, hence they are constant prey to new religious adventurers. We have seen little evidence of genuine religiosity among Negroes. They have invented no religion of their own. The one that comes closest to it, that of Father Divine, encourages a grotesque flight into unreality by the crude device of denying the real world and creating an artificial one. What accounts for its success is not its ideology, but its practice, which frees its "angels" of any responsibility for themselves.

In conclusion, we can say that our society has a system of internal balance which places a heavy load on personal adaptation. The self-preservation anxiety is enormous, has spread through all classes, and within the past half century has infiltrated the international scene. It is the intensity of this anxiety which leads to perversions of this "instinct" in the form of power or wealth, and leaves the lowest social strata in the worst situation. Apart from making the personal lot of the lower classes extremely difficult, the aspect of the problem that concerns the society as a whole is the one that affects the family structure, the induction of affectivity, and the social cohesion of this group. This is the price that the entire community pays for the dubious gratifications of social discrimination.

We are in no position to say how far the findings of the lower-class Negro apply to lower-class whites. This would require special study. The situation cannot possibly be as bad in these latter groups, because they do not have the caste situation to contend with, and among the disastrous effects that register their impact on Negro life, that of caste is the worst. It is this influence which colors to a marked degree the class tensions in Negro society, and affects all classes, however different their manifestations.

The lesson that this study teaches is that social homeostasis at the cost of discrimination against a group does not remain confined to the particular individuals who are concerned. There is a feed-back into the entire culture. Discrimination against the Negro does not alter his needs or wants. These are determined by the culture as a whole. Class distinctions further circumscribe the range of opportunity, particularly for the lower classes. Social discrimination narrows the opportunities still more—to the bare subsistence level and even below. The effects of this cannot be confined to the individual who can accommodate himself to this fate by a variety of intrapsychic devices; but a very considerable part of this marginal adaptation flows over into the community as a whole. This back flow takes its impetus from the derangements of the family structure, the affectivity potential, and the social cohesion of the affected group.

We started this chapter by asking a question: Is this laborious technique worth while and does it give us information we cannot get in any other way? We think it does. The information we get from statistics are crude sociological data. They do not give us the picture of how the facts recorded are worked into the lives of the people under study. We cannot tell how the social institutions are integrated into the life of the individual until we study the personalities individually. Thus, for example, without such studies, we could not have determined the impact on the Negro group of the simple statistical fact that the male has fewer opportunities for employment than the female. The same is true of all the recorded statistical findings about the broken homes, the higher death rate, the greater incidence of crime, and so on. Furthermore, this psychodynamic survey points to a great many more features of Negro life that can and ought to be studied in quantity. In other words, the psychodynamic approach to the study of sociological data has a specific function to perform: it can show us how these factors are integrated into the life of the individual. Hence, to those disposed to social action, such studies can give particular indications. Whether we accept these indications or not depends on our willingness to see the mutilating marks that oppression leaves on the human mind, and on our readiness to be moved by them.

The psychosocial expressions of the Negro personality that we have described are the *integrated* end products of the process of oppression. Can these be changed by *education* of the Negro? The answer is, no. They can never be eradicated without removing the forces that create and perpetuate them. Obviously, Negro self-esteem cannot be retrieved, nor Negro self-hatred destroyed, as long as the status is quo. What is needed by the Negro is not education, but *re-integration.* It is the white man who requires the education. *There is only one way that the products of oppression can be dissolved, and that is to stop the oppression.*

Index

CPSIA information can be obtained
at www.ICGtesting.com
Printed in the USA
BVHW081955050720
582970BV00005B/484